Lecture Notes in Operations Research

Lecture Notes in Operations Research is an interdisciplinary book series which provides a platform for the cutting-edge research and developments in both operations research and operations management field. The purview of this series is global, encompassing all nations and areas of the world.

It comprises for instance, mathematical optimization, mathematical modeling, statistical analysis, queueing theory and other stochastic-process models, Markov decision processes, econometric methods, data envelopment analysis, decision analysis, supply chain management, transportation logistics, process design, operations strategy, facilities planning, production planning and inventory control.

LNOR publishes edited conference proceedings, contributed volumes that present firsthand information on the latest research results and pioneering innovations as well as new perspectives on classical fields. The target audience of LNOR consists of students, researchers as well as industry professionals.

Pascal Alphonse • Karima Bouaiss •
Pascal Grandin • Constantin Zopounidis
Editors

Essays on Financial Analytics

Applications and Methods

 Springer

Editors

Pascal Alphonse
IAE
University of Lille
Lille, France

Karima Bouaiss
IAE
University of Lille
Lille, France

Pascal Grandin
IAE
University of Lille
Lille, France

Constantin Zopounidis
School of Production Engineering &
Management
Technical University of Crete
Chania, Greece

ISSN 2731-040X   ISSN 2731-0418   (electronic)
Lecture Notes in Operations Research
ISBN 978-3-031-29049-7   ISBN 978-3-031-29050-3   (eBook)
https://doi.org/10.1007/978-3-031-29050-3

This Springer imprint is published by the registered company Springer Nature Switzerland AG
The registered company address is: Gewerbestrasse 11, 6330 Cham, Switzerland

Paper in this product is recyclable.

Contents

Part IV   Portfolio Management and Fintech

Part I
Risk Assessment and Growth Models

Foreign Exchange Risk Hedging Policy: Evidence from France

Ghassen Nouajaa and Jean-Laurent Viviani

Abstract This paper examines foreign exchange risk hedging determinants for a sample of 82 French non-financial firms. Starting from the observation that firms, often, use both currency derivatives and foreign debt, we find evidence that foreign debt can be considered as hedging tool in addition to currency derivatives. Our results show that currency derivatives' hedging depends from firm size, financial distress risk, liquidity level, foreign sales and future growth opportunities. Foreign debt level depends from firm size, debt level, foreign sales and its future growth opportunities.

We demonstrate, further, that foreign debt and currency derivatives are quite different hedging tools. Our results show that the level of operational hedging with foreign debt seems to be loosely correlated with that of currency derivatives.

Keywords Foreign exchange risk · Hedging · Currency derivatives · Foreign debt

JEL Classifications: F31, G15

G. Nouajaa (✉)
Esprit School of Business (ESB), Ariana, Tunisia
e-mail: ghassen.nouajaa@esprit.tn

J.-L. Viviani
University of Rennes, Rennes, France
e-mail: jean-laurent.viviani@univ-rennes1.fr

© The Author(s), under exclusive license to Springer Nature Switzerland AG 2023
P. Alphonse et al. (eds.), *Essays on Financial Analytics*, Lecture Notes in Operations Research, https://doi.org/10.1007/978-3-031-29050-3_1

1 Introduction

The theory of corporate FX[1] risk hedging is quiet diverse, and there are various empirical studies that investigate about determinants of this policy. In this content, we distinguish between "classical" studies (e.g. Nance et al., 1993) that believe that hedging is limited to the use of financial derivatives and other more recent studies (e.g. Eliott et al., 2003) that take into account other FX risk hedging tools such as foreign debt. Starting with Géczy et al. (1997), these studies assume that we must consider relation between financial hedging with derivatives and firm capital structure to define all dimensions of FX risk hedging. This hypothesis supposes that financial hedging depends from firm other financial policies such as the debt structure.

We hypothesize that FX risk hedging policy has two main components; the first is financial hedging with currency derivatives and the second one is hedging using foreign debt. This implies that both of these hedging instruments can, eventually, be interdependent since currency derivatives' use influences firm's capital structure and so is the debt and vice versa.

There are many reasons to believe that financial hedging with derivatives is not the only way for the firm to hedge FX risk. First, the optimal hedging theory, by Smith and Stulz (1985), assumes that the higher firm financial distress risk is, the more are its incentives to hedge to reduce probability of default. This implies positive relationship between debt level and hedging. As we know that foreign debt is part of firm's total debt and an increase in its level raises total value of debt, we assume that foreign debt can have an impact on firm financial hedging with derivatives. In this same pattern, Clark and Judge (2008) demonstrate that foreign debt use influences the relationship between firm financial distress risk and FX risk hedging with currency derivatives. Second, foreign debt itself can be used as a FX risk hedging tool. For a firm with sales abroad, FX risk arises when foreign currency exchange rate goes down. This can be hedged even with currency derivative contract (e.g. a currency forward or future contract, etc.) or with foreign debt issuance for the same amount of the transaction. Thus, foreign debt can be used as an operational hedging tool of FX risk other than currency derivatives. Besides, foreign debt, as part of firm total debt, is related to derivatives. Fazillah et al. (2008) argue that distress cost reduction due to financial hedging increases debt capacity of the firm. As there is tax savings in the debt, firms will go, further, into debt, and this raises financial distress probability. Consequently, they will have to increase, over, hedging using derivatives. Moreover, Schiozer and Saito (2009) empirical findings confirm foreign debt role in currency derivatives' hedging. Their results demonstrate that the decision to issue foreign debt leads to that of using currency derivatives.

Recent empirical studies on FX risk hedging determinants (e.g. Eliott et al., 2003; Clark & Judge, 2008; Schiozer & Saito, 2009) emphasize the role of foreign debt

---

[1] FX is an abbreviation for foreign exchange.

as hedging instrument in addition to currency derivatives. They consider that there is interdependence between currency derivatives' usage and level of foreign debt since corporate FX risk hedging includes derivatives and foreign currency funds. We notice that results of these studies do not converge about the nature of this relationship (whether these hedging tools are complements or substitutes) or even confirm each one of them, possibly, determines or not the use of the other. Eliott et al. (2003) find that foreign debt and currency derivatives act as substitutes as there is a negative relationship between them. On the other hand, Clark and Judge (2008) find that foreign debt constitutes a real motive for hedging with currency derivatives since it increases total debt level, so financial distress risk that makes firm increase FX risk hedging.

As both of these hedging tools are different in terms of employment, hedging purpose and prevalence, [2] empirical studies suggest different determinants for each one. Most of these studies refer to optimal hedging theory (by Smith & Stulz, 1985; Nance et al., 1993) empirical study for determinants of derivatives' hedging to test factors that influence currency derivatives' hedging. The factors, often used, are firm size, financial distress risk, liquidity level, exposure to FX risk and firms' future growth opportunities. For firm foreign debt use, the main determinants are firm size, debt level, profitability rate, level of exposure to FX risk and future growth opportunities.

Our paper aims to study factors that influence decision and level of both financial and operational FX risk hedging and to check about possible link between them. This paper adds to FX risk hedging theory in different ways. First, it questions about the existence of interdependence between currency derivatives and foreign debt as hedging instruments rather than "classical" approach limited to financial hedging with derivatives. Besides, it is the first empirical work to check for a more realistic definition of FX risk hedging and gives findings about French firms. Also, we use a new methodology comparing the use of one of these hedging tools in addition to the other. Our empirical results support evidence that currency derivatives and foreign debt hedging are two separate hedging instruments.

This paper is organized as follows: Sect. 2 discusses about factors that determine currency derivatives and foreign debt hedging. Our dataset and methodology are presented in Sect. 3. Empirical results are detailed in Sect. 4. We conclude in Sect. 5.

---

[2] Aabo (2006) study examines determinants of the relative importance of foreign debt to currency derivatives. Results demonstrate that foreign debt is, often, used as an alternative for currency derivatives' hedging and most firms tend to prefer foreign debt to derivatives when hedging long-term exposure.

2   Determinants of FX Risk Financial and Operational Hedging

As we assumed, FX risk hedging cannot be limited to financial hedging with currency derivatives. Recent empirical studies confirm that operational hedging using foreign debt is an important component of corporate FX risk hedging policy. In what follows, we explain the impact of firm financial characteristics on hedging policy using derivatives and foreign debt.

2.1   Currency Derivatives' Hedging Determinants

The theory of corporate risk management suggests that hedging level depends, mainly, from firm size, financial distress risk, exposure to FX rate risk, its growth opportunities and the level of liquidity.

2.1.1   Firm Size

According to Nance et al. (1993), large firms benefit more from scale economies that give them opportunity to implement a hedging policy at lower costs compared to smaller ones. Most empirical researches on FX risk hedging determinants (e.g. Géczy et al., 1997) find a positive relationship between firm size and currency derivatives' use. Thus, we hypothesize that the larger is the firm, the higher is the level of FX risk hedging with currency derivatives. We expect a positive relationship between firm size and currency derivatives' hedging. We choose natural logarithm of total assets as a proxy for size of the firm.

2.1.2   Financial Distress Risk

Optimal hedging theory suggests that distress risk is positively related to hedging. Smith and Stulz (1985) assume that higher financial distress costs give firm a reason to hedge to reduce the variability of its future value, so lowering the probability of bankruptcy. This implies that firms with higher financial distress risk tend to hedge more their FX risk with derivatives. However, empirical studies' results are not consistent about this relationship because some studies (e.g. Davies et al., 2006; Gonzalez et al., 2010) find no significant effect. In our study, we use two variables to proxy for firm financial distress risk: the debt-to-total assets ratio and fixed charge coverage ratio.[3] The debt-to-total assets ratio represents leverage of the firm. Fixed charge coverage ratio is defined as earnings before interest and taxes divided by interest expenses and preferred dividends. This variable represents the number of times firm's earnings can cover its fixed charges (interests and preferred dividends). So, the greater is the firm fixed charge coverage, the lower is the default probability and the less are the incentives to hedge. We hypothesize, then, that the higher is the firm debt level and/or the lower is its fixed charge coverage, the higher will be the currency derivatives' hedging.

2.1.3 Exports Level

Level of exports measures for firm's international sales exposed to foreign exchange rate variations.[4] Most empirical studies (such as Goldberg et al., 1998; Géczy et al., 1997) find a positive relationship between firm's exposure level and currency derivatives' hedging. It is common that firm with higher level of sales abroad tends to hedge more its FX risk using currency derivatives to reduce variability in value of its sales. To measure exposure level for our sample firms in the study period,[5] we construct our own *foreign sales ratio* because exports of French companies in the eurozone do not generate direct exchange rate risk.

For every firm and every year, we collect data about geographical segments sales, and we compute total value of international sales out of the eurozone. We, then, divide this value by the total net sales to obtain exports level measure. Therefore, we assume that there is a positive relationship between firm exports level and currency derivatives' hedging.

2.1.4 Growth Opportunities

Myers (1977) argue that, for firms with higher growth opportunities, agency conflicts (between shareholders and bondholders) occur when shareholders forego future investment projects if profits could go, first, to bondholders. This situation is defined as the underinvestment problem. Bessembinder (1991) affirms that firm can resolve this problem and assure bondholders about fixed claims payment by hedging. Therefore, we assume that firms with higher growth opportunities tend to hedge more with derivatives to assure funds for future investment opportunities and

---

[3] Fixed charge coverage ratio is as follows: earnings before interest and taxes/((interest expense on debt + preferred dividends)/(1−tax rate)). DataStream data type WC08251.

[4] The foreign sales ratio, here, is manually computed using data about international sales by different geographical areas in DataStream (not as presented with data type WC08731 in the same database, which includes sales in the eurozone). It is equal to the sum of international sales out of the eurozone divided by the total of net sales for each firm and each year of the study period.

[5] The euro common currency is, officially, adopted since 1999.

to face higher underinvestment costs. In line with these assumptions, we suppose that there is a positive relationship between firm's future growth opportunities and currency derivatives' hedging. The market-to-book ratio is used as a proxy for growth opportunities.

2.1.5 Liquidity

Firm financial policy suggests that it should invest in more liquid assets in order to reduce the probability of default. Nance et al. (1993) assume that firms with more liquid assets are less likely to engage in risk management because liquidity can be used as a substitute for hedging. In line with this assumption, we suppose that there is a negative relationship between liquidity level and currency derivatives' hedging. As a proxy for firm liquidity, we use the ratio of cash to total assets. We notice that firm cash level is defined as money and equivalents available for use in the current operations.

2.2 Foreign Debt Use Determinants

Recent empirical studies on FX risk hedging (e.g. Eliott et al., 2003; Schiozer & Saito, 2009) emphasize the role of foreign debt, in addition to currency derivatives, in hedging. In what follows, we analyse firm characteristics that can explain firm foreign debt use for hedging.

2.2.1 Firm Size

It is supposed to have a positive relation with the probability and level of foreign debt use. In fact, firms must benefit from economies of scale to have access to foreign loan markets since foreign debt issue can be an expensive hedging method for smaller ones. We assume, then, that there is a positive relation between firm size and foreign debt use. We notice that Eliott et al. (2003) and Aabo (2006) find a positive relationship between firm size and foreign debt. These findings are consisting with the assumption of scale economies' role in hedging using foreign debt. We chose natural logarithm of total assets as a proxy for firm size.

2.2.2 Debt Level

There is a specific relationship between firm debt level and foreign debt. First, firms with higher level of debt (so higher financial distress risk) can hedge FX risk with foreign debt to reduce bankruptcy costs, as it has the same role as derivatives in hedging. Moreover, foreign debt is a component of firm's total debt, and firms with higher level of debt are more likely to use foreign debt than firms with lower level as they, probably, have relatively higher level of foreign currency debt. Most empirical studies find a positive relationship between firm's debt level and foreign debt use; Aabo (2006) finds that foreign debt is positively related to firm debt ratio. In addition, Eliott et al. (2003) find a positive relationship between firm's debt ratio and level of foreign debt. We suppose that there is a positive relationship between firm debt level and foreign debt use. As a proxy for debt level, we use the debt-to-total assets ratio.

2.2.3 Profitability

There are two possible effects of firm profitability on its foreign debt use. The first is that highly profitable firms have better and easier access to foreign loan markets. In this case, there is a positive effect of profitability rate on foreign debt issue. The second hypothesis, as detailed by the pecking order theory (by Myers & Majluf, 1984 [6]), is that firm tends to use internally generated resources (e.g. profits) rather than costly external financing. In line with Myers and Majluf (1984) assumption, we suppose that there is a negative relationship between firm's ability to generate internal resources and foreign debt use. We choose the return-on-assets ratio as a proxy for firm profitability level.

2.2.4 Exposure to FX Risk

This variable is the main factor that can explain firms going on foreign indebtedness. The level of international sales to total sales is as follows: firm yearly international sales out of the eurozone divided by total net sales (the same method as for exports level measure in the previous subsection). This ratio represents better firm exposure to FX risk because it sizes up level of its activity running this risk. Most empirical studies find a positive effect of foreign sales level on the decision (Gelos, 2003; Keloharju & Niskanen, 2001; Nguyen & Faff, 2006) and on the level of foreign debt (Eliott et al., 2003; Gonzalez et al., 2010). Therefore, we assume that there is a positive relationship between exposure to FX risk and foreign debt use. As a proxy for exposure level, we choose the foreign sales ratio as described above.

2.2.5 Growth Opportunities

Optimal hedging theory (as by Smith & Stulz, 1985) affirms that firms go on hedging to reduce variability of future cash flows or revenues. This assumption

---

[6] Myers, S., Majluf, N., 1984. "Corporate financing and investment decisions when firms have information that investors do not have". Journal of Financial Economics. 13 (2), 187–222

highlights firm derivatives' role in reducing volatility of future revenues to, finally, pay lower taxes and/or reduce default payment probability. This hypothesis concerns firm financial hedging with derivatives in relation with its growth opportunities and cannot be, necessarily, true for other hedging ways such as foreign debt use. In fact, foreign debt is defined as an external funding and possibly a hedging instrument. Myers and Majluf (1984) argue that firm with greater growth opportunities, so with future investment projects' cash flows, gives priority to internally generated funds over debt because of uncertain future investments' performance and the relative expensive cost of external financing. Thus, we assume that there is a negative relationship between firm's future growth opportunities and its foreign debt use. We choose the market-to-book ratio as a measure for future growth opportunities.

2.2.6 Information Asymmetries

It is supposed that firms with foreign business face less information asymmetries if it has more foreign investors or shareholders compared to the other ones. Kedia and Mozumdar (2003) demonstrate that firms with greater operations abroad (e.g. with foreign subsidiaries) benefit from less informational disadvantage and obtain more foreign financing. In fact, the existence of information asymmetries makes more difficult for the firm to have access to foreign currency debt. We argue that firms with more foreign investors (more capital foreign investments) have less of this asymmetry, so they hedge more using foreign debt. We choose the foreign holdings ratio as a proxy for lower information asymmetries. This ratio represents the percentage of firm shares held by foreign investors to total shares. We suppose, then, that there is a positive relationship between foreign holdings ratio and foreign debt use.

3 Dataset and Methodology

3.1 Dataset

Our study focuses on analysing the determinants of FX risk hedging with derivatives as well as foreign debt for French non-financial firms. Data about currency derivatives' contracts and foreign debt (out of currency derivatives' hedging) are hand collected from firms' published annual reports. The rest of our data, concerning firms' financial characteristics, are collected from both DataStream and Thomson One Banker databases. We choose French firms listed in the SBF 120 with complete data during the study period (2004–2012). We exclude financial firms from the first sample because of the different nature of their business activities and their eventual use of derivatives for speculative purpose. The final sample consists of 82 French non-financial firms with a set of 568 firms' year observations.

3.2 Methodology

Our aim is, first, to check which factors have an influence on FX risk hedging using currency derivatives and foreign debt, separately. Then, we try to test whether these hedging instruments are interdependent.

To estimate determinants of currency derivatives' hedging, we implement the following model:

$$
\begin{aligned}
\text{FCDeriv}_{i,t} = \alpha_0 + \alpha_1 \text{Size}_{i,t} + \alpha_2 \text{DebtTA}_{i,t} + \alpha_3 \text{FixCh}_{i,t} + \alpha_4 \text{FSales}_{i,t} \\
+ \alpha_5 \text{MTBV}_{i,t} + \alpha_6 \text{CashTA}_{i,t} + \varepsilon_{i,t}
\end{aligned}
\tag{1}
$$

where FCDeriv_i represents firm currency derivatives' hedging (probability or level). Size_i is the size of firm i calculated by the natural logarithm of total assets. DebtTA_i is the ratio of total debt to total assets. FixCh_i is the fixed charge coverage ratio (as explained in footnote 2). FSales_i is the foreign sales ratio. MTBV_i is the market-to-book ratio. CashTA_i represents firm's cash level divided by total assets.

To estimate determinants of foreign debt hedging, we implement the following model:

$$
\begin{aligned}
\text{FDebt}_{i,t} = \beta_0 + \beta_1 \text{Size}_{i,t} + \beta_2 \text{DebtTA}_{i,t} + \beta_3 \text{ROA}_{i,t} + \beta_4 \text{FSales}_{i,t} \\
+ \beta_5 \text{MTBV}_{i,t} + \beta_6 \text{ForHol}_{i,t} + \delta_{i,t}
\end{aligned}
\tag{2}
$$

where FDebt_i represents firm foreign debt hedging (probability or level). Size_i is the size of firm i calculated by the natural logarithm of total assets. DebtTA_i is the ratio of total debt to total assets. ROA_i is the return-on-assets ratio. FSales_i is the foreign sales ratio. MTBV_i is the market-to-book ratio. ForHol_i is firm percentage of shares held by foreign investors.

To test whether there is interdependence between currency derivatives and foreign debt hedging, we run a two-stage regression estimation model.

The following equations detail this regression method:

$$
\begin{aligned}
\text{FCDeriv}_{i,t} = \lambda_0 + \lambda_1 \text{Size}_{i,t} + \lambda_2 \text{DebtTA}_{i,t} + \lambda_3 \text{FixCh}_{i,t} + \lambda_4 \text{FSales}_{i,t} \\
+ \lambda_5 \text{MTBV}_{i,t} + \lambda_6 \text{CashTA}_{i,t} + \lambda_7 \widehat{\text{FDebt}}_{i,t} + \omega_{i,t}
\end{aligned}
\tag{3}
$$

where FCDeriv_i represents firm currency derivatives' hedging level measured by nominal value of currency derivatives to total sales. $\widehat{\text{FDebt}}_i$ is the forecasted value foreign debt level estimated by eq. (2).

$$
\begin{aligned}
\text{FDebt}_{i,t} = \theta_0 + \theta_1 \text{Size}_{i,t} + \theta_2 \text{DebtTA}_{i,t} + \theta_3 \text{ROA}_{i,t} + \theta_4 \text{FSales}_{i,t} + \theta_5 \text{MTBV}_{i,t} \\
+ \theta_6 \text{ForHol}_{i,t} + \theta_7 \widehat{\text{FCDeriv}}_{i,t} + \upsilon_{i,t}
\end{aligned}
\tag{4}
$$

where FDebt$_i$ represents firm foreign debt hedging level measured by value of foreign debt to total assets. $\widehat{FCDeriv}_i$ is the forecasted value currency derivatives' level estimated by eq. (1).

Our empirical analysis for determinants of FX risk hedging consists, first, of studying determinants of probability of using only currency derivatives and that of using currency derivatives combined with foreign debt. For this, we implement a multinominal logit model whose dependent variable is equal to 0 if firm does not use currency derivatives, 1 if it uses only currency derivatives and 2 if it uses currency derivatives combined with foreign debt. We do the same method for estimation of determinants of foreign debt use probability. The multinominal logit model dependent variable is equal to 0 if firm does not use foreign debt, 1 if it uses only foreign debt and 2 if it uses foreign debt combined with currency derivatives. Second, we study determinants of FX risk hedging level using currency derivatives and foreign debt, separately. For this, we use three different empirical models: tobit, OLS (ordinary least square) and GLS (generalized least square) models. The last step of our empirical analysis will be to test whether there is interdependence between currency derivatives and foreign debt hedging methods.

4 Empirical Results

4.1 Univariate Analysis

Descriptive statistics for determinants of currency derivatives and foreign debt are presented in Table 1. We notice that firms of our sample have an average size of 8.865. This indicates that most of our sample firms are quiet large. The debt level represents, on average, 24.8% of our sample firms' total assets, and fixed charge coverage ratio mean and median values are equal to 22.94 and 6.01, respectively. These statistics show the low level of financial distress risk among French exporting firms. Liquidity level measured by the ratio of cash to total assets has a mean value of 6.2% and that of return-on-assets is equal to 5.06. This result shows, strangely, low liquidity level among our sample firms despite the high level of profitability. This can be interpreted by important level of fixed costs for our sample firms.

We notice, further, that exports level mean and median values are relatively high. On average, 41.3% of French firms' total sales are out of the eurozone. The percentage of shares held by foreign investors has a mean value of 6.6%. This low level of foreign capital investments could reflect high information asymmetries and, probably, a more restricted access to foreign loan markets. The average value of the market-to-book ratio is equal to 2.24, and median value is equal to 1.81. This result indicates the high level of future growth opportunities for our sample firms.

Table 2 reports Student test mean comparison results for determinants of currency derivatives' hedging. Results show that firms that use currency derivatives have, on average, higher level of exports (out of the eurozone). This finding

Table 1 Descriptive statistics

	N	Mean	Median	Minimum	Maximum	SD
Firm size	569	8.865	8.877	5.239	12.415	1.527
Debt to total assets	569	0.248	0.232	0	0.613	0.129
Fixed charge ratio	569	22.949	6.014	−33.125	1562.5	105.89
Cash to total assets	569	0.062	0.05	0.002	0.383	0.05
Return on assets	569	5.065	4.806	−16.343	49.251	5.211
Foreign holdings	569	0.066	0	0	0.75	0.107
Foreign sales ratio	569	0.413	0.397	0	1	0.193
Market to book value	568	2.244	1.815	0.22	43.39	2.339

This table reports summary descriptive statistics of currency derivatives and foreign debt explanatory variables. Currency derivatives' explanatory variables are firm size, which is a natural logarithm of total assets; ratio of debt to total assets; fixed charge ratio, which is the ratio of earnings before interest and taxes by interests on debt and firm preferred dividends multiplied by (1−tax rate); cash to total assets, which is firm cash and equivalents divided by total assets; foreign sales ratio, which is international sales divided by total sales; and market to book value, which is the ratio of firm market to book value. The sample consists of 82 French non-financial firms for the period 2004–2012

N represents the number of observations. SD is the standard deviation

highlights the importance of exposure to FX risk in currency derivatives' hedging decision. Results of the same table show, also, that firms that use currency derivatives in combination with foreign debt are larger and have higher level of debt. This result shows the important role of scale of economies (measured by firm size) and financial distress risk in the choice of a FX risk hedging policy including both currency derivatives and foreign debt.

Results of Student test mean comparison for determinants of foreign debt hedging are presented in Table 3. Results of this test show that firms that use foreign debt, compared to other firms that do not use it, are more indebted and have lower level of future growth opportunities. Our results indicate that firms with more debt tend to hedge using foreign debt and/or those with higher average level of growth opportunities tend to not use foreign debt.

Results of the same table indicate that firms that use foreign debt in combination with currency derivatives are on average larger and lower indebted and have higher exports than those that use only foreign debt. This finding indicates the importance of economies of scales and lower level of debt charges in the choice of both foreign debt and currency derivatives to hedge FX risk. The higher mean value of exports for firms' hedging with both of these tools emphasizes the relative importance of currency derivatives (compared to foreign debt) to hedge higher exposure level. We notice, also, that firms that use both foreign debt and currency derivatives have higher growth opportunities compared to firms that use only foreign debt. This reflects the important role of firm's future growth opportunities in the choice of currency derivatives in combination with foreign debt.

Table 2 Student mean test for determinants of currency derivatives' hedging

	Currency derivatives' non-users (N = 71)		Only currency derivatives' users (N = 35)		Currency derivatives' and foreign debt users (N = 463)		Only currency derivatives' users–currency derivatives' non-users	Currency derivatives' and foreign debt users–only currency derivatives' users
	Mean	SD	Mean	SD	Mean	SD	t statistic (p-value)	t statistic (p-value)
Firm size	7.453	1.246	7.601	0.822	9.177	1.434	−0.729 (0.233)	−10.221 (0.000)
Debt to total assets	0.321	0.173	0.286	0.16	0.234	0.114	1.003 (0.159)	1.887 (0.033)
Fixed charge ratio	17.702	51.942	22.781	51.215	23.766	114.7	−0.477 (0.317)	−0.096 (0.461)
Cash to total assets	0.061	0.038	0.063	0.047	0.062	0.052	−0.244 (0.403)	0.073 (0.471)
Foreign sales ratio	0.288	0.237	0.451	0.106	0.429	0.184	−4.886 (0.000)	1.097 (0.138)
Market to book value	2.393	1.551	2.508	1.269	2.201	2.497	−0.406 (0.342)	1.258 (0.106)

This table reports the mean and standard deviation statistics for currency derivatives' explanatory variables. Student test of mean is between currency derivatives' users and non-users and between currency derivatives and foreign debt users and only currency derivatives users. Explanatory variables are firm size, which is a natural logarithm of total assets; ratio of debt to total assets; fixed charge ratio, which is the ratio of earnings before interest and taxes by interests on debt and firm preferred dividends multiplied by (1−tax rate); cash to total assets, which is firm cash and equivalents divided by total assets; foreign sales ratio, which is international sales divided by total sales; and market to book value, which is the ratio of firm market to book value. The sample consists of 82 French non-financial firms for the period 2004–2012

N represents the number of observations. SD is the standard deviation

Table 3 Student mean test for determinants of foreign debt use

	Foreign debt non-users ($N = 69$)		Only foreign debt users ($N = 37$)		Foreign debt and currency derivatives' users ($N = 463$)		Only foreign debt users–non-users	Foreign debt and currency derivatives' users–only foreign debt users
	Mean	SD	Mean	SD	Mean	SD	t statistic (p-value)	t statistic (p-value)
Firm size	7.419	1.038	7.656	1.264	9.177	1.434	−0.98 (0.165)	−6.964 (0.000)
Debt to total assets	0.294	0.179	0.338	0.147	0.234	0.114	−1.377 (0.086)	4.203 (0.000)
Return on assets	5.446	4.121	4.84	3.737	5.026	5.457	0.767 (0.222)	−0.28 (0.39)
Foreign holdings	0.075	0.133	0.054	0.078	0.065	0.105	1.011 (0.157)	−0.806 (0.787)
Foreign sales ratio	0.33	0.195	0.363	0.254	0.429	0.184	−0.683 (0.751)	−1.546 (0.065)
Market to book value	2.688	1.619	1.951	0.945	2.201	2.497	2.956 (0.001)	−1.287 (0.10)

This table reports the mean and standard deviation statistics for foreign debt explanatory variables. Student test of mean is between foreign debt users and non-users and between foreign debt and currency derivatives' users and only foreign debt users. Explanatory variables are firm size, which is a natural logarithm of total assets; ratio of debt to total assets; return-on-assets ratio; foreign holdings, which is firm percentage of shares held by foreign investors; foreign sales ratio, which is international sales divided by total sales; and market to book value, which is the ratio of firm market to book value. The sample consists of 82 French non-financial firms for the period 2004–2012

N represents the number of observations. SD is the standard deviation

4.2   Multivariate Analysis

4.2.1   FX Risk Hedging Probability

Table 4 reports empirical results for determinants of currency derivatives' hedging probability using multinominal logit model. Results show that firm size has a significant positive impact on probability of hedging using currency derivatives and that of using both currency derivatives and foreign debt. This result is in line with Nance et al. (1993) empirical results of scale of economies' positive effect on probability of hedging using derivatives. French larger firms benefit from scale of economies to implement a FX risk hedging using either currency derivatives or both of currency derivatives and foreign debt. Results of the same table show that financial distress risk has a negative significant effect on probability of hedging with currency derivatives and foreign debt compared to that with only currency derivatives (column 1 in the middle of Table 4). The sign of debt-to-total assets ratio coefficient is not in accordance with optimal hedging theory assumption of positive effect of distress risk on hedging. Therefore, we suppose that there is non-linearity in the distribution of the debt ratio, and we introduce squared value of the debt-to-total assets ratio as an explanatory variable in our model. Results of this new regression are presented in column II of Table 4. We notice that the more firm is indebted, the higher is the probability of use of foreign debt in addition to currency derivatives to hedge. It is obvious that French firms with higher financial distress risk use more foreign debt in order to attenuate default risk. Results of Table 4 show, also, that exports level has a significant positive impact on currency derivatives' hedging probability. This result is consistent with most empirical studies' results (e.g. Géczy et al., 1997; Davies et al., 2006) about positive relationship between exposure to FX risk and the use of currency derivatives.

Results about determinants of foreign debt use probability are reported in Table 5. Our results show that firm size has a significant positive effect on probability of hedging with foreign debt in combination with currency derivatives compared to hedging with foreign debt only. This finding confirms the importance of scale of economies in hedging with both of these instruments compared to only foreign debt use. Besides, we find that firm debt level has a significant positive effect on the probability of foreign debt use (columns I and II in the left of Table 5). This result is in accordance with our assumptions of positive relationship between financial distress risk and hedging with foreign debt. We find, further, that debt level has a negative impact on probability of hedging with foreign debt and currency derivatives compared to that of foreign debt use only. As we have supposed for determinants of currency derivatives' hedging (non-linearity in the distribution of the debt ratio), we introduce squared value of the debt-to-total assets ratio as an explanatory variable in the model. Results for this variable (column II in the middle of Table 5) show that probability of hedging with both foreign debt and derivatives is positively related to firm debt level. Our result show that the more firm is indebted, the higher will be the

Table 4 Multinomial logit model estimates for currency derivatives' hedging decision

	Expected sign	Only currency derivatives' use compared to non-use of currency derivatives		Currency derivatives and foreign debt use compared to non-use of currency derivatives		Currency derivatives and foreign debt use compared to only use of currency derivatives	
		(I) Coefficient p-value	(II) Coefficient p-value	(I) Coefficient p-value	(II) Coefficient p-value	(I) Coefficient p-value	(II) Coefficient p-value
Firm size	+	0.46 (0.013)	0.486 (0.009)	1.485 (0.000)	1.55 (0.000)	1.024 (0.000)	1.064 (0.000)
Debt to total assets	+	−1.89 (0.248)	2.783 (0.539)	−6.338 (0.000)	11.354 (0.011)	−4.448 (0.006)	8.57 (0.053)
(Debt to total assets)^2	±		−6.714 (0.377)		−30.974 (0.000)		−24.259 (0.005)
Fixed charge ratio	−	−0.0003 (0.619)	0.0013 (0.52)	−0.0011 (0.11)	0.0015 (0.433)	−0.0007 (0.318)	0.0002 (0.827)
Cash to total assets	−	−4.246 (0.437)	−4.745 (0.372)	1.821 (0.646)	1.592 (0.665)	6.067 (0.236)	6.338 (0.197)
Foreign sales ratio	+	6.207 (0.000)	6.125 (0.000)	6.764 (0.000)	6.193 (0.000)	0.556 (0.477)	0.067 (0.934)
Market to book value	+	0.019 (0.786)	0.032 (0.699)	0.011 (0.897)	0.094 (0.335)	−0.0087 (0.908)	0.061 (0.526)
		(I)		(II)			
Wald chi²		154.66		125.9			
Prob > chi²		0.000		0.000			
Pseudo R²		0.328		0.358			
N		568		568			

The dependent variable is equal to 0 if the firm does not use currency derivatives, 1 if it uses only currency derivatives and 2 if it uses currency derivatives and foreign debt. Independent variables are firm size, which is a natural logarithm of total assets; ratio of debt to total assets; (debt to total assets)^2, which is debt-to-total assets ratio squared; fixed charge ratio, which is the ratio of earnings before interest and taxes by interests on debt and firm preferred dividends multiplied by (1−tax rate); cash to total assets, which is firm cash and equivalents divided by total assets; foreign sales ratio, which is international sales divided by total sales; and market to book value, which is the ratio of firm market to book value. The sample consists of 82 French non-financial firms for the period 2004–2012

(I) and (II) denote currency derivatives' use multinomial logit model separate eqs. N represents the number of observations

Table 5 Multinomial logit model estimates for foreign debt use decision

	Expected sign	Only foreign debt use — Compared to non-use of foreign debt		Foreign debt and currency derivatives' use — Compared to non-use of foreign debt		Foreign debt and currency derivatives' use — Compared to only use of foreign debt	
		(I) Coefficient p-value	(II) Coefficient p-value	(I) Coefficient p-value	(II) Coefficient p-value	(I) Coefficient p-value	(II) Coefficient p-value
Firm size	+	0.062 (0.73)	0.04 (0.824)	1.335 (0.000)	1.394 (0.000)	1.272 (0.000)	1.354 (0.000)
Debt to total assets	+	4.054 (0.029)	8.625 (0.084)	−5.226 (0.000)	11.807 (0.003)	−9.28 (0.000)	3.182 (0.574)
(Debt to total assets)^2	±		−8.817 (0.235)		−31.66 (0.000)		−22.843 (0.028)
Return on assets	−	0.024 (0.34)	0.033 (0.268)	−0.068 (0.006)	−0.053 (0.062)	−0.093 (0.001)	−0.087 (0.003)
Foreign holdings	+	−3.473 (0.192)	−2.659 (0.287)	1.496 (0.315)	3.123 (0.049)	4.97 (0.055)	5.782 (0.033)
Foreign sales ratio	+	1.945 (0.131)	1.857 (0.144)	5.306 (0.000)	4.538 (0.000)	3.361 (0.012)	2.681 (0.051)
Market to book value	−	−0.402 (0.008)	−0.396 (0.011)	−0.011 (0.904)	0.089 (0.361)	0.39 (0.012)	0.485 (0.004)
		(I)		(II)			
Wald chi^2		140.86		121.39			
Prob > chi^2		0.000		0.000			
Pseudo R^2		0.321		0.351			
N		568		568			

The dependent variable is equal to 0 if the firm does not use foreign debt, 1 if it uses only foreign debt and 2 if it uses foreign debt and currency derivatives. Independent variables are firm size, which is a natural logarithm of total assets; ratio of debt to total assets; (debt to total assets)^2, which is debt-to-total assets ratio squared; return-on-assets ratio; foreign holdings, which is firm percentage of shares held by foreign investors; foreign sales ratio, which is international sales divided by total sales; and market to book value, which is the ratio of firm market to book value. The sample consists of 82 French non-financial firms for the period 2004–2012

(I) and (II) denote foreign debt use multinomial logit model separate eqs. N represents the number of observations

probability of use of both of these hedging tools but financial distress risk mitigates the impact.

Results of the same table show that return-on-assets ratio has a significant negative effect on probability of hedging with foreign debt and currency derivatives compared to that of foreign debt use only. Firms with higher level of profitability give up currency derivatives and foreign debt hedging as they have more funds to face exposure to FX risk. We find, also, that firm's capital foreign holdings have a significant positive effect on probability of hedging with foreign debt and currency derivatives compared to that of foreign debt. This supposes that foreign investors prefer a combined hedging policy rather than hedging with foreign debt only. This result is in contradiction with our hypothesis of negative relationship between information asymmetries (represented by lower value of capital foreign investors) and foreign debt use. Exports level has a significant positive effect on probability of hedging with foreign debt and currency derivatives' use. This is in line with our assumptions and with results of most empirical research studies on determinants on foreign debt use (e.g. Eliott et al., 2003) and on currency derivatives hedging (e.g. Géczy et al., 1997; Davies et al., 2006). We notice, also, that exports level ratio coefficients are positive and almost significant for probability of foreign debt use only. Firm future growth opportunities measured by the market-to-book ratio have significant negative impact on probability of hedging with foreign debt. This is in line with pecking order theory (by Myers & Majluf, 1984) hypothesis. It is obvious, here, that firms with higher future growth opportunities prefer to use internally generated funds rather than external costly financing. Moreover, our results show that firm growth opportunities have significant positive effect on hedging with foreign debt and currency derivatives compared to that of foreign debt use only. This is in accordance with Nance et al. (1993) empirical results of positive relationship between firm growth opportunities and use of derivatives.

4.2.2   FX Risk Hedging Level

Results for determinants of currency derivatives' hedging level (with tobit, [7] OLS and GLS models) are presented in Table 6. Results show that firm size is positively related to the level of currency derivatives' hedging. An increase in firm size by 1% leads to an increase in currency derivatives' level by 0.094%. This result is in line with Nance et al. (1993) finding about economies of scale role in hedging using derivatives. Larger firms, as they benefit from scale economies, can more hedge using currency derivatives at lower cost compared to smaller ones.

We notice that debt-to-total assets ratio coefficient sign is not consistent with optimal hedging theory assumption about financial distress risk impact on hedging. We explain this by non-linear distribution of debt-to-total assets ratio. To resolve this, we add squared value of debt ratio as an explanatory variable in our empirical

---

[7] The tobit model is left censored (censored at zero).

Table 6 Currency derivatives' level determinants empirical estimates

	Expected sign	Tobit model		OLS model		GLS model	
		Coefficient p-value	Coefficient p-value	Coefficient p-value	Coefficient p-value	Coefficient p-value	Coefficient p-value
Firm size	+	0.094 (0.000)	0.095 (0.000)	0.073 (0.000)	0.075 (0.000)	0.069 (0.000)	0.069 (0.000)
Debt to total assets	+	−0.427 (0.001)	−0.708 (0.025)	−0.313 (0.000)	−0.982 (0.000)	−0.046 (0.629)	0.008 (0.977)
(Debt to total assets)^2	±		0.51 (0.377)		1.196 (0.005)		−0.101 (0.845)
Fixed charge ratio	−	−6.4e-06 (0.94)	−0.00002 (0.73)	4.88e-06 (0.955)	−0.00004 (0.513)	0.00001 (0.88)	0.00001 (0.862)
Cash to total assets	−	0.766 (0.008)	0.76 (0.009)	0.705 (0.012)	0.689 (0.014)	0.463 (0.014)	0.463 (0.014)
Foreign sales ratio	+	0.354 (0.000)	0.356 (0.000)	0.236 (0.000)	0.247 (0.000)	0.176 (0.014)	0.176 (0.014)
Market to book value	+	0.008 (0.002)	0.008 (0.004)	0.009 (0.000)	0.008 (0.002)	0.004 (0.136)	0.004 (0.137)
		p-value 0.000	0.000	p-value 0.000	0.000	p-value 0.00	0.000
		Pseud R^2 0.475	0.477	R^2 0.198	0.2	R^2 0.174	0.172
		N 568	568	N 568	568	N 568	568

The dependent variable is represented by the ratio of nominal value of currency derivatives to total sales. Independent variables are firm size, which is a natural logarithm of total assets; ratio of debt to total assets; (debt to total assets)^2, which is debt-to-total assets ratio squared; fixed charge ratio, which is the ratio of earnings before interest and taxes by interests on debt and firm preferred dividends multiplied by (1 − tax rate); cash to total assets, which is firm cash and equivalents divided by total assets; foreign sales ratio, which is international sales divided by total sales; and market to book value, which is the ratio of firm market to book value. The sample consists of 82 French non-financial firms for the period 2004–2012

R^2 represents the R-squared obtained from the model. N represents the number of observations

models. Results show negative effect of debt-to-total assets ratio and positive effect of squared value of the same ratio. We can conclude that the more the firm is indebted, the lower will be the level of currency derivatives' hedging and financial distress risk attenuates this effect.

Surprisingly, firm cash level has significant positive effect on currency derivatives' level. An increase of firm cash level by 1% raises currency derivatives' hedging level by 0.766%. Our result is not in line with Nance et al. (1993) assumption about negative relationship between liquidity level and derivatives' use. This can be interpreted by the fact that French firms with more liquid assets profit from the situation to increase their currency derivatives' level as the liquidity expended can be recovered, afterwards, from additional derivatives purchased at their maturity dates. Exports level has significant positive effect on currency derivatives' hedging level. A 1% increase in international sales raises currency derivatives' hedging by 0.354%. This is in line with most empirical studies' (e.g. Davies et al., 2006) findings about positive relationship between exports and hedging. In fact, foreign sales increase raises FX risk transactions exposure, thus making firms increase their currency derivatives' hedging level. Moreover, we find that firm's future growth opportunities have significant positive impact on currency derivatives' hedging level. An increase of 1% in the market to book value of the firm leads to an increase of 0.008% on currency derivatives' level. Our result is in the same line with Bessembinder (1991) assumptions and with Nance et al. (1993) finding about positive relationship between growth opportunities and derivatives' use.

Table 7 reports empirical results for determinants of foreign debt level (using tobit, [8] OLS and GLS models). Results show that firm size has significant positive effect on level of foreign debt. This is in the same line with most empirical studies in the subject (e.g. Kedia & Mozumdar, 2003; Eliott et al., 2003). Economies of scale allow French firms to have easier access to foreign capital markets and at lower costs compared to smaller ones. Debt-to-total assets ratio coefficient is positive and that of its squared value is negative. This finding indicates that the more the firm is indebted, the higher foreign debt level will be and financial distress risk mitigates this effect. We notice, here, that positive effect of firm debt level on foreign debt is in accordance to our assumptions and to Clark and Judge (2008) finding of positive link between financial distress risk and foreign indebtedness. Exports level has significant positive effect on foreign debt level. An increase of foreign sales ratio by 1% leads to an increase of 0.125% in foreign debt level. Our result confirms the assumption that foreign debt is, often, used for hedging purpose. It is, also, in accordance with most empirical studies on foreign debt determinants (e.g. Eliott et al., 2003). Three out of six of the market-to-book ratio coefficients are significant. This result is in the same line with Myers and Majluf (1984) assumption of negative relationship between firm's future growth opportunities and external financing. Our result confirms that French firms with higher growth opportunities prefer to finance

---

[8] The tobit model is left censored (censored at zero).

Table 7 Foreign debt level determinants empirical estimates

	Expected sign	Tobit model		OLS model		GLS model	
		Coefficient p-value	Coefficient p-value	Coefficient p-value	Coefficient p-value	Coefficient p-value	Coefficient p-value
Firm size	+	0.008 (0.000)	0.007 (0.000)	0.006 (0.000)	0.005 (0.000)	−0.001 (0.658)	−0.001 (0.602)
Debt to total assets	+	0.157 (0.000)	0.416 (0.000)	0.145 (0.000)	0.327 (0.000)	0.106 (0.000)	0.178 (0.001)
(Debt to total assets)^2	±		−0.474 (0.001)		−0.331 (0.006)		−0.129 (0.149)
Return on assets	−	0.0004 (0.323)	0.0006 (0.145)	0.0004 (0.272)	0.0006 (0.148)	−0.00004 (0.884)	−0.00002 (0.927)
Foreign holdings	+	0.004 (0.862)	0.013 (0.558)	−0.001 (0.946)	0.005 (0.773)	−0.011 (0.435)	−0.01 (0.473)
Foreign sales ratio	+	0.125 (0.000)	0.118 (0.000)	0.103 (0.000)	0.098 (0.000)	0.032 (0.012)	0.031 (0.014)
Market to book value	−	−0.001 (0.062)	−0.001 (0.093)	−0.001 (0.049)	−0.0009 (0.116)	0.0007 (0.15)	−0.0008 (0.14)
		p-value 0.000	0.000	p-value 0.000	0.000	p-value 0.00	0.000
		Pseud R^2 −0.09	−0.11	R^2 0.19	0.21	R^2 0.11	0.12
		N 582	568	N 568	568	N 568	568

The dependent variable is presented by the ratio of foreign debt to total assets value. Independent variables are firm size, which is a natural logarithm of total assets; ratio of debt to total assets; (debt to total assets)^2, which is debt-to-total assets ratio squared; return-on-assets ratio; foreign holdings, which is firm percentage of shares held by foreign investors; foreign sales ratio, which is international sales divided by total sales; and market to book value, which is the ratio of firm market to book value. The sample consists of 82 French non-financial firms for the period 2004–2012

R^2 represents the R-squared obtained from the model. N represents the number of observations

their activities at lower costs by internally generated resources rather than the use of foreign debt.

4.2.3 Currency Derivatives and Foreign Debt Interdependence

Our empirical results, so far, confirm the assumption of foreign debt use as a hedging instrument in addition to currency derivatives. We demonstrate that firm exports level has significant positive effect on probability and level of foreign debt use. In what next, we try to check for possible interdependence between currency derivatives and foreign debt hedging levels. For this, we run a two-stage regression procedure as detailed in Sect. 3. Results for this empirical regression method are presented in Table 8. We notice, first, that firm size has significant positive effect on currency derivatives and foreign debt levels. This confirms what we have, previously, found for determinants of currency derivatives' hedging and foreign debt in Tables 6 and 7, respectively. Larger firms benefit from scale of economies to increase level of currency derivatives' hedging and that of foreign debt. Results of Table 8 show, also, that firm foreign debt is positively related to total debt level and to foreign sales. Our finding about positive impact on total debt confirms Clark and Judge (2008) result of positive effect of financial distress risk on hedging using foreign debt. In addition, the positive relationship between exports level and that of foreign debt is in accordance with our result in Table 6 and confirms, once more, the use of foreign debt as an instrument for FX risk hedging.

Results of Table 8 show, further, that foreign debt level has no significant effect on that of currency derivatives. Similarly, currency derivatives have no significant effect on foreign debt level. Although non-significant, both of the predicted explanatory variable coefficients are negative and their p-values are not so far from 10% limit. Our result is interpreted by the fact that each one of these hedging tools is independent from the other. It is obvious, so far, that currency derivatives and foreign debt are different in terms of the access to costs and maturity. In this same line of reasoning, Géczy et al. (1997) find that transactions abroad (imports and exports) have positive effect on the choice of currency forwards rather than swap contracts. We can deduce that exposure to FX risk in the short term is different from that for long term. Corporate short-term FX risk can be hedged by currency derivatives, and long-term FX risk (concerning foreign investments and assets) can be hedged by currency swaps and/or foreign debt.

5   Conclusion

Our paper presents a new empirical approach in the study of determinants of FX risk hedging policy for French non-financial firms. We follow recent empirical studies'

Table 8 2SLS model estimates results for dependence between currency derivatives and foreign debt

	Currency derivatives' hedging determinants		Foreign debt level determinants	
	Expected sign	Coefficient (p-value)	Expected sign	Coefficient (p-value)
Firm size	+	0.128 (0.007)	+	0.011 (0.014)
Debt to total assets	+	1.008 (0.305)	+	0.112 (0.000)
Fixed charge ratio	−	−0.00008 (0.521)		
Cash to total assets	−	0.181 (0.753)		
Return on assets			−	0.00008 (0.859)
Foreign holding			+	0.011 (0.644)
Foreign sales ratio	+	1.278 (0.113)	+	0.126 (0.000)
Market-to-book ratio	+	−0.0009 (0.93)	−	−0.0003 (0.683)
Foreign debt (predicted)	±	−9.596 (0.186)		
Currency derivatives (predicted)			±	−0.081 (0.198)
Wald chi^2 (7)	30.48		123.76	
Prob > F	0.000		0.000	
R^2	NA		0.013	
N	568		568	

The first equation concerns currency derivatives' hedging where the dependent variable is represented by the ratio of nominal value of currency derivatives to total sales. Independent variables are firm size, which is a natural logarithm of total sales; ratio of debt to total assets; fixed charge ratio, which is the ratio of earnings before interest and taxes by interests on debt and firm preferred dividends multiplied by (1−tax rate); cash to total assets, which is firm cash and equivalents divided by total assets; foreign sales ratio, which is international sales divided by total sales; market to book value, which is the ratio of firm market to book value; and foreign debt (predicted), which is the estimated value of foreign debt from first-stage regression of 2SLS model. The second equation concerns foreign debt level determinants. The dependent variable is presented by the ratio of foreign debt to total assets value. Independent variables are firm size, which is a natural logarithm of total assets; ratio of debt to total assets; return-on-assets ratio; foreign holdings, which is firm percentage of shares held by foreign investors; foreign sales ratio, which is international sales divided by total sales; and market to book value, which is the ratio of firm market to book value. Currency derivatives (predicted) are the estimated value of currency derivatives from first-stage regression of 2SLS model. The sample consists of 82 French non-financial firms for the period 2004–2012

R^2 represents the R-squared obtained from the model. N represents the number of observations

definition of firm hedging policy, which combines currency derivatives and foreign debt use.

The empirical analyses consist of studying FX risk hedging determinants and testing for eventual interdependence between currency derivatives and foreign debt hedging for French non-financial firms. The main assumption is that firm hedging policy is composed of financial hedging with currency derivatives and hedging using foreign debt. Empirical results show that currency derivatives' hedging and foreign debt use are positively related to firm size and exports level. This finding indicates the importance, of both, of scale of economies and transactions exposure in firm FX risk hedging policy. Our results show, also, that financial hedging with currency derivatives depends from financial distress risk, liquidity level and future growth opportunities. The more the firm is indebted, the lower is hedging with currency derivatives as more debt generates higher financial costs. The higher liquidity level and/or growth opportunities is/are, the more important is currency derivatives' level.

We find, also, that foreign debt level is positively related to level of debt and negatively related to firm's future growth opportunities. In fact, financial distress risk makes firms hedge FX risk with foreign debt and firms with higher growth opportunities prefer to use internally generated funds, rather than foreign indebtedness. Our results show, further, that French firms' operational (with foreign debt) and financial (with currency derivatives) hedging are two weakly related hedging tools.

References

Aabo, T. (2006). The importance of corporate foreign debt in managing exchange rate exposures in non-financial companies. *European Financial Management, 12*(4), 633–649.

Bessembinder, H. (1991). Forwards contracts and firm value: Investment incentives and contracting effects. *Journal of Financial and Quantitative Analysis, 26*(4), 519–532.

Clark, E., & Judge, A. (2008). The determinants of foreign currency hedging: Does foreign currency debt induce a bias? *European Financial Management, 14*(3), 445–469.

Davies, D., Eckberg, C., & Marshall, A. (2006). The determinants of Norwegian exporters' foreign exchange risk management. *The European Journal of Finance, 12*(3), 217–240.

Eliott, W., Huffman, S., & Makar, S. (2003). Foreign-denominated and foreign currency derivatives: Complements or substitutes in hedging foreign currency risk? *Journal of Multinational Financial Management, 13*(2), 123–139.

Fazillah, M., Azizan, N., & Hui, T. (2008). The relationship between hedging through forwards, futures and swaps and corporate capital structure in Malaysia. *The ICFAI Journal of Derivatives Markets, 5*(2), 37–52.

Géczy, C., Minton, B., & Schrand, C. (1997). Why firms use currency derivatives. *Journal of Finance, 52*(4), 1323–1354.

Gelos, R. (2003). Foreign currency debt in emerging markets: Firm-level evidence from Mexico. *Economic Letters, 78*(3), 323–327.

Goldberg, S., Tritschler, C., Godwin, J., & Kim, M. (1998). On the determinants of corporate usage of financial derivatives. *Journal of International Financial Management and Accounting, 9*(2), 132–166.

Gonzalez, L., Bua, M., Lopez, S., & Santomil, P. (2010). Foreign debt as a hedging instrument of exchange rate risk: A new perspective. *The European Journal of Finance, 16*(7), 677–710.

Kedia, S., & Mozumdar, A. (2003). Foreign currency-denominated debt: An empirical examination. *Journal of Business, 76*(4), 521–546.

Keloharju, M., & Niskanen, M. (2001). Why do firms raise foreign currency denominated debt? Evidence from Finland. *European Financial Management, 7*(4), 481–496.

Myers, S. (1977). Determinants of corporate borrowing. *Journal of Financial Economics, 5*(2), 147–175.

Myers, S., & Majluf, N. (1984). Corporate financing and investments decisions when firms have information investors do not have. *Journal of Financial Economics, 13*(2), 187–222.

Nance, D., Smith, C., & Smithson, C. (1993). On the determinants of corporate hedging. *Journal of Finance, 48*(1), 267–284.

Nguyen, H., & Faff, R. (2006). Foreign debt and financial hedging: Evidence from Australia. *International Review of Economics and Finance, 15*(2), 184–201.

Schiozer, R., & Saito, R. (2009). The determinants of currency risk management in Latin America non-financial firms. *Emerging Markets Finance & Trade, 45*(1), 49–71.

Smith, C., & Stulz, R. (1985). The determinants of firms' hedging policies. *Journal of Financial and Quantitative Analysis, 20*(4), 391–405.

Ghassen Nouajaa is a finance assistant professor at Esprit School of Business (ESB), Ariana Tunis.

Jean-Laurent Viviani is a finance professor at University of Rennes 1.

Monetary Utility Functions and Risk Functionals

Christos Floros, Konstantinos Gkillas, and Christos Kountzakis

Abstract This paper's content is devoted to the study of the monetary utility functions and their use in optimal portfolio choice and optimal risk allocation. In most of the relative papers, the domain of a monetary utility function is a dual space. This approach implies that closed and convex sets are weak-star compact. The main contribution of the present paper is the definition of such a function on any Riesz space, which is not necessarily a dual space, but it formulates a symmetric Riesz dual pair together with its topological dual. This way of definition implies the weak compactness of the sets usually needed for the solution of the above optimization problems.

Keywords Monetary risk measures · Risk functionals · Premium calculation principles · Monetary utility functions · Optimal portfolio choice · Optimal risk allocation

AMS (2020) Classification Numbers: 90C44, 91B05

JEL Classification Numbers: C44, G22

C. Floros (✉) · K. Gkillas
Department of Accounting and Finance, Hellenic Mediterranean University, Herakleion, Crete, Greece
e-mail: cfloros@hmu.gr; gillask@hmu.gr

C. Kountzakis
Department of Statistics and Actuarial-Financial Mathematics, University of the Aegean, Karlovassi, Samos, Greece
e-mail: chr_koun@aegean.gr

© The Author(s), under exclusive license to Springer Nature Switzerland AG 2023
P. Alphonse et al. (eds.), *Essays on Financial Analytics*, Lecture Notes in Operations Research, https://doi.org/10.1007/978-3-031-29050-3_2

1 Monetary Utility Functions and Risk Metrics

We obtain the following definition of a monetary utility function:

Definition 1.1 A finite-valued function $U : L^1(\Omega, \mathcal{F}, \mathbb{P}) \to \mathbb{R}$ is called **monetary utility function** if it enjoys the following properties:

(1) $U(X) \geq U(Y)$, if $X(\omega) \geq Y(\omega)$, $\mathbb{P}-$ a.e. (Monotonicity)
(2) $U(t \cdot X + (1 - t) \cdot Y) \geq tU(X) + (1 - t)U(Y)$, for any $t \in [0, 1]$, where $\cdot$ denotes the usual scalar product (Concavity)
(3) $U(X + m \cdot \mathbf{1}) = U(X) + m$, where $\mathbf{1}(\omega) = 1$, $\mathbb{P}$-a.e. (Cash Invarianve)

A value of some Monetary Utility Function corresponds to an amount of capital, alike in the case of the Principles of Premium Calculation in insurance.

The above definition of a monetary utility function is obtained from Jouini et al. (2007) in $L^\infty(\Omega, \mathcal{F}, \mathbb{P})$, where the optimal risk sharing problem is studied. Equilibrium pricing under monetary utility functions is studied in Filipoviĉ and Kupper (2008) in $L^\infty(\Omega, \mathcal{F}, \mathbb{P})$ as well. As it is well-known, coherent risk measures are established in Artzner et al. (1999) and convex risk measures in Föllmer and Schied (2002). The main contribution of this paper is that convex and coherent risk measures may be replaced by monetary utility functions and vice versa, under the properties of equivalence defined below. Optimal portfolio selection is the main application of the monetary utility function. Another use of monetary utility functions is that their continuity provides that the optimal risk allocation problem has a non-empty solution. The optimal risk allocation problem is initially studied in Borch (1962). Recent works on the same theme are Kiesel and Rüschendorf (2009), Righi and Moresco (2022). We also provide a way to produce monetary utility functions and corresponding monetary risk measures by Young functions. In general, we notice that a monetary convex risk measure ρ implies the definition of a monetary utility function $u = -\rho$. On the other hand, a monetary utility function u implies the definition of a monetary convex risk measure $\rho = -u$.

2 Risk Functionals and Their Equivalence

Definition 2.1 A **risk measure**, with respect to a nonatomic probability space $(\Omega, \mathcal{F}, \mathbb{P})$, is some $\rho : L^0 \times \mathcal{F} \to \mathbb{R}$, such that $\rho(X, A) = \rho(X^{-1}(A))$.

Definition 2.2 A **risk functional**, with respect to the probability space $(\Omega, \mathcal{F}, \mathbb{P})$, is some $f : \mathbb{P} \times L^0 \times \mathcal{F} \to \mathbb{R}$, such that $f(\mathbb{P}, X, A) = \mathbb{P}(X^{-1}(A))$.

Remark 2.3 A **law-invariant** risk measure is a risk functional. We recall that a risk measure ρ is law invariant if $\mathbb{P}_X = \mathbb{P}_Y$ implies that $\rho(X) = \rho(Y)$, where $\mathbb{P}_Z$ is the distribution probability measure of Z. A monetary risk measure corresponds to the notion of **regulatory capital**. A risk functional which is not a risk measure is value at risk (VaR). Hence, the notion of risk functional is a generalization of the notion of risk measure.

Definition 2.4 Two risk functionals f_i, f_j are called **equivalent**, and we write $f_i \sim f_j$, if for some strictly positive M_i, $M_j \in \mathbb{R}$ we have $M_i f_j \leq f_i \leq M_j f_j$,. A risk functional is called **nontrivial** if it is not equal to the zero function on $\mathcal{F}$.

Proposition 2.5 *The equivalence of risk functionals is actually an equivalence relation in terms of set theory. It is reflexive, symmetric, and transitive.*

Proof If $f_1 \sim f_2$, obviously $f_1 \sim f_1$. If $f_1 \sim f_2$, then $f2 \sim f_1$. Finally, if $f_1 \sim f_2$ and $f_2 \sim f_3$, then $f_1 \sim f_3$. $f_i, i = 1, 2, 3$ are risk functionals according to the above definition. □

We notice that:

Lemma 2.6 *Value at risk and expected shortfall are not equivalent.*

Proof As it is well -known, $ES_a(X) = -\frac{1}{a} \int_0^a VaR_u(X)du$, for any level of significance $a \in (0, 1)$ and any $X \in L^1(\Omega, \mathcal{F}, \mathbb{P})$. □

Proposition 2.7 *Let $f_i, f_j : \mathcal{F} \to \mathbb{R}$ be two risk functionals which are nontrivial and $f_i \sim f_j$. Moreover, let f_i be coherent. Then, f_j is coherent as well.*

Proof Direct from the properties of coherent risk measures. □

Proposition 2.8 *Let $f_i, f_j : \mathcal{F} \to \mathbb{R}$ be two risk functionals which are nontrivial and $f_i \sim f_j$. Moreover, let f_i be convex. Then, f_j is convex as well.*

Proof Direct from the properties of convex risk measures. □

Another proof of the non-coherence of value at risk is the following one.

Corollary 2.9 *Value at risk is a noncoherent risk functional.*

Proof Direct, from the above proposition and $ES_a(X) = -\frac{1}{a} \int_0^a VaR_u(X)du$, for any level of significance $a \in (0, 1)$ and any $X \in L^1(\Omega, \mathcal{F}, \mathbb{P})$. □

An example of a premium principle, which does not satisfy the properties of a coherent risk measure, is the **Exponential Principle of Premium Calculation**:

$$P_b(X) := \frac{1}{b} \log \mathbb{E}(e^{bX}), \tag{2.1}$$

for any strictly positive $b \in \mathbb{R}$.

The subset of those $X \in L^0$ in which $\mathbb{E}(e^{bX})$ is not equal to infinity is related to the Orlicz spaces, mentioned below.

Definition 2.10 The parameter b is called **risk aversion coefficient**.

Proposition 2.11 *The monetary utility function $-P_b$ arising from the Exponential Principle of Premium Calculation P_b satisfies the properties of a coherent risk measure, except positive homogeneity.*

Proof First we do prove that $-P_b$ does not satisfy the positive homogeneity: if $t > 0$ is a positive, nonzero real number, then

$$P_b(t \cdot X) = \frac{1}{b} log \mathbb{E}(e^{b(tX)}) = \frac{1}{b} log \mathbb{E}(e^{bt} e^{bX}) = P_b(X) + t,$$

where $\cdot$ denotes the scalar product:

(i) (Translation Invariance): $P_b(X + c\mathbf{1}) = \frac{1}{b} \log \mathbb{E}(e^{b(X+c1)}) = \frac{1}{b}(\log(e^{bc}) + P_b(X) = c + P_b(X)$, for any $c \in \mathbb{R}$. $-P_b$ satisfies the translation invariance property.
(ii) (Monotonicity): If $X \geqslant Y$, $\mathbb{P}$-a.s., then $e^{bX} \geqslant e^{bY}$, $\mathbb{P}$-a.s. This implies $\mathbb{E}(e^{bX}) \geqslant \mathbb{E}(e^{bY})$ and consequently $P_b(X) \geqslant P_b(Y)$.
(iii) (Subadditivity):

$$\frac{1}{b} \log \mathbb{E}(e^{b(X+Y)}) \geqslant \frac{1}{b} \log \mathbb{E}(e^{bX}), \frac{1}{b} \log \mathbb{E}(e^{bY}),$$

hence

$$\frac{1}{b} \log \mathbb{E}(e^{b(X+Y)}) \geqslant \max \left\{ \frac{1}{b} \log \mathbb{E}(e^{bX}), \frac{1}{b} \log \mathbb{E}(e^{bY}) \right\},$$

namely,

$$P_b(X + Y) \geqslant \max\{P_b(X), P_b(X)\}.$$

Hence, $P_b(X + Y) \geqslant -\min\{-P_b(X), -P_b(X)\}$, and consequently $-U_b(X + Y) \geqslant -\min\{U_b(X), U_b(X)\}$, which implies $\min\{U_b(X), U_b(X)\} \leqslant U_b(X + Y)$. Finally, we get that $U_b(X + Y) \leqslant U_b(X) + U_b(Y)$. $\qquad\square$

The last inequality in the above theorem relies on the following:

Lemma 2.12 $P_b(X) \geqslant \mathbb{E}(X)$, for any $X \in L^1_+$. Thus, for any $X \in L^1(\Omega, \mathcal{F}, \mathbb{P})$ taking almost everywhere positive values. For such a X, $P_b(X) \geq 0$.

Proof It suffices to prove that $\frac{1}{b} \log \mathbb{E}(e^{bX}) \geqslant \mathbb{E}(X)$. From Jensen's inequality, we get that $e^{b\mathbb{E}(X)} \leqslant \mathbb{E}(e^{bX})$. Hence, $b\mathbb{E}(X) \leqslant \log \mathbb{E}(e^{bX})$. $\qquad\square$

2.1 The Case of Conditional Value at Risk

As it is well-known expected shortfall ES_a is Conditional Value -at- Risk $CVaR_a$ are equal for any real-valued random variable $X \in L^0(\Omega, \mathcal{F}, \mathbb{P})$, and for any $a \in (0, 1)$. This is true if cumulative distribution function F_X is continuous, except a set $A_a(X) \in \mathcal{B}[0, 1]$, such that $\lambda(A_a(X)) = 0$. $\mathcal{B}[0, 1]]$ denotes the σ-algebra of Borel sets in $[0, 1]$. λ is the Lebesgue measure on $[0, 1]$.

3 Monetary Utility Functions and Equilibrium

Monetary utility functions' impact on investors' decisions may be summarized in terms of "best" portfolio choice for a single investor. That's because the essential problem for any investor is to determine the set of portfolios, which maximizes her monetary utility function U defined on $L^1(\Omega, \mathcal{F}, \mathbb{P})$. $\mathbf{1}$ is the ranodm variable, such that $\mathbf{1}(\omega) = 1$, $\mathbb{P}$ -a.e. Since the order interval $[-e\mathbf{1}, e\mathbf{1}]$ is weakly compact and convex set of $L^1(\Omega, \mathcal{F}, \mathbb{P})$, then $B(p, e, w) = \{X \in L^1_+ | p(X) = w, X \in [-e\mathbf{1}, e\mathbf{1}]\}$ is a weakly compact and convex set. $p \in L^\infty(\Omega, \mathcal{F}, \mathbb{P})$, such that $p(\omega) > 0$, $\mathbb{P}$ a.e. and $w > 0$ is the cash wealth of the investor.

Then, for any monetary utility function $U : L^1(\Omega, \mathcal{F}, \mathbb{P}) \to \mathbb{R}$, we obtain the following.

Theorem 3.1 *The problem of maximization of a monetary utility function U over $B(p, e, w)$ has a solution if U is weakly continuous.*

Proof $< L^1(\Omega, \mathcal{F}, \mathbb{P}), L^\infty(\Omega, \mathcal{F}, \mathbb{P}) >$ is a symmetric Riesz pair. Hence $[-e\mathbf{1}, e\mathbf{1}]$ is a weakly compact and convex set. The conclusion arises from the Bauer maximization principle. □

Hence, the Marshallian demand correspondence is well-defined for any investor whose monetary utility function U is convex and weakly continuous. This is a result of special importance if markets are **incomplete**, or else the portfolio payoffs lie in a nontrivial and weakly closed subspace M of $L^1(\Omega, \mathcal{F}, \mathbb{P})$.

4 Optimal Risk Allocations

Monetary utility functions are also related to problems of collective minimization of regulatory capital. We consider a set $\{1, 2, ..., I\}$ consisted of regulators or financial institutions. Risk functionals arise in the problems related to the inf -convolution, which is actually the value functional of the following optimization problem:

$$\inf \left\{ \sum_{i=1}^{I} r_i \rho_i(X_i) \; \middle| \; \sum_{i=1}^{I} X_i = X \in L^p, \; X_i \in L^p \right\}.$$

$r_i > 0$ for any $i = 1, 2, ..., I$ such that $\sum_{i=1}^{I} r_i = 1$, and ρ_i is some risk measure defined on $L^p := L^p(\Omega, \mathcal{F}, \mathbb{P})$ for $p \geq 1$ and $p < \infty$. r_i for any $i = 1, ..., I$ denotes the market power of each $i = 1, ..., I$. Since the optimal risk allocations are related to some class of utility functions, we may consider the class of monetary utility functions. A monetary utility function, which arises from a monetary risk measure $\rho : L^0 \to \mathbb{R}$, is the function $u = -\rho$. On the other hand, a utility function u implies a monetary risk measure $\rho = -u$.

These spaces are in general L^p spaces on a nonatomic probability space $(\Omega, \mathcal{F}, \mathbb{P})$, and $1 \leq p < \infty$. A unified result is the following one:

Proposition 4.1 *The above inf-convolution is well-defined on the symmetric Riesz pair, if ρ_i is weakly continuous, for any $i = 1, ..., I$.*

Proof The conclusion arises from Bauer maximization principle. $\qquad\square$

The case of $p = 1$ is of special interest since the probability distributions of the heavy-tailed random variables lie in this one Lebesgue space. We recall that a heavy-tailed random variable is any element $X \in L^0(\Omega, \mathcal{F}, \mathbb{P})$ whose exponential moments $\mathbb{E}(e^{rX}) = +\infty$ for any positive, nonzero real number r. In order to make things more simple, we assume that $X(\omega) \geq 0$, $\mathbb{P}$-a.e.

5 Creating Monetary Utility Functions

As we did notice above, Jensen's inequality implies that for any convex and finite -valued function $C : \mathbb{R} \to \mathbb{R}$:

$$C(\mathbb{E}(X)) \leq \mathbb{E}(C(X)),$$

namely, convex functions imply a way to establish monetary utility functions, whose form is actually an expected utility form. It suffices to assume that $\mathbb{E}(C(X))$ is finite for a subset of L^0. A large class of convex functions is the one of Young functions.

We call *Young function* any convex, even, continuous function Φ satisfying the relations $\Phi(0) = 0$, $\Phi(-x) = \Phi(x) \geq 0$ for any $x \in \mathbb{R}$ and

$$\lim_{x \to \infty} \Phi(x) = \infty.$$

The *conjugate function* of Φ is defined by

$$\Psi(y) = \sup_{x \geq 0}\{xy - \Phi(x)\}, \qquad \forall\, y \geq 0.$$

Definition 5.1 An N-Young function is a Young function Φ defined on $\mathbb{R}$, which satisfies the conditions:

(1)

$$\lim_{x \to 0} \frac{\Phi(x)}{x} = 0,$$

(2)

$$\lim_{x \to \infty} \frac{\Phi(x)}{x} = \infty \,,$$

(3) If $\Phi(x) = 0$, then $x = 0$.

Definition 5.2 We say that a Young function Φ satisfies the Δ_2-property if there exist a constant $k > 0$ and a $x_0 \in \mathbb{R}$ such that holds

$$\Phi(2x) \leq k\Phi(x), \quad \forall \, x \geq x_0 \,.$$

Let us mention some examples of Young functions: $\Phi_0(x) = |x|$ is a Young function. $\Phi_1 = \frac{1}{2}|x|^2$ is a Young function, which satisfies both N and Δ_2 properties. If we would like to specify some Young function which is not of the type of $\Phi_p(x) = \frac{1}{p}|x|^p, p > 1$ and satisfies both N properties and Δ_2 properties, then we may mention $\Phi_\ell(x) = (1 + |x|)log(1 + |x|) - |x|$. About the class ∇_2 of Young functions, see (Rao and Ren, 1991, p. 22): a Young function Φ is a ∇_2 -Young function if

$$\Phi(x) \leq \frac{1}{2g}\Phi(x), x \geq x_0 > 0$$

for some $g > 1$. x_0 may be equal to zero. An example of ∇_2 Young function is the conjugate of Φ_ℓ, which is the function $\Psi(x) = e^{|x|} - |x| - 1$.

The book Rao and Ren (1991) is devoted to a complete study on Young functions and Orlicz spaces.

Thus, the monetary utility function implied by some Young function Φ is the following one $\phi : L^0 \to \mathbb{R}$, where $\phi(X) := -\mathbb{E}(\Phi(X))$. Any monetary utility function defined by the way shown above is a **Young monetary utility function**.

In Rao and Ren (1991), the (sub) -set of $X \in L^0(\Omega, \mathcal{F}, \mathbb{P})$ such that $(E)(U(X)) < +\infty$ if $-U$ is a Young function is called *Orlicz Heart M_U*. M_U is in general a convex subset of $L^0(\Omega, \mathcal{F}, \mathbb{P})$. Monetary risk measures defined on Orlicz hearts and Orlicz spaces are initially studied in Cheridito and Li (2009).

6   Analysis Notions and Results Used in the Paper

We add this section in order to make the content of the paper understood in a better manner. The partially ordering implied by some cone K on the vector space E is defined in the following way: $x \geq y \leftrightarrow x - y \in K$. A more detailed study of partially ordered linear spaces and all of the content of this section is obtained from Aliprantis and Border (2006). A non-empty subset K of a vector space E, such that $K + K \subseteq K$, $tK \subset K$ for any $t \in \mathbb{R}_+$ and $K \cap (-K) = \{0\}$ is a cone. Any set of the form $[a, b] = (a + K) \cap (b - K)$, where $a, b \in E$ is an order-interval with respect to the cone K.

The set of upper bounds of $a \in E$, with respect to the cone K, is the set $a + K$. Lower bound of $b \in E$ with respect to the cone K is the set $b - K$. A partially ordered vector space E is a Riesz space (or else a vector lattice) if $\sup\{x, y\} = x \vee y \in E$ and $\inf\{x, y\} = x \wedge y \in E$, where supremum and infimum are the minimum upper bound and the maximum lower bound of $\{x, y\}$, respectively (with respect to the cone K). In such a case, the absolute value of any $x \in E$ is equal to $x \vee (-x) = |x|$ alike in the case of real numbers. The space of all real-valued linear functionals defined on some vector space E is called algebraic dual space of E. A linear functional defined on some partially ordered space E, such that the cone K implying the partially ordering is the cone K, is called order-bounded if it actually maps an order-interval $[a, b]$ to a closed interval of the real numbers. The vector space of all the order-bounded linear functionals of the partially ordered linear space E is called order dual. We denote the order dual of E by E'. An ideal of some Riesz space is any subspace S of E, such that if $|x| \geq |y|$ and $x \in S$, implies that $y \in S$. A dual pair $< E, E^* >$ is called Riesz pair if both E, E^* are Riesz spaces and E^* is an ideal of the order dual E' of E. A dual pair $< E, E^* >$ is called symmetric Riesz pair, if and only if $< E^*, E >$ is a Riesz Pair as well. If $< E, E^* >$ is a symmetric Riesz pair, then the non-empty order intervals of E are weakly compact. The set F of maximizers of some weakly continuous function f is non-empty if the domain of it is some weakly compact set C of E. Moreover, F actually it is an extreme set of C. An extreme set of some convex set is any subset A of it; then every element of $z \in A$, such that $z = tx + (1 - t)y \in A$, where $t \in (0, 1)$; then $x, y \in A$. An extreme point is any extremal set consisted of a singleton. This is a proof of Bauer maximization principle refers to the maximization of semicontinuous functions: if C is a compact convex subset C of a locally convex Hausdorff space, then every upper semicontinuous convex function on C has a maximum point that is an extreme point of it. The analog of the above theorem is valid for the minimization of a concave function, which is weakly continuous. The topology under use here is the weak topology over a Riesz pair $< E, E^* >$ as well.

7   Further Research

Further research may be related to the functional form of the efficiency frontiers or the demand functions under different classes of concave functions. This study relies on the equivalence structure for risk functionals as it is defined here.

References

Aliprantis, C. D., & Border, K. C. (2006). *Infinite dimensional analysis: A Hitchhiker's Guide* (3rd ed.). Springer.

Artzner, P., et al. (1999). Coherent measures of risk. *Mathematical Finance, 9*(3), 203–228.

Borch, K. (1962). Equilibrium in a reinsurance market. *Econometrica, 30*, 424–444.

Cheridito, P., & Li, T. (2009). Risk measures on Orlicz hearts. *Mathematical Finance, 19*, 189–214.

Filipoviĉ, D., & Kupper, M. (2008). Equilibrium prices for monetary utility functions. *Journal of Theoretical and Applied Finance, 11*(3), 325–343.

Föllmer, H., & Schied, A. (2002). Convex measures of risk and trading constraints. *Finance and Stochastics, 6*, 429–447.

Jouini, E., Schachermayer, W., & Touzi, N. (2007). Optimal risk sharing for law invariant monetary utility functions. *Mathematical Finance, 18*(2), 269–292.

Kiesel, S., & Rüschendorf, L. (2009). Characterization of optimal risk allocations for convex risk functionals. *Statistics and Risk Modeling, 26*, 303–319.

Rao, M. M., & Ren, Z. D. (1991). *Theory of Orlicz spaces.* New York: M. Dekker, Inc.

Righi, M. B., & Moresco, M. R. (2022). Inf-convolution and optimal risk sharing with countable 226 sets of risk measures. *Annals of Operations Research.* https://doi.org/10.1007/s10479-022-04593-8

Koopman Operators and Extended Dynamic Mode Decomposition for Economic Growth Models in Terms of Fractional Derivatives

John Leventides, Evangelos Melas, Costas Poulios, and Paraskevi Boufounou

Abstract We apply the Koopman operator theory and Extended Dynamic Mode Decomposition (EDMD) in a non-linear dynamical system. This system describes the capital accumulation, and it is similar to the Solow-Swan model and the Ramsey-Cass-Koopmans model. However, the usual derivative is replaced with a fractional derivative. This dynamical system is approximated by a finite-dimensional linear system which is defined in some augmented state space. However, because of the presence of the fractional derivative, one expects that the dimension of the linear system will be quite bigger.

Keywords Koopman operator · Extended dynamic mode decomposition · Solow-Swan model · Ramsey-Cass-Koopmans model · Capital accumulation · Fractional calculus

1 Introduction

Economic growth plays a central role in the long-run development of every economy. Since many decades, the process of economic growth is one of the most important topics of research in dynamic macroeconomic analysis. Furthermore, the sources of differences in economic performance across countries have been the central issue in many social studies.

Traditional growth models, such as the basic Solow-Swan (or exogenous growth) model and the neoclassical models, provided a good starting point for the theoretical research and understanding of the mechanics of economic growth. Later, these models were extended to several directions. The Solow-Swan model consists of a single ordinary non-linear differential equation that describes the evolution of the per capita stock of capital. Cass and Koopmans combined this system with

J. Leventides (✉) · E. Melas · C. Poulios · P. Boufounou
Department of Economics, National and Kapodistrian University of Athens, Athens, Greece
e-mail: ylevent@econ.uoa.gr; emelas@econ.uoa.gr; konpou@econ.uoa.gr;
pboufounou@econ.uoa.gr

© The Author(s), under exclusive license to Springer Nature Switzerland AG 2023
P. Alphonse et al. (eds.), *Essays on Financial Analytics*, Lecture Notes in Operations
Research, https://doi.org/10.1007/978-3-031-29050-3_3

Ramsey's analysis of consumer optimization and created the so-called Ramsey-Cass-Koopmans model.

The equation for capital accumulation is one of the key equations in the aforementioned model. It is similar to the differential equation in Solow-Swan model, and it can be derived as follows. The model starts with an aggregate production function which satisfies the Inada conditions, and it is a standard Cobb-Douglas function. Hence, it is of the form $F(K, L) = AK^\alpha L^\beta$, where K denotes capital, L is the labour input and A is the (constant) total factor productivity. If $\alpha + \beta = 1$, then $F(K, L)$ is homogeneous of degree 1, and it can be written in the next form

$$F(K, L) = L \cdot F\left(\frac{K}{L}, 1\right) = L \cdot f(k),$$

where $k = \frac{K}{L}$ is the capital per person. The amount of labour L is assumed to be equal to the population in the economy, and it is given by $L = L_0 \cdot e^{nt}$. Hence, we assume that the population grows at a constant rate n.

In Ramsey-Cass-Koopmans model, the capital accumulation is described by the following first-order non-linear differential equation:

$$\frac{dk}{dt} = f(k) - (n + \delta) \cdot k - c \tag{1}$$

where δ is a constant expressing the depreciation rate of the capital and c stands for the consumption per person. In the case where the population remains constant, i.e. $n = 0$, Eq. (1) indicates that the growth in capital per person is the part of the output that is not consumed ($f(k) - c$) minus the rate of the depreciation of capital.

In the present work, our primary objective is to study the dynamical system arising from the previous equation that models the dynamics of capital accumulation. Our investigation in this topic is oriented towards two directions. First of all, we modify Eq. (1) by replacing the derivative of k with some fractional derivative. Thus, we have the dynamical system given by

$$D_t^{\alpha, \rho} k = f(k) - (n + \delta) \cdot k - c. \tag{2}$$

This system has already been considered by Traore and Sene (2020) where a stability analysis can be found. However, in this work, our purpose is to study the above system using tools and methods from the Koopman operator theory combined with the Extended Dynamic Mode Decomposition (EDMD).

The reason for this approach is twofold. On the one hand, fractional calculus has found seminal applications not only in mathematics but also in many research fields, such as in physics and fluid mechanics. It has been observed that sometimes fractional-order derivatives enjoy many advantages in comparison with the usual derivatives.

On the other hand, the theory of Koopman operators has become a popular formalism of dynamical systems and especially in the case of non-linear system.

2 Fractional Calculus

There are several ways to generalize the ordinary differentiation and integration to non-integer (arbitrary real or complex) order. These definitions of fractional derivatives do not give the same results, even for smooth functions. In this work, we consider the Riemann-Liouville fractional derivative and the Grünwald-Letnikov fractional derivative. The latter allows us in general to construct numerical methods for differential equations of fractional order, and also it allows us in particular later on to construct the necessary extension to the Koopman-EDMD theory needed to accommodate the presence of fractional derivatives in the differential equations which drive the dynamics of the system under consideration.

2.1 The Riemann-Liouville Fractional Derivative

The Riemann-Liouville fractional derivative is defined as follows. For a function $f : [c, d] \rightarrow \mathbb{R}$ and a (not necessarily integer) number α, the α-fractional derivative of f is given by

$$_c D_t^\alpha f(t) = \frac{1}{\Gamma(n - \alpha)} \cdot \frac{d^n}{dt^n} \int_c^t \frac{f(\tau)}{(t - \tau)^{\alpha - n + 1}} \, d\tau,$$

where n is the smallest integer greater than α (i.e. $n = \lceil \alpha \rceil$).

2.2 The Grünwald-Letnikov Fractional Derivative

Nearly simultaneous with the development of the Riemann-Liouville definition of fractional integration and differentiation, another definition for a non-integer derivative was developed independently by Grünwald and Letnikov. The Grünwald-Letnikov fractional derivative is defined as follows. Let $\alpha \in \mathbb{R}^+$. The operator defined by

$$D^\alpha f(x) = \lim_{h \to 0} \frac{(\Delta_h^\alpha f)(x)}{h^\alpha} = \lim_{\substack{h \to 0, \\ mh = x - \alpha}} \frac{1}{h^\alpha} \sum_{k=0}^m (-1)^k \binom{\alpha}{k} f(x - kh),$$

$$(3)$$

for $\alpha \leq x \leq b$ is called the Grünwald-Letnikov fractional derivative of order α. In this definition, the term $(\Delta^{\alpha} f)(x)$ is a fractional formulation of a backward difference which is reminiscent of the discretization of higher-order positive integer derivatives.

3   Koopman Operator and Extended Dynamic Mode Decomposition

We start by giving the bare essentials of Koopman operator theory and the associated EDMD method in the form they are applied to dynamical systems whose dynamics is driven by differential equations, ordinary or partial, which do not involve fractional derivatives. Then we give the necessary extension to the Koopman-EDMD method in order to make it applicable to the case where fractional derivatives appear in the differential equation which governs the dynamics. The generalized Koopman-EDMD scheme presented here does not claim full generality; it is written instead with the view to be applied to the particular problem under consideration.

3.1   Koopman-EDMD Theory

Assume that we have an autonomous dynamical system of the form $\dot{x}(t) = f(x(t))$. Any function $\phi : \mathbb{R} \to \mathbb{R}$ is called an observable of the system. The flow of the system is also defined as follows: $S^t(x)$ is the state of the system after time t when starting from the initial condition x. We assume that $\mathcal{F}$ is a vector space of observables which is closed under composition with the flow (i.e. if $\phi \in \mathcal{F}$, then $\phi \circ S^t \in \mathcal{F}$). The Koopman operator (which was introduced by Koopman (1931) and is actually a family of operators) is defined as follows:

$$K_t(\phi) = \phi \circ S^t,$$

for any $t > 0$. As usual, we refer to the Koopman operator and we will denote the operator by K.

The operator is linear and its spectral properties describe completely the dynamics of the original system (see, for example, Mezić, 2005). However, it is infinite dimensional, and its spectral decomposition cannot be found with numerical methods. For this reason, we seek for finite-dimensional approximations of this operator. The EDMD provides a systematic way to devise such a finite-dimensional approximation of the operator. The method is data-driven and it can be applied even if the dynamics are unknown or strongly non-linear.

More precisely, we start by choosing a *dictionary*, which is a set $\{\phi_j\}_{j=1}^m$ of observables. This choice is very crucial, since the dictionary will determine the approximation properties. We next collect the data. We assume that k trajectories of the dynamical system are executed starting from initial conditions $x_{j0} \in \mathbb{R}^n, j = 1, 2, \ldots, k$. Each trajectory is witnessed for some time horizon T, and it is sampled at a fixed time interval Δt. Hence, we obtain $n_0 + 1 = \frac{T}{\Delta t}$ snapshots of each trajectory. Therefore, the data are given by

$$\left(\left(x_{js} \right)_{s=0}^{n_0} \right)_{j=1}^k.$$

Observe that we have considered fixed time horizon T and also uniform sampling in time. However, this is not obligatory, and one may collect the data using different sampling strategy.

The augmented (or lifted) stated space consists of vectors of the form

$$y = [x, \phi(x)]^T,$$

where $\phi(x) = [\phi_1(x), \ldots, \phi_m(x)]^T$. Observe that the augmented space has dimension $m + n$, i.e. if one wishes to approximate the original non-linear system with a linear one, they have to consider more dimensions. The number m of additional coordinates varies and depends on the behaviour of the original system. If our data indicate that the dynamical system, although non-linear, has a "smooth" behaviour, then it suffices to consider only a few additional coordinates. For systems with extreme behaviour and complex trajectories, the number m should be large enough to obtain good approximation properties (if this is possible).

Each trajectory of the original system corresponds to a trajectory in the lifted space. Therefore, the collected data $\left(\left(x_{js} \right)_{s=0}^{n_0} \right)_{j=1}^k$ correspond to data in the augmented state space which have the form

$$y_{j0}, y_{j1}, \ldots, y_{jn_0},$$

for initial values $y_{j0}, j = 1, 2, \ldots, k$. For any $j = 1, 2, \ldots, k$, we set

$$Y_{j[0,n_0-1]} = \left[y_{j0}, y_{j1}, \ldots, y_{j,n_0-1} \right] \quad \text{and} \quad Y_{j[1,n_0]} = \left[y_{j1}, y_{j1}, \ldots, y_{j,n_0} \right].$$

Finally, a best-fit (finite-dimensional) linear operator $A \in \mathbb{R}^{(n+m) \times (n+m)}$ is obtained such that $Y_{j[1,n_0]} \approx A \cdot Y_{j[0,n_0-1]}$, for all $j = 1, 2, \ldots, k$. The matrix A is constructed with least square regression methods. For instance, one may consider

$$A = \operatorname{argmin}_{\widetilde{A} \in \mathbb{R}^{(n+m) \times (n+m)}} \sum_{j=1}^k \left\| Y_{j[1,n_0]} - \widetilde{A} \cdot Y_{j[0,n_0-1]} \right\|^2.$$

The (finite-dimensional) linear operator A can now be used to approximate the trajectories of the original dynamical system. More precisely, given the initial condition $x_0 \in \mathbb{R}^n$, one has to move into the lifted space and to consider the initial condition $y = [x_0, \phi(x_0)]^T$. Then, the trajectory $\{y_n\}$ of the linear system $y_{n+1} = A \cdot y_n$ can also be obtained. The projection of this trajectory to the first n coordinates gives rise to an approximation of the trajectory of the original system, provided that the choice of dictionary is proven to be suitable.

Approximating a non-linear system with a linear one has many advantages. The dynamics of the linear system $y_{n+1} = A \cdot y_n$ are completely determined by the spectral properties of the matrix A. Therefore, if, for instance, A has $n + m$ distinct eigenvalues, then it can be decomposed as $A = P\Lambda P^{-1}$, where Λ is diagonal and P is the matrix whose columns are eigenvectors of A. Consequently, $y_{n+1} = P\Lambda^n P^{-1} \cdot y_0$, or equivalently

$$P^{-1} y_{n+1} = P\Lambda^n P^{-1} \cdot y_0$$

for every positive integer n. This shows, for example, that if the eigenvalue λ is bigger than 1 but the coordinates of y_{n+1} are small, then the initial condition y_0 is orthogonal to the corresponding eigenvector.

3.2 Koopman-EDMD Theory with Fractional Derivatives Present

The Koopman-EDMD method given in Sect. 3.1 cannot approximate the trajectories of the dynamics determined by Eqs. (2) and (3) no matter how many observables we are going to include in the dictionary. The reason is that in the usual Koopman-EDMD method, the values of the observables at an instant of time are determined by their values at a time step Δt before as it is indicated by the equation $Y_{j[1,n_0]} \approx A \cdot Y_{j[0,n_0-1]}$ for all $j = 1, \ldots, k$. However, when fractional derivatives appear in the dynamical law, the values of the observables at an instant of time not only are determined by their values one time step Δt before but they are also determined by their values at more than one previous time steps. Therefore, we need to modify the Koopman-EDMD method in order to apply it to the dynamics given by Eqs. (2) and (3). We do so by introducing a hybrid method which combines the standard Koopman-EDMD theory with the autoregressive model.

Therefore, motivated by Eq. (3), the values of the observables at an instant are not determined only by the values of the observables a time step Δt before, but they retain the memory of the values of the observables μ steps before. Therefore, $Y_{j[1,n_0]} \approx A \cdot Y_{j[0,n_0-1]}$ for all $j = 1, \ldots, k$ is now generalized to

$$Y_{j[\mu,n_0]} \approx A_1 \cdot Y_{j[0,n_0-\mu]} + A_2 \cdot Y_{j[1,n_0-(\mu-1)]} + \cdots + A_\mu \cdot Y_{j[\mu-1,n_0-1]}. \tag{4}$$

Equation (4) is conveniently written as

$$
Y_{j[\mu,n_0]} \approx \begin{bmatrix} A_1 & A_2 \cdots & A_\mu \end{bmatrix} \cdot \begin{bmatrix} Y_{j[0,n_0-\mu]} \\ Y_{j[1,n_0-(\mu-1)]} \\ \vdots \\ Y_{j[\mu-1,n_0-1]} \end{bmatrix} \tag{5}
$$

Equation (5) implies that

$$
\begin{bmatrix} A_1 & A_2 \cdots & A_\mu \end{bmatrix} \approx Y_{j[\mu,n_0]} \cdot \begin{bmatrix} Y_{j[0,n_0-\mu]} \\ Y_{j[1,n_0-(\mu-1)]} \\ \vdots \\ Y_{j[\mu-1,n_0-1]} \end{bmatrix}^{+}
$$

where A^+ denotes the pseudoinverse of a matrix A.

4 Conclusions

The standard mathematical language, which is actively used in mathematical modelling of economy, is the calculus of derivatives and integrals of integer orders, the differential and difference equations. These operators and equations allowed economists to formulate models in mathematical form and, on this basis, to describe a wide range of processes and phenomena in economy. It is known that the integer-order derivatives of functions are determined by the properties of these functions in an infinitely small neighbourhood of the point, in which the derivatives are considered. As a result, economic models, which are based on differential equations of integer orders, cannot describe processes with memory and nonlocality. As a result, this mathematical language cannot take into account important aspects of economic processes and phenomena.

Fractional calculus is a branch of mathematics that studies the properties of differential and integral operators that are characterized by real or complex orders. The methods of fractional calculus are powerful tools for describing the processes and systems with memory and nonlocality. There are various types of fractional integral and differential operators that have been proposed by Riemann, Liouville, Grünwald, Letnikov, Sonine, Marchaud, Weyl, Riesz, Hadamard, Kober, Erdelyi, Caputo and other mathematicians. In this paper, we have concentrated on the Riemann-Liouville fractional derivative and on the Grünwald-Letnikov fractional derivative which allows to construct numerical methods for differential equations of fractional order.

The fractional derivatives have a set of nonstandard properties such as a violation of the standard product and chain rules. The violation of the standard form of the product rule is a main characteristic property of derivatives of non-integer orders that allows us to describe complex properties of processes and systems. Recently, fractional integro-differential equations are actively used to describe a wide class of economical processes with power-law memory and spatial nonlocality. Generalizations of basic economic concepts and notions of the economic processes with memory by using fractional derivatives have been proposed.

However, the mathematical treatment of differential equations with fractional derivatives poses significant challenges. In this paper, we propose a method in order to apply the Koopman-EDMD theory in the study of differential equations with fractional derivatives. Thus, we associate a linear operator to the non-linear dynamics driven by fractional derivatives, and we therefore can employ the full machinery of the linear operator theory, spectra analysis, etc., in order to probe the fractional derivative dynamics.

Koopman operator theory and EDMD provide an alternative theory to study the discrete or the continuous flow on M of some discrete or continuous, respectively, dynamical system. Specifically, for a subset $X_0 \subseteq M$ and horizons $[0, n_0]$, $[0, T] \subseteq [0, \infty)$, EDMD simplifies the orbits by

(a) Extending the state space M to $\overline{M}$ and defining a linear system on the new space $\overline{M}$ (this is done via the Koopman operator) which is infinite dimensional
(b) Approximating the orbits on $\overline{M}$ with a finite-dimensional linear system of dimension m: $m \gg \dim M$
(c) Using the flow of the linear system of [(b)] to approximate the flow (orbits) of the original non-linear system

The dynamical system described in Eq. (2) not only is non-linear but also the usual derivative has been replaced with the fractional derivative D^α. Consequently, one expects that the augmented state space $\overline{M}$, constructed by the dictionary of observables, should have bigger dimension, so that the orbits of the finite-dimensional linear system can approximate the orbits of the original system (2).

References

Koopman, B. O. (1931). Hamiltonian systems and transformation in Hilbert space. *Proceedings of the National Academy of Sciences, 17*, 315–318.
Mezić, I. (2005). Spectral properties of dynamical systems, model reduction and decompositions. *Nonlinear Dynamics, 41*, 309–325.
Traore, A., & Sene, N. (2020). Model of economic growth in the context of fractional derivative. *Alexandria Engineering Journal, 59*, 4843–4850.

Part II
Cryptocurrency and Investment Policy

Efficiency, Taxation, and Solvency Issues for SMEs: The Case of Greece, Italy, and Spain

Christos Floros, Christos Lemonakis, Efthalia Tabouratzi, Alexandros Garefalakis, and Constantin Zopounidis

Abstract This paper provides new insights into the efficiency of European firms using accounting and financial ratios. In particular, we discuss how the data envelopment analysis (DEA) method can be used with accounting and financial data to highlight the importance of firm profitability as a counterbalance to crisis-induced weakness in demand. We consider several DEA models for studying the technical, financial, and financing efficiency of firms, including a unique set of variables (inputs/outputs) for productivity analysis. Our results provide recommendations for financial managers and analysts dealing with European firms, especially from the southern parts of Europe, i.e., Greece, Italy, and Spain.

Keywords Efficiency · Accounting ratios · Financial ratios · DEA · European firms

---

C. Floros (✉) · E. Tabouratzi
Department of Accounting & Finance, Hellenic Mediterranean University, Crete, Greece
e-mail: cfloros@hmu.gr; tamthal@hmu.gr

C. Lemonakis
Department of Management Science and Technology, Hellenic Mediterranean University, Crete, Greece
e-mail: lemonakis@hmu.gr

A. Garefalakis
Department of Business Administration and Tourism, Hellenic Mediterranean University, Crete, Greece
e-mail: agarefalakis@hmu.gr

C. Zopounidis
Financial Engineering Laboratory, Technical University of Crete, Chania, Greece

Audencia Business School, Nantes, France
e-mail: kzopounidis@tuc.gr

1   Introduction

Businesses play an important role in all economies and are the main generators of employment and income as well as the drivers of innovation and growth. They are the engine of growth (Beck & Demirguc-Kunt, 2006). The manufacturing sector is a feature of fast-growing economies. What mechanism and how much tax and efficiency ratios affect the profitability index (return on assets—ROA) and solvency ratio are one of the main objectives of this research.

Profitability ratios are considered the most important financial ratios of a company that can be used to evaluate the desirable performance of a company in profitable situations. To relate taxes to profitability ratios, a company's costs and debt can be used. By determining the ratio of debt to assets and profits, as well as the return on assets, a correct decision can be made about granting different types of financial facilities to the companies under study.

Little attention has been paid to the relationship between ROA and solvency ratio with company values, especially for Greece, Italy, and Spain. Taxes can increase ROA and the solvency ratio and thus have a positive effect. Efficiency can increase ROA and solvency ratio and thus have a positive effect. Negative effects: Debtors have a negative impact on the solvency ratio.

Q1) Is ROA a key factor in explaining differences in taxation, efficiency, and other explanatory variables?
Q2) To what extent do efficiency and taxation affect solvency?

2   Methodology: Two-Stage Approach

Reviewing the efficiency and profitability of European (Greek, Spanish, and Italian) companies is important because many companies tend to negotiate their existence in competitive markets, change their business models, and increase their market shares (Voulgaris & Lemonakis, 2014). The economic crisis has been particularly hard on Greek companies. This study contributes to the existing literature in two ways: It is the first empirical study on the relationship between ROA, efficiency, taxation, and solvency ratio; we use two commonly accepted methods: data envelopment analysis (DEA) and panel regression.

In this study, we use data envelopment analysis (DEA), a nonparametric method for measuring relative efficiency, taxation, and solvency issues for SMEs of the European South, within a group of homogeneous decision-making units (DMUs) with multiple inputs and multiple outputs.

We use efficiency scores as indicators of firm performance (Mok et al., 2007; Floros et al., 2014). The efficiency estimates in our study are obtained using the DEA, which dates back to Charnes et al. (1978). We then examine the relationships between the efficiency scores of DEA and return on equity, taxation, and solvency.

3 DEA Description

The foundations of the data envelopment analysis (DEA) method were laid by Charnes et al. (1978), later developed further by Banker et al. (1984). Several DEA models have been developed; one of the well-known is the model of Charnes et al. (1978), known as the CCR model, and its extension by Banker et al. (1984), known as the BCC model. Depending on their orientation, these models are divided into input-oriented models (for a given level of output to minimize inputs) and output-oriented models (for a given level of input to maximize outputs) and by returns to scale into constant returns to scale (CRS model) and variable returns to scale (VRS model).

Data envelopment analysis (DEA) is a nonparametric mathematical programming approach to estimating frontiers. DEA is a method best suited for measuring relative efficiency by input and output elements of decision-making units (DMUs). DEA is an effective tool for analyzing the efficiency of many groups of companies, while it works relatively well with small samples of units. In addition, DEA can handle multiple inputs and outputs reported in different units of measurement and does not require knowledge of the functional form of the frontier (Charnes et al., 1994), while DEA can provide robust results (Seiford & Thrall, 1990).

Input (output)-oriented technical efficiency—TE measures address the questions, "By how much can input (output) quantities be proportionally reduced (expanded) without changing the output (input) quantities produced (used)?"

(a) DEA-CRS and DEA VRS Models

Charnes et al. (2018) proposed DEA and assumed constant returns to scale (CRS). It measures the efficiency of each decision-making unit (DMU), which is the maximum of the ratio of weighted output to weighted input. Banker et al. (1984) proposed a variable return to scale (VRS) model. The VRS assumption allows the measurement of purely technical efficiency (PTE), i.e., the measurement of technical efficiency without the scale efficiency. If the efficiency scores obtained from CRS model and the VRS model are different, this indicates that the DMU has scale inefficiency.

(b) DEA-CRS Model

Theoretical Formulation of the DEA-CRS Model
To measure the efficiency of each DMU, T.J. Coelli (1996) presented a mathematical linear programming equation calculating the ratio of all outputs over all inputs. The formula is as follows:

$$\min_{\theta, \lambda} \theta, \text{ s.t.}$$

$$-y_i + Y\lambda \geq 0, \theta x_i - X\lambda \geq 0, \ \lambda \geq 0.$$

where the symbol θ is a scalar and refers to the efficiency of a unit and takes values within the closed interval [0, 1]. Also, λ is an $N*1$ vector of constants, where it represents the percentage of the other units in the virtual unit.

In DEA method, the problem to be solved is to determine the values of θ. DMUs with values of θ equal to 1 operate at optimal efficiency, while DMUs with values of θ less than 1 are inefficient.

The linear programming problem above is under the assumption of constant returns to scale (CRS), introduced by Charnes, Cooper, and Rhodes in 1978. In difference, another condition, $N1'\lambda = 1$, is added to the linear programming problem under the variable returns to scale (VRS), introduced by Banker, Charnes, and Cooper in 1984—leading to different results in terms of efficiency.

(c) Theoretical Formulation of the DEA-VRS Model

The total technical efficiency (OTE: overall technical efficiency) is equal to the result obtained from the application of the data envelopment analysis methodology, under constant scale odds (CRS model). SE (scale efficiency) is achieved by using the VRS model. The relationship between CSR and VRS is given below:

$$^{TE}CRS = {}^{TE}VRS^{X\,SE}$$

The CRS linear programming problem can be easily modified to account for VRS by adding the convexity constraint, $N1'\lambda = 1$, to provide

$$\min\theta, \lambda\ \theta,$$

$$\text{s.t.}$$

$$-yi + Y\lambda \geq 0, \theta xi - X\lambda \geq 0, N1'\lambda = 1,$$

$$\lambda \geq 0.$$

where $N1$ is an $N \times 1$ vector of ones. This approach forms a convex hull of interesting plans which envelop the data points more tightly than the CRS conical hull; this provides pure technical efficiency scores which are greater than or equal to those obtained using the CSR model.

1. Panel Regression

In this study, EGLS models are used, with a balanced panel data. Data were treated for outliers at 5% level. There is no indication that the data structure is characterized by period specific efficiency, competitiveness, and exports of agricultural firms in the referring period heteroskedasticity and contemporaneous and between-period covariance. The independent variables were selected on the basis of theory and international literature.

More specifically, we propose the following model (Model 1):

$$\text{ROA} \quad \text{BEFORETAX}_i \text{ or Solvency Ratio}_i$$
$$= a1 + a2 \text{ COLLECTIONPERIOD}_i + a3$$

$$\text{LOGTAX} + a4 \text{ VRSOUTPUT}_i \text{ (or CRSOUTPUT)}$$
$$+a5 \text{ LOGDEPRAMORT}_i + a6 \text{ LOGDEBTORS}_i + a7 \text{ LOGINTERPAID}_i$$
$$+a8 \text{ LOGWORKINGCAPITAL}_i + a9 \text{ LOGENTERPRISEVALUE}_i$$
$$+a10 \text{ LOGPROVISIONS}_i + \varepsilon_i \text{ (Model 1)}$$

where

Dependent Variables
- ROA = return on assets ratio (with income before taxes)

- Solency_ratio: Solvency ratio is a measure of a firm's ability to meet its debt and other obligations. It indicates whether a company's cash flow is sufficient to meet its short-term and long-term liabilities [= (Net income + depreciations) / (short- + long-term liabilities)]

Independent Variables
- vrsoutput: VRS output orientation for DEA analysis
- crsoutput: CRS output orientation for DEA analysis
- Collection_period: collection period of demand in days
- Log_Tax: logarithm of taxes paid in the EUR
- Log_DeprAmort: logarithm of depreciation and amortizations account from firms'
    financial statements
- Log_Debtors: logarithm of the debtors' account in the EUR
- Log_Interpaid: logarithm of interest paid in banking institutions and elsewhere in the EUR
- Log_Workingcapital: logarithm of firms' working capital = current assets – current liabilities per year
- Log_Enterpricevalue: logarithm of firms' market value in the EUR
- LogProvisions: logarithm of firms' provisions accounts per year

The above variables are used to derive relationships between dependent variables and independent ones, on the basis of the results obtained from the application of DEA methods for the countries under review.

2. Data

We consider a large amount of recent data (source: Amadeus DataBase) and apply several DEA methods (DEA-CRS vs. DEA VRS) and panel regressions to examine our hypotheses for Greece, Italy, and Spain.

Sectors: sample firms sectors—mainly in manufacturing and services. Type of firms—very large firms. Sample firms: Greece, 132 firms; Spain, 98 firms; Italy, 150 firms; total = 380 firms; for the period 2007–2015

(a) *Firms' Descriptive statistics*

Type of firms—very large firms
Table 1 presents the sample firms sectors—mainly in manufacturing and services.
Table 2 presents the sample's firms' descriptives statistics.
The average of 9 years was intentionally chosen to avoid including misleading information about the volumes of total assets, current assets, and working capital and the procedures delivered by them in the analysis to be made.

3. Empirical Results: DEA

The nonparametric approach DEA is mainly applied to estimate efficiencies with the use of the following parameters:

(a) *DEA Analysis*

Outputs

• Output1—Sales account
• Output2—Net income account

Inputs

• Input1—Gearing (leverage), financial ratio
• Input2—Equity capital
• Input3—Net fixed assets

We take the following orientation—CRS output and VRS output orientations— and we run the DEA model for firms from selected countries.

(b) *Results of DEA*

The mean values per year for the whole sample (i.e., all countries' firms) are depicted in Table 3.
Mean Values of DEA Scores per Country

DEA Scores
Tables 4, 5, and 6 show that the companies in the Italian sample have the highest average values for CRS output per year (%) and VRS output per year (%) during the audit period, while the sampled companies from Greece have the lowest scores in all DEA analysis options. The year 2011 shows the sharpest decline in efficiency

Table 1 Sample firms sectors—mainly in manufacturing and services

1.	Trade of gas through mains (very large companies)
2.	Activities of holding companies (very large companies)
3.	Construction of other civil engineering projects (very large companies)
4.	Postal activities under universal service obligation (very large companies)
5.	Passenger air transport (very large companies)
6.	Wholesale of clothing and footwear (very large companies)
7.	Production of electricity (very large companies)
8.	Manufacture of air and spacecraft and related machinery (very large companies)
9.	Construction of residential and nonresidential buildings (very large companies)
10.	Retail sale in nonspecialized stores with food, beverages, or tobacco predominating (very large companies)
11.	Wholesale of electrical household appliances (very large companies)
12.	Manufacture of refined petroleum products (very large companies)
13.	Wholesale of metals and metal ores (very large companies)
14.	Collection of nonhazardous waste (very large companies)
15.	Operation of dairies and cheese making (very large companies)
16.	Restaurants and mobile food service activities (very large companies)
17.	Water collection, treatment, and supply (very large companies)
18.	Manufacture of cement (very large companies)
19.	Gambling and betting activities (very large companies)
20.	Building of ships and floating structures (very large companies)
21.	Engineering activities and related technical consultancy (very large companies)
22.	Private security activities (very large companies)
23.	Wired telecommunications activities (very large companies)
24.	Accounting, bookkeeping, and auditing activities; tax consultancy (very large companies)
25.	Retail sale of clothing in specialized stores (very large companies)
26.	Service activities incidental to air transportation (very large companies)
27.	Distribution of electricity (very large companies)
28.	Development of building projects (very large companies)
29.	Other information technology and computer service activities (very large companies)
30.	Construction of railways and underground railways (very large companies)
31.	Manufacture of machinery for metallurgy (very large companies)
32.	Freight transport by road (very large companies)
33.	Wholesale of computers, computer peripheral equipment, and software (very large companies)
34.	Transmission of electricity (very large companies)
35.	Manufacture of other parts and accessories for motor vehicles (very large companies)
36.	Construction of utility projects for electricity and telecommunications (very large companies)
37.	Computer programming activities (very large companies)
38.	Hotels and similar accommodation (very large companies)
39.	Business and other management consultancy activities (very large companies)
40.	Manufacture of beverages (very large companies)
41.	Other business support service activities not elsewhere classified (very large companies)

Table 2 Firms' descriptives

	Total assets—average values	Current assets—average values	Working capital—average values
2015	2.083.389,39€	683.528,42€	129.467,78€
2014	2.175.872,59€	718.413,81€	142.457,96€
2013	2.262.989,32€	737.912,38€	148.833,14€
2012	2.272.748,99€	726.935,51€	163.046,13€
2011	2.306.798,55€	736.580,63€	163.164,40€
2010	2.077.650,65€	675.500,92€	177.180,30€
2009	2.006.586,63€	701.979,12€	168.195,37€
2008	1.866.506,67€	643.491,97€	133.899,40€
2007	1.644.196,60€	533.034,96€	145.069,18€

Table 3 Average of CRS and VRS output values per year (%)

Years	Average of CRS output values per year (%)	Average of VRS output values per year (%)
2007	30.29	37.05
2008	28.62	35.98
2009	25.63	31.87
2010	23.24	31.25
2011	23.38	31.77
2012	24.68	32.56
2013	24.22	32.83
2014	23.15	31.86
2015	27.19	35.89
Average	*25.60*	*33.45*

Table 4 Average of crs and vrs output values per year (%) for Spain

Years	Average of CRS output values per year (%)	Average of VRS output values per year (%)
2007	32.84	44.55
2008	28.18	39.71
2009	24.52	35.39
2010	19.83	29.96
2011	19.84	29.25
2012	23.13	32.39
2013	21.26	34.25
2014	20.69	30.92
2015	24.27	35.62
Average	*23.84*	*34.67*

Table 5 Average of CRS and VRS output values per year (%) for Italy

Years	Average of CRS output values per year (%)	Average of VRS output values per year (%)
2007	35.11	41.92
2008	32.32	39.75
2009	32.30	37.71
2010	30.44	40.12
2011	31.49	42.46
2012	29.70	40.94
2013	29.47	38.73
2014	26.47	37.78
2015	34.52	42.93
Average	*31.31*	*40.26*

Table 6 Average of CRS and VRS output values per year (%) for Greece

Years	Average of CRS output values per year (%)	Average of VRS output values per year (%)
2007	22.91	25.93
2008	24.74	28.92
2009	18.86	22.63
2010	17.59	22.14
2011	16.80	21.49
2012	20.11	23.16
2013	20.45	25.06
2014	21.19	25.82
2015	21.01	28.08
Average	*20.41*	*24.80*

for companies in Spain and Greece, while these data are collected 1 year later, in 2012, for Italy, although the crisis period continues for all companies in the sample in the following years.

4 Econometric Results

We use econometric analysis in order to relate the taxes to the profitability indices, and the costs and the debts of a corporation can be referred.

In case of determining a relationship between debts ratio to the assets and profits as well as asset return, a correct decision over granting various types of financial facilities to the studied companies can be made.

In particular, in this part of the study, we run the following regression models, i.e., Options 1–4. We have as follows:

Option 1

$$\text{ROA BEFORETAXi} = \text{a1} + \text{a2 COLLECTIONPERIODi} + \text{a3 LOGTAX} \\ + \text{a4 VRSOUTPUTi}$$

$$+ \text{a5LOGDEPRAMORTi} + \text{a6LOGDEBTORSi} + \text{a7 LOGINTERPAIDi} \\ + \text{a8 LOGWORK}-$$

$$\text{INGCAPITALi} + \text{a9 LOGENTERPRISEVALUEi} \\ + \text{a10 LOGPROVISIONSi} + \varepsilon i$$

For each firm $i(i = 1, 2, 3, \ldots, 380)$, for 9 consecutive years, e.g., 2007–2015 we run Option 1.

Because cross-section random has a probability of 0.000, we reject the null hypothesis (H0) that the model follows the random effects method, and we accept the alternative, i.e., the H1 that the model follows the fixed effects method (Table 7).

We run the fixed effects method with the use of White test to reduce heteroskedasticity of the model (Table 8).

We run four options of the econometric models as follows:

We use White cross-section standard errors and covariance (d.f. corrected) and estimated coefficient covariance matrix which is of a reduced rank. We found positive relation of the ROA with the variables of taxation, efficiency (VRSOUTPUT) and enterprise value (at 1% significance level), and negative relation with depreciation and amortization firms' accounts (at 1% significance level).

Table 7 Correlated random effects—Hausman test/test cross-section random effects

Test summary	Chi-sq. statistic	Chi-sq. d.f.	Prob.
Cross-section random	99.878440	9	0.0000

Table 8 ROA as the dependent variable and VRS output orientation set for DEA

Variable	Coefficient	Std. error	t-statistic	Prob.
C	5.776542	7.237436	0.798148	0.4249
COLLECTION_PERIOD	−0.016543	0.013593	−1.217045	0.2238
LOG_TAX (*)	3.594140	0.407739	8.814807	0.0000
VRSOUTPUT (*)	0.070879	0.011138	6.363975	0.0000
LOG_DEPRAMORT (*)	−10.74640	2.680054	−4.009769	0.0001
LOG_DEBTORS	1.703278	2.017213	0.844372	0.3986
LOG_INTERPAID	−1.317873	1.401529	−0.940311	0.3473
LOG_WORKINGCAPITAL	−0.575234	0.666136	−0.863539	0.3880
LOG_ENTERPRISEVALUE (*)	5.222291	0.830273	6.289846	0.0000
LOG_PROVISIONS	0.115271	0.419956	0.274484	0.7838

(*) refers to significance at 1%, R-squared = 0.770354, prob. (F-stat) = 0.000000

Option 2

Because cross-section random has a probability of 0.000, we reject the null hypothesis (H0) that the model follows the random effects method, and we accept the alternative, i.e., the H1, that the model follows the fixed effects method (Table 9).

We run in Option 2 the econometric formulation of Model 1, under the fixed effects method with the use of White test to reduce heteroskedasticity of the model. We get the results in Table 10.

We find that the signs remain the same in both models with the use of CRS or VRS output orientation. Also, the results show a positive relation of ROA with taxation, efficiency (CRSOUTPUT) and enterprise value (at 1% significance level), and negative relation with depreciation and amortization firms' accounts (at 1% significance level).

Option 3

In this option, because cross-section random has a probability of 0.000, we reject the null hypothesis (H0) that the model follows the random effects method and we accept the alternative, i.e., the H1 hypothesis, that the model follows the fixed effects method (Table 11).

We also run Model 1 formation with the use of White test to reduce heteroskedasticity (See Table 12).

We find that Option 3 results in a positive relation of solvency with taxation, efficiency (CRS output orientation from DEA) at a1% significance level, and

Table 9 Correlated random effects—Hausman test/test cross-section random effects

Test summary	Chi-sq. statistic	Chi-sq. d.f.	Prob.
Cross-section random	90.640246	9	0.0000

Table 10 ROA as the dependent variable and CRS output orientation set for DEA

Variable	Coefficient	Std. error	t-statistic	Prob.
C	2.522917	7.442011	0.339010	0.7347
COLLECTION_PERIOD	−0.015425	0.013078	−1.179407	0.2385
LOG_TAX(*)	3.513639	0.448369	7.836495	0.0000
CRSOUTPUT(*)	0.086022	0.007530	11.42381	0.0000
LOG_DEPRAMORT(*)	−10.07192	2.475968	−4.067873	0.0001
LOG_DEBTORS	1.877144	1.846427	1.016636	0.3095
LOG_INTERPAID	−1.132858	1.290667	−0.877731	0.3803
LOG_WORKINGCAPITAL	−0.703548	0.700718	−1.004038	0.3156
LOG_ENTERPRISEVALUE(*)	5.249635	0.866008	6.061876	0.0000
LOG_PROVISIONS	0.011614	0.433382	0.026800	0.9786

(*) refers to significance at 1%, R-squared = 0.770354, prob. (F-stat) = 0.000000

Table 11 Correlated random effects—Hausman test/test cross-section random effects/option No3

Test summary	Chi-sq. statistic	Chi-sq. d.f.	Prob.
Cross-section random	84.443644	9	0.0000

Table 12 Solvency ratio as the dependent variable and CRS output orientation set for DEA

Variable	Coefficient	Std. error	t-statistic	Prob.
C	83.12246	13.72051	6.058264	0.0000
COLLECTION_PERIOD	−0.010725	0.014577	−0.735755	0.4620
LOG_TAX	*2.102207*	*0.590000*	*3.563064*	*0.0004*
CRSOUTPUT	*0.097030*	*0.015760*	*6.156708*	*0.0000*
LOG_DEPRAMORT	1.481268	2.999619	0.493819	0.6215
LOG_DEBTORS	−4.164500	1.809575	−2.301369	0.0215
LOG_INTERPAID	*−7.661831*	*0.941772*	*−8.135548*	*0.0000*
LOG_WORKINGCAPITAL (**)	*1.040409*	*0.532561*	*1.953596*	*0.0510*
LOG_ENTERPRISEVALUE	−1.080738	0.810070	−1.334129	0.1824
LOG_PROVISIONS	*−1.668313*	*0.523974*	*−3.183960*	*0.0015*

(*), (**) refer to significance at 1 and 85%, respectively, R-squared 0.899396, prob. (F-stat) = 0.000000

Table 13 Correlated random effects—Hausman test/test cross-section random effects/option No4

Test summary	Chi-sq. statistic	Chi-sq. d.f.	Prob.
Cross-section random	77.536557	9	0.0000

Table 14 Solvency ratio as the dependent variable and VRS output orientation set for DEA

Variable	Coefficient	Std. error	t-statistic	Prob.
C	86.05583	13.23303	6.503107	0.0000
COLLECTION_PERIOD	−0.012948	0.014457	−0.895631	0.3706
LOG_TAX (*)	*2.281449*	*0.614982*	*3.709782*	*0.0002*
VRSOUTPUT (*)	*0.067166*	*0.016008*	*4.195682*	*0.0000*
LOG_DEPRAMORT	0.659181	3.140555	0.209893	0.8338
LOG_DEBTORS (**)	*−4.266500*	*1.912720*	*−2.230593*	*0.0259*
LOG_INTERPAID (*)	*−7.922536*	*1.016243*	*−7.795908*	*0.0000*
LOG_WORKINGCA PITAL (**)	*1.193687*	*0.497158*	*2.401022*	*0.0165*
LOG_ENTERPRISEVALUE	−0.900786	0.797082	−1.130105	0.2587
LOG_PROVISIONS	−1.611173	0.504215	−3.195407	0.0014

(*), (**) refer to significance at 1 and 85%, respectively, R-squared 0.897181, prob. (F-stat) = 0.000000

working capital of the sample firms (= current assets – current liabilities) at 5% significance level. Also, negative relation of solvency with interest paid and provisions accounts at 1% significance does exist.

Option 4

In this option, we also reject the null hypothesis (H0) that the model follows the random effects method, and we accept the alternative, i.e., the H1 that the model follows the fixed effects method—Hausman test (Table 13).

Now, we run the fixed effects method with the use of White test to reduce heteroskedasticity of the model (Table 14).

Also, the results show a positive relation of solvency with taxation, efficiency (VRS output orientation from DEA) at 1%, and working capital of the sample firms (= current assets – current liabilities) at a 5% significance level for Option 4 settings.

Additionally, we find a negative relation of solvency with interest paid and provisions accounts at 1% significance as well as with debtors at 5% significance level.

Overall, we see a positive relation of ROA with taxation, efficiency (VRSOUT-PUT), and enterprise value. Furthermore, there is a negative relation with depreciation and amortization firms' accounts, while a positive relation of solvency with taxation, efficiency (CRS output orientation from DEA), and working capital of the sample firms (= current assets – current liabilities) does exist. Also, negative relation of solvency with interest paid and provisions accounts is found.

5 Conclusions: Considerations

Businesses play an important role in all economies and are the main generators of employment and income as well as the drivers of innovation and growth. They are the engine of growth (Beck & Demirguc-Kunt, 2006; Makridou et al., 2016). The manufacturing sector is a feature of fast-growing economies. Which mechanism and how much tax and efficiency ratios affect the profitability index (ROA) and the solvency ratio are one of the main objectives of this research. Reviewing the efficiency and profitability of European (i.e., Greek, Spanish, and Italian) companies is important because the percentage of companies is declining. In particular, the economic crisis has severely affected Greek companies during the period under review.

Theoretically, there are several variables that can affect the performance of companies, as survival or business success depends mainly on company profitability, market value, and other explanatory variables. However, there is limited evidence on the link between firms' profitability or their solvency ratio and tax level.

Therefore, the present study was initiated to determine the effects of differences in taxation, efficiency, and other explanatory variables in relation to firms' characteristics and activities. It is found that there is a positive effect of the profitability of the companies with their tax obligations. This means that there is a growing tax base in these three countries, mainly coming from very large companies (in terms of total assets) in the manufacturing and services sectors.

Consistent with this concept, this research also finds a positive relationship between firms' profitability and their level of efficiency, indicating that firms are operating profitably in their market. In contrast, efficiency reduces firms' depreciation balances, as their increased profitability makes it easier for them to absorb larger amounts of fixed asset depreciation.

The literature also indicates that studies on the impact of firms' market value on their profitability have made solid claims about a positive relationship between these variables (e.g., Berger and Bonaccorsi di Patti (2006), Becchetti and Sierra (2003),

Shen and Rin (2012), Murillo (2007), Agustinus and Rachmadi (2008), Floros et al. (2014), Fragkiadakis et al. (2016)). In our study, we likewise confirm this positive relationship.

Moreover, a higher solvency ratio has significant positive effects on corporate taxation, efficiency, and working capital, which in other words indicates a better allocation of resources at the firm level. On the other hand, the results of the econometric analysis show that there is a negative relationship between profitability and the balance of debtor accounts and interest payments on loans and other liabilities. This is an important result that highlights the value of corporate profitability in reducing debt, especially for countries in crisis. Overtaxation also limits the growth opportunities of companies, especially those that meet their tax obligations despite the unfavorable conditions in their countries (e.g., Greece).

This firms' tax policy needs to be improved by national tax authorities, with a focus on gradually reducing the high tax burden of consistent taxpayers so that these businesses can continue to grow their operations. The focus should also be on gradually reducing the tax burden from consistent taxpayers to tax avoiders, so that the former can enjoy a balanced and fair environment and improve their competitiveness and the latter can pay an affordable tax burden in accordance with their respective laws.

This study contributes to the existing literature in two ways: It is one empirical study that highlights the relationship between several firms' focused factors, e.g., ROA, efficiency, taxation, and solvency ratio; also, we apply two commonly accepted methods: data envelopment analysis (DEA) and panel regression.

References

Agustinus, P., & Rachmadi, P. (2008). *Determinants of corporate performance of listed companies in Indonesia, MPRA.* http://mpra.ub.un.muenchen.de/id/eprint/6777

Banker, R., Charnes, A., & Cooper, W. (1984). Some model for estimating technical and scale inefficiencies in data envelopment analysis. *Management Science, 30*, 1078–1092.

Becchetti, L., & Sierra, J. (2003). Bankruptcy risk and productive efficiency in manufacturing firms. *Journal of Banking & Finance, 27*(11), 2099–2120.

Beck, T., & Demirguc-Kunt, A. (2006). Small and medium-size enterprises: Access to finance as a growth constraint. *Journal of Banking & Finance, 30*(11), 2931–2943.

Berger, A. N. & Bonaccorsi di Patti, E. (2006). Capital structure and firm performance: A new approach to testing agency theory and an application to the banking industry. *Journal of Banking & Finance, 30*(4), 1065–1102. Elsevier.

Charnes, A., Cooper, W., & Rhodes, F. (1978). Measuring the efficiency of decision- making units. *European Journal of Operational Research, 2*(4), 429–444.

Charnes, A., Cooper, W., Lewin, A., & Seiford, L. (1994). *Data envelopment analysis: Theory, methodology, and applications.* Kluwer Academic.

Coelli, T. J. (1996). *A guide to DEAP version 2.1: A data envelopment analysis (computer) program.* University of New England; Armidale, CEPA working paper 96/08.

Floros, C., Voulgaris, Z., & Lemonakis, C. (2014). Regional firm performance: The case of Greece. *Procedia Economics and Finance, 14*, 210–219.

Fragkiadakis, G., Doumpos, M., Zopounidis, C., & Germain, C. (2016). Operational and economic efficiency analysis of public hospitals in Greece. *Annals of Operations Research, 247*, 787–806.

Makridou, G., Andriosopoulos, K., Doumpos, M., & Zopounidis, C. (2016). Measuring the efficiency of energy-intensive industries across European countries. *Energy Policy, 88*, 573–583.

Mok, V., Yeung, G., Han, Z., & Li, Z. (2007). Leverage, technical efficiency and profitability: An application of DEA to foreign-invested toy manufacturing firms in China. *Journal of Contemporary China, 16*(51), 259–274.

Murillo, C. (2007). *Asset tangibility and firm performance under external financing: Evidence from product markets*. Retrieved March 20, 2014, from https://doi.org/10.2139/ssrn.971170.

Seiford, L., & Thrall, R. (1990). Recent developments in DEA: The mathematical programming approach to frontier analysis. *Journal of Econometrics, 46*, 7–38.

Shen, G., & Rin, M. (2012). *How does capital structure affect firm performance? Recent evidence from Europe countries*. Retrieved March 12, 2013, from http://edubb.uvt.nl/webapps/blackboard/execute/viewcat-alo?type=course&id=21

Voulgaris, F., & Lemonakis, C. (2014). Creating a business competitiveness index: An application to Greek manufacturing firms. *Journal of Transnational Management, 19*(3), 191–210.

Use of Financial Instruments Among the Chilean Households

Carlos Madeira

I would like to thank Francisco Olivares for excellent research assistance. All errors are my own.

Abstract Using the Household Finance Survey (EFH), this work shows that the use of financial instruments—whether financial assets or insurance contracts—among Chilean households increased substantially since 2007. Complementing this analysis with the Family Expenditures Survey (EPF) between the years of 1987 and 2017, I show that the share of financial goods in expenditures dropped significantly, while the share of insurance products in consumption roughly doubled in this period. This indicates that financial goods are now much less expensive and the number of its users increased significantly. The use of the different insurance contracts (life and health, vehicles, home, and loan insurance) increased across all income levels. Overall, the widespread use of financial goods, insurance contracts, and purchase of durable goods among the Chilean population across all the income levels shows that the financial access to goods and services increased significantly over the last 35 years.

Keywords Financial access · Insurance · Credit · Financial markets · Inequality

JEL Classifications: D14, E21, G11, G20, G50, O16, O54

Data Availability Statement: All the data used in this article is openly available in a public repository that does not issue DOIs. The EFH dataset is publicly available from the Central Bank of Chile: https://www.efhweb.cl/. The EPF dataset is publicly available from the Chilean Bureau of Statistics: https://www.ine.cl/estadisticas/sociales/ingresos-y-gastos/encuesta-de-presupuestos-familiares.

C. Madeira (✉)
Central Bank of Chile, Santiago, Chile
e-mail: carlosmadeira2009@u.northwestern.edu

© The Author(s), under exclusive license to Springer Nature Switzerland AG 2023
P. Alphonse et al. (eds.), *Essays on Financial Analytics*, Lecture Notes in Operations Research, https://doi.org/10.1007/978-3-031-29050-3_5

1 Introduction

Household finance surveys, such as the Household Finance and Consumption Survey (HFCS) in Europe or the Survey of Consumer Finance in the United States, are increasingly used to study families' decisions on savings, investments, and borrowing (Dynan & Kohn, 2007; Christelis et al., 2013, 2017; Le Blanc et al., 2015; Bover et al., 2016). Survey information on finances is important, especially because many households and small enterprises rely on a diversity of funding sources, including bank and non-bank lenders (Gallardo & Madeira, 2022). For this reason, in the last 20 years, several projects improved the survey measurement of economic and financial variables (Le Blanc et al., 2015). This paper is related to microeconomic studies of household debt (Ampudia et al., 2016; Madeira, 2019a). This study is also related to a growing literature on how surveys of small firms and households can inform about the financial problems faced by families and entrepreneurs, especially in developing countries (Gallardo & Madeira, 2022).

The study uses the Chilean Household Finance Survey (Encuesta Financiera de Hogares, in Spanish, from hence on EFH) to summarize the ownership of financial assets, loans, and insurance contracts since 2007 until 2017. Furthermore, I complement this study with an analysis using the Family Expenditures Survey (in Spanish, *Encuesta de Presupuestos Familiares*, hence on EPF) of how the consumption of financial goods (such as loans, bank accounts, and other services) and insurance products has evolved since 1987 until 2017. I also look at the change in the consumption of durable goods (which are large items, expensive and infrequently purchased) to document if the increased financial access has relaxed the consumption smoothing restrictions of the households.

This work fits in a growing literature studying credit access in developing economies and middle-income countries (Madeira, 2014; Gallardo & Madeira, 2022). Previous research for Chile focused on the factors leading low-income families toward indebtedness (Madeira, 2015) and their difficulties of repayment (Madeira, 2014), while neglecting their choices for assets and insurance, a gap that is filled in this article. Finally, this study is related to research on the alternatives of bank versus non-bank credit (Madeira, 2018b; Roa et al., 2022) and its implications for financial stability (Madeira, 2018a).

This work is organized as follows. Section 2 summarizes the EFH dataset. Section 3 shows the fraction of households with different kinds of assets, debts, and insurance contracts between 2007 and 2017. I also show an international comparison of the household indebtedness in Chile relative to other Organisation for Economic Co-operation and Development (OECD) countries. Section 4 summarizes the consumption of financial services, insurance, and durable goods in the Santiago capital region. Finally, Sect. 5 concludes.

2 The EFH Dataset

This study uses the cross-sectional national waves of the EFH 2007, 2011, 2014, and 2017, which covered a total of 16,938 urban households. Each sampled household had one member which was selected for the interview, with this member being the household person with the greatest knowledge of the family finances or the highest income. The EFH survey, however, elicits demographic, net wealth, asset, debt, and income information for all the household members. The sample selection of the survey was based on an exhaustive list of homes from the Chile Internal Tax Service and is therefore representative of the national urban population after expansion factors are applied to each unit (Madeira, 2018a). The Chilean Household Finance Survey (EFH) has detailed information on assets, debts, income, insurance contracts, and financial behavior and is broadly comparable to similar surveys in the United States and Europe. This survey has detailed measures of income, assets (financial portfolio, vehicles, and real estate), and debts, including mortgage, educational, auto, retail, and banking consumer loans. To cover the debts exhaustively, the survey elicits the loan terms (debt service, loan amount, maturity) for the four main loans in each category.

The real assets include the main home of the household, plus up to three other properties such as land parcels, agricultural land or industrial property, parking lots, business space, office units, or commercial stores, plus hotels or accommodation space. The financial assets include stocks or equity, fixed-income instruments, savings accounts, voluntary pension funds (such as "Cuenta 2" or "APV"), participation in companies, mutual funds or investment vehicles, life insurance contracts with a savings component, and other financial assets (such as derivatives or exotic instruments). The debts of the household include the mortgage of the main home, the mortgages of up to three other real estate properties, and debts associated with the mortgage contracts, plus retail store credit cards and loans, banking consumer loans, banking credit cards, union and cooperatives consumer loans, and auto loans. For simplicity, I exclude educational loans (which are repaid several years after the college degrees are obtained) and informal loans (such as loans with relatives or pawnshops), although such debts are used by only a small fraction of the population. Finally, the EFH survey also includes information on whether households have life insurance contracts, voluntary auto insurance, fire and earthquake insurance, theft insurance, and other insurance policies.

Since the EFH is a small sample and some variables such as certain types of financial assets are concentrated in a minority of richer households, it is difficult to include too many degrees of heterogeneity. For this reason, I report the heterogeneity of results using a classification with just three categories based on the total household income: strata 1, corresponding to the percentiles 1–50 of the national household income distribution (i.e., the poorest households); strata 2, corresponding to the percentiles 51–80 of the national household income (i.e., the middle-class households right above the median income); and strata 3, corresponding to the families belonging to the top 20 percentiles (81–100) of the national household income distribution.

3 Use of Financial Instruments in Chile

3.1 Real Assets, Financial Assets, and Debt Ownership

Figure 1 shows the asset and debt ownership of households since 2007. The fraction of households with real assets (usually, the main home) and with financial assets increased substantially since 2007, although with a brief fall in 2011 possibly due to the Global Financial Crisis. Around 82.2% of the households had some assets in 2007, a number which increase to 89.5% in 2017. This growth in the households with assets was mostly due to stronger holdings of financial assets. In 2007, only 19% of the households were financial asset owners, a fraction of which dropped to 8.5% in 2011 but then increased again to 27.1% in 2014 and reached 34% in 2017

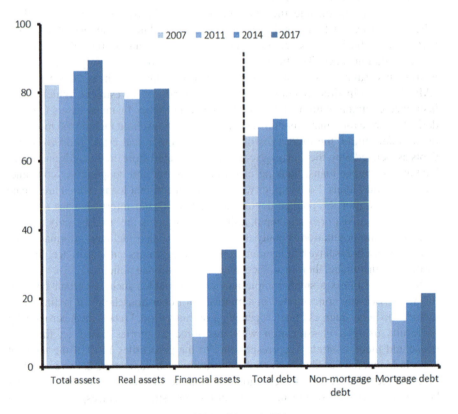

Fig. 1 Assets and debt ownership since 2007 (all households)

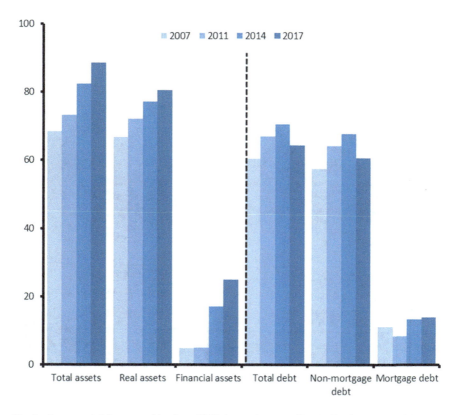

Fig. 2 Assets and debt ownership since 2007 (strata 1: percentiles 1–50 of the national income, i.e., the poorest households)

(almost twice as many as in 2007). The fraction of households with real assets grew slightly from 79.9% in 2007 to 81% in 2017. Meanwhile, the fraction of borrowers grew from 66.9% in 2007 to 72.1% in 2014, but then it dropped significantly to just 66% in 2017. This reduction is explained by the fall in non-mortgage debts, which fell from 67.6% in 2014 to just 60.5% in 2017. The fraction of households with mortgages grew during the last decade, from 18.2% in 2007 to 21.1% in 2017.

Across income levels in Figs. 2 (strata 1), 3 (strata 2), and 4 (strata 3), I find that it was among the poorest households where the ownership of both real assets and financial assets grew the most. Figure 2 shows the evolution of the fraction of households with asset and debt ownership in strata 1 (the households below the national median income level). It shows that among the poor Chilean households, the fraction of real asset and financial asset ownership grew from 66.7 and 4.9% in 2007 to 80.7 and 25.1% in 2017, respectively. Notice that the current fraction of real asset ownership for the households in strata 1 is now almost the same as for the households in strata 3 (with 84.8% of real asset ownership in 2017; see Fig. 4) and strata 2 (with 79% of real asset ownership in 2017; see Fig. 3). In fact, the

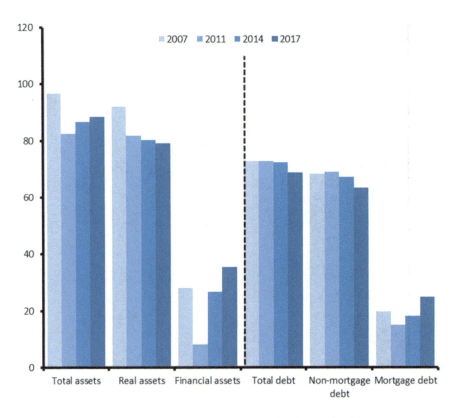

Fig. 3 Assets and debt ownership (strata 2: percentiles 51–80 of the national income)

fraction of middle- and upper-income households with real assets actually fell from 92.1 to 98.1%, respectively, in 2007 to the lower levels around 80% nowadays. This development could be due to a preference for renting in some of the middle- and upper-income households in younger generations. The fraction of financial asset ownership is still higher for the middle- and upper-income households, although just like for the households in strata 1, there was a deep fall in asset ownership in the year 2011, perhaps as a consequence of the financial crisis. In the most recent year of 2017, around 35.4 and 54.3% of the households in stratas 2 and 3 have some financial asset ownership.

It is noticeable that the fraction of borrowers fell across all income levels between 2014 and 2017, showing perhaps a more conservative use of this financial instrument. In particular, Figs. 2, 3, and 4 show that the share of households with non-mortgage debt fell across all levels in a roughly similar way, from 67.7, 67.3, and 68.1% in 2014 to 60.7, 63.3, and 56.1% in 2017 for stratas 1, 2, and 3, respectively. However, the share of mortgages grew across all income levels, from 13.4, 18.2, and 28.5% in 2014 to 14.1, 24.8, and 33.2% in 2017 for stratas 1, 2, and 3, respectively. Therefore, households are treating debt instruments less as a short-

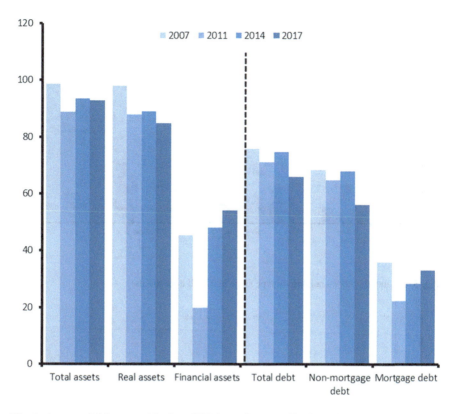

Fig. 4 Assets and debt ownership since 2007 (strata 3: percentiles 81–100 of the national income, i.e., the richest households)

term option for consumption and more as a means of financing long-term durables such as home purchases.

3.2 Financial Assets and Insurance Contracts by Type

Now Fig. 5 shows the financial asset ownership of the Chilean household across different types of asset classes since 2007, while Fig. 6 shows the same for the different classes of insurance contracts. As shown before in Fig. 1, the fraction of financial asset owning households increased from 19% in 2007 to 34% in 2017. Ownership of financial assets and insurance contracts grew across all contract classes since 2007–2017, although all the classes of instruments fell in 2011 after the Global Financial Crisis. This makes sense since households tend to reduce their investments after being scarred by a financial crisis (Malmendier, 2021). Savings accounts are by far the most popular type of financial asset, having grown from

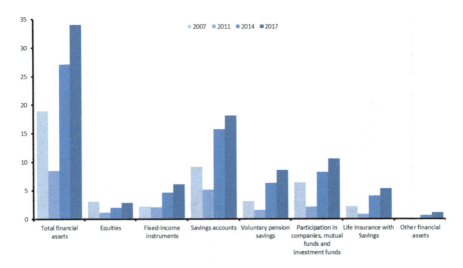

Fig. 5 Financial asset ownership by type since 2007 (all households)

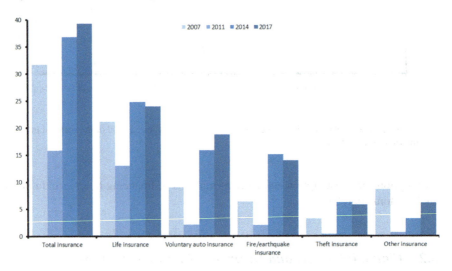

Fig. 6 Insurance ownership by type since 2007 (all households)

9.1% of the households in 2007 to 18.1% in 2017. In fact, savings accounts have been the preferred financial savings of households in every year since 2007.

In the most recent year of 2017, the fraction of households with any type of financial asset was 34%. Across each type of asset in 2017, the ownership of assets in 2017 is higher in terms of managed and diversified investment instruments, with 18.1, 10.6, 8.6, 6.1, and 5.3% of the households having savings accounts, mutual funds, voluntary pension funds, fixed income, and life insurance with savings. The fraction of households in 2017 with investments in equities and other financial assets (such as exotic instruments), respectively, is just 2.9 and 1.2%.

The use of insurance contracts grew from 31.7% in 2007 to 39.3% in 2017, with life insurance being the most important class in every year. Again, the use of all insurance contracts fell significantly in 2011 after the Global Financial Crisis. The use of life insurance contracts grew from 21.1% of the households in 2007 to 24% in 2017. The use of voluntary auto insurance and fire-earthquake home insurance are the second and third types of most common insurance contracts, having grown from 9 and 6.3% in 2007 to 18.7 and 14% in 2017, respectively. In the most recent year of 2017, there is also a significant fraction of households with theft insurance (5.8%) and other insurance (6.1%), but the use of these insurance types has remained stable over the last decade (theft and other insurance represented 11.8% of the households in both 2007 and 2017).

3.3   Debts

As seen in Fig. 1, there was a reduction in the fraction of households with consumer loans since 2014, although the fraction of mortgages has kept steadily increasing. Figure 7 shows the evolution of debt ownership in the recent years across different loan types. It shows that there was an increase in bancarization. The fraction of borrowers with consumer loans only in banks increased since 2014, while the fraction of borrowers with consumer loans in retail stores only or with a mix of loans in both retail stores and banks decreased. Furthermore, there was also a small reduction in the number of borrowers with loans in both retail stores and non-banking lenders.

In 2017, around 21.1% of the households had some type of mortgage debt (Fig. 1). Now Fig. 8 shows the evolution of households with other properties and mortgage debt for other properties, which show a steady increase for both the median and upper-income households (stratas 2 and 3). In fact, for the upper-income households in Chile, it is now very common to have secondary properties besides their main home. In 2017, around 41% of the households in the upper-income strata owned other properties, and 18.5% of those households had mortgages that were contracted for the purchase of those properties. This illustrates that Chile is now a country with many small investors in real estate. This aspect could present a risk for financial stability, since this phenomenon of households buying properties as a rental investment (despite large fractions of unused properties) was one of the factors during the last subprime crisis (Albanesi, 2018).

Finally, Fig. 9 shows that the indebtedness ratios of the median borrower increased between 2007 and 2017. In terms of the ratio of monthly debt service (interest plus loan amortization) to income (DSR), its value increased from 21.1% in

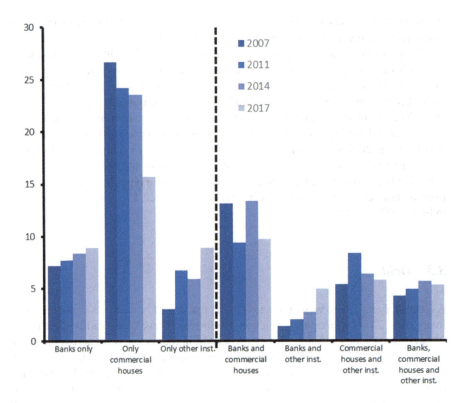

Fig. 7 Debt ownership by lender type

2007 to 24.7% in 2017. The DSR is a measure of the liquidity of the household, since it measures the payment necessary to fulfill the loan commitments in this period. As a measure of long-term solvency, I also report the debt to asset ratio (DAR, for the households with both debts and assets), which has also increased from 11% in 2007 to 14.9% in 2017. Furthermore, the total debt to annual income ratio (DIR) of the median borrower also increased from 2.43 in 2007 to 3.45 in 2017. Therefore, not only did households increase their financial access in terms of mortgages over the last decade, but households also increased their overall debt amounts, whether as a ratio of their income or of their assets.

To summarize the households' balance sheets, I calculate each household's real assets (main home, other properties, and vehicles) plus its financial assets and the debts in terms of their monetary amounts. The financial assets include nine distinct categories of assets, including stocks, mutual funds, bonds and savings accounts, voluntary pension funds, exotic instruments (such as derivatives, swaps,

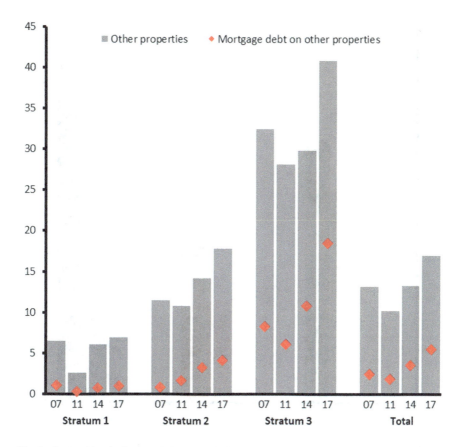

Fig. 8 Ownership of other properties and mortgage debt for other properties

or forward-future contracts), equity in non-public companies and funds,[1] insurance contracts with savings components, and uncategorized financial contracts. Among the financial assets, the categories of stocks, mutual funds, bonds, and savings accounts, plus voluntary pension funds, are considered to be liquid financial assets, since those accounts can be withdrawn in an emergency with a small penalty. Table 1 summarizes the fraction of households with different categories of assets (real assets, financial assets, and financial liquid assets) and the ratio of asset value relative to debt (for the households with both positive assets and debts). As an emerging economy, the Chilean households have few financial assets (such as stocks, bonds, or savings accounts) in comparison with developed countries (Le

---

[1] Here non-public equity is defined as equity in companies that are not tradeable in the stock market, for instance, ownership or participation of your family's company or participation in a society with other entrepreneurs.

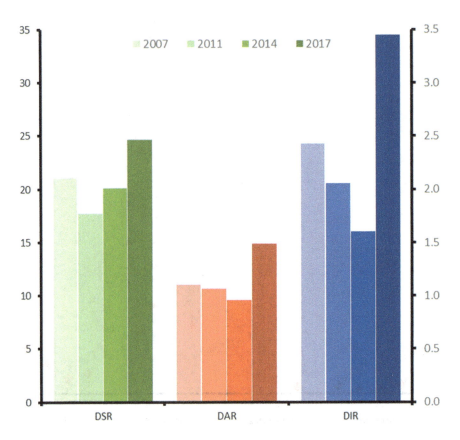

Fig. 9 Indebtedness ratios: debt service to monthly income ratio (DSR), total debt to monthly income ratio, and debt to asset ratio (median values for the borrowing households)

Blanc et al., 2015; Christelis et al., 2013). Almost 75% of the Chilean population have no financial assets at all, and 83% of the households have no liquid financial assets. Among households with some debt, less than 19% of them have liquid financial assets, and even the median household with some liquid assets can only cover 17% of its debts by using such assets. For most households, their only asset is the main home, with Chile having a high fraction of home ownership due to state subsidized low-cost housing. Seventy-six percent of the households have some real assets, and even the borrowers with the lowest real assets (those in the percentile 25 of the real asset to debt ratio) can cover more than twice their debts. Therefore, the large majority of the Chilean borrowers are solvent if they can tap into their real wealth.

Table 1 Real and financial assets by borrower type

Borrower type:	Fraction of households (in %) with no assets across asset classes				Ratios of assets to debt[a]: for households with assets								
	Any	Real	Financial	Liquid	Real assets to debt			Financial assets to debt			Liquid assets to debt		
					pc 25	pc 50	pc 75	pc 25	pc 50	pc 75	pc 25	pc 50	pc 75
Non-debtor	31.2	34.5	81.8	86.2	N/A			N/A			N/A		
Any debt	15.4	18.3	70.9	81.4	2.04	6	33.9	0.02	0.15	1.29	0.03	0.17	0.97
Consumer	16.5	19.6	71.6	82	2.04	6.73	40.48	0.02	0.16	1.51	0.03	0.19	1.25
Mortgage	3.4	4.3	60.9	77.1	1.7	2.69	5.31	0	0.05	0.26	0.01	0.06	0.25
Consumer and mortgage	3	3.6	59.5	77.8	1.6	2.43	4.71	0	0.04	0.21	0.01	0.05	0.24
Borrowers by income strata:													
Strata 1 (pc 1–50)	26.3	30.1	82	86.8	2.77	13.5	63.32	0.03	0.22	1.92	0.04	0.23	1.56
Strata 2 (pc 51–80)	12.1	15.6	74.5	83.6	1.85	5.3	30.1	0.01	0.11	0.97	0.02	0.14	1
Strata 3 (pc 81–100)	4.9	6	51.8	71.3	1.86	3.59	13.83	0.02	0.17	0.98	0.03	0.16	0.67
All households:													
Strata 1 (pc 1–50)	32.7	36.5	85.3	88.6									
Strata 2 (pc 51–80)	14.3	17.7	74.5	82.9									
Strata 3 (pc 81–100)	7.6	8.9	54.7	72.6									
All households	21.1	24.2	74.9	83.1									

EFH wave of 2017
[a]Values are in number, meaning that 1 implies assets equal debts. All values use household weights (not adjusted for the size of the household debt)

3.4   International Comparison of the Chilean Household Debt Use

Now I compare Chile with other countries with similar household finance surveys, using data from the Wealth Distribution Database of the OECD (based on surveys mostly from 2014), the United States' Survey of Consumer Finances (wave 2013), the ECB's Household Finance and Consumption Survey (using wave 2, based on surveys implemented mostly in 2013 and 2014), and the Uruguay's Encuesta Financiera de los Hogares Uruguayos (EFHU, from 2014). The sample includes 31 countries, mostly developed economies from the OECD, although some variables are not available for all countries. Table 2 compares the Chilean household indebtedness in 2017 relative to the other countries, but the results are similar with the Chilean 2014 survey. Since most countries in the sample are richer than Chile, the last column includes the predictions made from an Ordinary Least Squares (OLS) and quantile (QREG) linear regressions of each debt statistic and the GDP per capita (in Purchasing Power Party (PPP) measured in USD) estimated from all countries in the sample, but with the outcome prediction for a country with the same GDP per capita as Chile. Therefore, I compare the Chilean debt statistics with the range of countries in the sample (summarized by their minimum, median, and maximum statistics) and with a hypothetical country similar to Chile obtained from the OLS and QREG predictions. The OLS gives a comparable prediction for a country similar to Chile, while the quantile 75 give a high indebtedness value for countries with similar GDP per capita as Chile.

Relative to a country of similar GDPpc, Chile has a large fraction of households with any debt, non-mortgage debt, and debt in credit cards/lines, since these values are well above the quantile 75 of similar countries and also well above the median in the sample of all countries. The percentage of Chilean households with a mortgage is close to the quantile 75 of similar countries, while the share of households with "No access to credit" is slightly below its quantile 75. Also, the share of non-mortgage debt in terms of the aggregate household debt of 24.6% is slightly above the quantile 75 of similar countries, confirming that Chile is a country with a large use of non-mortgage (or consumer) debt. Chile is also below the median country in terms of the debt to income ratio, whether one uses the median (P50) or the percentiles 75 and 90 of the population of borrowers. However, Chile is very close to the median country in terms of its population's debt service to income ratio. Finally, in terms of the debt motives, relative to comparable countries, the Chilean borrowers are less likely to use consumer loans for expenses related to their home and real estate, but they are more likely to use debt for both "Pay other debts" and "Education" purposes.

In summary, Chile is a country with a large number of borrowers with non-mortgage and credit card debt, besides a robust fraction of mortgage borrowers. However, Chile has a normal debt amount and debt service (as measured by the DIR and DSR) relative to comparable countries.

Table 2 Comparison of household debt indicators in Chile versus other countries

Indicators (in %)	No. of countries	Chile (2017)	Min	Median	Max	OLS[a]	Q-75[a]
Households with:							
Any debt	31	66.4	21.2	47	84.9	42.2	46.2
Mortgages	30	21.2	6.5	25	47.6	17.4	18.9
Non-mortgage debt	30	60.9	10.3	33.2	68	33.8	37
Debt in credit cards and lines	23	44.1	3.8	13.2	81.6	19.2	22.6
No credit access	21	8.7	3.4	7.6	20.8	8.2	9
Non-mortgage debt/household debt:							
Aggregate ratio	27	24.6	1.6	14.2	63.5	20.9	24.2
Debt to income ratio:							
P50 of country's debtors	22	24.8	11.5	63.4	242.8	57.2	54.3
P75 of country's debtors	21	88.6	54.7	188.2	611.7	164.4	173
P90 of country's debtors	21	191.7	149.6	343.2	1450.6	356.5	406.1
Debt service ratio (no credit cards and lines of credit):							
P50 of country's debtors	22	14.0	8.4	13.4	35.3	14.4	16.2
P75 of country's debtors	21	24.5	15.8	23	62.5	25.3	26.6
P90 of country's debtors	21	41.3	26.2	38.3	143	47.5	51.2
Debt motivations (as a % of the total consumer debt in the country):							
Residence and real estate	21	8.9	1.4	20.8	50.2	24.1	32.6
Vehicles	21	15.7	6.6	24.5	70.3	13.9	20.6
Entrepreneurship/investment	21	5.6	0.2	2.7	16.4	5.6	5.6
Pay other debts	21	19.1	0	5.4	25.2	9.7	13.5
Education	21	21.7	0	7.2	38.3	8.4	13.8

Sources: EFH (Chile), EFHU (Uruguay), HFCS (Europe), Survey of Consumer Finances (USA), Wealth Distribution Database (OECD)

[a] The OLS and quantile regression use a constant and the log GDP per capita in PPP for each country and year t as controls. The models then provide a prediction for a generic country with the same GDP per capita as Chile in 2017

4   Consumption of Financial Goods and Insurance

How much do households spend on financial assets and insurance? To answer this question, I use the Chilean Expenditure Survey (EPF) waves of 1987, 1997, 2007, 2012, and 2017. This survey was implemented every 10 years until 2007[2] and every 5 years since then, collecting information from 5076, 8445, 10,092, 10,473, and 15,239 households in the years of 1987, 1997, 2007, 2012, and 2017. This study uses the pooled cross-section waves between 1987 and 2017, with a total of 49,325 household observations. Since expenditure surveys are expensive, requiring a mix of recall and diary measurement of expenditures (Battistin et al., 2020), the 1987 and 1997 waves only cover the Great Santiago capital area, which concentrates around 40% of the country's population, but with survey waves since 2007 collecting around 1/3 of their samples in the other regions. The EPF survey provides a high-quality measure of durable and non-durable expenditures classified for a list of 1570 product categories, with interviewers visiting households multiple times during a period of 1 month, asking for their bills and receipts from expenditures, plus memory reports of non-receipt expenses made during the period and of infrequent expenses, similar to the best international procedures (Battistin et al., 2020). One extremely relevant difference regarding the EFH survey is that the EPF registers all the expenses of the household, but it does not denote whether the products such as life, home, and loan insurance were voluntary or compulsory associated with other goods such as the mortgage. Since the EFH survey registers voluntary insurance, then its numbers are likely to be somewhat smaller than in the EPF survey.

To obtain comparable measures of income and consumption across households, I express all household income and consumption variables in terms of their equivalized measures (Krueger et al., 2010; OECD, 2008). The equivalized measures are similar to a "per capita" measure, but, instead of dividing by the total number of household members n_i, the equivalized measures take into account that there are some scale economies in terms of the consumption of joint goods within the household. In this paper, I apply the OECD-modified scale (OECD, 2008), which assigns a value of 1 to the household head, 0.5 to each additional adult member (above age 15), and 0.3 to each child: $ne_i^{OECD} = 1 + 0.5 \ (adults_i - 1) + 0.3 \ children_i$. Other measures are possible, with, for instance, some articles using the square root of all household members ($ne_i = \sqrt{n_i}$) or the Oxford scale which assigns a value of 1 to the first household member, 0.7 to each additional adult, and 0.5 to each child ($ne_i^{Oxford} = 1 + 0.7 \ (adults_i - 1) + 0.5 \ children_i$). The results in this article are qualitatively similar if one uses the Oxford or the square-root household equivalence measures.

To analyze the consumption of different goods in real value over time, I apply different consumer price indexes (CPIs) to each good (Krueger & Perri, 2006). This option is made to take into account that some goods may have decreased or

---

[2] There were also EPF surveys in 1967 and 1977, but the microdata for those waves is no longer available.

increased their prices relative to the general CPI, with, for example, computers becoming cheaper, while healthcare and education become more expensive. There is not an individual CPI for each product category (1570 product categories); therefore, I match each product category to 1 of the 144 CPI categories published by Carlomagno et al. (2021) with a standardization of 1 in December of 2007. Therefore, the consumption of household i at time t for each product j is calculated as $c_{i,j,t} = \frac{\text{expenditure}_{i,j,t}}{\text{CPI}_{j,t} \times ne_i^{\text{OECD}}}$, with the total consumption of household i at time t given by $c_{i,t} = \sum_j c_{i,j,t}$. Another reasonable option is to calculate the total consumption standardized by the CPI of the period t (instead of the individual CPIs): $c2_{i,t} = \frac{\sum_j \text{expenditure}_{i,j,t}}{\text{CPI}_t \times ne_i^{\text{OECD}}}$. However, both measures of consumption, $c_{i,t}$ and $c2_{i,t}$, are very similar, showing a correlation coefficient of 98.6% for the pooled EPF dataset (1987–2017).

I then classify the product lists in terms of their use, with three categories: medical expenses, financial, and insurance. Table 3 shows the share of expenditures dedicated to these three different uses as a fraction of the total household consumption in the Great Santiago area. It shows that households have been devoting a

Table 3 Consumption dedicated to medical, financial, and insurance as a fraction of the total household consumption (in %) in the Great Santiago region—mean statistics for all the households and across income levels

Year	Income Strata	Consumption as a fraction of total consumption (in %)			Fraction of households with positive consumption (in %)		
		Medical	Financial	Insurance	Medical	Financial	Insurance
1987	All households	2.4	2.5	0.3	74.9	59.5	11.9
1997	All households	3.9	1.4	0.4	63.1	51.3	24.1
2007	All households	3.8	1.4	0.6	66.3	61.5	35.6
2012	All households	3.7	2.0	0.6	71.2	73.6	38.1
2017	All households	4.2	1.5	0.7	84.8	91.1	44.5
1987	Strata 1 (pc 1–50)	1.8	1.9	0.1	63.9	50.6	3.1
1997	Strata 1 (pc 1–50)	2.8	0.9	0.2	52.5	38.3	15.8
2007	Strata 1 (pc 1–50)	2.7	1.4	0.4	54.4	52.5	20.9
2012	Strata 1 (pc 1–50)	2.9	1.2	0.3	59.6	61.3	21.7
2017	Strata 1 (pc 1–50)	3.8	1	0.2	74.1	83.4	19.6
1987	Str. 2 (pc 51–80)	2.7	2.8	0.2	81.6	67.9	8.6
1997	Str. 2 (pc 51–80)	4.3	1.5	0.3	68.8	57.5	27.3
2007	Str. 2 (pc 51–80)	4.3	1.4	0.6	72.1	69.0	41.6
2012	Str. 2 (pc 51–80)	4.1	2.1	0.6	76.1	81.3	45.6
2017	Str. 2 (pc 51–80)	4.1	1.6	0.5	88.9	96.4	44.5
1987	Str. 3 (pc 81–100)	3.3	3.3	0.9	90.3	67.5	37.0
1997	Str. 3 (pc 81–100)	5.8	2.5	0.9	78.4	71.0	37.8
2007	Str. 3 (pc 81–100)	5.2	1.3	1.1	82.7	70.0	57.3
2012	Str. 3 (pc 81–100)	5.0	3.7	1.2	91.1	91.4	65.6
2017	Str. 3 (pc 81–100)	5.1	2.3	1.5	95.8	96.4	81.7

stronger fraction of their consumption to medical expenses since 1987, with this share increasing from 2.4 to 4.2% for the average household. Furthermore, since 1987, more than 60% of the households put some out-of-pocket expenditures for medical consumption. Although the share of households with some out-of-pocket medical expenditures fell between 1987 and 1997 due to the expansion of the state-sponsored medical program FONASA[3] (Sapelli & Vial, 2003; Sapelli, 2004), the share of households with medical expenditures grew again in 2007, 2012, and 2017, reaching 84.8% of the households in the most recent year. Even today, Chile has the fifth highest out-of-pocket payments among OECD countries (OECD, 2019).

The share of financial expenditures in total consumption actually dropped substantially from 2.5% in 1987 to 1.4% in 1997 and then persisting at a similar level afterward, with a value of 1.5% in 2017. Therefore, financial products became less important relative to other goods, which makes sense, since financial products are mostly an expense made by households in order to transfer income to other time periods. If households can now devote less expenses to such products due to their relative decreasing costs over time, then this implies a welfare gain. In fact, the share of households with some financial expenses grew throughout this period from 59.5% of the households in 1987 to 91.1% in 2017; therefore, there is more widespread access to financial services now. The fraction of consumption dedicated to insurance products increased from 0.3% in 1987 to 0.7% in 2017, while the fraction of households with insurance products grew from 10.6% in 1987 to 44.5% in 2017. In summary, this shows that in 2017 there is more widespread access to both insurance products (44.5% of the population) and other financial products (91.1% of the population).

Finally, the consumption of medical goods and services, financial products, and insurance is increasing with household income, even taking into account that values are standardized as a fraction of the total household consumption. For instance, the share of medical, financial, and insurance products in total consumption in 2017 was 5.1, 2.3, and 1.5% for strata 3 (the upper income); 4.1, 1.6, and 0.5% for strata 2 (the upper-middle-class-income households); and 3.8, 1.0, and 0.2% for strata 1 (households below the median income). The out-of-pocket medical expenses grew for all the income strata between 1987 and 2017, in the same way as the insurance expenses increased during the same period. Since life and health insurance are also related to medical expenses, then it is possible that the aging of the Chilean society is a factor pushing up both the consumption of medical and insurance goods (Madeira, 2021). However, it is also noticeable that the consumption of financial goods (as a share of the total consumption in the average household of each stratum) fell 0.9–1.2% across all income levels. This fall in the consumption of financial goods could be explained by a reduction in fees for such goods and services over the last few decades. In fact, the number of households with positive consumption of financial

---

[3] FONASA (National Health Fund) is the Chilean's public health insurance that is mandated to cover the entire population, with FONASA being given from its acronym in Spanish, "Fondo Nacional de Salud"

goods increased across all income levels, changing from 50.6, 67.9, and 67.5% in 1987 to 83.4, 96.4, and 96.4% in 2017 for stratas 1, 2, and 3, respectively. This confirms that in 2017 the access to financial goods is almost universal in Chile, even among the lower-income households (strata 1). The share of households with out-of-pocket medical expenses was high already in 1987, but it dropped significantly in 1997 (perhaps due to the expansion of the FONASA), and it increased since then across all income levels. Finally, the number of households consuming insurance products also grew across all income levels, but especially among the higher-income families (strata 3). The fraction of households consuming insurance increased from 3.1, 8.6, and 37% in 1987 to 19.6, 44.5, and 81.7% in 2017 for stratas 1, 2, and 3, respectively. Therefore, in 2017, the consumption of insurance products is quite common among the middle-class (44.5% of the families in strata 2) and almost universal among the upper-income families (81.7% of the households in strata 3).

What kinds of financial goods and services and insurance products are purchased by the Chilean households? Table 4 shows that in 1987 the most common type of financial products were "mortgages and bank loans," which were used by 46.1% of the households, while "credit cards, retail loans, and other non-bank lenders" were used by 28.9% of the families. By 2017, the use of "credit cards, retail loans, and other non-bank lenders" had grown to 80.8% of the population, while "bank accounts and other financial products" grew from almost 0% (between 1987 and 2007) to 51.7% of the population. However, the share of households paying mortgages or other bank loans in the Santiago capital area had fallen from 46.1% in 1987 to 26.5% in 1997 and 22.6% in 2017. This pattern was common to families across all income levels. The share of families using "mortgages and other bank loans" fell substantially (especially among the poor-income families in strata 1), while the share of users of "credit cards, retail loans, and other non-bank lenders" and "bank accounts and other financial products" grew significantly.

In terms of insurance, there are no categories in 1997 and 2007 because the EPF survey questionnaire was reduced substantially in those waves and there is not enough detail to know which insurance products were being used. However, for the waves of 1987, 2012, and 2017, the use of insurance products is classified into four categories: (1) life, health, and personal accidents insurance; (2) home and property insurance; (3) automobile, vehicle, and travel insurance; and (4) other financial insurance (such as insurance for the delinquency of loan products). Just like in the EFH survey depicted in Fig. 6, the most popular insurance products are life and vehicle insurance. The results show that all the types of insurance products grew substantially between 1987 and 2012 and 2017. Life and health insurance grew from 4.5% of the households in 1987 to 5.8% in 2012 and 24.4% in 2017. Vehicle and travel insurance grew from 4.0% of the families in 1987 to 9.7% in 2012 and 22.1% in 2017. Home and other insurance products grew, respectively, from 1.8 and 0.3% in 1987 to 6.0 and 19.9% in 2017, although the category of other loan insurance fell a bit since 2012. This drop in the use of other insurance since 2012 is consistent with the fall in the use of consumer loans in recent years (as shown in Fig. 1), perhaps as a result of the lower interest rate ceiling introduced in 2013 and which substantially reduced the use of high-cost small loans (Madeira, 2019b). Just

Table 4 Fraction of the households (in %) purchasing different financial and insurance products in the Great Santiago region

Year	Education	Financial products			Insurance products			
		Mortgages and bank loans	Credit cards, retail, and other lenders	Bank accounts and other products	Life and health	Home	Vehicle and travel	Others (e.g., loan insurance)
1987	All households	46.1	28.9	0.3	4.5	1.8	4.0	0.3
1997	All households	26.5	35.4	1.1				
2007	All households	24.0	54.6	0.0				
2012	All households	24.5	67.2	29.6	5.8	2.8	9.7	31.1
2017	All households	22.6	80.8	51.7	24.4	6.0	22.1	19.9
1987	Strata 1 (pc 1–50)	34.3	27.6	0.0	0.7	0.1	0.2	0.1
1997	Strata 1 (pc 1–50)	22.2	20.6	0.4				
2007	Strata 1 (pc 1–50)	11.9	48.9	0.0				
2012	Strata 1 (pc 1–50)	10.7	55.5	19.6	1.3	0.2	1.8	19.1
2017	Strata 1 (pc 1–50)	10.0	65.2	56.1	8.7	1.6	4.9	8.7
1987	Str. 2 (pc 51–80)	52.4	41.8	0.0	2.9	1.2	1.6	0.2
1997	Str. 2 (pc 51–80)	27.7	42.5	0.5				
2007	Str. 2 (pc 51–80)	26.4	62.4	0.0				
2012	Str. 2 (pc 51–80)	28.8	74.6	35.8	6.5	1.7	6.2	38.6
2017	Str. 2 (pc 51–80)	23.0	90.2	58.6	23.2	3.4	15.3	20.4
1987	Str. 3 (pc 81–100)	63.9	12.8	1.5	15.7	6.6	16.1	1.0
1997	Str. 3 (pc 81–100)	34.2	57.9	3.4				
2007	Str. 3 (pc 81–100)	45.2	56.0	0.0				
2012	Str. 3 (pc 81–100)	50.7	83.8	44.0	15.1	10.4	32.8	48.5
2017	Str. 3 (pc 81–100)	41.0	92.9	36.7	49.5	15.8	56.0	36.1

like for each type of financial goods, the use of all the types of insurance products increases with the income level, and therefore, all the insurance products are more widely used among the upper-income (strata 3) than the middle-class (strata 2) and more common among the middle-class than the low-income (strata 1) families. The evolution of insurance use is similar across all income strata, with the use of all insurance products increasing between 1987 and 2017, while other insurance fell a bit in use since 2012. However, it is noticeable that life and health is more common than vehicle insurance for stratas 1 and 2, while vehicle insurance is more common than life and health for the upper-income families (strata 3).

Are households able to purchase more durable goods in recent years due to their access to finance? To answer this question, I classify the product lists of the EPF surveys in terms of their durability, with four categories: services (non-durable), non-durable goods, semi-durable goods (goods that can last more than 1 year but less than 3 years), and durable goods (goods that can last more than 3 years). Durable goods can be more affected by financial conditions, because these products are more expensive and infrequently purchased and their use must be smoothed over longer periods. Table 5 confirms that the share of durable goods increased

Table 5 Consumption (in %) dedicated to services (non-durable), non-durable goods, and semi-durable and durable goods in the Great Santiago region—mean statistics for all the households and across income levels

Year	Education	Consumption as a fraction of total consumption (in %)				Households with positive durables
		Services	Non-durable	Semi-durable	Durable	consumption (in %)
1987	All levels	25.3	40.0	28.8	5.9	53.7
1997	All levels	34.2	53.0	9.3	3.5	49.4
2007	All levels	42.7	41.1	6.8	9.3	75.6
2012	All levels	52.6	29.4	8.0	10.0	73.8
2017	All levels	51.1	25.1	11.2	12.5	75.3
1987	Strata 1 (pc 1–50)	23.1	47.7	25.5	3.7	32.0
1997	Strata 1 (pc 1–50)	30.6	58.2	8.7	2.5	36.1
2007	Strata 1 (pc 1–50)	39.8	46.7	6.2	7.3	66.6
2012	Strata 1 (pc 1–50)	52.6	33.1	6.7	7.7	62.7
2017	Strata 1 (pc 1–50)	51.1	28.7	11.1	9.0	61.5
1987	Str. 2 (pc 51–80)	25.2	37.8	30.1	6.8	62.2
1997	Str. 2 (pc 51–80)	33.3	52.7	10.1	3.9	55.1
2007	Str. 2 (pc 51–80)	43.6	39.4	7.1	9.9	81.3
2012	Str. 2 (pc 51–80)	50.9	29.6	9.2	10.2	80.0
2017	Str. 2 (pc 51–80)	49.4	25.6	11.7	13.3	78.1
1987	Str. 3 (pc 81–100)	30.6	25.3	34.3	9.8	91.3
1997	Str. 3 (pc 81–100)	43.4	42.1	9.5	5.1	70.8
2007	Str. 3 (pc 81–100)	47.6	32.1	7.7	12.6	86.6
2012	Str. 3 (pc 81–100)	54.9	20.6	9.5	15.0	90.9
2017	Str. 3 (pc 81–100)	53.3	19.2	10.7	16.8	92.5

from 5.9% of the consumption in 1987 to 12.5% in 2017, while the number of households with positive consumption of durable goods increased from 53.7% in 1987 to roughly 75% during the period of 2007–2017. The share of non-durables and semi-durables in consumption decreased between 1987 and 2017, although the share of services increased substantially. This pattern is similar across all income levels, with the share of durables in consumption roughly doubling between 1987 and 2017 for each income strata. It is noticeable, however, that the share of upper-income families consuming durables remained roughly constant around 90% during this period, while the share of families with positive durable consumption in the low income (strata 1) and middle class (strata 2) increased significantly from 31 and 62.2% in 1987 to 61.5 and 78.1% in 2017, respectively. Durables are therefore twice as widespread among poor families in recent years. This is an indicator that financial access and credit constraints fell significantly in Chile during this period, especially among poor families.

5 Conclusions

Using the Chilean Household Finance Survey (EFH), this work shows that the use of financial assets, insurance, and mortgage loans increased substantially since 2007, although there was some fall in the use of non-bank consumer debt, perhaps as a consequence of an increased bancarization. Financial owners and users of insurance contracts grew, respectively, from 19 and 31.7% in 2007 to 34 and 39.3% in 2017, with savings accounts and life-health insurance being the most popular types of financial assets and insurance. Relative to other OECD countries, however, Chile still has a low fraction of mortgages and a high number of households with consumer loans.

Complementing this analysis with the Family Expenditures Survey (EPF), I show that the share of financial goods in consumption dropped significantly, while the share of insurance products in consumption roughly doubled in this period. However, the users of financial services and insurance increased from 59.5 and 10.6% of the families in 1987 to 91.1 and 44.5% in 2017, respectively, with usage of financial instruments being now common among all income levels. Finally, the results also show that the share of durable goods in the total consumption of the average household grew from 5.9 to 12.5% between 1987 and 2017, while the fraction of households reporting purchase of durables increased from 53.7 to 75.3% during the same period. This is a reliable indicator that households are better able to use available financial instruments for consumption smoothing and to finance purchases of better goods. In summary, the access to financial assets, financial services, and insurance products grew substantially in Chile over the last 35 years. This expansion in the access to finance in Chile (Berstein & Marcel, 2019) may have important implications for future growth and a reduction in inequality (Demirgüç-Kunt & Levine, 2009; Cihak & Sahay, 2020).

References

Albanesi, S. (2018). *The role of investors in the 2007–2009 housing crisis: An anatomy.* NBER, mimeo.

Ampudia, M., van Vlokhoven, H., & Zochowski, D. (2016). Financial fragility of euro area households. *Journal of Financial Stability, 27*, 250–262.

Battistin, E., De Nadai, M., & Krishnan, N. (2020). *The insights and illusions of consumption measurements.* Research working paper 9255.

Berstein, S., & Marcel, M. (2019). *Sistema Financiero en Chile: Lecciones de la Historia Reciente.* Economic policy papers 67, Central Bank of Chile.

Bover, O., Casado, J., Costa, S., Du Caju, P., McCarthy, Y., Sierminska, E., Tzamourani, P., Villanueva, E., & Zavadil, T. (2016). The distribution of debt across euro-area countries: The role of individual characteristics, institutions, and credit conditions. *International Journal of Central Banking, 12*(2), 71–128.

Carlomagno, G., Fornero, J., & Sansone, A. (2021). *Price indexes for 144 product categories in Chile.* mimeo, Central Bank of Chile.

Christelis, D., Georgarakos, D., & Haliassos, M. (2013). Differences in portfolios across countries: Economic environment versus household characteristics. *Review of Economics and Statistics, 95*(1), 220–236.

Christelis, D., Ehrmann, M., & Georgarakos, D. (2017). *Exploring differences in household debt across the United States and Euro area countries.* CSEF working papers 465.

Cihak, M., & Sahay, R. (2020). *Finance and inequality.* IMF WP 20–01.

Demirgüç-Kunt, A., & Levine, R. (2009). Finance and inequality: Theory and evidence. *Annual Review of Financial Economics, 1*(1), 287–318.

Dynan, K., & Kohn, D. (2007). *The rise in U.S. household indebtedness: Causes and consequences.* FEDS working paper no. 2007–37, Board of Governors of the Federal Reserve System.

Gallardo, S., & Madeira, C. (2022). Chapter 36: The role of financial surveys for economic research and policy making in emerging markets. In *Handbook of banking and finance in emerging markets* (pp. 676–686).

Krueger, D., & Perri, F. (2006). Does income inequality lead to consumption inequality? Evidence and theory. *Review of Economic Studies, 73*(1), 163–193.

Krueger, D., Perri, F., Pistaferri, L., & Violante, G. (2010). Cross sectional facts for macroeconomists. *Review of Economic Dynamics, 13*(1), 1–14.

Le Blanc, J., Porpiglia, A., Teppa, F., Zhu, J., & Ziegelmeyer, M. (2015). *Household saving behaviour and credit constraints in the Euro area.* ECB working paper no. 1790.

Madeira, C. (2014). El Impacto del Endeudamiento y Riesgo de Desempleo en la Morosidad de las Familias Chilenas. *Economía Chilena, 17*(1), 88–102.

Madeira, C. (2015). Motivaciones del Endeudamiento en las Familias Chilenas. *Economía Chilena, 18*(1), 90–106.

Madeira, C. (2018a). Explaining the cyclical volatility of consumer debt risk using a heterogeneous agents model: The case of Chile. *Journal of Financial Stability, 39*, 209–220.

Madeira, C. (2018b). Priorización de pago de deudas de consumo en Chile: el caso de bancos y casas comerciales. *Economía Chilena, 21*(1), 118–132.

Madeira, C. (2019a). Measuring the covariance risk of consumer debt portfolios. *Journal of Economic Dynamics and Control, 109*, 21–38.

Madeira, C. (2019b). The impact of interest rate ceilings on households' credit access: Evidence from a 2013 Chilean legislation. *Journal of Banking and Finance, 106*, 166–179.

Madeira, C. (2021). The long term impact of policy reforms on Chilean savings and pensions. *Journal of the Economics of Ageing, 19*, 100326.

Malmendier, U. (2021). Exposure, experience, and expertise: Why personal histories matter in economics. *Journal of the European Economic Association, 19*(6), 2857–2894.

OECD. (2008). *Growing unequal? Income distribution and poverty in OECD countries.*

OECD. (2019). *Health at a glance 2019: OECD indicators.*

Roa, M. J., Villegas, A., & Garrón, I. (2022). Interest rate caps on microcredit: Evidence from a natural experiment in Bolivia. *Journal of Development Effectiveness, 14*(2), 125–142.

Sapelli, C. (2004). Risk segmentation and equity in the Chilean mandatory health insurance system. *Social Science & Medicine, 58*(2), 259–265.

Sapelli, C., & Vial, B. (2003). Self-selection and moral hazard in Chilean health insurance. *Journal of Health Economics, 22*(3), 459–476.

Investor Attention and Bitcoin Trading Behaviors

Wang Chun Wei and Dimitrios Koutmos

> Disgraced football coach Mark Thompson admitted to obsessively trading cryptocurrencies for 12 hours a day in the lead up to his arrest ... and that he'd been consumed by watching YouTube tutorials.
>
> – *Sydney Morning Herald, June 26, 2019*

Abstract The rise of cryptocurrencies and social media platforms has given us unique insight on the impact of investor attention on investor trading behavior. In this paper, we focus specifically on the impact of news and social media attention on Bitcoin across five major global exchanges: Bitfinex, Bitstamp, BTC-e, Coinbase, and Kraken. We break attention into three categories: social media attention by existing investors proxied through Reddit posts (*seasoned attention*), social media attention by new investors proxied through Reddit subscribers (*novice attention*), and traditional online media attention proxied through the number of Bloomberg news articles. We find that new entrants have a greater impact on Bitcoin than discussions and posts by existing Bitcoin holders. This suggests that rise in Bitcoin prices is driven by new investors entering into the market rather than by existing investors adjusting their valuations and beliefs. In short, the increase in attention by new investors has pushed Bitcoin prices and induced extra noise in the market. We

The views expressed in the text belong solely to the authors and do not reflect the authors' employers. The research was conducted during the time where Wang Chun Wei was employed as an Assistant Professor at the University of Queensland, St Lucia, QLD, Australia. All errors are our own.

W. C. Wei
Realindex Investments, First Sentier Investors, Sydney, NSW, Australia

D. Koutmos (✉)
College of Business, Texas A&M University, Corpus Christi, TX, USA
e-mail: dimitrios.koutmos@tamucc.edu

also document some asymmetries in the transmission of investor attention to Bitcoin trades depending on exogenous news shocks.

Keywords Investor attention · Cryptocurrency · VAR · Asymmetric impact

How investors digest information for trading has always been integral in the understanding of financial markets. Increased investor attention should, in theory, lead to more informed trading. In the seminal works of Merton (1987) and Grossman and Stiglitz (1980), more information leads to more informative prices and greater market efficiency. However, Da et al. (2011) find that for retail investors, increased investor attention simply amounts to greater noise, and a subsequent decrease in market efficiency. This paper analyzes the impact of increased investor attention in Bitcoin markets. We examine attention both from traditional online news format and from social media activity. The latter is important, as it allows us to discern between *novice* and *seasoned* attention.

Early researchers using Bitcoin data highlighted its unique or novel setting due to their isolation from real economics (see Kristoufek, 2013). However, over the last 2 years, we have seen increasing mainstream interest in Bitcoin and cryptocurrencies (such as Bitcoin futures on the CME and cryptocurrency-based ETFs) to an extent that it is no longer isolated but an important part of the investment ecosystem. Nevertheless, traditional fundamental valuation methods fail to provide an adequate fair value, and thus trading in this market has largely hinged on sentiment traders. We argue that a lack of direction regarding intrinsic value causes higher degrees of investor ambiguity. In this paper, we discern the role of investor attention in markets where higher levels of investor ambiguity exist. In Peress (2014), attention via traditional media contributed in improving market efficiency of stock markets, reducing both share turnover and volatility. For equity indices, Vozlyublennaia (2014) shows a link between index returns and investor attention. She shows that increased investor attention, as proxied by Google search probability, resulted in diminished return predictability and improved market efficiency. Vozlyublennaia (2014) finds that increased attention by investors uncovered new information that subsequently moved traded prices closer to a more efficient price This contradicts Da et al.'s (2011) and Barber and Odean (2008) that investors are more likely to buy than sell a stock that have attracted their attention. By employing high-frequency tick data, we analyze investor attention in Bitcoin markets, and focus on its impact to returns, trading volumes, intraday volatility, and order imbalance. In light of information ambiguity and low information quality in Bitcoin markets, we hypothesize in favor of Da et al.'s (2011) explanation for Bitcoin markets. When increased investor attention does not yield more information, we argue this leads to more noise trading and a decrease in efficiency. Our findings intend to shed light on similarities between Bitcoin investors and Da et al.'s (2011) research on retail investors.

Furthermore, we examine the impact of investor attention in the context of news events. We test whether the impact of attention on returns is more pronounced for negative events than positive events, i.e., investors pay more attention during periods of negative news than during periods of positive returns. Asymmetric reaction has widely been documented in the literature. For instance, Vozlyublennaia (2014) shows that negative returns in US index returns draw greater investor attention than positive returns.

We analyze investor attention from two dimensions: (1) social media attention and (2) traditional media attention. For the former dimension, we use the social news platform, Reddit.[1] A survey conducted by a Reddit user on 331 subredditors in December 2017 provides some intriguing evidence on Bitcoin investor attention.[2] Results indicate that 94% of crypto investors check the price of cryptocurrencies daily, 80% check the price at least 3 times per day and over 40% check over 10 times per day. This suggest crypto investors are in general very active in absorbing any new information out on Internet platforms. Furthermore, 50% were drawn into investing cryptocurrencies because they read about them. Therefore, the impact of news articles, whether in be traditional or through social media, is likely to have an impact on investor trading behavior. By measuring the percentage change in subreddit *r/bitcoin* subscribers and also the number of new subreddit posts, we are able to measure investor interest and attention in Bitcoin. Subreddit activity serves as a proxy for investor attention in Bitcoin; however, one cannot be certain that users posting on the Bitcoin subreddit are all Bitcoin traders. Nevertheless, we believe this to be a reasonable proxy as there are no professional trading platforms such as Bloomberg and Thomson Reuters available for Bitcoin traders, and therefore Internet platforms are an important information source for even "seasoned" Bitcoin traders. Furthermore, we are able to separate between new Bitcoin subreddit participants versus existing participants. Change in subscription is reflective of new participants who have just subscribed. A surge of subscriptions would therefore indicate an increase in novice interest. Change in subreddit posts is reflective of "chatter" or attention by existing subredditors, and hence would indicate an increase in seasoned interest. To the best of the authors' knowledge, no existing research paper distinguishes between the two.

There are several papers that pursue a similar path in the literature. Kristoufek's (2013) seminal paper finds a positive correlation between Google Trends and Wikipedia data with Bitcoin prices. He argues, in the absence of fundamental traders, online sentiment plays a major role in exacerbating the price reactions. Increased *Internet interest* drives prices higher when they are above trend, and prices lower when they are below trend. Our paper extends on this analysis. Instead of arbitrarily identifying above or below trend periods, we explicitly label positive and negative fundamental news events and subsequently examine the impact of attention

---

[1] Since the Bitcoin investor demographic is largely dominated by young men, which correlated well with the Reddit user base. source: from a survey of 5,700 adults in 2018 by the Global Blockchain Business Council, the majority of crypto investors are young males, source: http://fortune.com/2018/01/24/young-men-buying-bitcoin.

[2] https://docs.google.com/document/d/1Y2fKK1cJla7r14lPz3y7w7AlkYgg_AM46_RkB-tggEM/edit.

under each type of event. The news events are based on government policy changes (such as the Chinese ban on Bitcoin), major exchange hacks, technological updates (such as SegWit), and significant market game changes. We test if social media attention drives prices higher in periods where there are positive news events, and prices lower in periods where there are exogenous negative news. The hypothesis is that social media attention exacerbates or exaggerates Bitcoin trading. Phillips and Gorse (2017) also examine the impact of social media on cryptocurrency bubbles via a hidden Markov model. They motivate by suggesting Bitcoin trading behavior during a bubble mimics psychological contagion, where further social media content spurs investor enthusiasm which spreads contagiously across the Internet population. Barclays Capital released a similar report in 2018 where they model Bitcoin price using an infectious disease model from epidemiology.[3] The rationale is that prices rise when interest in investing in Bitcoin spread from one buyer to a new buyer. When no new buyers are left (market participants reaching herd immunity), prices would subsequently fall, marking the end of the bubble.

We estimate traditional media activity by collecting the number of Bitcoin articles published on a leading financial news provider, Bloomberg. We use the daily article count to be a proxy for traditional media attention. Bloomberg is the premier financial news website for investors; an increased number of Bloomberg articles are likely to represent a broad increase in investor attention to Bitcoin. Media activity is a key driver in financial markets. For instance, Peress (2014) finds that the traditional print media has a causal impact on financial markets in key European countries. Over the period 1989–2010, he examined 52 national newspaper strikes in France, Italy, Norway, and Greece and found a decrease in both volume and intraday volatility. Shen et al. (2017) similarly document the impact of Baidu news coverage on Chinese stocks.

We find that investor attention in Bitcoin has a significant impact on subsequent Bitcoin returns. This is true for both social media attention and traditional news media attention. We find the impact is stronger with new *novice* investors, as they tend to be most enthusiastic, than existing *seasoned* investors, which partially validates claims by Phillips and Gorse (2017) and the Barclays Capital model that new investors ("just infected") impact Bitcoin prices more than existing investors ("already infected").

Our contribution is threefold. Firstly, if Bitcoin markets are inefficient (see Urquhart, 2016; Wei, 2018a), we expect both social media and traditional media to play a significant role in information dissemination. This is tested via Granger causality tests and vector autoregression (VAR) models similar to that discussed in Vozlyublennaia (2014), where we analyze the impact of news on returns. Secondly, we discern between novice and seasoned social media attention, by examining the impact of subscribers vs. posters. Thirdly, we analyze the impact of investor attention has on orderbook imbalance and intraday volatility. This is achieved

---

[3] Source: https://www.theguardian.com/technology/2018/apr/10/bitcoin-soaring-value-buyers-infectious-disease-barclays-economists-say.

through tick data from key Bitcoin global exchanges. We also analyze the impact of exogenous news stocks on trading behavior. In particular, we examine if the relationship between investor attention and Bitcoin trading changes when there is positive or negative news shock.

The paper is organized as follows. Section 1 provides an overview of the data we use as well as summary statistics. Section 2 documents the empirical methodologies and tests employed, and Sect. 3 documents subsequent results. Section 4 concludes.

1   Data

In order to examine the impact of attention in the form of social media and traditional media on Bitcoin returns, we use multiple sources of data. In subsection A to D, we document these.

A. Bitcoin Exchange Tick Data
We collect Bitcoin high-frequency tick data from five large liquid global exchanges: Coinbase, Bitfinex BTC-e, Bitstamp, and Kraken. Bitstamp is a European-focused Bitcoin exchange based in Luxembourg. It is one of the earlier exchanges, established in August 2011 in Slovenia. Coinbase and Kraken are Californian-based Bitcoin exchanges founded in June 2012 and July 2011, respectively. Bitfinex is a Hong Kong-based Bitcoin exchange founded in late 2012. BTC-e is a Russian-based Bitcoin exchange founded in July 2011; it has currently ceased operations. Tick data history was obtained from Kaiko. Table 1 documents the start and end dates of our tick data sample.

The tick data we receive comes with seven fields, a unique trade ID, an exchange identifier, currency pair symbol, timestamp in milliseconds (epoch timestamp), price, base currency value (largely in USD), and buy/sell initiation. These fields are sufficient for us to calculate returns, volume, order imbalance, and intraday volatility. As buy and sell initiations are explicitly recorded by the exchanges, this bypasses any issues associated with trade misclassification.

B. News Shocks
Peress (2014) points out identification issues in drawing a causal relationship between the media and stock market returns, as both variables may be resultant of unobserved news shock. This *omitted variable bias* is hard to rectify as identifying news shocks, idiosyncratic and systematic, is problematic for a large cross section of stocks. In our study, identification of news shocks is possible. Unlike Peress (2014) who examines a large cross section of European stocks, we only examine one asset, Bitcoin.

To proxy for exogenous news shocks on Bitcoin, we use a relatively complete set of the historical events for Bitcoin that may have had fundamental influence on the intrinsic value of Bitcoin. We construct two dummy variables associated with these historical events, denoted $NEWS^{POS}$ and $NEWS^{NEG}$. We use the event

Table 1 Summary statistics on Bitcoin exchanges. Below we tabulate basic summary statistics on five major Bitcoin exchanges in our study. Daily volume-weighted average price (VWAP) is in USD. Daily traded value is also denoted in USD, and refers to the total value of all Bitcoin/USD pair trades. Bitstamp and BTC-e BTC/USD pairs have a trading history, but Bitfinex is the most liquid in our sample

		Date	Daily VWAP	Daily traded value
Bitfinex BTC/USD	Mean		2208.9	23, 442.6
	Sd		3376.8	25, 010.3
	Min	1/04/2013	67.2	399.4
	Max	6/11/2018	19, 252.8	274, 470.2
Bitstamp BTC/USD	Mean		1744.3	10, 090.0
	Sd		3130.7	11, 004.0
	Min	19/08/2011	2.2	1.9
	Max	5/11/2018	19, 110.2	137, 070.2
BTC-e BTC/USD	Mean		1720.0	6361.3
	Sd		3306.4	8820.5
	Min	14/08/2011	2.1	2.3
	Max	5/11/2018	18, 240.4	147, 419.6
Coinbase BTC/USD	Mean		3044.7	10, 024.8
	Sd		3816.8	9059.3
	Min	1/12/2014	155.8	0.0
	Max	6/11/2018	19, 461.5	165, 542.8
Kraken BTC/USD	Mean		2438.7	2179.8
	Sd		3487.8	3210.4
	Min	8/10/2013	124.0	0.0
	Max	5/11/2018	19, 135.5	28, 799.4

set documented by Feng et al. (2018) in their research on informed trading in Bitcoin markets. We find their events to be complete from December 2011 to March 2017. footnoteFeng et al.'s (2018) event set begins on the December 19, 2011, and ends on March24, 2017, and consists of policy, hacking, technology, regulatory, and market-related events. From March 2017 to November 2018, we use Zakon's (2018) blockchain timeline[4] and https://www.Bitcoinwiki.org[5] to help piece together more recent history events. Feng et al. (2018) have labeled their events positive and negative, which we use for constructing our two dummy variables. We also document the country and the event type, i.e., hacking (e.g., DDoS attacks on Mt. Gox), policy-related (e.g., Bitcoin subject to tax), investigative and crime (e.g., Mark Karpeles of Mt. Gox arrested), and market based (e.g., Dell accepts Bitcoins). In Tables 2, we tabulate our events.

---

[4] Zakon (2018) blockchain timeline: https://www.zakon.org/robert/blockchain/timeline/.

[5] Bitcoinwiki bitcoin timeline: https://en.bitcoinwiki.org/wiki/Bitcoin_history#Bitcoin_in_2018.

Table 2 Bitcoin news events. We document Bitcoin news shocks. From December 2011 to March 2017, we use Feng et al. (2018) Bitcoin event data set. From March 2017 to November 2018, we use Zakon's (2018) blockchain timeline and Bitcoinwiki.org to piece together recent history

Date	Event type	Sentiment	Country	Event
1/03/2012	Hacking	Negative	US	Linode, an American privately owned virtual private server provider company, was hacked. Over 46,000BTC was stolen
17/08/2012	Crime	Negative	US	Bitcoins Savings & Trust, halted payments, which turned out to be a Ponzi scheme
5/09/2012	Hacking	Negative	US	Bitfloor, which was the fourth largest exchange dealing in US dollars, announced to be hacked. 24,000 BTC was stolen
12/03/2013	Tech	Negative	US	Bitcoin 0.8 caused a feather hard fork of Bitcoin
25/03/2013	Policy	Positive	EU	The tax haven Cyprus made a deal with the Europe to get €10 billion bailout, conditioning on levying large bank accounts. Many account holders and followers began buying Bitcoin, making Bitcoin double its price in 10 days.
14/05/2013	Investigation	Negative	US	The US Homeland Security Investigations (DHS) seized $2,915,507.40 from an account owned by a Mt. Gox subsidiary, with the warrant
29/06/2013	Policy	Positive	US	The US Financial Crimes Enforcement Network (FinCEN) issued license to Mt. Gox, the largest Bitcoin exchange at that time.
2/10/2013	Investigation	Negative	US	The US FBI seized around 26,000 BTC from Silk Road, an online black market, during the arrest of its owner Ross William Ulbricht
23/10/2013	Hacking	Negative	AU	Inputs.io, an Australian wallet provider, was hacked. 4100 Bitcoins (worth over a million USD) was stolen.
18/11/2013	Policy	Positive	US	The US Senate held a hearing on Bitcoin. The general consensus is summed up by the director of the FinCEN "We want to operate in a way that does not hinder innovation"
5/12/2013	Policy	Negative	CN	The People's Bank Of China (PBOC) declared prohibiting financial institutions from handling Bitcoin transactions, which led to a market panic
18/12/2013	Market	Negative	CN	China's biggest Bitcoin exchange at that time, BTCChina, announced to stop accepting deposits in RMB.
8/01/2014	Policy	Positive	CN	The Financial Services and the Treasury of Hong Kong addressed that "Hong Kong at present has no legislation directly regulating Bitcoin and other similar virtual currencies."
27/01/2014	Policy	Negative	RU	The Russia Central Bank recommended that Russians and legal entities refrain from dealing with Bitcoins.
7/02/2014	Hacking	Negative	JP	Mt. Gox, Bitstamp, and BTC-e all experienced a stoppage of trading due to massive DDoS attacks.
24/02/2014	Hacking	Negative	JP	Mt. Gox Closed. An alleged leaked internal document showed that over 744,000 BTC were lost by the company
7/03/2014	Policy	Negative	JP	The Japanese government made a cabinet decision, prohibiting banks and securities companies from dealing Bitcoins
26/03/2014	Policy	Negative	US	the US Internal Revenue Service (IRS) declared that Bitcoin is a property subject to tax
10/04/2014	Policy	Negative	CN	The PBOC's restrictions against Bitcoin finally pressured some Chinese banks to issue a deadline against several Bitcoin exchanges, requiring them to close their accounts by 4/15/2014
4/07/2014	Policy	Negative	EU	The European Banking Authority (EBA) recommended that national supervisory authorities discourage financial institutions from dealing visual currencies.
18/07/2014	Market	Positive	US	Dell announced to accept Bitcoin
11/12/2014	Market	Positive	US	Microsoft announced to accept Bitcoin
4/01/2015	Hacking	Negative	LU	Bitstamp's operational hot wallets were hacked, and 18,866 BTC was stolen (roughly $5.2 million)
26/01/2015	Market	Positive	US	Coinbase Launched a US-Licensed exchange

(continued)

Table 2 (continued)

Date	Event type	Sentiment	Country	Event
14/02/2015	Hacking	Negative	CN	BTER, a Chinese top ranking Bitcoin exchange, was hacked. 7170 BTC (roughly $2.1million) was stolen.
3/06/2015	Policy	Positive	US	New York State announced to release BitLicense application.
1/08/2015	Investigation	Negative	JP	Mark Karpeles, the CEO of the failed Bitcoin exchange Mt. Gox, was arrested in Japan on charges of fraud and embezzlement in relation to the collapse of Mt. Gox
15/08/2015	Tech	Negative		Bitcoin XT Fork Released and caused market fear
22/09/2015	Policy	Positive	US	New York State Department of Financial Services (NYDFS) approved the first BitLicense application, to Circle Internet Financial

(continued)

Table 2 (continued)

Date	Event type	Sentiment	Country	Event
22/10/2015	Policy	Positive	EU	European Court of Justice (ECJ), the highest court in Europe, ruled that Bitcoin is a payment method, not a property; buying and selling Bitcoin are tax-free.
31/10/2015	Market	Positive	UK	Bitcoin featured on the front page of the magazine The Economist
14/01/2016	Market	Negative	CH	Mike Hearn, who had been heavily involved in the Bitcoin community since the beginning of Bitcoin, announced to quit Bitcoin.
24/02/2016	Policy	Positive	JP	Japanese legislators officially proposed virtual currencies to be payment methods.
27/04/2016	Market	Positive	US	Steam, a popular gaming platform, announced to accept Bitcoin
25/05/2016	Policy	Positive	JP	Japan officially recognized Bitcoin and digital currencies as "means of payment that is not a legal currency"
2/08/2016	Hacking	Negative	CN	Bitfinex was hacked, announcing that 119,756 BTC (around 72 million) was stolen
29/11/2016	Policy	Positive	RU	Russia's Federal Tax Service stated that there is no legal prohibition of cryptocurrencies in a document.
11/01/2017	Investigation	Negative	CN	Chinese authorities announced plans to investigate Bitcoin exchanges
9/02/2017	Policy	Negative	CN	Department of Business Administration of the PBOC stated four banning rules on the Bitcoin exchanges. Multiple Chinese Bitcoin exchanges delayed or paused Bitcoin withdraw services
10/03/2017	Policy	Negative	US	The US Securities and Exchange Commission (SEC) rejected the Winklevoss Bitcoin ETF application
24/03/2017	Policy	Positive	JP	Japan's Financial Services Agency (FSA) announced that a new law will be implemented from April 1, 2017, which categorizes Bitcoin as a legal payment method.
11/04/2017	Market	Negative	US	The cryptocurrency exchange Poloniex announces it is suspending services in Washington State
13/06/2017	Policy	Positive	US	Gemini, the digital currency exchange started by the Winklevoss twins, begins operating in Washington State after it is granted a license to do so.
20/07/2017	Tech	Positive		Bitcoin Improvement Proposal 91, to trigger Segregated Witness (SegWit) activation, is locked in
1/08/2017	Tech	Positive		A hard fork of bitcoin known as Bitcoin Cash
8/09/2017	Policy	Negative	RU	Russia's Finance Minister Anton Siluanov announces plan to regulate the circulation of bitcoin and other cryptocurrencies involving Russian citizens and firms
29/09/2017	Policy	Positive	JP	Japan's Financial Services Agency (FSA) issues operating licenses to 11 bitcoin exchanges
11/10/2017	Policy	Negative	RU	The Central Bank of Russia announces it would support moves to block websites dealing in bitcoin and other virtual currencies, amid declarations of President Vladimir Putin denouncing the cryptocurrency as risky and used by criminals
16/10/2017	Market	Positive	US	IBM and a network of banks begin using digital currency and blockchain software to move money across borders throughout the South Pacific.
28/11/2017	Policy	Negative	US	Coinbase is ordered to disclose information on 14,355 users with Bitcoin transactions greater than US$20,000 during 2013–2015, one year after the IRS sought information on all Coinbase user
1/12/2017	Policy	Positive	US	Unites States regulator Commodity Futures Trading Commission (CFTC) announces it would let the Chicago Mercantile Exchange and Chicago Board Options Exchange trade in Bitcoin-related financial contracts.
6/12/2017	Tech	Positive		Lightning Network Protocol 1.0 released
28/12/2017	Policy	Negative	KR	South Korea's government announces imposition of additional measures to regulate speculation in cryptocurrency trading within the country.

(continued)

Table 2 (continued)

Date	Event type	Sentiment	Country	Event
14/01/2018	Market	Positive	US	Capital One announces it is blocking purchases of cryptocurrencies using its credit cards
22/01/2018	Policy	Negative	KR	South Korea brought in a regulation that requires all the bitcoin traders to reveal their identity, thus putting a ban on anonymous trading of bitcoins.
30/01/2018	Market	Negative	US	Facebook bans people entirely from advertising bitcoin and other cryptocurrencies amid fears they are used for fraud
7/03/2018	Policy	Negative	US	The US securities and exchange Commission confirmed that many online trading platforms for digital assets should be registered with the Agency as exchanges. Statement the SEC has heightened concerns about the fact that the regulation tightening might restrict trade.
14/03/2018	Market	Negative	US	Google announced that it prohibits online advertising promoting cryptocurrency
26/03/2018	Market	Negative	US	Twitter announced that it would ban advertising for cryptocurrencies, after overclocking Google and Facebook, which aims to protect investors from fraud.
2/05/2018	Market	Positive	US	Goldman Sachs announces a cryptocurrency trading desk
24/05/2018	Investigation	Negative	US	The justice Department opened a criminal case about whether traders manipulate the price of bitcoins and other digital currencies. The investigation focuses on illegal activities that can affect prices such as spoofing or flooding the market with fake orders to trick other traders into buying or selling.
10/06/2018	Hacking	Negative	KR	South Korean exchange Coinrail loses more than $ 40 million in tokens after hacking.

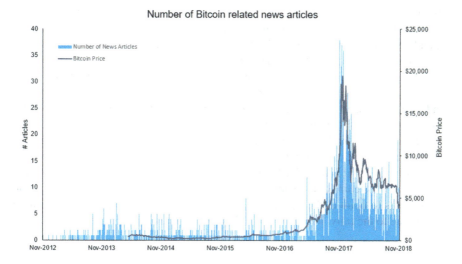

Fig. 1 Traditional Media: the total number of Bitcoin-related news articles across time The total number of Bitcoin-related news articles published by Bloomberg across time. We find that the height of media frenzy coincided with the height in Bitcoin prices

C. Traditional Media

We proxy for traditional media coverage of Bitcoin by examining the aggregate number of Bitcoin-related news articles, videos, and photo essays on Bloomberg, a key financial news provider. We collect this data directly from the Bloomberg website. The majority of these articles are news articles such as:

```
https://www.bloomberg.com/news/articles/2018-02-07/
canada-s-first-blockchain-etf-launches-amid-bitcoin-volatility
```

while others are more nuanced opinion-based pieces:

```
https://www.bloomberg.com/view/articles/2018-01-30/
let-telegram-try-to-build-a-digital-nation
```

As our focus is on investor attention rather than investor sentiment, we examine only the number of articles published rather than the sentiment of each article. In Fig. 1, we show the increase in Bitcoin-related articles, and how it correlates positively with Bitcoin price trend. In particular, we note that the height of media frenzy, where Bloomberg published more than 30 Bitcoin-related articles per day, coincided with the height of Bitcoin bubble.

D. Social Media

We use Reddit activity as a proxy for social media attention on Bitcoin. Reddit claims to be "the front page of the internet" aggregating social news and web content. It currently has an Alexa rank of 21 with 542 million monthly visitors.[6]

---

[6] As of March 2019.

With such a broad online presence, there is a significant overlap between Reddit users and Bitcoin investors. For instance, there are more than one million unique members on the *r/Bitcoin* subreddit. In our paper, social media attention is estimated using data on (i) the number of daily Reddit posts and (ii) new Reddit subscribers to the subreddit *r/Bitcoin*. These metrics are plotted in Fig. 2. The rationale for the former (i) is that increased posting on the Bitcoin subreddit by existing users indicates increased interest or debate. It could also be in due to a third-party exogenous news shock; we account for news events section B and in our modeling. The rationale for the later (ii) is that increased subscribers to the subreddit indicate new interest/attention for Bitcoin by fresh members. We find that while daily posting activity by existing Bitcoin Reddit participants did not increase during the late 2017 bubble, new Bitcoin Reddit subscriptions increased significantly during the bubble. This seems to point to the fact that increased attention by existing investors did not contribute to the rally, but rather the influx of new market participants.

2 Empirical Methodology

2.1 Statistical Causality Between Attention and Bitcoin Trading

To analyze the statistical causality between investor attention and Bitcoin performance, we employ Granger causality tests via an autoregressive distributed lag (ADL) model. Let r_t be Bitcoin daily return and a_t be investor attention. We test for three different cases of attention a_t: (i) Reddit daily posts, (ii) Reddit new subscribers, and (iii) Bloomberg daily news articles. The former two are proxies for social media attention and the latter traditional media attention. A general categorization is that Reddit daily posts capture *chatter* and attention by existing Bitcoin traders while Reddit new subscribers reflect the attention of uninformed investors who are new to Bitcoin. This is illustrated in Fig. 2 where new subscribers increased along with the rally, where greater attention by new investors followed after a rise in Bitcoin price. We do not see this effect with Reddit daily posts, which reflects attention by existing investors.

$$\text{Null model: } r_t = \alpha_0 + \sum_{i=1}^{p} \alpha_i r_{t-i} + \varepsilon_t$$

$$\text{Full model: } r_t = \alpha_0 + \sum_{i=1}^{p} \alpha_i r_{t-i} + \sum_{i=1}^{q} \beta_i a_{t-i} + \varepsilon_t$$

$$(1)$$

A joint F-test on the ADL(p,q) is used to test statistical causality. We extend beyond Bitcoin returns r_t, and also examine the causality between attention and

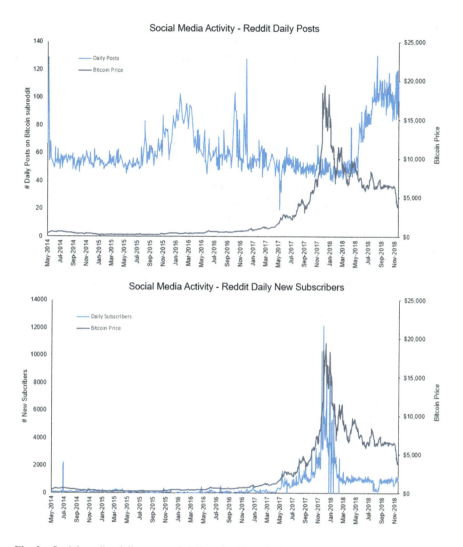

Fig. 2 Social media: daily post and daily subscribers Daily posts reflect attention and activity among existing Bitcoin subreddit members, while daily subscribers reflect new entrants into the Bitcoin subreddit. The former is a proxy for attention by existing Bitcoin holders, while the latter is a proxy for new Bitcoin enthusiasts

volume v_t, volatility σ_t, and order imbalance OI_t. Details on these metrics are provided in Sect. 2.2. These tests are also employed in Vozlyublennaia (2014), who uses it to analyze the impact of Google search probability on US index returns, and Wei (2018b) uses a similar approach to examine the impact of Tether grants on Bitcoin returns. Shen et al. (2019) also use a similar VAR approach to examine the impact of Tweets on Bitcoin. We extend on existing research in the area of investor attention by discerning between traditional media and social media, as well as distinguishing between new investor attention vs. existing investor attention. We believe these Granger causality tests provide us with a simplistic initial impression on the impact of attention on Bitcoin trading. In Sect. 2.2, we detail a more comprehensive model specification.

2.2 Asymmetric Impact of Attention on Bitcoin Trading

As discussed in Peress (2014), establishing a causal link via standard Granger causality test between media (or attention) and financial markets can be problematic as they both can be resultant from a fundamental news event. We account for this here by incorporating both positive and negative exogenous news shocks ($NEWS^{POS}$, $NEWS^{NEG}$). Let Bitcoin returns be denoted r_t, and social media attention and traditional media attention to be denoted SM_t and TM_t, respectively. Furthermore, we split social media attention into two categories, Reddit daily posts SM_t^{posts} and Reddit new subscribers SM_t^{subs}.

Our model specification is as follows:

$$
r_t = \sum_{i=1}^{n} \alpha_i r_{t-i}
$$

$$
+ \sum_{i=1}^{n} \left(\beta_{i,posts}^{SM} + \gamma_{i,posts}^{POS} NEWS_{t-i}^{POS} + \gamma_{i,posts}^{NEG} NEWS_{t-i}^{NEG} \right) SM_{t-i}^{posts}
$$

$$
+ \sum_{i=1}^{n} \left(\beta_{i,subs}^{SM} + \gamma_{i,subs}^{POS} NEWS_{t-i}^{POS} + \gamma_{i,subs}^{NEG} NEWS_{t-i}^{NEG} \right) SM_{t-i}^{subs}
$$

$$
+ \sum_{i=1}^{n} \left(\beta_i^{TM} + \delta_i^{POS} NEWS_{t-i}^{POS} + \delta_i^{NEG} NEWS_{t-i}^{NEG} \right) TM_{t-i}
$$

$$
+ \sum_{i=1}^{n} \left(\phi^{POS} NEWS_{t-i}^{POS} + \phi^{NEG} NEWS_{t-i}^{NEG} \right) + \varepsilon_t
$$

$$
(2)
$$

First, ϕ^{POS} and ϕ^{NEG} account for the impact of current news events on Bitcoin returns. We expect $\phi^{POS} > 0$ and $\phi^{NEG} < 0$, as positive (negative) event is likely to have a positive (negative) reaction on returns. Second, we incorporate lagged returns to account for the impact of serial autocorrelation in Bitcoin returns. Existing research on cryptocurreny market efficiency documents a high level of autocorrelation among daily returns (see Urquhart, 2016 and Wei, 2018a). This could in part be due to extrapolative behavior among Bitcoin investors. Furthermore, this approach is consistent with the standard Granger causality approach. Third, we examine the impact of social media and traditional media attention on Bitcoin returns. The general impact of attention on returns is captured by $\beta_{i,posts}^{SM}$, $\beta_{i,subs}^{SM}$, and β_i^{TM}. We allow for asymmetric response between good and bad exogenous news shocks, as we expect the transmission between attentions and returns would be different under these scenarios.

Next we examine the impact of investor attention on daily traded volume in US dollars (V_t) under the same specifications. Aggregate traded daily volume provides us with a proxy on trading activity. We expect trading activity to increase as investor attention increases. In particular, we expect new Reddit Bitcoin subscriptions, SM_t^{subs}, which proxies fresh interest by novice Bitcoin enthusiasts to be positively correlated to trading activity. Our model specification is

$$
V_t = \sum_{i=1}^{n} \alpha_i V_{t-i}
$$

$$
+ \sum_{i=1}^{n} \left(\beta_{i,posts}^{SM} + \gamma_{i,posts}^{POS} NEWS_{t-i}^{POS} + \gamma_{i,posts}^{NEG} NEWS_{t-i}^{NEG} \right) SM_{t-i}^{posts}
$$

$$
+ \sum_{i=1}^{n} \left(\beta_{i,subs}^{SM} + \gamma_{i,subs}^{POS} NEWS_{t-i}^{POS} + \gamma_{i,subs}^{NEG} NEWS_{t-i}^{NEG} \right) SM_{t-i}^{subs}
$$

$$
+ \sum_{i=1}^{n} \left(\beta_i^{TM} + \delta_i^{POS} NEWS_{t-i}^{POS} + \delta_i^{NEG} NEWS_{t-i}^{NEG} \right) TM_{t-i}
$$

$$
+ \sum_{i=1}^{n} \left(\phi^{POS} NEWS_{t-i}^{POS} + \phi^{NEG} NEWS_{t-i}^{NEG} \right) + \varepsilon_t
$$

$$(3)$$

Here ϕ^{POS} and ϕ^{NEG} account for the impact of current news events on Bitcoin traded value regardless of media attention.

Next we examine order flow imbalance (OI_t) with similar specifications. Order imbalance signals private information, which should reduce liquidity and move market price. Random large order imbalances increase the inventory problem faced by private exchanges or market makers, who would respond by revising bid-ask spreads. There is a large volume of extant literature analyzing order imbalance around earnings announcements (Lee, 1992), institutional buying and selling (Sias and Starks, 1997), and financial crashes (Blume et al., 1987). We extend by examining how investor attention impacts order imbalance. As our tick data history explicitly labels buy/sell initiation, we are able to calculate daily aggregate buy and sell trades. From this, order flow imbalance is defined as

$$OI_t = \frac{|B_t - S_t|}{B_t + S_t}$$

where B_t and S_t are the number of buy-initiated and sell-initiated trades for day t, respectively. Our model specification for the impact of media attention on order imbalance is as follows:

$$
\begin{aligned}
OI_t = &\sum_{i=1}^{n} \alpha_i OI_{t-i} \\
&+ \sum_{i=1}^{n} \left(\beta_{i,posts}^{SM} + \gamma_{i,posts}^{POS} NEWS_{t-i}^{POS} + \gamma_{i,posts}^{NEG} NEWS_{t-i}^{NEG} \right) SM_{t-i}^{posts} \\
&+ \sum_{i=1}^{n} \left(\beta_{i,subs}^{SM} + \gamma_{i,subs}^{POS} NEWS_{t-i}^{POS} + \gamma_{i,subs}^{NEG} NEWS_{t-i}^{NEG} \right) SM_{t-i}^{subs} \\
&+ \sum_{i=1}^{n} \left(\beta_i^{TM} + \delta_i^{POS} NEWS_{t-i}^{POS} + \delta_i^{NEG} NEWS_{t-i}^{NEG} \right) TM_{t-i} \\
&+ \phi^{POS} NEWS_{t-i}^{POS} + \phi^{NEG} NEWS_{t-i}^{NEG} + \varepsilon_t
\end{aligned}
\tag{4}
$$

Last, we examine the impact of attention on intraday volatility. We hypothesize that an increase in attention by Bitcoin investors is likely to cause greater intraday trading volatility. Da et al. (2011) document that increased retail attention created extra noise and reduced market efficiency. Here we test whether increased attention yielded greater volatility in intraday Bitcoin trading.

We choose the Parkinson (1980) high-low measure to be an estimate for historical intraday volatility. Let H_t and L_t denote the highest and lowest price of Bitcoin on a given day t. The high low measure is defined as

$$\hat{\sigma}_t^2 = \frac{1}{4 \log(2)} (\log(H_t) - \log(L_t))^2 \tag{5}$$

We deliberately ignore extensions such as the Garman and Klass (1980) volatility estimator and the Yang and Zhang (2000) methodologies. The former is an extension of the Parkinson (1980) measure by accounting for open and close prices, while the latter handles overnight jumps. Since Bitcoin trading is continuous with no overnight period, these extensions are deemed unnecessary. Our model specification are as follows:

$$\sigma_t = \sum_{i=1}^{n} \alpha_i \sigma_{t-i}$$

$$+ \sum_{i=1}^{n} \left(\beta_{i,posts}^{SM} + \gamma_{i,posts}^{POS} NEWS_{t-i}^{POS} + \gamma_{i,posts}^{NEG} NEWS_{t-i}^{NEG} \right) SM_{t-i}^{posts}$$

$$+ \sum_{i=1}^{n} \left(\beta_{i,subs}^{SM} + \gamma_{i,subs}^{POS} NEWS_{t-i}^{POS} + \gamma_{i,subs}^{NEG} NEWS_{t-i}^{NEG} \right) SM_{t-i}^{subs}$$

$$+ \sum_{i=1}^{n} \left(\beta_i^{TM} + \delta_i^{POS} NEWS_{t-i}^{POS} + \delta_i^{NEG} NEWS_{t-i}^{NEG} \right) TM_{t-i}$$

$$+ \phi^{POS} NEWS_{t-i}^{POS} + \phi^{NEG} NEWS_{t-i}^{NEG} + \varepsilon_t$$

$$(6)$$

3 Empirical Results

A. The Impact of Attention on Bitcoin Trading

First we examine whether there is any sign of statistical causality between investor attention and Bitcoin performance. We use Granger causality tests outlined in Sect. 2.1. We examine three different types of attention:

(i) New investor attention (novice attention), proxied using Reddit daily new subscribers. The rationale being only relatively new investors (who has just recently gained interest in Bitcoin) would subscribe to the Bitcoin subreddit. Existing Bitcoin investors would have already subscribed to the subreddit.

(ii) Existing investor attention, proxied using Reddit daily posts and shows activity and discussion among existing Reddit members.

(iii) Traditional news attention, proxied by the number of Bitcoin-related articles on Bloomberg.com. A rise in the number of articles by journalists should impact public interest and attention.

Table 3 shows that there is strong evidence for statistical causality between attention and Bitcoin trading. Among some of the most liquid Bitcoin exchanges, we find the following:

1. In general, all aspects of attention have some impact Bitcoin trading
2. Novice attention (Reddit subscribers) and traditional news media (Bloomberg news articles) attention have a stronger impact on Bitcoin returns than existing investor attention (Reddit posts). This suggests that Bitcoin trading is impacted more by incoming participants as opposed to existing participants. This provides

Table 3 Statistical causality between attention and Bitcoin trading We use Granger causality to examine if there is any statistical causality between different forms of investor attention and different dimensions of Bitcoin trading. In general, we find that all three forms of attention impact Bitcoin trading. We find that Coinbase trading is less impacted by news and investor attention. This is in part due to the fact that Coinbase is used by novice Bitcoin investors with more user-friendly functions such as mobile app trading. It is also less liquid than Bitfinex and Bitstamp in our sample set

		Bitfinex			Bitstamp			BTCe			Coinbase			Kraken		
		F-test	p-value		F-test	p-value		F-test	p-value		F-test	p-value		F-test	p-value	
Returns	Reddit posts	0.77	0.575		0.58	0.718		0.48	0.791		0.40	0.852		0.48	0.794	
	Reddit subscribers	5.56	0.000	***	4.94	0.000	***	2.44	0.033	**	3.05	0.010	***	4.37	0.001	***
	Bloomberg articles	3.24	0.006	***	2.86	0.014	**	2.06	0.067	*	2.09	0.064	*	1.99	0.078	*
Volume	Reddit posts	2.46	0.031	**	2.99	0.011	**	1.94	0.084	*	3.13	0.008	***	1.36	0.235	
	Reddit subscribers	4.00	0.001	***	1.47	0.197		2.60	0.024	**	10.77	0.000	***	2.67	0.021	**
	Bloomberg articles	5.60	0.000	***	4.09	0.001	***	3.89	0.002	***	11.43	0.000	***	5.64	0.000	***
Order imbalance	Reddit Posts	2.38	0.036	**	1.24	0.290		1.91	0.090	*	0.21	0.960		1.97	0.081	*
	Reddit subscribers	3.50	0.004	***	2.65	0.022	**	2.84	0.015	**	1.38	0.229		3.46	0.004	***
	Bloomberg articles	3.74	0.002	***	3.59	0.003	***	2.29	0.043	**	0.73	0.598		2.41	0.034	**
Volatility	Reddit posts	2.68	0.020	**	2.65	0.022	**	2.38	0.037	**	0.51	0.771		3.18	0.007	***
	Reddit subscribers	16.15	0.000	***	14.22	0.000	***	6.14	0.000	***	0.05	0.999		10.35	0.000	***
	Bloomberg articles	15.35	0.000	***	12.78	0.000	***	4.87	0.000	***	0.08	0.996		6.61	0.000	***

evidence in favor of psychological contagion, where investor enthusiasm spreads contagiously across the Internet population. Similar to the Barclay's Capital model, prices are impacted by new buyers that have been infected with Bitcoin FOMO through media attention rather than by existing buyers.

3. Coinbase Bitcoin trading volatility and order imbalance are least impacted by media attention. We believe this is due to a shorter history (since 2014) and its focus on mobile app trading.

We conclude that increased media and social media attention impacts Bitcoin trading behavior. In the subsequent sections, we further analyze the asymmetric impact of investor attention on Bitcoin trading conditional and accounting for fundamental news events.

B. Asymmetric Impact of Attention on Bitcoin Returns

Table 4 documents the impact of news and attention on Bitcoin returns for all five exchanges.

First, we notice a statistically significant autocorrelation in Bitcoin returns across all five exchanges, which suggests a degree of market inefficiency. In Bitfinex and Bitstamp exchanges, $\alpha_1 = 0.235 \sim 0.238$, respectively. BTC-e, Coinbase, and Kraken exhibited lower levels of autocorrelation with α_1 between 0.104 and 0.149.

Second, similar to our findings in Section A, we find an increase in Reddit subscribers to be more informative than Reddit posts. Overall, across all five exchanges, we did not find Reddit posting activity to impact subsequent Bitcoin returns. However, when there is an exogenous negative news event (as tabulated in Tables 2, we find that Reddit postings did yield significant negative impact on Bitcoin returns in four of our five exchanges (BTC-e being the exception). We did not find similar results for exogenous positive new events. This suggests Reddit posting activity only impacts returns negatively in periods with cryptocurrency pessimism. Contrary to Reddit posting activity, we find Reddit new subscriber activity to be statistically significant (and positive) in its impact on Bitcoin returns.

Third, we find traditional media activity (Bloomberg news articles) has a strong positive impact on Bitcoin returns for all exchanges during periods with positive exogenous news events. This impact seems to be significant across several lags, which indicates investors might take a few days to process the positive news article before buying Bitcoin. It may also reflect the fact that novice investors might take a few days to set up an account and buy Bitcoin. For negative news events, the impact of traditional media attention has a significant negative impact on only one lag. Once investors have set up an account, it is a lot quicker for them to react and sell Bitcoin after reading bad news; thus, we do not see the same lagged significance on the negative side.

Furthermore, we also find that exogenous news shocks have an impact on Bitcoin returns. The coefficient of positive news events ϕ_i^{POS} is positive and statistically significant at the 10% level. Similarly, the coefficient of negative news events ϕ_i^{NEG} is negative and statistically significant between the 5% level and the 10% level. We

Table 4 Asymmetric impact on Bitcoin returns

		Bitfinex			Bitstamp			BTCe			Coinbase			Kraken		
		Coef	T-stat	p-value	Coef	T-stat	p-value	Coef	T-stat	p-value	Coef	T-stat	p-value	Coef	T-stat	p-value
Returns	α_1	2.35E-01	9.34	0.000 ***	2.38E-01	9.44	0.000 ***	1.42E-01	5.49	0.000 ***	1.49E-01	5.49	0.000 ***	1.04E-01	4.11	0.000 ***
	α_2	-1.13E-01	-4.46	0.000 ***	-1.10E-01	-4.34	0.000 ***	-8.34E-02	-3.23	0.001 ***	-8.48E-02	-3.12	0.002 ***	-3.24E-03	-0.13	0.898
	α_3	2.00E-02	0.80	0.424	2.96E-02	1.19	0.236	9.19E-03	0.36	0.720	5.67E-02	2.10	0.036 **	-1.70E-02	-0.68	0.498
Posts	$\beta_{1,posts}^{SM}$	4.53E-05	0.42	0.674	1.32E-05	0.12	0.901	8.46E-06	0.07	0.946	2.09E-05	0.16	0.872	-3.09E-05	-0.27	0.786
	$\beta_{2,posts}^{SM}$	-1.67E-04	-1.08	0.281	-1.07E-04	-0.70	0.485	-5.23E-05	-0.29	0.771	-1.31E-05	-0.07	0.944	-4.61E-05	-0.28	0.780
	$\beta_{3,posts}^{SM}$	1.32E-04	1.23	0.219	1.01E-04	0.95	0.341	6.33E-05	0.51	0.612	5.54E-06	0.04	0.966	8.78E-05	0.77	0.442
Posts (Pos)	$\gamma_{1,posts}^{POS}$	6.13E-04	1.44	0.149	7.68E-04	1.84	0.066 *	6.36E-04	1.29	0.198	6.70E-04	1.37	0.170	8.74E-04	1.94	0.053 *
	$\gamma_{2,posts}^{POS}$	1.73E-04	0.41	0.685	3.49E-05	0.08	0.934	7.13E-05	0.14	0.886	3.16E-05	0.06	0.949	-1.61E-04	-0.35	0.723
	$\gamma_{3,posts}^{POS}$	-4.44E-05	-0.10	0.917	-2.02E-04	-0.48	0.629	-9.84E-05	-0.20	0.842	-1.09E-04	-0.22	0.823	5.27E-05	0.12	0.907
Posts (Neg)	$\gamma_{1,posts}^{NEG}$	-1.34E-03	-2.13	0.033 **	-1.24E-03	-2.01	0.045 **	-1.18E-03	-1.54	0.123	-1.34E-03	-1.79	0.074 *	-1.10E-03	-1.65	0.099 *
	$\gamma_{2,posts}^{NEG}$	-6.61E-04	-1.05	0.294	-6.88E-04	-1.11	0.268	-4.51E-04	-0.59	0.555	-6.72E-04	-0.89	0.373	-7.56E-04	-1.13	0.259
	$\gamma_{3,posts}^{NEG}$	-4.70E-04	-0.75	0.456	-2.47E-05	-0.04	0.968	-3.01E-04	-0.39	0.693	-1.97E-04	-0.26	0.794	-2.78E-04	-0.42	0.678
Subscribers	$\beta_{1,subs}^{SM}$	4.73E-06	2.67	0.008 ***	4.46E-06	2.56	0.011 **	3.20E-06	1.54	0.125	3.67E-06	1.79	0.073 *	5.79E-06	3.09	0.002 ***
	$\beta_{2,subs}^{SM}$	-5.96E-06	-3.23	0.001 ***	-5.49E-06	-3.03	0.003 ***	-4.04E-06	-1.88	0.061 *	-4.59E-06	-2.17	0.031 **	-5.38E-06	-2.75	0.006 ***
	$\beta_{3,subs}^{SM}$	6.43E-07	0.38	0.705	6.29E-07	0.38	0.706	1.55E-06	0.78	0.436	-9.62E-07	-0.49	0.623	-5.27E-07	-0.29	0.770
Subscribers (Pos)	$\gamma_{1,subs}^{POS}$	4.21E-06	0.67	0.500	6.29E-06	1.03	0.306	6.80E-06	0.94	0.349	6.17E-06	0.86	0.391	1.31E-06	0.20	0.843
	$\gamma_{2,subs}^{POS}$	-2.92E-05	-4.69	0.000 ***	-3.01E-05	-4.92	0.000 ***	-2.41E-05	-3.32	0.001 ***	-3.01E-05	-4.19	0.000 ***	-2.93E-05	-4.43	0.000 ***
	$\gamma_{3,subs}^{POS}$	-2.10E-05	-3.39	0.001 ***	-2.27E-05	-3.72	0.000 ***	-2.79E-05	-3.88	0.000 ***	-2.48E-05	-3.48	0.001 ***	-2.45E-05	-3.73	0.000 ***
Subscribers (Neg)	$\gamma_{1,subs}^{NEG}$	2.99E-05	2.87	0.004 ***	2.96E-05	2.89	0.004 ***	2.76E-05	2.20	0.028 **	2.74E-05	2.29	0.022 **	2.41E-05	2.19	0.029 **
	$\gamma_{2,subs}^{NEG}$	-3.56E-05	-3.41	0.001 ***	-3.09E-05	-3.01	0.003 ***	-1.71E-05	-1.36	0.175	-2.39E-05	-1.99	0.047 **	-2.50E-05	-2.26	0.024 **
	$\gamma_{3,subs}^{NEG}$	3.53E-05	3.37	0.001 ***	2.80E-05	2.71	0.007 ***	1.58E-05	1.25	0.211	2.05E-05	1.70	0.090 *	2.16E-05	1.95	0.052 *

(continued)

Table 4 (continued)

		Bitfinex				Bitstamp				BTCe				Coinbase				Kraken			
		Coef	T-stat	p-value		Coef	T-stat	p-value		Coef	T-stat	p-value		Coef	T-stat	p-value		Coef	T-stat	p-value	
Bloomberg	β_1^{TM}	5.09E-04	1.63	0.103		5.74E-04	1.87	0.061	*	3.77E-04	1.01	0.312		8.56E-04	2.37	0.018	**	4.91E-04	1.49	0.136	
	β_2^{TM}	-6.67E-04	-2.05	0.041	**	-5.96E-04	-1.86	0.063	*	-9.36E-06	-0.02	0.981		-5.88E-04	-1.56	0.118		-5.82E-04	-1.70	0.090	*
	β_3^{TM}	6.69E-04	2.17	0.030	**	5.48E-04	1.81	0.071	*	-1.41E-04	-0.38	0.704		5.75E-04	1.61	0.108		5.56E-04	1.71	0.088	*
Bloomberg (Pos)	δ_1^{POS}	3.34E-03	2.57	0.010	**	3.24E-03	2.53	0.011	**	4.02E-03	2.65	0.008	***	4.43E-03	2.97	0.003	***	5.10E-03	3.70	0.000	***
	δ_2^{POS}	3.73E-03	2.86	0.004	***	3.35E-03	2.61	0.009	***	2.87E-03	1.88	0.061	*	3.75E-03	2.51	0.012	**	2.95E-03	2.13	0.033	**
	δ_3^{POS}	1.99E-03	1.52	0.128		2.16E-03	1.68	0.093	*	3.34E-03	2.19	0.029	**	2.29E-03	1.53	0.126		2.65E-03	1.91	0.056	*
Bloomberg (Neg)	δ_1^{NEG}	-5.38E-03	-2.43	0.015	**	-5.65E-03	-2.59	0.010	***	-5.84E-03	-2.18	0.030	**	-4.97E-03	-1.87	0.062	*	-3.96E-03	-1.69	0.092	*
	δ_2^{NEG}	2.40E-03	1.08	0.280		1.15E-03	0.53	0.599		-9.79E-05	-0.04	0.971		7.51E-04	0.28	0.778		5.22E-04	0.22	0.824	
	δ_3^{NEG}	-4.94E-03	-2.22	0.027	**	-3.45E-03	-1.58	0.115		-3.22E-03	-1.20	0.231		-3.40E-03	-1.27	0.203		-3.48E-03	-1.48	0.140	
News (Pos)	ϕ_1^{POS}	7.27E-02	1.77	0.078	*	6.89E-02	1.70	0.089	*	5.78E-02	1.14	0.254		6.65E-02	1.31	0.191		4.94E-02	1.13	0.258	
	ϕ_2^{POS}	4.66E-02	1.13	0.259		5.51E-02	1.35	0.176		3.02E-02	0.59	0.552		4.85E-02	0.95	0.341		5.99E-02	1.37	0.171	
	ϕ_3^{POS}	1.74E-02	0.42	0.674		-1.00E-02	-0.25	0.805		1.79E-02	0.35	0.724		7.66E-03	0.15	0.881		8.45E-03	0.19	0.847	
News (Neg)	ϕ_1^{NEG}	-5.20E-02	-1.79	0.074	*	-6.65E-02	-2.33	0.020	**	-5.83E-02	-1.70	0.089	*	-6.28E-02	-1.85	0.064	*	-7.66E-02	-2.49	0.013	**
	ϕ_2^{NEG}	-9.17E-04	-0.03	0.975		1.06E-02	0.37	0.712		2.27E-03	0.07	0.947		8.53E-03	0.25	0.802		2.82E-02	0.91	0.363	
	ϕ_3^{NEG}	2.56E-02	0.88	0.380		3.53E-02	1.23	0.219		2.51E-02	0.73	0.464		3.45E-02	1.01	0.311		1.50E-02	0.49	0.627	

find that negative news events have a statistically more significant impact on Bitcoin returns than positive returns.

C. Asymmetric Impact of Attention on Bitcoin Trading Volumes

Similar to Bitcoin returns, we note a strong degree of autocorrelation in Bitcoin trading volumes across all five exchanges (Table 5).

We note that Reddit posts on Bitcoin do influence the level of Bitcoin trading on four of the five major exchanges (Kraken being the exception). This means increased chatter on social media platforms does induce greater trading by investors. We find that Reddit posts during negative exogenous news shocks tend to drive higher volumes. However, during positive news shocks, Reddit posts have no impact on Bitcoin trading.

We find some level of positive significance between Reddit new subscribers and Bitcoin trading volumes for four of the five major exchanges (BTC-e being the exception). The positive significance occurred in lags 1 and 2, suggesting a some delay between a new user subscribing onto the Bitcoin subreddit and then subsequently choosing an online exchange to trade. Since Coinbase is a relatively more user-friendly than the other exchanges, there is a 1-day lag between an increase in subreddit subscribers and an increase in trading volumes. For other exchanges, there is a 2-day lag.

We do not find a relationship between traditional media attention and trading volumes. However, in periods with negative exogenous news shocks, we find that Bloomberg news articles tended to increase trading activity as investors scramble to sell. This triangulates well with our results in Table 4, where we find that the traditional media attention during negative news events strongly affected Bitcoin returns negatively.

Overall, we find that existing investor attention or *chatter* on social Internet platforms had more impact on Bitcoin daily turnover than new entrants and traditional news media attention. However, during periods with positive exogenous news events, an influx of new subscribers has a lagged positive impact on volumes. Similarly, during periods with negative exogenous new events, an increase in traditional media articles also increases trading volumes as market participants rush to sell their holdings.

D. Asymmetric Impact of Attention on Bitcoin Intraday Volatility

First we estimate Bitcoin intraday volatility using the Parkinson (1980) high-low measure; then, we subsequently examine the impact social media and traditional media attention on volatility. Existing research by Da et al. (2011) find that increased retail attention yielded extra noise and volatility. We find similar results in Bitcoin markets.

First, we note that increased attention by existing Bitcoin investors, as measured through Reddit posts, had a negligible impact on Bitcoin volatility. This suggests chatter by existing investors on social media platforms does not result in market destabilization. This is also supported by our results in Table 4, which find Reddit posts to be insignificant as an explanatory variable for Bitcoin returns.

Table 5 Asymmetric impact of Bitcoin trading volumes

		Bitfinex				Bitstamp				BTCe				Coinbase				Kraken			
		Coef	T-stat	p-value		Coef	T-stat	p-value		Coef	T-stat	p-value		Coef	T-stat	p-value		Coef	T-stat	p-value	
Volume	α_1	6.78E-01	26.12	0.000	***	7.26E-01	28.13	0.000	***	6.01E-01	23.47	0.000	***	3.04E-01	10.46	0.000	***	6.69E-01	25.45	0.000	***
	α_2	-7.40E-02	-2.38	0.017	**	-1.11E-01	-3.50	0.000	***	5.49E-02	1.84	0.066	*	2.67E-01	9.15	0.000	***	-1.92E-02	-0.61	0.545	
	α_3	1.42E-01	5.49	0.000	***	1.81E-01	7.02	0.000	***	1.42E-01	5.55	0.000	***	8.15E-02	2.81	0.005	***	2.49E-01	9.50	0.000	***
Posts	$\beta^{SM}_{1,posts}$	1.38E+02	2.19	0.029	**	4.33E+01	1.85	0.064	*	3.56E+01	2.35	0.019	**	5.50E+01	2.22	0.027	**	4.43E+00	0.77	0.439	
	$\beta^{SM}_{2,posts}$	-1.03E+02	-1.13	0.257		-3.15E+01	-0.94	0.349		-4.08E+01	-1.87	0.062	*	-1.34E+01	-0.37	0.708		-1.81E+00	-0.22	0.826	
	$\beta^{SM}_{3,posts}$	4.87E+01	0.77	0.443		2.11E+01	0.90	0.366		2.56E+01	1.69	0.091	*	-4.49E+00	-0.18	0.857		1.12E+00	0.20	0.844	
Posts (Pos)	$\gamma^{POS}_{1,posts}$	1.20E+02	0.48	0.629		5.30E+01	0.58	0.565		5.41E+00	0.09	0.928		3.53E+00	0.04	0.970		-2.50E+00	-0.11	0.912	
	$\gamma^{POS}_{2,posts}$	-3.00E+01	-0.12	0.904		-1.22E+02	-1.32	0.186		-2.66E+01	-0.44	0.659		-4.90E+01	-0.52	0.601		-5.21E+00	-0.23	0.818	
	$\gamma^{POS}_{3,posts}$	-3.97E-02	-1.59	0.112		-8.89E-01	-0.97	0.335		-6.61E-01	-1.10	0.271		-8.49E-01	-0.91	0.364		2.16E-01	0.96	0.339	
Posts (Neg)	$\gamma^{NEG}_{1,posts}$	1.19E+03	3.24	0.001	***	5.00E+02	3.67	0.000	***	1.80E+02	1.95	0.052	*	3.99E+02	2.78	0.006	***	2.14E+01	0.64	0.520	
	$\gamma^{NEG}_{2,posts}$	-2.20E+02	-0.59	0.552		-1.28E+02	-0.94	0.349		1.50E+02	1.62	0.106		-3.86E-01	-0.27	0.789		-1.32E-01	-0.40	0.692	
	$\gamma^{NEG}_{3,posts}$	9.43E+01	0.25	0.799		-3.72E+00	-0.03	0.978		-1.30E+02	-1.41	0.159		-2.33E-01	-0.16	0.872		4.33E+01	1.30	0.195	
Subscribers	$\beta^{SM}_{1,subs}$	-6.00E-01	-0.57	0.566		-6.93E-02	-0.18	0.857		-8.44E-02	-0.34	0.737		8.12E-01	2.02	0.044	**	-4.63E-02	-0.49	0.623	
	$\beta^{SM}_{2,subs}$	2.73E+00	2.50	0.012	**	1.21E+00	3.02	0.003	**	-2.20E-03	-0.01	0.993		4.57E-01	1.10	0.270		3.84E-01	3.89	0.000	***
	$\beta^{SM}_{3,subs}$	1.10E+00	1.09	0.276		1.37E-01	0.37	0.711		2.34E-02	0.10	0.922		5.71E-01	1.47	0.142		9.35E-04	0.01	0.992	
Subscribers (Pos)	$\gamma^{POS}_{1,subs}$	5.47E+00	1.50	0.135		1.95E-01	1.45	0.148		4.26E-01	0.48	0.628		1.02E+00	0.74	0.460		6.58E-01	1.98	0.047	**
	$\gamma^{POS}_{2,subs}$	1.40E+01	3.82	0.000	***	2.94E+00	2.18	0.029	***	-7.93E-02	-0.09	0.928		6.43E+00	4.67	0.000	***	8.02E-01	2.43	0.015	**
	$\gamma^{POS}_{3,subs}$	-4.50E-03	-0.00	0.999		2.87E-01	0.22	0.829		-5.77E-01	-0.67	0.505		2.97E+00	2.18	0.029	**	4.76E-01	1.46	0.144	
Subscribers (Neg)	$\gamma^{NEG}_{1,subs}$	-4.37E+00	-0.72	0.472		-2.38E+00	-1.06	0.288		-8.04E-01	-0.53	0.596		-3.50E-01	-0.15	0.879		-4.86E-01	-0.88	0.380	
	$\gamma^{NEG}_{2,subs}$	4.70E+00	0.77	0.441		1.56E+00	0.69	0.487		-6.43E-01	-0.42	0.673		-6.62E-01	-0.29	0.773		2.09E-04	0.00	1.000	
	$\gamma^{NEG}_{3,subs}$	-8.19E+00	-1.34	0.181		-1.42E+00	-0.63	0.529		8.57E-01	0.56	0.574		-1.06E+00	-0.46	0.646		-1.51E+00	-2.71	0.007	***

(continued)

Table 5 (continued)

		Bitfinex			Bitstamp			BTCe			Coinbase			Kraken		
		Coef	T-stat	p-value	Coef	T-stat	p-value	Coef	T-stat	p-value	Coef	T-stat	p-value	Coef	T-stat	p-value
Bloomberg	β_1^{TM}	−8.12E+01	−0.44	0.659	−8.00E+01	−1.17	0.241	−4.26E+01	−0.94	0.345	1.54E+02	2.21	0.028 **	6.84E+00	0.40	0.686
	β_2^{TM}	2.28E+02	1.18	0.237	1.49E+01	0.21	0.835	3.64E+01	0.76	0.445	−9.62E+01	−1.32	0.187	−2.73E+01	−1.55	0.121
	β_3^{TM}	−5.06E+02	−2.76	0.006 ***	−2.48E+02	−3.66	0.000 ***	−9.13E+01	−2.04	0.042 **	−1.92E+02	−2.76	0.006 ***	−6.50E+01	−3.87	0.000 ***
Bloomberg (Pos)	δ_1^{POS}	2.99E+02	0.39	0.694	7.98E+01	0.28	0.776	9.42E+01	0.51	0.608	3.18E+02	1.12	0.264	−7.16E+01	−1.04	0.298
	δ_2^{POS}	−2.16E+03	−2.84	0.005 ***	−5.41E+02	−1.92	0.054 *	−3.64E+01	−0.20	0.843	−7.64E+02	−2.69	0.007 ***	−1.02E+02	−1.48	0.139
	δ_3^{POS}	−1.57E+03	−2.06	0.040 **	−4.35E+02	−1.55	0.121	3.03E+00	0.02	0.987	−9.66E+02	−3.39	0.001 ***	−1.17E+02	−1.70	0.089 *
Bloomberg (Neg)	δ_1^{NEG}	3.16E+03	2.44	0.015 **	1.28E+03	2.67	0.008 ***	3.12E+02	0.96	0.337	8.70E+02	1.72	0.086 *	2.79E+02	2.37	0.018 **
	δ_2^{NEG}	−8.55E+01	−0.07	0.947	−5.98E+01	−0.12	0.901	3.78E+02	1.16	0.244	2.96E+02	0.58	0.560	7.06E+01	0.60	0.548
	δ_3^{NEG}	1.27E+03	0.97	0.330	1.69E+02	0.35	0.725	−1.53E+02	−0.47	0.640	1.86E+02	0.36	0.716	3.55E+02	3.00	0.003 ***
News (Pos)	ϕ_1^{POS}	−7.75E+04	−3.21	0.001 ***	−3.54E+04	−3.97	0.000 ***	−1.14E+04	−1.86	0.064 *	−2.53E+04	−2.61	0.009 ***	−2.67E+03	−1.22	0.221
	ϕ_2^{POS}	9.46E+03	0.39	0.697	7.03E+03	0.78	0.434	−1.14E+04	−1.84	0.066 *	1.73E+03	0.18	0.859	8.37E+02	0.38	0.702
	ϕ_3^{POS}	−5.83E+03	−0.24	0.810	5.23E+02	0.06	0.954	7.42E+03	1.20	0.229	1.20E+03	0.12	0.902	−3.20E+03	−1.46	0.144
News (Neg)	ϕ_1^{NEG}	−2.01E+04	−1.18	0.239	−7.39E+03	−1.17	0.241	−1.77E+03	−0.43	0.670	−1.85E+03	−0.28	0.776	9.14E+00	0.01	0.995
	ϕ_2^{NEG}	9.22E+03	0.54	0.591	1.11E+04	1.76	0.078 *	3.04E+03	0.73	0.465	3.29E+03	0.50	0.614	2.84E+02	0.18	0.854
	ϕ_3^{NEG}	3.31E+04	1.94	0.053 *	7.61E+03	1.21	0.228	6.28E+03	1.51	0.132	8.04E+03	1.24	0.217	−1.41E+03	−0.91	0.362

Second, we find that an increase in Bitcoin subreddit subscribers had a lagged positive impact on Bitcoin volatility. This supports Da et al.'s (2011) findings that increased novice attention only yielded extra noise and reduced market efficiency. New subscribers are an indicator for new/novice attention. We find that it takes 2 days for an increase in subscription to result in an increase in Bitcoin volatility on the major exchanges. In periods where there is a positive exogenous news shock, we find further statistical significance in the impact of subscription on Bitcoin volatility. Contrary to Reddit, Bloomberg news articles in periods of positive exogenous news shocks had a negative impact on volatility. This suggests when traditional media reported positive news on Bitcoin, this in turn had an effect of taming Bitcoin trading. However, increased attention by new Bitcoin traders that opened accounts in the wake of good news tended to increase volatility through their trading (Table 6).

E. Asymmetric Impact of Attention on Bitcoin Order Imbalance
We find order imbalance in major Bitcoin exchanges to be highly autocorrelated. However, we do not find any significant relationship between social media and traditional media attention on Bitcoin order imbalance. High-order imbalance is a sign for private information. In probability of informed trading (PIN) models, buy and sell initiation imbalance is evidence for informed trading. Our non-result shown in Table 7 confirms that media attention through Bloomberg news articles and social media attention through Reddit activity does not yield any private information, and therefore increased attention does not lead to a reduction of liquidity and an increase in order imbalance.

4 Conclusion

The rise of cryptocurrencies and social media platforms has given us unique insight on the impact of investor attention on investor trading behavior. In this paper, we focus specifically on Bitcoin across five major global exchanges: Bitfinex, Bitstamp, BTC-e, Coinbase, and Kraken. We break attention into three categories, social media attention by existing investors (or at least people familiar with Bitcoin) proxied through Reddit posts, social media attention by new investors proxied through Reddit subscribers, and traditional media attention proxied through Bloomberg news articles. We find that new entrants, i.e., novice Bitcoin investors, have a greater impact on Bitcoin returns and volatility than discussions and posts by existing Bitcoin holders. This suggests that rise in Bitcoin prices is driven by new investors entering into the market rather than by existing investors adjusting their valuations and beliefs. In short, the increase in attention by new investors has pushed Bitcoin prices and increased extra noise. We also document evidence of asymmetric impact between Bitcoin attention and Bitcoin trading. First, we note a greater lag between Reddit subscribers and Bitcoin returns, volume and volatility when there is positive exogenous news compared to negative exogenous news. This, in part, is reflective of the fact that it takes time for new investors to get set up

Table 6 Asymmetric impact of Bitcoin intraday volatility

		Bitfinex				Bitstamp				BTCe				Coinbase				Kraken			
		Coef	T-stat	p-value		Coef	T-stat	p-value		Coef	T-stat	p-value		Coef	T-stat	p-value		Coef	T-stat	p-value	
Volatility	α_1	3.54E-01	13.71	0.000	***	4.89E-01	18.33	0.000	***	1.54E-01	5.92	0.000	***	-2.04E-04	-0.01	0.994		3.65E-01	14.12	0.000	***
	α_2	-4.63E-03	-0.17	0.862		-5.00E-02	-1.72	0.086	*	6.74E-02	2.58	0.010	***	-9.31E-04	-0.03	0.973		8.95E-02	3.26	0.001	***
	α_3	1.32E-02	0.52	0.604		5.06E-02	1.92	0.055	*	1.72E-02	0.66	0.507		-1.33E-03	-0.05	0.961		-3.06E-02	-1.18	0.239	
Posts	$\beta_{1,posts}^{SM}$	1.55E-05	1.26	0.208		1.31E-05	1.22	0.223		1.29E-05	0.75	0.454		2.16E-03	0.63	0.530		1.74E-05	1.39	0.166	
	$\beta_{2,posts}^{SM}$	-5.66E-06	-0.32	0.750		-8.76E-06	-0.56	0.573		-1.46E-05	-0.59	0.558		-5.97E-03	-1.20	0.229		-6.89E-06	-0.38	0.703	
	$\beta_{3,posts}^{SM}$	-1.41E-06	-0.11	0.909		3.45E-06	0.32	0.749		1.23E-05	0.71	0.476		4.34E-03	1.26	0.209		-1.54E-06	-0.12	0.902	
Posts (Pos)	$\gamma_{1,posts}^{POS}$	-3.10E-06	-0.06	0.949		-5.42E-06	-0.13	0.898		-4.33E-05	-0.63	0.528		5.85E-04	0.05	0.964		-6.81E-05	-1.38	0.168	
	$\gamma_{2,posts}^{POS}$	-2.30E-05	-0.47	0.636		-2.96E-05	-0.70	0.487		-2.75E-05	-0.40	0.690		2.48E-03	0.19	0.849		-3.83E-05	-0.77	0.441	
	$\gamma_{3,posts}^{POS}$	-1.27E-06	-0.03	0.979		6.95E-06	0.16	0.870		-4.32E-05	-0.63	0.529		-1.25E-03	-0.10	0.923		-5.73E-05	-1.16	0.248	
Posts (Neg)	$\gamma_{1,posts}^{NEG}$	1.46E-04	2.03	0.043	**	9.46E-05	1.51	0.132		9.81E-05	0.93	0.354		3.58E-04	0.02	0.986		1.02E-04	1.40	0.162	
	$\gamma_{2,posts}^{NEG}$	-3.66E-05	-0.51	0.612		-3.20E-05	-0.51	0.611		-4.88E-07	-0.00	0.996		4.57E-04	0.02	0.982		-4.57E-05	-0.62	0.533	
	$\gamma_{3,posts}^{NEG}$	9.11E-05	1.26	0.206		-1.71E-05	-0.27	0.786		-4.22E-05	-0.40	0.690		-6.84E-04	-0.03	0.973		1.93E-05	0.26	0.792	
Subscribers	$\beta_{1,subs}^{SM}$	-3.27E-07	-1.58	0.114		-2.81E-07	-1.55	0.122		1.40E-07	0.48	0.629		5.50E-06	0.10	0.919		-3.27E-07	-1.57	0.116	
	$\beta_{2,subs}^{SM}$	8.46E-07	3.92	0.000	***	8.28E-07	4.37	0.000	***	3.57E-07	1.19	0.234		-2.62E-06	-0.05	0.963		5.85E-07	2.70	0.007	***
	$\beta_{3,subs}^{SM}$	3.09E-07	1.55	0.122		7.55E-08	0.43	0.667		1.66E-07	0.60	0.549		4.63E-07	0.01	0.993		2.75E-07	1.37	0.170	
Subscribers (Pos)	$\gamma_{1,subs}^{POS}$	8.66E-07	1.21	0.225		8.00E-07	1.28	0.200		-5.27E-08	-0.05	0.958		7.78E-07	0.00	0.997		-1.73E-07	-0.23	0.815	
	$\gamma_{2,subs}^{POS}$	5.39E-06	7.57	0.000	***	4.41E-06	7.08	0.000	***	3.82E-06	3.80	0.000	***	1.71E-05	0.09	0.929		4.85E-06	6.61	0.000	***
	$\gamma_{3,subs}^{POS}$	2.91E-07	0.41	0.682		9.85E-07	1.58	0.113		2.06E-06	2.07	0.039	**	1.22E-05	0.06	0.948		1.08E-06	1.50	0.135	
Subscribers (Neg)	$\gamma_{1,subs}^{NEG}$	6.20E-07	0.52	0.601		3.93E-07	0.38	0.705		8.12E-07	0.47	0.640		3.59E-07	0.00	0.999		9.40E-07	0.78	0.437	
	$\gamma_{2,subs}^{NEG}$	2.33E-06	1.96	0.050	**	1.65E-06	1.58	0.113		1.32E-06	0.76	0.450		1.03E-05	0.03	0.974		1.21E-06	1.00	0.319	
	$\gamma_{3,subs}^{NEG}$	-1.17E-06	-0.98	0.329		-1.06E-06	-1.02	0.310		-3.97E-07	-0.23	0.820		-2.33E-06	-0.01	0.994		-5.95E-07	-0.49	0.624	

(continued)

Table 6 (continued)

		Bitfinex			Bitstamp			BTCe			Coinbase			Kraken		
		Coef	T-stat	p-value	Coef	T-stat	p-value	Coef	T-stat	p-value	Coef	T-stat	p-value	Coef	T-stat	p-value
Bloomberg	β_1^{TM}	−4.88E−05	−1.37	0.171	−4.42E−05	−1.41	0.158	−7.21E−06	−0.14	0.889	−2.04E−03	−0.21	0.830	4.77E−07	0.01	0.989
	β_2^{TM}	1.47E−04	3.92	0.000 ***	1.15E−04	3.52	0.000 ***	5.23E−05	0.96	0.337	7.52E−05	0.01	0.994	6.05E−05	1.60	0.109
	β_3^{TM}	−8.91E−05	−2.51	0.012 **	−9.45E−05	−3.03	0.003 ***	−2.88E−05	−0.56	0.575	−2.45E−03	−0.26	0.796	−1.58E−05	−0.44	0.661
Bloomberg (Pos)	δ_1^{POS}	−1.65E−05	−0.11	0.911	3.08E−05	0.24	0.812	−7.84E−05	−0.37	0.710	4.97E−03	0.13	0.900	−2.41E−04	−1.58	0.114
	δ_2^{POS}	−6.83E−04	−4.60	0.000 ***	−6.27E−04	−4.83	0.000 ***	−5.76E−04	−2.72	0.007 ***	9.84E−04	0.02	0.980	−7.40E−04	−4.85	0.000 ***
	δ_3^{POS}	−1.33E−04	−0.89	0.372	−1.48E−04	−1.14	0.255	−3.91E−04	−1.85	0.065 *	1.67E−03	0.04	0.966	−3.92E−04	−2.58	0.010 **
Bloomberg (Neg)	δ_1^{NEG}	2.05E−04	0.81	0.417	2.39E−04	1.08	0.280	1.68E−05	0.05	0.964	2.02E−03	0.03	0.977	1.51E−04	0.59	0.557
	δ_2^{NEG}	−2.97E−04	−1.18	0.240	−1.90E−04	−0.86	0.390	−1.26E−04	−0.34	0.734	8.86E−04	0.01	0.990	−1.83E−04	−0.71	0.477
	δ_3^{NEG}	−2.67E−04	−1.05	0.293	1.20E−04	0.54	0.588	−9.80E−06	−0.03	0.979	4.17E−03	0.06	0.953	−1.41E−04	−0.54	0.587
News (Pos)	ϕ_1^{POS}	−1.00E−02	−2.13	0.033 **	−8.34E−03	−2.03	0.043 **	−5.64E−03	−0.80	0.422	−3.87E−02	−0.03	0.977	−7.80E−03	−1.63	0.103
	ϕ_2^{POS}	1.76E−03	0.37	0.709	1.86E−03	0.45	0.653	−4.31E−04	−0.06	0.951	−4.74E−02	−0.03	0.972	2.41E−03	0.50	0.616
	ϕ_3^{POS}	1.08E−03	0.23	0.820	1.27E−03	0.31	0.758	3.03E−03	0.43	0.667	1.58E−02	0.01	0.991	2.08E−03	0.43	0.664
News (Neg)	ϕ_1^{NEG}	−7.03E−04	−0.21	0.833	−4.74E−04	−0.16	0.871	3.35E−03	0.71	0.481	−6.80E−02	−0.08	0.940	5.53E−03	1.63	0.102
	ϕ_2^{NEG}	1.43E−03	0.43	0.668	2.16E−03	0.74	0.459	2.04E−03	0.43	0.668	−1.70E−01	−0.19	0.851	2.66E−03	0.78	0.434
	ϕ_3^{NEG}	5.85E−04	0.18	0.860	−5.12E−04	−0.18	0.860	3.44E−03	0.72	0.470	4.18E−02	0.05	0.963	5.89E−03	1.74	0.083 *

Table 7 Asymmetric impact of Bitcoin order imbalance

		Bitfinex			Bitstamp			BTCe			Coinbase			Kraken		
		Coef	T-stat	p-value	Coef	T-stat	p-value	Coef	T-stat	p-value	Coef	T-stat	p-value	Coef	T-stat	p-value
Order imbalance	α_1	2.57E-01	10.40	0.000 ***	4.45E-01	17.93	0.000 ***	1.77E-01	6.87	0.000 ***	4.02E-01	15.09	0.000 ***	3.09E-01	12.48	0.000 ***
	α_2	8.18E-02	3.20	0.001 ***	1.49E-01	5.53	0.000 ***	1.37E-01	5.27	0.000 ***	2.58E-01	9.20	0.000 ***	2.37E-01	9.36	0.000 ***
	α_3	1.35E-01	5.43	0.000 ***	1.28E-01	5.12	0.000 ***	1.06E-01	4.11	0.000 ***	1.90E-01	7.02	0.000 ***	1.91E-01	7.66	0.000 ***
Posts	$\beta^{SM}_{1,posts}$	1.47E-04	0.51	0.611	-1.21E-04	-0.39	0.693	7.52E-04	3.23	0.001 ***	4.58E-04	1.40	0.162	8.63E-04	1.28	0.202
	$\beta^{SM}_{2,posts}$	-2.32E-05	-0.06	0.955	-1.55E-07	-0.00	1.000	-7.32E-04	-2.19	0.029 **	-8.08E-05	-0.17	0.863	3.61E-04	0.37	0.710
	$\beta^{SM}_{3,posts}$	7.36E-04	2.55	0.011 **	6.01E-04	1.95	0.051 *	5.88E-04	2.52	0.012 **	-7.21E-05	-0.22	0.826	-2.57E-04	-0.38	0.703
Posts (Pos)	$\gamma^{POS}_{1,posts}$	-3.11E-05	-0.03	0.978	5.42E-04	0.45	0.655	1.06E-04	0.12	0.908	7.90E-04	0.64	0.521	-4.84E-03	-1.82	0.069 *
	$\gamma^{POS}_{2,posts}$	-7.20E-05	-0.06	0.950	1.99E-03	1.64	0.101	1.00E-03	1.08	0.279	-2.35E-04	-0.19	0.849	-1.74E-04	-0.07	0.948
	$\gamma^{POS}_{3,posts}$	3.41E-04	0.30	0.764	-1.29E-04	-0.11	0.915	6.28E-04	0.68	0.496	-1.12E-03	-0.91	0.362	1.15E-03	0.43	0.664
Posts (Neg)	$\gamma^{NEG}_{1,posts}$	-1.23E-03	-0.73	0.463	1.44E-03	0.80	0.422	-7.45E-04	-0.52	0.600	3.61E-04	0.19	0.849	-4.36E-03	-1.11	0.268
	$\gamma^{NEG}_{2,posts}$	1.73E-03	1.03	0.305	-1.11E-03	-0.62	0.535	-1.67E-03	-1.17	0.240	2.77E-04	0.15	0.884	-1.23E-03	-0.31	0.755
	$\gamma^{NEG}_{3,posts}$	1.72E-03	1.02	0.307	-1.72E-03	-0.96	0.339	-1.69E-03	-1.19	0.235	-2.15E-03	-1.13	0.258	1.70E-03	0.43	0.665
Subscribers	$\beta^{SM}_{1,subs}$	-1.73E-06	-0.37	0.713	3.76E-06	0.74	0.457	-1.02E-06	-0.26	0.794	-4.86E-06	-0.94	0.348	-1.09E-05	-0.99	0.324
	$\beta^{SM}_{2,subs}$	-4.00E-07	-0.08	0.935	-7.41E-06	-1.41	0.158	8.67E-06	2.15	0.031 **	-3.88E-07	-0.07	0.942	-1.28E-07	-0.01	0.991
	$\beta^{SM}_{3,subs}$	-1.32E-06	-0.29	0.770	4.60E-06	0.96	0.339	5.93E-06	1.60	0.109	4.04E-06	0.82	0.411	-2.68E-06	-0.25	0.800
Subscribers (Pos)	$\gamma^{POS}_{1,subs}$	1.16E-05	0.69	0.488	-1.82E-05	-1.02	0.306	3.97E-05	2.93	0.003 ***	-8.13E-06	-0.45	0.654	-6.56E-05	-1.67	0.094 *
	$\gamma^{POS}_{2,subs}$	-6.46E-07	-0.04	0.969	-8.16E-06	-0.46	0.645	-6.13E-06	-0.45	0.651	-1.29E-05	-0.71	0.475	-5.91E-06	-0.15	0.879
	$\gamma^{POS}_{3,subs}$	-1.48E-05	-0.90	0.368	-2.65E-05	-1.51	0.131	-7.78E-06	-0.58	0.560	-1.99E-05	-1.11	0.266	2.77E-06	0.07	0.942

(continued)

Table 7 (continued)

		Bitfinex			Bitstamp			BTCe			Coinbase			Kraken		
		Coef	T-stat	p-value	Coef	T-stat	p-value	Coef	T-stat	p-value	Coef	T-stat	p-value	Coef	T-stat	p-value
Subscribers (Neg)	$\gamma_{1,subs}^{NEG}$	−3.23E−06	−0.12	0.907	−1.44E−05	−0.49	0.625	−3.08E−06	−0.13	0.895	−1.20E−05	−0.40	0.690	2.15E−05	0.33	0.741
	$\gamma_{2,subs}^{NEG}$	1.91E−05	0.69	0.490	−4.43E−05	−1.49	0.135	−1.49E−05	−0.63	0.526	−3.36E−05	−1.11	0.265	3.75E−05	0.58	0.564
	$\gamma_{3,subs}^{NEG}$	5.20E−07	0.02	0.985	1.66E−05	0.56	0.576	9.45E−06	0.40	0.688	−3.10E−06	−0.10	0.918	−2.49E−05	−0.38	0.703
Bloomberg	β_1^{TM}	−8.30E−04	−1.00	0.316	−1.81E−04	−0.20	0.838	7.30E−04	1.05	0.293	9.54E−04	1.05	0.292	−1.04E−04	−0.05	0.957
	β_2^{TM}	6.89E−04	0.79	0.427	1.72E−03	1.85	0.064 *	−2.74E−04	−0.37	0.708	8.80E−04	0.93	0.354	−3.35E−04	−0.17	0.869
	β_3^{TM}	−7.07E−04	−0.86	0.390	1.59E−03	1.81	0.070 *	−8.89E−04	−1.29	0.198	5.23E−04	0.58	0.561	4.77E−04	0.25	0.804
Bloomberg (Pos)	δ_1^{POS}	−1.14E−03	−0.33	0.742	2.93E−03	0.79	0.428	−8.17E−03	−2.88	0.004 ***	2.19E−03	0.58	0.559	5.22E−03	0.64	0.521
	δ_2^{POS}	−2.31E−04	−0.07	0.947	−5.02E−03	−1.36	0.175	−3.01E−03	−1.06	0.290	−1.12E−05	−0.00	0.998	−1.39E−03	−0.17	0.864
	δ_3^{POS}	4.01E−04	0.12	0.908	4.18E−03	1.13	0.258	6.96E−05	0.02	0.980	−1.62E−03	−0.43	0.666	2.93E−03	0.36	0.718
Bloomberg (Neg)	δ_1^{NEG}	8.59E−04	0.15	0.884	4.60E−03	0.73	0.465	−4.57E−03	−0.91	0.361	−1.50E−04	−0.02	0.982	−7.18E−03	−0.52	0.604
	δ_2^{NEG}	−1.44E−03	−0.24	0.808	5.39E−03	0.86	0.392	−8.65E−04	−0.17	0.863	4.59E−03	0.69	0.493	−5.69E−03	−0.41	0.681
	δ_3^{NEG}	−3.64E−03	−0.61	0.540	−8.46E−03	−1.34	0.182	−3.88E−04	−0.08	0.938	−2.12E−03	−0.32	0.752	3.00E−03	0.22	0.829
News (Pos)	ϕ_1^{POS}	4.62E−02	0.42	0.674	−9.04E−02	−0.77	0.440	4.20E−02	0.44	0.657	−3.06E−02	−0.24	0.811	2.37E−01	0.92	0.357
	ϕ_2^{POS}	−1.07E−01	−0.97	0.330	5.22E−02	0.44	0.657	1.02E−01	1.08	0.279	−4.54E−02	−0.35	0.724	7.02E−02	0.27	0.786
	ϕ_3^{POS}	−1.83E−02	−0.17	0.868	1.32E−01	1.13	0.260	8.94E−02	0.94	0.345	1.54E−01	1.20	0.230	−6.43E−02	−0.25	0.803
News (Neg)	ϕ_1^{NEG}	9.46E−03	0.12	0.904	−4.83E−02	−0.58	0.560	4.84E−03	0.08	0.940	−7.13E−02	−0.83	0.405	3.79E−01	2.08	0.037 **
	ϕ_2^{NEG}	−8.52E−03	−0.11	0.913	−6.94E−02	−0.84	0.403	−6.01E−02	−0.94	0.348	4.79E−03	0.06	0.956	4.13E−02	0.23	0.821
	ϕ_3^{NEG}	5.02E−02	0.65	0.518	1.25E−02	0.15	0.880	−4.86E−02	−0.76	0.447	1.19E−01	1.39	0.166	−9.33E−02	−0.51	0.609

for buying Bitcoin, but subsequently it is a lot easier for them to sell Bitcoin when their sentiment changes. Second, we find that Reddit posts had more impact when inducing volumes during negative exogenous events than positive events. This is suggestive of greater disagreement between investors during negative events than positive events. Furthermore, we find little evidence to suggest that social media attention has an impact on Bitcoin liquidity and order imbalance. This is suggestive that no "informed" information is being transferred through social media channels.

References

Barber, B., & Odean, T. (2008). All that glitters: The effect of attention and news on the buying behavior of individual and institutional investors. *The Review of Financial Studies, 21*(2), 785–818.

Blume M. E., MacKinlay, A. C., & Terker, B. (1987). Order imbalances and stock price movements on October 19 and 20, 1987. *The Journal of Finance, 44*(4), 827–848.

Da, Z., Engelberg, J., & Gao, P. (2011). In search of attention. *Journal of Finance, 66*, 1461–1499.

Feng, W., Wang, Y., & Zhang, Z. (2018). Can cryptocurrencies be a safe haven: A tail risk perspective analysis. *Applied Economics, 50*(44), 4745–4762.

Garman, M. B., & Klass, M. J. (1980). On the estimation of security price volatilities fom historical data. *The Journal of Business, 53*(1), 67–78.

Grossman, S. J., & Stiglitz, J. E. (1980). On the impossibility of informationally efficient markets. *The American Economic Review, 70*(3), 393–408.

Kristoufek, L. (2013). Bitcoin meets Google Trends and Wikipedia: Quanitifying the relationship between phenomena of the Internet era. *Nature: Scientific Reports, 3*, 3415.

Lee, C. (1992). Earnings news and small traders: An intraday analysis. *Journal of Accounting and Economics, 15*(2), 265–302.

Merton, R. C. (1987). A simple model of capital market equilibrium with incomplete information. *The Journal of Finance, 42*(3), 483–510.

Parkinson, M. (1980). The extreme value method for estimating the variance of the rate of return. *The Journal of Business, 53*(1), 61–65.

Peress, J. (2014). The media and the diffusion of information in financial markets: Evidence from newspaper strikes. *Journal of Finance, 69*(5), 2007–2043.

Phillips, R. C., & Gorse, D. (2017). Predicting cryptocurrency price bubbles using social media data and epidemic modelling. *IEEE Symposium Series on Computational Intelligence*, 1–7

Shen, A., Li, X., & Zhang, W. (2017). Baidu news coverage and its impacts on order imbalance and large-size trade of Chinese stocks. *Finance Research Letters, 23*, 210–216.

Shen, D., Urquhart, A., & Wang, P. (2019). A three-factor pricing model for cryptocurrencies. *Finance Research Letters, 34*, 1012–1048.

Sias, R. W., & Starks, L. T. (1997). Return autocorrelation and institutional investors. *Journal of Financial Economics, 46*(1), 103–131.

Urquhart, A. (2016). The inefficiency of Bitcoin. *Economics Letters, 148*, 80–82.

Vozlyublennaia, N. (2014). Investor attention, index performance, and return predictability. *Journal of Banking & Finance, 41*, 17–35.

Wei, W. C. (2018a). Liquidity and market efficiency in cryptocurrencies. *Economics Letters, 168*, 21–24.

Wei, W. C. (2018b). The impact of Tether grants on Bitcoin. *Economics Letters, 171*, 19–22.

Yang, D., & Zhang, Q. (2000). Drift-independent volatility estimation based on high, low, open, and close prices. *The Journal of Business, 73*(3), 477–491.

Zakon, R. H. (2018). Hobbes' Blockchain timeline. www.zakon.org.

Cryptocurrency Portfolios Using Heuristics

Emmanouil Platanakis and Charles Sutcliffe

Abstract Given the support from academic studies for heuristic (naive) asset allocation strategies, this study compares the performance of seven heuristics, including
four new heuristics, in forming a portfolio of six popular cryptocurrencies. As many
cryptocurrency traders are retail investors, they are likely to use heuristics, rather
than sophisticated optimization procedures. Our empirical analysis shows little
difference in the out-of-sample performance of these seven strategies, indicating that
it does not matter which heuristic is used by cryptocurrency investors. Therefore,
retail investors might as well use the simplest heuristic (*1/N*) strategy, whose
performance has been widely studied and found to be comparable with that of
portfolio optimization models.

Keywords Cryptocurrencies · Heuristic asset allocation strategies · Portfolio
management

JEL G11

Highlights

- We compare seven heuristics in forming portfolios of six cryptocurrencies.
- Heuristics are relevant for the retail investors who dominate cryptocurrencies.

(continued)

E. Platanakis (✉)
School of Management, University of Bath, Bath, UK
e-mail: E.Platanakis@bath.ac.uk

C. Sutcliffe
The ICMA Centre, Henley Business School, University of Reading, Reading, UK
e-mail: c.m.s.sutcliffe@rdg.ac.uk

- There is little out-of-sample performance difference between the seven heuristics.
- We suggest using the widely studied and very simple *1/N* heuristic.

1 Introduction

The main problem with Markowitz (1952) portfolio theory is that parameter estimation errors often lead to poor out-of-sample performance, and this phenomenon has been extensively investigated, e.g. Kan and Zhou (2007), Platanakis and Sutcliffe (2017), Platanakis et al. (2019) and Platanakis et al. (2021), among others. For this reason, several influential academic studies support using heuristic asset allocation strategies (e.g. *1/N*). For instance, DeMiguel et al. (2009) show that *1/N* with rebalancing is not consistently beaten by any of 14 portfolio optimization methods across 7 datasets in an out-of-sample setting. Kirby and Ostdiek (2012) propose two heuristic portfolio strategies, volatility timing and reward-to-risk timing, that beat *1/N* in the presence of transaction costs, while Hsu et al. (2018) evaluate the out-of-sample performance of several portfolio construction techniques relative to *1/N* and find that none can consistently beat *1/N* after controlling for data-snooping biases.

Cryptocurrencies have attracted much attention from individual investors, fund managers, academics and the media; and in June 2019, the total market capitalization of cryptocurrencies was over \$330 billion.[1] Since many cryptocurrency traders are retail investors (Dyhrberg et al., 2018), they are unlikely to use sophisticated portfolio optimization procedures and rely on a heuristic. Therefore, the performance of heuristics is of particular importance in cryptocurrency markets.

This is the first paper to apply a wide range of heuristics to forming portfolios of cryptocurrencies and to investigate whether any heuristic is superior. We build on Platanakis et al. (2018), who showed there is very little difference in performance between the *1/N* rule and Markowitz when applied to cryptocurrency portfolios. We apply three popular heuristics (*1/N*, risk parity and reward-to-risk timing), together with four new heuristics which we propose, to a portfolio of six popular and very liquid cryptocurrencies (Bitcoin, Litecoin, Ripple, Dash, Stellar and Monero). Overall, our results show there is little to choose between these seven heuristics.

The rest of this paper is organized as follows. Section 2 presents our data and methodology, Sect. 3 contains a description of our performance metrics and transaction costs, and Sect. 4 presents our results. We conclude in Sect. 5.

---

[1] For a review of the cryptocurrency literature, see Corbet et al. (2019).

Table 1 Correlation matrix of cryptocurrency returns and annualized means and standard deviations and Sharpe ratios

Correlation matrix	Bitcoin	Litecoin	Ripple	Dash	Stellar	Monero
Bitcoin	1.0000	–	–	–	–	–
Litecoin	0.5535	1.0000	–	–	–	–
Ripple	0.2866	0.5639	1.0000	–	–	–
Dash	0.3755	0.3376	0.1742	1.0000	–	–
Stellar	0.3333	0.3015	0.5859	0.1629	1.0000	–
Monero	0.4209	0.3048	0.1679	0.4300	0.1700	1.0000
Mean return %	97.71	186.36	698.81	233.54	712.02	381.56
SD of returns %	35.57	60.77	92.36	57.70	102.03	72.53
Sharpe ratio	2.73	3.05	7.56	4.03	6.97	5.25

2 Data and Methodology

2.1 Data

We analyse weekly data on Bitcoin, Litecoin, Ripple, Dash, Stellar and Monero over the period 15 August 2014 to 22 February 2019 (237 weeks/observations) from www.coinmarketcap.com.[2] The risk-free rate is from the Kenneth French website. Table 1 reports the correlations and the means, standard deviations and Sharpe ratios of the six cryptocurrencies. The highest correlation is between Ripple and Stellar at 0.5859, and the lowest is between Stellar and Dash at 0.1629.

2.2 Methodology: Portfolio Construction Techniques

1/N We apply the *1/N* heuristic with re-balancing, as in DeMiguel et al. (2009), which assigns a weight of *1/N* to each asset at every re-balancing:

$$x_i^{1/N} = \frac{1}{N}, \forall i \qquad (1)$$

where x_i^j represents the portfolio weights for each asset i and heuristic$j$. N denotes the total number of assets.

Risk Parity (RP) Risk parity has the intuitive appeal of achieving an equal contribution by each asset to total portfolio risk. We use a simplified version of

---

[2] Consistent with Platanakis and Urquhart (2020), we use weekly rather than monthly returns since monthly returns would not provide an adequate number of observations.

the risk-parity method, as in Oikonomou et al. (2018). The portfolio weights are:

$$x_i^{RP} = \frac{1/\sigma_i^2}{\sum\limits_{\iota=1}^{N} \left(1/\sigma_\iota^2\right)}, \forall i \tag{2}$$

where σ_ι^2 denotes the sample variance of asset i.

Reward-to-Risk Timing (RRT) Reward-to-risk timing assigns greater weight to assets with a higher sample reward-to-risk ratio and is characterized by lower turnover than other approaches. The RRT asset weights are:

$$x_i^{RRT} = \frac{\mu_\iota^+/\sigma_\iota^2}{\sum\limits_{\iota=1}^{N} \left(\mu_\iota^+/\sigma_\iota^2\right)}, \forall i \tag{3}$$

where σ_ι^2 is the sample variance of asset i, and $\mu_\iota^+ = \max(0, \mu_i)$ to avoid short selling (μ_i denotes the historical (sample) mean return of asset i).

Value-at-Risk Heuristic (VaRH) The value-at-risk heuristic is based on the value-at-risk (VaR) of each asset. Inspired by the risk-parity approach, we overweight assets with lower VaR at the 99th percentile. This is particularly important since cryptocurrencies are much riskier than traditional assets, e.g. equities, and can generate huge losses (Chaim & Laurini, 2018; Fry, 2018). The VaR asset weights of this new heuristic are:[3]

$$x_i^{VaRH} = \frac{1/VaR_{99\%,i}}{\sum\limits_{\iota=1}^{N} \left(1/VaR_{99\%,i}\right)}, \forall i \tag{4}$$

Reward-to-VaR Timing (RVT) We propose a reward-to-VaR timing heuristic, which is an extension of the RRT heuristic. We use the VaR as a risk measure instead of the sample variance. Since cryptocurrencies are more exposed to extreme events, the VaR may be a more appropriate risk measure than the sample variance. The RVT asset weights are:

$$x_i^{RVT} = \frac{\mu_\iota^+/VaR_{99\%,i}}{\sum\limits_{\iota=1}^{N} \left(\mu_\iota^+/VaR_{99\%,i}\right)}, \forall i \tag{5}$$

where $\mu_\iota^+ = \max(0, \mu_i)$, $\forall i$, to prohibit short selling.

---

[3] None of the values of $VaR_{99\%,i}$ is positive.

Naïve Combination (NC) and Optimal Combination (OC) Heuristics We also propose two more heuristics that are based on a combination of the five heuristics we have described so far (1/N, RP, RRT, VaRH and RVT). We take the average of the asset weights across these five heuristics in an attempt to diversify away the estimation errors of each heuristic.

We compute the portfolio weights for the naïve (equally) weighted combination heuristic as:

$$x_i^{NC} = \frac{1}{5} \times \left(x_i^{1/N} + x_i^{RP} + x_i^{RRT} + x_i^{VaRH} + x_i^{RVT} \right), \forall i \tag{6}$$

We compute the portfolio weights for the optimal combination heuristic (OC) as:

$$x_i^{OC} = \left(\alpha_1 x_i^{1/N} + \alpha_2 x_i^{RP} + \alpha_3 x_i^{RRT} + \alpha_4 x_i^{VaRH} + \alpha_5 x_i^{RVT} \right), \forall i \tag{7}$$

where $\alpha_i \geq 0, \forall i$. The OC heuristic is attractive since it applies the shrinkage approach directly to the portfolio weights by computing the optimal combination of the five heuristic portfolios. The coefficients (α_i) for the OC heuristic are computed by minimizing the portfolio variance, subject to no-short selling and normalization of the portfolio weights. Hence, the optimization problem for the OC heuristic is:

$$\begin{aligned} \min_{\mathbf{x}^{OC}} & \quad \left\{ \left(\mathbf{x}^{OC} \right)^T \Sigma \mathbf{x}^{OC} \right\} \\ \text{s.t.} & \quad x_i^{OC} \geq 0, \ \forall i \ , \\ & \quad \sum_{i=1}^{N} x_i^{OC} = 1 \end{aligned} \tag{8}$$

3 Performance Metrics and Transaction Costs

3.1 Performance Metrics

The Sharpe ratio (Sharpe, 1966) is probably the most popular metric for measuring portfolio risk-adjusted performance and is computed as the average out-of-sample portfolio excess return, divided by the out-of-sample portfolio standard deviation. We also use certainty equivalent returns (CERs) as an additional performance metric. Assuming mean-variance investors, this is computed as:

$$CER = \overline{\mu}_{portfolio} - \frac{\lambda}{2} \sigma^2_{portfolio}, \tag{9}$$

where $\overline{\mu}_{portfolio}$ denotes the average out-of-sample portfolio return and $\sigma_{portfolio}$ represents the out-of-sample portfolio standard deviation. Following DeMiguel et al. (2009), we set the risk aversion parameter (λ) to unity.

We also compute the Omega ratio (Shadwick & Keating, 2002) as our third risk-adjusted performance metric. This ratio does not depend on any assumption about the distribution of asset returns and is computed as:

$$\text{Omega} = \frac{\frac{1}{T}\sum_{t=1}^{T}\max\left(0, +R_{p,t}\right)}{\frac{1}{T}\sum_{t=1}^{T}\max\left(0, -R_{p,t}\right)}, \tag{10}$$

where $R_{p,t}$ is the portfolio return at time t.

3.2 Transaction Costs

Total transaction costs, which are subtracted from portfolio returns, are computed as:

$$\text{TC}_t = \sum_{i=1}^{N} T_i \left(\left|x_{i,t} - x_{i,t-1}^{+}\right|\right). \tag{11}$$

We follow Platanakis et al. (2018) and Platanakis and Urquhart (2019) and set T_i (proportional transaction costs) to 50 bps (0.5%) for all the cryptocurrencies. $x_{i,t}^{+}$ denotes the weight of asset i in the portfolio at the end of period t (just before re-balancing).

4 Results

We use a 52-week (1-year) expanding estimation window with weekly re-balancing. Figures 1, 2 and 3 plot the annualized out-of-sample Sharpe ratios, CERs and Omega ratios, allowing for transaction costs. These show very little difference between the seven heuristics. Table 2 has the mean values of the seven strategies in Figs. 1, 2 and 3. VaRH has the highest Sharpe ratio, while *1/N* is the best heuristic according to both the CERs and Omega ratios. But using the test of Lo (2002), there are no significant differences between the seven Sharpe ratios. In Table 3, we report the means and standard deviations of the portfolio weights of the seven strategies; and Figs. 4, 5, 6, 7, 8 and 9 plot the asset allocation over the entire out-of-sample period for each heuristic. The portfolio weights differ across the seven heuristics, with Bitcoin having the highest average weight for every heuristic except *1/N* and Stellar having the lowest average weight for four heuristics. Bitcoin has the lowest average

Fig. 1 Out-of-sample Sharpe ratios (annualized) of the seven heuristics

Fig. 2 Out-of-sample CERs (annualized) of the seven heuristics

return (98%) and standard deviation (36%), while Stellar has the highest average return (712%) and standard deviation (102%). So Bitcoin has the greatest appeal to more risk-averse investors, and Stellar has the least appeal. These differences in portfolio weights do not have a significant impact on out-of-sample performance.

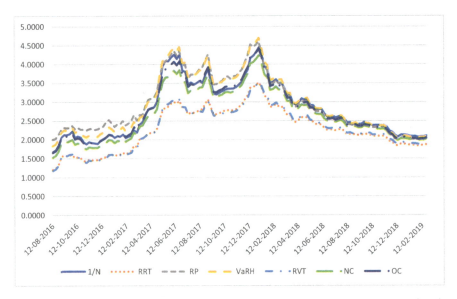

Fig. 3 Out-of-sample Omega ratios (annualized) of the seven heuristics

Table 2 Mean annualized out-of-sample performance of the seven heuristics

	1/N	RRT	RP	VaRH	RVT	NC	OC
Mean Sharpe ratio	1.7059	1.5476	1.7410	1.7438	1.5369	1.6826	1.7148
Mean CER	1.2470	1.0407	1.1297	1.2057	1.0783	1.1614	1.1837
Mean Omega ratio	2.0974	1.8753	2.0361	2.0865	1.9046	2.0154	2.0436

Table 3 Portfolio weights for the seven heuristics

		Bitcoin	Litecoin	Ripple	Dash	Stellar	Monero
1/N	Mean	0.1667	0.1667	0.1667	0.1667	0.1667	0.1667
	SD	0.0000	0.0000	0.0000	0.0000	0.0000	0.0000
RRT	Mean	0.2265	0.0899	0.2116	0.2047	0.1368	0.1306
	SD	0.1277	0.0614	0.1677	0.0891	0.1007	0.0659
RP	Mean	0.4688	0.1651	0.0710	0.1430	0.0571	0.0950
	SD	0.0322	0.0201	0.0091	0.0230	0.0130	0.0230
VaRH	Mean	0.2994	0.1760	0.1181	0.1675	0.1042	0.1347
	SD	0.0135	0.0091	0.0065	0.0124	0.0109	0.0152
RVT	Mean	0.1231	0.0824	0.2507	0.1950	0.1823	0.1664
	SD	0.0703	0.0592	0.1465	0.0842	0.0958	0.0931
NC	Mean	0.2569	0.1360	0.1636	0.1754	0.1294	0.1387
	SD	0.0407	0.0233	0.0626	0.0350	0.0392	0.0261
OC	Mean	0.2776	0.1418	0.1478	0.1750	0.1190	0.1388
	SD	0.0290	0.0163	0.0378	0.0267	0.0241	0.0177

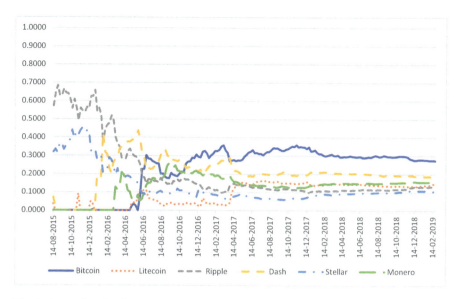

Fig. 4 Asset allocation for RRT

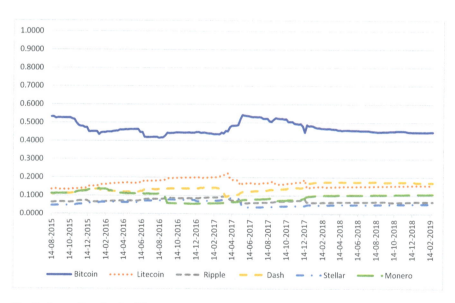

Fig. 5 Asset allocation for RP

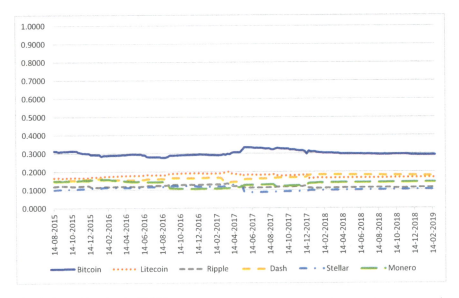

Fig. 6 Asset allocation for VaRH

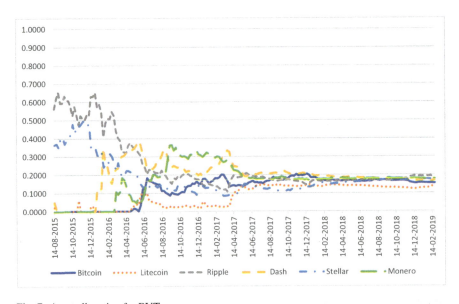

Fig. 7 Asset allocation for RVT

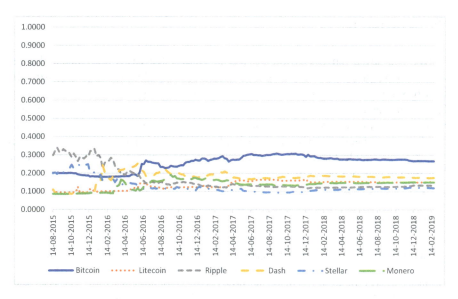

Fig. 8 Asset allocation for NC

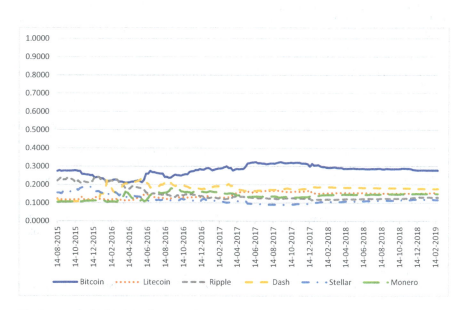

Fig. 9 Asset allocation for OC

5 Conclusions

Given the strong support from influential studies for easily implemented asset allocation strategies, we contribute to the cryptocurrency literature by comparing the out-of-sample performance of seven heuristics for forming portfolios of six popular cryptocurrencies. Although they have different average asset allocations, using three performance metrics, we find very little difference in the out-of-sample performance of these seven heuristics. Our findings imply that unsophisticated retail investors can use *1/N*, the simplest heuristic, to form cryptocurrency portfolios, although this may not lead to superior performance.

References

Chaim, P., & Laurini, M. P. (2018). Volatility and return jumps in bitcoin. *Economics Letters, 173*, 158–163.

Corbet, S., Lucey, B., Urquhart, A., & Yarovaya, L. (2019). Cryptocurrencies as a financial asset: A systematic analysis. *International Review of Financial Analysis, 62*, 182–199.

DeMiguel, V., Garlappi, L., & Uppal, R. (2009). Optimal versus naive diversification: How inefficient is the 1/N portfolio strategy? *Review of Financial Studies, 22*, 1915–1953.

Dyhrberg, A. H., Foley, S., & Svec, J. (2018). How investable is bitcoin? Analysing the liquidity and transaction costs of bitcoin markets. *Economics Letters, 171*, 140–143.

Fry, J. (2018). Booms, busts and heavy-tails: The story of bitcoin and cryptocurrency markets? *Economics Letters, 171*, 225–229.

Hsu, P. H., Han, Q., Wu, W., & Cao, Z. (2018). Asset allocation strategies, data snooping, and the 1/N rule. *Journal of Banking and Finance, 97*, 257–269.

Kan, R., & Zhou, G. (2007). Optimal portfolio choice with parameter uncertainty. *Journal of Financial and Quantitative Analysis, 42*, 621–656.

Kirby, C., & Ostdiek, B. (2012). It's all in the timing: Simple active portfolio strategies that outperform naïve diversification. *Journal of Financial and Quantitative Analysis, 47*, 437–467.

Lo, A. (2002). The statistics of Sharpe ratios. *Financial Analysts Journal, 58*, 36–52.

Markowitz, H. (1952). Portfolio selection. *Journal of Finance, 7*, 77–91.

Oikonomou, I., Platanakis, E., & Sutcliffe, C. (2018). Socially responsible investment portfolios: Does the optimization process matter? *British Accounting Review, 50*, 379–401.

Platanakis, E., & Sutcliffe, C. (2017). Asset–liability modelling and pension schemes: The application of robust optimization to USS. *The European Journal of Finance, 23*(4), 324–352.

Platanakis, E., & Urquhart, A. (2019). Portfolio management with cryptocurrencies: The role of estimation risk. *Economics Letters, 177*, 76–80.

Platanakis, E., & Urquhart, A. (2020). Should investors include bitcoin in their portfolios? A portfolio theory approach. *The British Accounting Review, 52*(4), 100837.

Platanakis, E., Sutcliffe, C., & Urquhart, A. (2018). Optimal vs naïve diversification in cryptocurrencies. *Economics Letters, 171*, 93–96.

Platanakis, E., Sakkas, A., & Sutcliffe, C. (2019). Harmful diversification: Evidence from alternative investments. *British Accounting Review, 51*, 1–23.

Platanakis, E., Sutcliffe, C., & Ye, X. (2021). Horses for courses: Mean-variance for asset allocation and 1/N for stock selection. *European Journal of Operational Research, 288*(1), 302–317.

Shadwick, W. F., & Keating, C. (2002). A universal performance measure. *Journal of Performance Measurement, 6*, 59–84.

Sharpe, W. F. (1966). Mutual fund performance. *Journal of Business, 39*, 119–138.

Part III
Financial Strategy and Analytics

Detecting Equity Style Information Within Institutional Media

Cédric Gillain, Ashwin Ittoo, and Marie Lambert

Abstract This study examines the detection of information related to small and large equity styles. Using a novel database of magazines targeting institutional investors, the institutional media, we compare the performance of dictionary-based and supervised machine learning algorithms (Naïve Bayes and support vector machine). Our three main findings are (1) restricted word lists are the most efficient approach, (2) bigram term frequency matrices are the best weighting scheme for algorithms, and (3) Naïve Bayes exhibits overfitting while support vector machine delivers encouraging results. Overall, our results provide material to construct small-cap and large-cap coverage indexes from specialized financial media.

Keywords Textual analysis · Machine learning · Style investing

1 Introduction

In their stock allocation process, some investors first allocate their funds between several categories before selecting individual stocks. Those categories are called "styles," and this investment behavior is called "style investing" (Barberis & Shleifer, 2003). Empirical studies (Froot & Teo, 2008; Kumar, 2009) have documented the importance of investor preference shifts between styles across time (small vs. large, value vs. growth). Change in style preferences provokes important inflow into one style to the detriment of its counterpart. Experts' recommendations within media are one potential major variable influencing the choice of investors between extreme styles. In this study, we document the most appropriate textual methodology to detect small and large style information within specialized advising magazines.

C. Gillain (✉) · A. Ittoo · M. Lambert (✉)
HEC Liège, Management School of the University of Liège, Liège, Belgium
e-mail: cedric.gillain@uliege.be; Ashwin.Ittoo@uliege.be; Marie.Lambert@uliege.be

© The Author(s), under exclusive license to Springer Nature Switzerland AG 2023   131
P. Alphonse et al. (eds.), *Essays on Financial Analytics*, Lecture Notes in Operations Research, https://doi.org/10.1007/978-3-031-29050-3_8

Investors cannot find directly or explicitly information about equity style investing into traditional financial newspapers (*The Wall Street Journal*, Dow Jones Newswires) or social network platforms (Twitter, StockTwits). Information in these media sources is often related at stock level or with a broader market vision. Therefore, we explore a new source of information to address our problem, namely, an institutional media database, which we created. It is composed of nine magazines targeting institutional investors, asset managers, advisers, and financial consultants. These magazines provide information focusing on different asset classes with an emphasis on strategic allocation. This way of relating financial market information is in accordance with style investing foundation, i.e., investors shifting preferences between assets sharing opposite characteristics. To our knowledge, no other publication suggests this type of analysis with a corpus targeting professional investors.

Whether existing textual analysis methodologies in finance are transposable to our problem is worth being addressed. The first and most widespread application is sentiment analysis, where researchers translate a qualitative piece of information into a score indicating polarity conveyed. Many sentiment indexes have been developed to study different asset classes (stock, housing, commodities, etc.) using dedicated source of information (newspapers, social media, company filings, etc.). These sentiment indicators exist with an important variation of methodologies applied in different context. For example, measuring sentiment should be different between a more formal newspaper content and informal social network language. In this study, we summarize major methodologies applied in sentiment analysis. We find that existing literature mainly uses word lists (i.e., dictionaries) or supervised machine learning algorithms. But many existing publications lack comparison between the two main solutions leaving a room for discussion. One comparison within an identical sample was documented by Henry and Leone (2016). They find similar performance between word lists and Naïve Bayes algorithms applied to earnings announcement. We formulate our detection problem as a classification task distinguishing between news with style content (i.e., style news) and news without style content (i.e., neutral news). We document the limits of dictionary-based, Naïve Bayes, and support vector machine classifiers, compare their performance, and provide recommendations on the optimal methodology to detect small and large style content.

We encounter three main challenges to detect style information in institutional media. First, we lack labelled data and have to proceed to manual annotation by ourselves. This task is required to train supervised machine learning algorithms so that they learn from data. In contrast to our difficulty, recent studies on social network now find annotated data available (Oliveira et al., 2016; Renault, 2017). This increasing amount of self-generated data improves algorithm efficiency. Second, style information does not necessarily constitute news headlines but mainly represents secondary information. The way that information is presented increases the difficulty of manual annotation. Third, style content is disseminated across various financial topics such as financial markets, retirement planning, or mutual funds industry-related news. In order to adapt our annotation process, we manually select neutral news and use dictionary detection for style news. This semi-automatic labelling process is only possible since dictionary-based approach delivers high precision: news classified within style class contains in vast majority style content.

We find promising results from support vector machine algorithms, especially with a term document matrix composed of bigrams. This methodology delivers balanced performance, limiting false detection (neutral news classified as style news) and missed detection (style news classified as neutral news). Naïve Bayes fails to limit false detection and is extremely sensitive to the size of annotated sample. Naïve Bayes is also more susceptible to overfitting, strongly modeling labelled data but weakly generalizing to an extended corpus such as the overall institutional media database. Compared to supervised algorithms, dictionary-based approach delivers the best performance. Restricted unigram and bigram lists with implicit stock content outperform supervised algorithms. The absence of existing labelled data is detrimental to the training phase of such algorithms.

Our research contributes to the literature on textual analysis in finance. We provide a critical analysis of the capacity of current methodologies to detect style information. We compare the use of human word lists with supervised machine learning algorithms. The results of our work provide style coverage indexes with applications focused on investor behavior, fund flows, and the importance of expert advices in the financial press.

The remainder of the paper is organized as follows. Section 2 discusses main methodologies applied in the financial domain. Section 3 introduces the institutional media database. Section 4 describes the different approaches selected to detect style investing-related content and the evaluation of their performance. Section 5 reports the empirical results. Section 6 concludes.

2 Literature Review

In this section, we present a review of existing classification methodologies applied to financial applications. As such, a classification methodology consists of identifying the class of a piece of information (word, sentence, or text), i.e., reducing the content of information to one or several categories. Most publications covered in our work concern sentiment analysis where the information is classified into positive or negative content. Table 1 summarizes publications covered in this review.

The usage and creation of expert dictionaries in financial publications is important. Tetlock (2007) uses the Harvard IV-4 psychosocial dictionary (hereafter H4N) to study the role of newspapers in the stock market. He counts the number of word occurrences from the 77 predetermined H4N categories. He finds that the "negative," "weak," "fail," and "fall" (i.e., pessimism factor) categories mostly influence stock market prices. In their seminal paper, Loughran and McDonald (2011, hereafter LM) develop financial word lists to better capture domain-specific information. They prove that many words from Harvard General Inquirer are misclassified in the financial context. A concrete example lies in the title of their paper, "When is a liability not a liability?". The word liability is erroneously

Table 1 Literature review of classification methodologies in finance

Approach	Publication	Application	Description of methodology	Sample
Dictionary-based	Tetlock (2007)	Tone content of stock market in newspapers (sentiment)	Selection of most pertinent lists within Harvard IV-4 psychosocial dictionary with a principal component factor analysis	*The Wall Street Journal*, "Abreast of the Market" daily news (3709 observations), from 1984 to 1999
	Loughran and McDonald (2011)	Tone content of company earnings filings (sentiment)	Creation of word lists dedicated to the financial domain (negative and positive, uncertainty, litigious, strong and weak modal)	37,287 MD&A section of 10-K filings (8341 different firms), from 1994 to 2008
	Larcker and Zakolyukina (2012)	Detection of deceptive narrative in conference calls	Selection of pertinent word lists from LIWC and WordNet	29,663 transcripts for US companies, from September 2003 to May 2007
	Garcia (2013)	Tone content of stock market in newspapers (sentiment)	Estimation of the fraction of positive and negative words classified by Loughran and McDonald (2011) dictionary	55,307 articles from *The New York Times* "Financial Markets" and "Topics in Wall Street" columns, from January 1905 to December 2005
	Bodnaruk et al. (2015)	Firm financial constraint	Creation of a word list referring to financial constraint	51,533 10-K filings (3607 different firms, excluding regulated financial firms and utilities), from 1996 to 2011
	Baker et al. (2016)	Economic policy uncertainty index	Use of three manually defined word lists (economy, uncertainty, and policy)	Articles in 10 US leadings newspapers, from 1985 to 2012
	Loughran et al. (2019)	Oil tone index	Creation of related oil word lists with inclusion of modifier words	41,432 Dow Jones Energy Services (DJES) oil-related articles from 2000 to 2016
	Soo (2018)	Housing sentiment index	Adaptation of four lists (increase, rise, decrease, and fall) from Harvard IV-4 psychosocial dictionary	37,357 articles in major newspapers of 34 US cities, from January 2000 to December 2013

(continued)

Table 1 (continued)

Approach	Publication	Application	Description of methodology	Sample
Machine learning	Antweiler and Frank (2004)	Sentiment analysis of message boards	Naïve Bayes trained on 1000 manually annotated messages	1.5 million messages from Yahoo Finance and Raging Bull over 45 firms in the Dow Jones Industrial Average and Dow Jones Internet Commerce Index during 2000
	Das and Chen (2007)	Sentiment analysis of message boards	Five distinct intuitive algorithms trained on 1000 manually annotated messages	145,110 messages from Yahoo Finance over 24 tech stocks between July and August 2001
	Li (2010)	Tone and content of forward-looking statements (FLS)	Naïve Bayes algorithms trained on 30,000 sentences. Multi-class into "tone" and "content" categories	140,000 FLS (13 million sentences) between 1994 and 2007
	Jegadeesh and Wu (2013)	Tone content of company earnings filings	Regression-based approach of tone content on market reaction	45,860 filings from 7606 firms, between 1995 and 2010
	Oliveira et al. (2016)	Sentiment analysis of StockTwits posts	Unigram and bigram classification using co-occurrence measures with a training set representing 75% of overall sample	350,000 messages on StockTwits platform, from June 2010 to March 2013
	Manela and Moreira (2017)	News implied volatility index (NVIX)	Support vector regression trained on a period ranging from 1996 to 2009	Title and abstract of The Wall Street Journal front page, from July 1889 to December 2009
	Renault (2017)	Sentiment analysis of StockTwits posts	Sentiment weight of unigrams and bigrams using 375,000 bearish and 375,000 bullish posts	Nearly 60 million messages from StockTwits platform, from January 2012 to December 2016

This table provides several key information about publications covered in our literature review. We provide a general description of the financial application and the methodology used. We give an overview of sample size and the related period of analysis

considered as negative by common dictionaries while exhibiting no valence in a financial context. Negative and positive word lists created by LM better capture tone content in financial information such as earnings filings. Using the LM dictionary, Garcia (2013) extends Tetlock (2007) findings: both positive and negative tones in media have predictive power on market returns, especially during recession (high uncertainty period). He confirms the importance of selecting an adapted dictionary to the financial domain.

Other word lists have been created subsequent to LM financial dictionary. Larcker and Zakolyukina (2012) analyze conference call transcripts to detect deceptive narrative from CEO and CFO. They manually form several word lists including general knowledge, emotions, hesitations, personal references, and shareholder value. False narratives contain more extreme positive emotion and references to general knowledge but less shareholder value terms. Soo (2018) creates an index for housing sentiment by quantifying tone in different local newspapers in the United States. He adapted four listed categories from Harvard IV-4 psychosocial dictionary: "Increase" and "Rise" (resp. "Decrease" and "Fall") for positive (resp. negative) sentiment. He manually removes misclassified words and expands lists with all inflections of remaining words. He shows that housing sentiment has higher potential to explain house price variations than a cluster of economic variable (such as rents, employment, or interest rates).

Baker et al. (2016) search terms related to economy ("economic" or "economy"), uncertainty ("uncertain" or "uncertainty"), and policy ("Congress," "deficit," "Federal Reserve," "legislation," "regulation," or "White House") within US newspapers. To define the policy list, authors conduct an audit consisting of 12,009 article readings. They compare human classification with automatic word detection from an enlarged word list (15 terms). They form the policy final list by minimizing coding misclassification (in comparison to manual labelling). The audit process was highly time-consuming, involving the construction of an extensive annotation guide and the participation of a research team. This work leads to the construction of an economic policy uncertainty index allowing further research about policy implications on financial markets. For example, authors show that policy uncertainty affects stock price volatility and reduces investment and employment in certain sectors. Finally, Loughran and McDonald extend their approach to other word list applications. Bodnaruk et al. (2015) study firm financial constraint with a list of related words. Based on their word list, they are able to predict firm liquidity events (such as dividend omission) from financial variables, proving again that textual analysis helps develop new pertinent (and low correlated) variables of interest. Loughran et al. (2019) manually create lists affecting oil prices. Their approach goes beyond the creation of two positive and negative lists. They define a third list of keywords whose effect on oil prices depends on an accompanied modifier word (such as "fall" or "surge"). They find investor overreaction to oil news.

Statistical algorithms are mainly used in absence of a reference dictionary or to alleviate limited size of restricted word lists. Antweiler and Frank (2004) were the first to construct a sentiment index with a Naïve Bayes methodology. Their model correctly classify more than 80% of 1000 messages manually labelled as {Buy, Sell,

Hold}. They show that talk from social media has an effect on trading volume and volatility, opening path for applications in event studies and insider trading. Das and Chen (2007) insist on web talk ambiguity and the difficulty to correctly classify message boards (even for humans). They suggest the combination of five different intuitive algorithms computationally efficient in such a way that they do not require important optimization. They find that a majority voting among algorithms delivers higher sentiment accuracy and reduces false positive.[1] Li (2010) annotated manually 30,000 sentences from 13 million included in forward-looking statements from firms' earnings filings. He trained a multi-class Naïve Bayes algorithms to categorize sentence tone ("positive," "neutral," "negative," and "uncertain") and content ("revenue," "cost," "profits," "operations," "liquidity," "investing," "financing," "litigation," "employees," "regulation," "accounting," "others"). By applying an N-fold cross-validation test, the algorithm correctly predicts sentence classes with an accuracy above 60%. He advocates that in absence of an adapted dictionary, researchers should rely on machine learning classifier instead of using general word lists.

From these pioneering studies, we learn that there is a compromise between sample training size and time spent for annotations. Moreover, existing dictionaries do not adjust to the informal content of Internet messages. But the recent evolution of social networks brings one green light to researchers: self-reported annotations. Oliveira et al. (2016) automatically construct dictionaries dedicated to StockTwits. From 350,000 users' labelled posts, they identify unigrams and bigrams co-occurring with bullish and bearish stance. They estimate co-occurrence with information gain, pointwise mutual information, and TF-IDF measures. Their automated methodology produces high classification rate outperforming classical dictionaries, which are not suitable to microblogging data. Renault (2017) attributes a sentiment weight to unigrams and bigrams by counting their occurrences in bearish and bullish posts from StockTwits. His methodology produces higher out-of-sample accuracy than LM and H4N dictionaries. Exploring nearly 60 million posts, he shows that sentiment is a predictor of intraday stock return, mainly driven by novice traders. These findings provide a direct empirical evidence of noise trading.

All previous studies require subjective interpretation: lists of words are constructed from experts' knowledge, while automatic labelling from microblogs still requires manual deletion or reclassification to improve algorithm efficiency.[2] Some researchers avoid intentionally any manual classification in their methodology. Jegadeesh and Wu (2013) use a regression-based approach to estimate word positive and negative weightings using market reaction to 10-K filings. They depart from the hypothesis that all words are equally relevant and suggest that market reaction should objectively determine this relative importance. They regress word content of 10-K filings on firms' abnormal returns during the releasing day: word coefficients

---

[1] Renault (2017) corrected manually misclassification using Oliveira et al. (2016) methodology. He finds, for example, that the words "further" or "commodity" are classified as negative.
[2] Ibid

representing a positive or negative power. They find that word power weightings differ significantly from proportional and TF-IDF weightings. They proved that the word power approach is robust while using combination of dictionaries and omitting some word from these dictionaries. Their approach gets rid of word classification subjectivity but requires to identify a market reaction to the information studied. Manela and Moreira (2017) apply a support vector regression (hereafter SVR) procedure where unigrams and bigrams from *The Wall Street Journal* were regressed on implied volatility index (VIX). The advantage of SVR is the reduction of term matrix into its most impactful constituents permitting a regression setting (otherwise impossible with OLS). They find that high news implied volatility index (NVIX) predicts above-average stock returns. Using WordNet to classify word in categories, they find that wars and government are driving the variation of equity risk premium. This last example demonstrates that all research tend usually to blend objective and subjective components.

3   Institutional Media Corpus

Several media groups deliver financial information through their portfolio of magazines. Their general mission statement includes production of trusted information targeting financial decision-makers (such as investment managers, advisers, pension trustees, and financial intermediaries). We identified nine different pension funds and institutional magazines from five well-known financial media groups: they form our institutional media corpus. Table 2 presents a description of institutional media and the related magazines. Although it might differ among our magazine sample, most of the readers are institutional investors, asset managers, advisers, and consultants. For instance, the Global Fund Media reach 43,000 active readers, and more than 60% have position in buy-side industry (fund managers, institutional investors, and advisers). The remaining readers occupy various positions in financial services. PLANSPONSOR magazine has 35,000 subscribers from corporate and plan pension-related positions.

The structure of information within our institutional media corpus is similar to newspapers content. News released in institutional media cover a broad range of topics such as macro-economics, market analysis, expert insight, and strategic portfolio allocation. Equity-related information is essentially discussed at category-based level, i.e., emerging market and developed market equities, equity investment style, or industry sectors. This departs from the information provided from conventional newspapers such as *The Wall Street Journal*, *Dow Jones News*, or other leading newspapers. Those media are featuring news on individual firms rather than opinions, recommendations, or performance analysis at a more aggregate level regarding equity style investment. One may have aggregated information from individual companies with regard to equity style portfolio. But two caveats are in order: first, this would assume investors are able to process all this information and, second, style rankings among companies are time-varying.

Table 2 Institutional media corpus

Media group	Magazines
Euromoney Institutional Investor: Euromoney Institutional Investor PLC ("Euromoney") is a global, multi-brand information business which provides critical data, price reporting, insight, analysis, and must-attend events to financial services, commodities, telecoms, and legal markets. Euromoney is listed on the London Stock Exchange and is a member of the FTSE 250 share index	*Euromoney*: *Euromoney*, founded in 1969 to chart the liberalization of cross-border capital flows, is the leading publisher on the world's banking and financial markets. Our coverage provides unrivalled insight into the finance houses at the heart of global finance through our privileged access to their senior leaders *Institutional Investor*: For 50 years, *Institutional Investor* has built its reputation on providing must-have information for the world's most influential decision-makers in traditional and alternative asset management
FTAdviser: FTAdviser.com is dedicated to the financial intermediary market covering investments, mortgages, pensions, insurance, regulation, and other key issues. The strength of FTAdviser.com comes from dedicated up-to-the-minute news articles and in-depth commentary written by the FTAdviser.com team, combined with the expertise of *Financial Advisor* and *Money Management* magazines, whose content feeds directly into the site	*Financial Advisor*: The premier weekly newspaper for the UK's financial intermediary community, *Financial Advisor* was launched in 1988 after the Financial Services Act 1986 defined for the first time the role of the independent financial advisor *Financial Advisor* offers comprehensive and in-depth coverage of the retail finance landscape
Global Fund Media: Founded in 2002, GFM Ltd. is the most targeted digital news publisher serving institutional investors/wealth managers and their investment managers/advisers across all asset classes with seven daily global newswires and real-time news-driven websites	*AlphaQ*: Compendium of investment ideas, skills, and talent across all asset classes *Institutional Asset Manager*: Institutional investors/pension funds and their managed funds/investment managers *Wealth Adviser*: Private client/wealth managers, family offices, trustees, and their investment advisers

(continued)

Table 2 Institutional media corpus

Media group	Magazines
IPE International Publishers Ltd.	*Investment & Pensions Europe (IPE):* IPE is the leading European publication for institutional investors and those running pension funds. It is published by IPE International Publishers Ltd., an independently owned company founded in July 1996
PLANSPONSOR: PLANSPONSOR/PLANADVISER, with its reputation for editorial integrity, objectivity, and leadership, is the trusted information and solutions resource for America's retirement benefits decision-makers. With its powerful array of customer-driven marketing programs, PLANSPONSOR/PLANADVISER offers industry providers an unparalleled ability to reach this influential audience. With all of the changes within the retirement industry, plan sponsors and advisers rely on PLANSPONSOR/PLANADVISER magazine to help them stay informed of crucial issues and important new innovative solutions	*PLANSPONSOR:* Since 1993, PLANSPONSOR has been the nation's leading authority on retirement and benefits programs and has been dedicated to helping employers navigate the complex world of retirement plan design and strategy *PLANADVISER:* Over the past 10 years, retirement plan advisers have reshaped the face of retirement benefits programs, and PLANADVISER has been there every step of the way—providing deep insight into the most pressing retirement plan challenges and strategies facing this specialized group. Our mission, through diverse media channels, is to identify and explore the most critical selling and servicing strategies and tactics facing retirement plan advisers and their clients

This table presents description of pension funds and institutional magazines forming our corpus

We use *Scrapy* library from Python[3] to collect news content from institutional media websites. Each news collected is converted in a plain text file with the following information: name of magazine, date, title, author, section, and textual content. We gather 108,638 news from January 1996 to June 2018 from the 9 identified magazines. PLANSPONSOR is the first contributor followed by *Wealth Adviser*, *Euromoney* and *Institutional Investor*. *AlphaQ, Institutional Asset Manager*, and *Financial Advisor* provide only recent releases but were nonetheless integrated in the corpus. More than 70% occurences of news are collected within the period ranging from 2009 to 2017. Table 3 present descriptive statistics of our database.

Figure 1 illustrates a news from institutional media corpus after collection. The title "What to expect from the markets in 2018" does not refer directly to equity styles. The author relates vision of managers for the coming year. While the article may certainly hold strategic content, it is not guaranteed that the author will speak about small or large styles. In this case, they are mentioned only in one sentence. With this example, we highlight that style information is often secondary topic within institutional media. In addition to the absence of existing annotation and the broad diversity of topics within institutional media, the way information is presented makes the detection of style information a challenge.

4 Methodology

We reformulate the detection of style information from institutional media as a classification problem. We intend to classify news into two categories: news containing style-related information (style class) or no style information (neutral class). One news potentially cover any one or two different style information. Since we want to disaggregate the information content by style, we will perform this classification for small- and large-cap styles separately. We investigate two approaches (1) dictionary-based and (2) a selection of machine learning methods. This methodology section will present our methodologies and the evaluation of their performance. Finally, we will discuss how we handle the construction of manually labelled sample to train machine learning algorithms.

4.1 Dictionary Approach

Dictionary-based method detects words (unigrams) and group of two words (bigrams) defining style investment strategies. Dictionary entries for style information include:

---

[3] https://scrapy.org/

Table 3 Descriptive statistics of institutional media corpus

	2000–2008	2009	2010	2011	2012	2013	2014	2015	2016	2017	2018 (*)	Total by magazines
Euromoney Institutional Investor												
Euromoney	5902	887	930	1285	1779	1071	900	748	730	677	365	15,274
Institutional Investor	0	328	736	3997	1278	871	1079	1422	1314	917	0	11,942
FTAdviser												
Financial Advisor	0	0	0	0	0	163	542	1158	2252	2618	1268	8001
Global fund Media												
AlphaQ	0	0	0	0	0	0	0	25	139	129	93	386
Institutional Asset Manager	0	0	0	0	0	0	0	0	722	1858	814	3394
Wealth Adviser	0	100	1583	1416	1448	1654	1789	2259	2133	2152	1102	15,636
IPE International Publishers												
Investment & Pensions Europe	163	118	114	272	239	254	756	853	645	1230	16	4660
PLANSPONSOR/PLANADVISER												
PLANSPONSOR	20,058	3309	3203	3520	2335	2227	1890	1456	1382	1308	653	41,341
PLANADVISER	1251	834	514	881	748	1018	541	441	718	688	370	8004
Total by year (*) until June 2018	*27,374*	*5576*	*7080*	*11,371*	*7827*	*7258*	*7497*	*8362*	*10,035*	*11,577*	*4681*	*108,638*

This table presents the distribution of news across time and magazines within our institutional media corpus. We group first years from 2000 to 2008 in one column (2000–2008). We only collect news until July for 2018

```
magazine : FTAdviser
section : Investments
date : 20180119
title : What to expect from the markets in 2018
author :Simoney Kyriakou
url : https://www.ftadviser.com/investments/2018/01/19/what-to-expect-from-the-markets-in-2018/


Cautious optimism: this seems to be the catchphrase as we enter 2018.

Fund managers have claimed there are many pockets of opportunity globally, whether this is in the rise of disruptive
technology or clean energy, Japanese large-caps or domestic small-caps in the US.

But with global political issues on the horizon, such as the Brexit negotiations and ongoing regulation in the financial world,
what sort of conversations should advisers be having with their clients?

What might be the potential pitfalls to watch out for this year - and avoid - and where might the new investment
opportunities be hiding?

According to Guy Stephens, technical investment director for Rowan Dartington: "When a market correction comes, it will
be sudden and savage as real fear returns."

Yet for others, such as Russ Mould of AJ Bell, the danger signs that usually presage a downturn in the markets, such as overly
high valuations, a sharp increase in volatility and a steep drop in copper prices, are just not flashing on the investment
dashboard right now.

 Peter Harrison, group chief executive of Schroders, commented: "The main risk we see lies in reflation, as governments turn
to lower taxes and higher infrastructure spending to stimulate economies, which could lead to overheating and unexpected
rises in inflation and interest rates.

"Overall, we carry a spirit of cautious optimism into 2018, albeit that caution may start to overwhelm optimism as the year
wears on."

The message, according to the contributors to this report, seems to be stay invested but stay alert and stay diversified.
```

Fig. 1 Example of news from institutional media corpus

- *Small style:* "microcap(s)," "micro cap(s)," "smallcap(s)," "small cap(s)," "mid-cap(s)," "mid cap(s)"
- *Large style:* "large cap(s)," "mega cap(s)"

The occurrence of each dictionary term is searched for in the news. If one news holds one (or several) terms in the lists above, the news belongs to the referred style class. The news is otherwise classified as neutral. While applying dictionary-based detection, we choose to restrain pre-processing steps to (1) removing {urls, special characters, and numbers}, (2) tokenization, and (3) lowering words. Since dictionary terms are nouns, we search for singular and plural forms.

4.2   Machine Learning Approaches

We apply supervised learning algorithms to detect style investment news. They are specifically adapted to classification problems when the number of classes is well defined. In supervised learning, the algorithms require a training phase, using a sub-sample of manually labelled data called training sample. Once algorithms are trained, they can perform classification on the overall corpus.

We select two different supervised methodologies for our work: Naïve Bayes (hereafter NB) and support vector machine (hereafter SVM). We choose NB since it is often used as the reference methodology in the literature (Antweiler & Frank, 2004; Das & Chen, 2007; Li, 2010; Henry & Leone, 2016). We complement the research by investigating SVM potentiality. Each method aims to solve the following problem: determine the class i of a news j containing n words. Considering each investment style separately, this is a binary classification problem where a news belongs to the style class or neutral class.

NB approach estimates the probability score of each word to belong to each class. It then predicts the best class based on the probability that words in the news belong to the class:

$$P\left(\text{class}_i | \text{news}_j\right) = P\left(w_1 | \text{class}_i\right) * P\left(w_2 | \text{class}_i\right) * \cdots * P\left(w_n | \text{class}_i\right)$$

where w_1, w_2, ..., w_n are words in the news j and class i refers to style or neutral news. This method makes two fundamental assumptions: (1) conditional independence (words occur independently from each other) and (2) positional independence (words have equal probabilities of occurring at all positions).

The SVM approach projects all news j in a space with n dimensions corresponding to each word. In this configuration, news j represents a point in the multi-dimensional word space. The algorithm then creates a boundary to separate the instances of each class i with the following rule: maximize the distance between the boundary and points from each class. SVM is an optimization method that produces the optimal boundary between components of each class. This boundary is constructed using linear or more complex kernel functions. We apply a linear kernel in this study.

We perform more in-depth pre-processing for machine learning algorithms than for the dictionary approach. We restrain vocabulary size to maximize algorithms efficiency. Our pre-processing steps include (1) removing {urls, special characters, and numbers}, (2) tokenization, (3) POS-tagging to select only {noun, verb, and adjective}, (4) lowering, (5) removing stop words, and (6) deleting term with less than three characters. Our pre-processing reduces around 40% of vocabulary size from 24,000 to 15,000 words.

4.3   Performance Assessment

Performance measurements are computed by comparing the actual class of news to the classification provided by the different methods. In our binary classification problem, we get four different results:

- True positive (TP): Style news is correctly classified within style class.
- False positive (FP): Neutral news is wrongly classified within style class.
- True negative (TN): Neutral news is correctly classified within neutral class.
- False negative (FN): Style news is wrongly classified within neutral class.

We estimate precision, recall, and F-score for dictionary-based and machine learning methods:

- Precision: $p = \frac{TP}{TP+FP}$
- Recall: $r = \frac{TP}{TP+FN}$
- Balanced F-score: $F = \frac{2*p*r}{p+r}$

Precision is the fraction of actual "style" news among news classified within "style" class by the method. Recall is the fraction of "style" news correctly retrieved among all existing style news. For example, suppose there exists 20 "style" news within a sample and the method classifies 10 news within style class. If eight of ten news classified within style class are really "style" news, precision is 0.8 (or 80%). And as the method has correctly retrieved 8 of 20 "style" news but fail to find the 12 remaining ones, recall is 0.4 (40%). We estimate the overall performance of the method with a balanced F-score.

We will promote the method exhibiting the best F-score. To construct the most efficient style coverage indexes, we intend to retrieve almost all style information included in our corpus, i.e., define a tolerable recall threshold. Moreover, we want to be sure that the retrieved information concerns style investing, i.e., we will maximize precision for accepted recall threshold.

4.4 Data Labelling, Training Sample, and Cross-Validation

The main benefit of dictionary-based approach is its high precision, attributed to the fact that terms are manually crafted. However, this method often exhibits poor recall since it is unlikely that a dictionary would contain all possible relevant terms. Machine learning methods, on the other hand, alleviate the issue of low recall since they can learn new instances of a given class, if properly trained. It is well-known that increasing the training data size results in more accurate methods.

We started our labelling task by parsing news titles in search of equity-related information. As such, we try to maximize manual detection of style news: we find more than 100 news referring to each style. We complete our sample with at least 100 neutral news. This initial labelled sample informed us on the performance of dictionary-based approach. We observe that style information represents a minority class within our corpus, i.e., there exists important imbalance between classes where neutral information is dominant. While increasing labelled sample size, we encounter high difficulty to find additional style news. Our manual labelling task became a tedious process.

To overcome this issue, we propose a semi-automatic labelling approach: we use dictionary detections as labelled data in order to avoid searching scarce style information. As previously mentioned, dictionaries exhibit high precision, i.e., detected style news are mainly true positives. Dictionary detections represent adequate candidates for labelled style data. We do not encounter difficulty to manually label neutral information since it represents the dominant class.

We annotate 800 neutral news and select 800 style news from our dictionary detections to form a balanced training sample. We document performance improvement related to the increasing size of training sample from 400 to 1600 news (equally weighted between style and neutral classes). We estimate performance scores of each algorithm with a fivefold cross-validation. We divide the training sample into five equally sized partitions. We use four partitions to train algorithms and estimate performance scores with the remaining fifth partition. We repeat the process five times by alternatively using each partition to assess performance (see Fig. 2). We compute average performance scores from these five estimations.

Finally, we extend our research to different integration of textual content, considering different term weighting estimations. First, we use word frequency as a base case. Second, we train algorithms with term frequency-inverse document frequency estimation. This evaluation adjusts word frequency by its number of observation across news. Such weighting scheme integrates the fact that words are more common than others. Third, we use bigram frequency to explore potential performance improvements as documented in Oliveira et al. (2016) and Renault (2017).

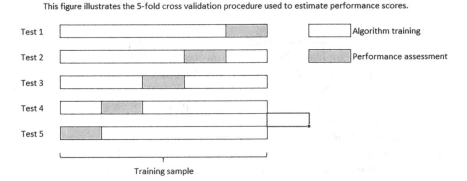

Fig. 2 Fivefold cross-validation. This figure illustrates the five-fold cross validation procedure used to estimate performance scores

5 Results

5.1 Performance of Style Dictionaries

We proceed to a performance assessment of our dictionary approach described in Sect. 4.1. Our results are summarized in Table 4. Small and large dictionaries have, respectively, balanced F-scores of 98 and 97%. They exhibit high precision and recall. Small-cap and large-cap terms defined in our dictionaries are so specific to the investments in style equity that we only find one false detection for each style (FP):

- "The fund invests in high-yield ('junk') bonds, foreign securities, emerging markets, liquidity risk, and small- and mid-cap *issuers*" [bond information].
- Non-US equities saw a median return of -4.80%, slightly ahead the Russell Developed ex-US Large Cap Index result of -5.79% [ex term, excluding large caps].

While we do not totally discard false detections, they remain exceptions. Second, small and large dictionaries detect the majority of related news. We find, respectively, four (resp. six) false negatives (FN) for small (resp. large) style. Dictionaries mainly fail to detect the information for two reasons: the presence of the other style in the sentence and the presence of the word "company" replacing the term "cap" from dictionary bigrams.

- "... investing in both *small and large-cap* based investment trusts" [fail to detect small information]
- "... as well as exposure to international and domestic *large- and mid-cap* equities" [fail to detect large information]
- "... dividends paid by *large companies* are more secure than those paid by *small and medium sized companies*, broadly speaking" [fail to detect small and large information]

We do not suggest the integration of terms such as "small company" or "large company" in dictionaries. The informational content is not specific to investments related to stocks and adds many false detections (FP). We do not suggest either adding extended n-gram to detect the opposite style. "Small" and "large" terms have too broad meanings. The power of small-cap and large-cap terms lies in their implicit stock content and their restricted size (unigram or bigram). To be exhaustive, we provide the reader with an Appendix presenting all false-positive and false-negative dictionary detection.

Table 4 shows that small-cap and large-cap terms are so specific to style investments that they are almost present when there is related style information within news. While we construct very restricted lists, our dictionaries are strongly efficient to detect small and large style information. We, respectively, find 2319

Table 4 Performance assessment of dictionary approach

Style	Initial sample			Dictionary classification				Performance measures		
	Total news	Style class	Neutral class	TP	FP	TN	FN	Precision	Recall	F-score
Small	233	121	112	117	1	111	4	0.99	0.98	0.98
Large	233	131	102	125	1	101	6	0.99	0.95	0.97

This table reports the performance scores of dictionary methodology for small and large equity style investments. We estimate performance scores from a manually labelled data sample. We refer the reader to section performance for more detail about dictionary classification and performance measures

small news and 1705 large news within our institutional media corpus of 108,638 news. This represents 1 to 2% of news confirming our previous observation: style information is relatively scarce among institutional media. The main drawback of our approach is the selection and size of our manual labelled sample. In the next section, we test the robustness of our results by investigating if our dictionaries fail to detect style news classified as such by machine learning algorithms.

5.2 Performance of Machine Learning Algorithms

In this section, we focused all tests and results on small style detection. Table 5 summarizes performance of Naïve Bayes and support vector machine approaches. We observe that SVM are more efficient than NB with term frequency weighting: F1 scores reach 84% for SVM compared to 76% for NB. Precision of NB is relatively low (from 62 to 66%): this algorithm tends to wrongly classified neutral news within style class. This is not the case with SVM which exhibits higher precision scores. We find that increasing sample size slightly increases precision of NB term frequency algorithm. Surprisingly, SVM precision is decreasing from 85 to 81% with increasing sample size. We attribute this observation to two possible reasons: the random selection of our training sample and the difficulty to construct a frontier clearly separating the two classes. First, while constructing our training sample, we randomly select 800 news among dictionary detection. This sample differs between each algorithm and therefore impacts their performances. Second, SVM frontier between classes becomes more difficult to construct with increasing number of news present in the multi-dimensional space. If SVM frontier is sensitive to increasing size, we should find similar trend regarding recall scores. However, recall scores seem more stable. We conclude that precision score discrepancy is more related to our random sampling selection.

Considering alternative term document matrices, bigram construction highlights important performance improvements. NB and SVM precision increases strikingly, while recall decreases slightly, leading to higher balanced F1 scores. These results indicate that bigrams add information to NB and SVM models. They are in accordance with observations in Sect. 5.1: bigrams hold more information and are more discriminant than unigrams. Oliveira et al. (2016) confirm our findings with their approach to automatically create sentiment lexicons. They advocate that bigrams present a better sentiment score than unigrams. We do not find the same evidence using term frequency-inverse document frequency weighting algorithms. NB precision, already its weakness, is decreasing to 60% leading to more false positives.

Table 5 Performance of machine learning algorithms

Training settings			In-sample performance scores			Holdout accuracy	Out-of-sample: small news
Method	Sample size	Term document matrix	Precision	Recall	F1 score		
Naïve Bayes	400	TF	0.62	0.89	0.73	0.90	32,094
	800	TF	0.63	0.89	0.73	0.93	28,855
	1600	TF	0.66	0.90	0.76	0.90	24,129
	1600	BF	0.77	0.84	0.80	0.89	22,098
	1600	TF-IDF	0.60	0.95	0.73	0.99	43,356
Support vector machine	400	TF	0.85	0.84	0.84	0.81	15,179
	800	TF	0.84	0.84	0.84	0.81	14,075
	1600	TF	0.81	0.83	0.81	0.85	15,875
	1600	BF	0.94	0.81	0.87	0.80	4569
	1600	TF-IDF	0.85	0.83	0.84	0.85	15,855

This table presents in-sample and out-sample performance assessment of Naïve Bayes and support vector machine approaches. We perform training phase with different sample sizes and term document matrices (*TF* term frequency, *BF* bigram frequency, *TF-IDF* term frequency-inverse document frequency). We compute in-sample performance scores following a fivefold cross-validation. The out-sample measures represent the number of news classified as small within the overall institutional media corpus

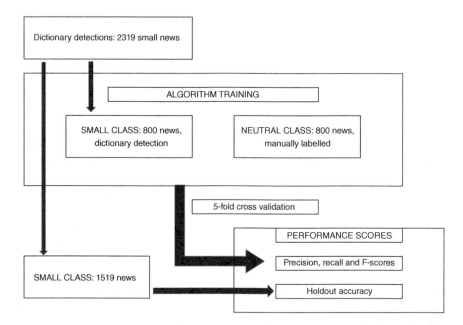

Fig. 3 Training procedure for Naïve Bayes and support vector machine algorithms. This figure illustrates training and performance evaluation for NB and SVM algorithms. We train algorithms with balanced class samples selected from our semi-automatic approach. We compute different in-sample performance scores: precision, recall, balanced F1-score and holdout accuracy

We document an additional performance measure, i.e., small class holdout accuracy. This measure represents the fraction of small news detected by the dictionary-based methodology and correctly classified as small by the algorithms. To compute the measure, we ask the algorithm to classify small news that were not used during the training phase. The overall procedure is presented in Fig. 3. Algorithms correctly classify between 80 and 99% of small news detected by our dictionary approach. As such, NB approach is more efficient to classify small news than SVM. As such, NB tends to retrieve more small news (higher recall) but with less precision.

While all measurements discussed indicate the best in sample performing method, they still not guarantee that algorithms will correctly retrieve style news in a sizable sample such as our institutional media corpus. It is possible that trained algorithms model too precisely the training data while not generalizing to new data. This problem is known as overfitting. We investigate out-of-sample performance by asking algorithms to classify all institutional media corpus news and record the number of small news afterwards. We expect this measure to be similar to the number of small news classified by dictionary-based methodology, i.e., 2319 small news detected. We find that NB approach classifies too much news as small in the institutional media corpus (from 22,098 to 43,356). The number of small news classified is 10–18 times more important than dictionary-based method. This suggests that we have an overfitting problem: term frequency algorithms model too precisely the training sample but fail to generalize to the institutional media corpus. SVM is more immune to overfitting, and it classifies between 4569 and 15,855 news as small depending on the algorithm.

The most promising algorithm is the SVM with bigram weighting scheme: it is more effective in out-of-sample classification than its NB counterpart. SVM trained with bigrams classify 4569 news (NB, respectively, 22,098 news) within a small class in the overall corpus. This algorithm is a potential substitute of our dictionary-based methodology. While dictionary methodology exhibits higher performance, measures are estimated from a smaller sample of manually annotated data (see Table 4. in Sect. 5.1). This manual annotation process may be biased. We may have inadvertently selected small news which contains dictionary terms and fail to select small news that do not contain those terms. In this case, we artificially inflate dictionary performance. We investigate this potential problem by comparing dictionary methodology and SVM using bigram term document matrix. We try to find if dictionary-based methodology fails to capture small news. We randomly read 100 news classified as small by SVM but classified as neutral by dictionary methodology. If the majority of news are really small news, our manual annotation process is biased, and the SVM approach is the best proposed methodology. On the contrary, if those news are mainly neutral ones, we will prefer the dictionary methodology. None of the news we read concern small-cap investments: dictionary-based methodology is still the best approach. We summarize our results in three points. First, best machine learning methodology (bigram SVM) captures 80% of small news detected by dictionary-based methodology (holdout accuracy). Second, news only detected as small by SVM are mainly false positive. Third, performance in dictionary-based section is reliable. We conclude that dictionary-based methodology will produce the most accurate small coverage indexes within institutional media.

6   Conclusions

This paper presents an original classification problem, detecting style content within a novel source of information, the institutional media corpus. We observe three main difficulties in our task: (1) the absence of labelled data, (2) an important class imbalance between neutral and style content, and (3) a diversity of topics within the corpus. This combination of problems makes the manual labelling task difficult for the minority style class.

We find that restricted word lists are the most promising methodology to detect small- and large-cap style information within institutional media corpus. Dictionaries composed of only five different terms (micro-, small-, mid-, large-, and mega-cap) efficiently capture style information. The explicit stock content of these terms avoids false detection (high precision) but also limits failed detection (acceptable recall). In comparison, supervised machine learning algorithms exhibit high recall but low precision scores. This comparison confirms that subjective handed crafted lists are more precise than high recall machine learning algorithms. One drawback of algorithms is their failure to generalize to the overall institutional media corpus. However, support vector machine trained with a bigram term frequency matrix presents encouraging results in alleviating this overfitting problem. One possible improvement for this method is the use of an alternative to linear kernel.

We delimit our research to the comparison of main methodologies applied in sentiment analysis. We do not cover any advanced techniques such as unsupervised learning (clustering, LDA, etc.) or deep learning (neural network), leaving a room for further comparison. Moreover, we do not extend our research to other equity style investments (growth vs. value, momentum vs. contrarian) due to manual labelling constraint. We expect that new source of data will fill the gap in the future, such as it exists user self-reported sentiment on social media. Data augmentation using generative model and semi-supervised learning are also alternative solutions.

Finally, this study opens a path for further research around media coverage and attention related to equity style investments. As such, style detections from dictionaries can be aggregated to construct small-cap and large-cap coverage indexes. With an appropriate fund flow analysis, researchers can investigate the potential impact of style information on institutional investors' behavior.

Appendix: Dictionary Approach: False Positives and False Negatives (Exhaustive List)

Style	Error	ID	Date	Title	Magazine	Sentence
Small	FP	54636	29/10/2012	Prudential launches mutual fund	PLANADVISER	The fund invests in high-yield ("junk") bonds, foreign securities, emerging markets, liquidity risk, and small- and mid-cap issuers.
	FN	51644	21/05/2012	European investors regain a wary confidence	Institutional investor	What is becoming clear to investors is that the best hopes for the next year or so lie in Europe's multinational corporations and smaller-cap companies that know how to build market share abroad, especially in the rapidly growing emerging markets of Asia and Latin America, and to some extent Russia, Eastern Europe and Africa.
	FN	62613	12/5/2014	Europe is moving back into favour	FT adviser	"Given the emerging economic stability appearing more broadly across the continent—including the previously struggling economies of Portugal, Ireland, Italy, Greece and Spain (the 'PIIGS')—investors are increasingly looking to capture a recovery in the region, following a long period of under-allocation to the region, investing in both small and large-cap based investment trusts."
	FN	91234	7/6/2017	Special report: large caps in uncharted waters	FT adviser	Despite the well publicised plight of Pearson, which earlier this year announced its intention to cut its dividend payout after issuing the latest in a string of profit warnings, dividends paid by large companies are more secure than those paid by small and medium sized companies, broadly speaking.
Large	FP	65724	########	Equities hurt master trust returns in Q3	PLANSPONSOR	Non-U.S. equities saw a median return of -4.80%, slightly ahead the Russell Developed ex U.S. Large Cap Index result of -5.79%.
	FN	29505	12/5/2009	Turner launches fund with access to long/short strategies	PLANADVISER	Turner Long/Short Equity strategy, directed by Christopher McHugh, lead portfolio manager, investing in stocks in all stock-market sectors, with a focus on mid-sized and large companies globally;

(continued)

(continued)

Style	Error	ID	Date	Title	Magazine	Sentence
	FN	53659	28/09/2012	Third avenue Nabs banker David Resnick	Institutional investor	With banks pulling back, Resnick believes many of the opportunities for Third Avenue will be found among midcap companies that don't have larger companies' ability to refinance.
	FN	76228	20/01/2016	Vanguard makes advisory changes for two active equity funds	Wealth adviser	The large- and mid-cap growth fund has been multi-managed since 1990, and following the transition, the allocation is expected to be as follows: Wellington, 48%; Jennison, 22%; Frontier, 15%; and Vanguard, 15%.
	FN	85585	14/12/2016	The universe of small-cap stocks is shrinking	Institutinal investor	In the decades since professors Eugene Fama and Kenneth French published their famous 1992 paper on company size being one of the three sources of equity returns, the edict that small stocks outperform their larger brethren has become conventional wisdom.
	FN	99186	15/03/2018	RBC global asset management strengthens US investment management team	Institutional asset manager	In his previous roles at Rutabaga Capital Management and MFS Investment Management, he had a focus on small- and micro-cap equities, as well as exposure to international and domestic large- and mid-cap equities.
	FN	100636	11/5/2018	Solactive releases media and communications index	Wealth adviser	Starting from the Solactive GBS Developed Markets Large & Mid Cap Index as the founding universe, the index implements a sector-based filtering strategy selecting companies operating in telecommunications, media and publishing services, communication equipment, web-based data, and game software.

References

Antweiler, W., & Frank, M. Z. (2004). Is all that talk just noise? The information content of internet stock message boards. *Journal of Finance, 59*(3), 1259–1294. https://doi.org/10.1111/j.1540-6261.2004.00662.x

Baker, S. R., Bloom, N., & Davis, S. J. (2016). Measuring economic policy uncertainty. *Quarterly Journal of Economics, 131*, 1593–1636.

Barberis, N., & Shleifer, A. (2003). Style investing. *Journal of Financial Economics, 68*(2), 161–199. https://doi.org/10.1016/S0304-405X(03)00064-3

Bodnaruk, A., Loughran, T., & McDonald, B. (2015). Using 10-K text to gauge financial constraints. *Journal of Financial and Quantitative Analysis, 50*, 623–646.

Das, S. R., & Chen, M. Y. (2007). Yahoo! For Amazon: Sentiment extraction from small talk on the web. *Management Science, 53*(9), 1375–1388. https://doi.org/10.1287/mnsc.1070.0704

Froot, K. A., & Teo, M. (2008). Style investing and institutional investors. *Journal of Financial and Quantitative Analysis, 43*, 883–906.

Garcia, D. (2013). Sentiment during recessions. *Journal of Finance, 68*(3), 1267–1300. https://doi.org/10.1111/jofi.12027

Henry, E., & Leone, A. J. (2016). Measuring qualitative information in capital markets research: Comparison of alternative methodologies to measure disclosure tone, *91*(1), 153–178. https://doi.org/10.2308/accr-51161

Jegadeesh, N., & Wu, D. (2013). Word power: A new approach for content analysis. *Journal of Financial Economics, 110*, 712–729.

Kumar, A. (2009). Dynamic style preferences of individual investors and stock returns. *Journal of Financial and Quantitative Analysis, 44*(03), 607. https://doi.org/10.1017/S0022109009990020

Larcker, D. F., & Zakolyukina, A. A. (2012). Detecting deceptive discussions in conference calls. *Journal of Accounting Research, 50*, 495–540.

Li, F. (2010). The information content of forward-looking statements in corporate filings – A naïve Bayesian machine learning approach. *Journal of Accounting Research, 48*(5), 1049–1102.

Loughran, T. I. M., & Mcdonald, B. (2011). When is a liability not a liability? Textual analysis, dictionaries, and 10-Ks, *66*(1), 35–65.

Loughran, T., McDonald, B., & Pragidis, I. (2019). Assimilation of oil news into prices. *International Review of Financial Analysis, 63*, 105–118.

Manela, A., & Moreira, A. (2017). News implied volatility and disaster concerns. *Journal of Financial Economics, 123*, 137–162.

Oliveira, N., Cortez, P., & Areal, N. (2016). Stock market sentiment lexicon acquisition using microblogging data and statistical measures. *Decision Support Systems, 85*, 62–73. https://doi.org/10.1016/j.dss.2016.02.013

Renault, T. (2017). Intraday online investor sentiment and return patterns in the U.S. stock market. *Journal of Banking and Finance, 84*, 25–40. https://doi.org/10.1016/j.jbankfin.2017.07.002

Soo, C. K. (2018). Quantifying sentiment with news media across local housing markets. *Review of Financial Studies, 31*, 3689–3719.

Tetlock, P. C. (2007). *Giving content to investor sentiment: The role of media in the stock market* published by: Wiley for the American Finance Association Stable URL: http://www.jstor.org/stable/4622297. The role of media in the stock market giving content to investor sentiment, *62*(3), 1139–1168.

Cédric Gillain is PhD candidate at HEC Liège, Management School of the University of Liège and Chief Research Officer at SOPIAD.

Ashwin Ittoo is Full Professor at HEC Liège, Management School of the University of Liège. Marie Lambert is Full Professor at HEC Liège, Management School of the University of Liège where she holds the Deloitte Chair in Sustainable Finance.

Marie Lambert is a fellow of Quantitative Management Research Initiative (QMInitiative.org).

Financial Analytics and Decision-Making Strategies: Future Prospects from Bibliometrix Based on R Package

Konstantina Ragazou ⓘ, Ioannis Passas ⓘ, Alexandros Garefalakis, and Constantin Zopounidis

Abstract Financial analytics involves the analysis of financial data by using statistical and quantitative methods to make decisions that improve businesses' results. Specifically, this system includes data mining, predictive analytics, and applied analytics and statistics and is delivered as a custom application to a business user. The integration of financial analytics by companies has already started changing their operational process while giving them the ability to leverage data from different sources, create easy-to-use dashboards, and visualize and predict future performance tools. This means that financial analytics offers the business a competitive edge and facilitates more the decision-making process. This chapter presents the importance of financial analytics and highlights the trends and prospects of it in the subject area of the decision-making process. To approach this issue, a Bibliometrix was applied based on R package. Data were retrieved from Scopus database and analyzed with the use of Biblioshiny and VOSviewer software.

Keywords Financial analytics · Decision-making process · Sustainability · Multiple criteria decision-making · Strategy

1 Introduction

Business analytics is a key factor in business arena. In the age of smart technology, which is characterized by fast pace and intense competition, the application of different techniques is applied to maintain the competitive advantage of each business

K. Ragazou (✉) · I. Passas · A. Garefalakis
Department of Business Administration and Tourism, Hellenic Mediterranean University, Heraklion, Greece
e-mail: kragazou@hmu.gr; ipassas@hmu.gr; agarefalakis@hmu.gr

C. Zopounidis
School of Production Engineering and Management, Technical University of Crete, Chania, Greece
e-mail: kostas@dpem.tuc.gr

P. Alphonse et al. (eds.), *Essays on Financial Analytics*, Lecture Notes in Operations Research, https://doi.org/10.1007/978-3-031-29050-3_9

(Gu et al., 2021; Shrivastava et al., 2021). A critical example is the collection of information from various sources as well as their analysis for predicting future trends and behaviors. All this approach is going to improve the strategy planning process and the operation of the business but also to promote the smart decision-making process. It is very important for every business to understand its customers, the competition, and the wider environment to be profitable, to adapt, and to be ready at any moment to face any challenge. Business analytics can contribute to this process, as its application discovers various patterns, trends, and a lot of information that can support specific actions (Shi et al., 2022). Through the ability to first understand different types of data and then decide what needs to be implemented for maintaining or gaining a competitive advantage (Ashrafi & Zareravasan, 2022; Escamilla-Solano et al., 2022).

Today, there are many types of business analytics. Knowledge of these is crucial for any business that wants to cope with the existing competitive environment and continue to be profitable and sustainable. Business analysts play a crucial role in the management, use, and implementation of business analytics (Hayajneh et al., 2022). Every business can either utilize or attract its own analysts or rely on external services. The selection of the analysts is considered as a very critical process. Analysts have the power to determine and influence the strategies, planning, and course of any business. This power can be acquired by applying business analytics, conducting information and business analyses, but also applying various financial models. When business analytics is efficient, each manager is allowed to confirm that the information is available and understood by the entire work team (Ashrafi & Zareravasan, 2022). By ensuring this situation, each team can be organized and at the end of the day determine the success rate. One of the advantageous applications of business analytics is the discovery and offering of valuable consumer characteristics and behaviors. Additionally, the implementation of a financial analysis can also identify important elements such as cost and profitability processes through cash flow analysis, budget analysis, etc. Overall, by combining a variety of applications and building the right way, each business manages to produce very important information (Abreu et al., 2021). Ending up in a competitive environment like this, none of a business can succeed once it is not able to understand its customers and insiders. The importance of business analytics is considered great for taking beneficial attitudes, but also for eliminating negative situations where a business is called to deal.

However, analytics is a priority not only for business analysts but also for financial experts too. Financial analytics is a new concept tool in the field of financial modeling, while it plays an important role in the increase of the value of the business (Anderson & Thoma, 2021; Bleibtreu et al., 2021). Financial is considered as an important function of the company and provides detailed information of all its sectors. The goal of financial executives is to optimize as much as they can the results of the business. So, this can be achieved by the application of financial technology and analytical skills. Especially, financial analytics indicate how financial experts can use the financial elements of their business to (1) solve daily common problems, (2) improve cash flow, and (3) improve profitability and competitive advantage of businesses. Moreover, financial analytics can contribute to the decision-making strategies for businesses. The purpose of this chapter is twofold: (1) to investigate the importance of financial analytics in the decision-making process of businesses and (2) to highlight the new trends in the decision-making strategies. Bibliometric analysis based on R package was used as the main methodological approach of this research work. Bibliometric analysis is the application of statistics and quantitative analysis of the publications of the most related research works in a scientific field and their references. It is worth mentioning that the quantitative assessment of publications and citations is done in almost all states and especially in universities and government laboratories, by researchers, and by research and decision-making policy-makers. The aim is to evaluate performance in the field of research. The fundamental reason that scientists all over the world have found bibliographic analysis to be so appealing in so many nations and institutions is because of the benefits it provides. Quantitative research analysis is done on a global scale and provides an overview of the work in each research field, complementing the local perception of the field. By also looking at each researcher's total publications and citations, conclusions are drawn without affecting characteristics such as place of production or pre-existing reputation, factors that determine people's perception of quality. For example, it is easy to think of the biggest producers of research (researchers, universities, countries, laboratories) when asked to find the best, which can lead to error, as they are not always the most important source of research. Thus, it is easy to understand the importance of bibliometric analysis and how it is an objective indicator of performance evaluation in the field of research.

In the context of this research, data were retrieved from Scopus database, while analysis and visualization of the findings were conducted via Biblioshiny and VOSviewer software. Content, keyword, co-citation, co-occurrence, MCA, and factorial analysis were applied for the identification of the gaps and opportunities of the research in financial analytics and decision-making strategies (Bhatnagar & Sharma, 2022; Khan, 2022).

2   The Evolution of Financial Analytics over the Time

Analytics in business dates back to Frederick Winslow Taylor in the late nineteenth century, with the application of the principles of scientific management of a company's processes, aimed at improving performance. Taylor's scientific management consisted of four principles: (1) replacement of empirical methods with methods based on a scientific study of processes; (2) scientific selection, training, and development of employees; (3) provision of a detailed job description and supervision of each employee during the execution of the tasks; and (4) separation of the working tasks between managers and employees, so that managers can apply scientific management principles for project planning and employees execute the project. Henry Ford later measured the time of each component on his new assembly line to optimize performance. With the advent of computers in decision support systems in 1960, business analytics received focused attention from experts and companies. Since then, analytics has evolved rapidly with the development of ERP systems (ERPs), data warehouses, and many other tools and processes. In the following years, business analytics reached a whole new level, providing countless opportunities for companies to understand and improve their performance.

Today, analytics has been integrated in every part of a business, like the financial department. Financial analytics can be characterized as an ad hoc analysis, which answers to specific questions of businesses, as well as forecast possible future financial scenarios. The development of such complex data analysis techniques has enabled the recording, diagnosis, and prediction of desired actions and automatic extraction of the optimal action to achieve the desired results. This study is among the first that aim to show, in a simple and concise way, the importance of financial analytics in the decision-making process of businesses and the new trends in the decision-making strategies based on the above techniques. A preliminary analysis of the data helps to capture the literature's basic overview. Our collection comprises 1095 articles that are published between 2014 and 2022. Table 1 presents an overview of the literature collected from Scopus database. Overall, the journals covered plenty of research areas, with the most common being decision, business management, and computer sciences. So, financial analytics has a wider field of application and a vital role in decision-making and strategic planning process. In addition, all these most cited and relevant journals in the studied field are indexed by Scopus and Scimago list, as well as by ABS list too. As for the h-index of the sources presented in the table, the average is close to 115, which indicated that the published research in the studied field of financial analytics received more than 115 citations each. This is a satisfactory metric which highlights the great importance, significance, and broad impact of authors' research in the role of financial analytics in the business arena.

Moreover, Fig. 1 shows that the studies on financial analytics and decision-making were barely existent between the studied timespans. Since the year 2013, there has been a gradual increase in the number of published articles, while in the year 2021, it has been highlighted the highest number of publications in the studied field. This is based on the COVID-19 pandemic, as businesses had to face different challenges, such as the decline of funding, issues with enrollments, and uncertainty with regard to endowment returns. To survive and adapt in the new environment, businesses choose to focus on the key parts of their purpose and make data-driven choices. This can contribute to the security of the optimal use of their resources and proper management of their time and human resources. Some of the companies that will follow this path may find difficult to maintain their financial solvency. However, these challenges can serve as an opportunity for businesses to better understand the levers and tools that have at their disposal to streamline their operations. So, financial analytics emerged as one of the most ideal and important tools for businesses, as it allows them to utilize their data to develop alternative management solutions for various challenges that arise from extreme situations, such as a crisis. Also, financial analytics can provide a business with opportunities for improving their operation and efficiency.

Table 1 Most related sources in the field of financial analytics within the timespan 2014–2022

Sources	Number of articles	Subject area	h-index	ABS ranking	Scimago ranking
European Journal of Operational Research	21	Decision Sciences	274	4****	Q1
Sustainability (Switzerland)	19	Management, Monitoring, Policy, and Law	109		Q1
Annals of Operations Research	14	Decision Sciences	111	3***	Q1
Decision Support Systems	11	Decision Sciences	161	3***	Q1
International Journal of Information Management	10	Decision Sciences	132	2**	Q1
Industrial Management and Data Systems	8	Business, Management, and Accounting	109	2**	Q1
Technological Forecasting and Social Change	8	Business, Management, and Accounting	134	3***	Q1
Computers and Industrial Engineering	7	Computer Science	136	2**	Q1
Expert Systems with Applications	7	Computer Science	225	1*	Q1
International Journal of Business Analytics	7	Business, Management, and Accounting	10		Q3
Journal of Business Analytics	7	Business, Management, and Accounting	5		Q2
Advances in Decision Sciences	6	Decision Sciences	16		Q4
Enterprise Information Systems	6	Decision Sciences	50	2**	Q1
Information and Management	6	Decision Sciences	170	3***	Q1
International Journal of Accounting Information Systems	6	Decision Sciences	56	2**	Q1
Journal of Business Research	6	Business, Management, and Accounting	217	3***	Q1
Journal of Enterprise Information Management	6	Decision Sciences	67	2**	Q1
Omega (United Kingdom)	6	Decision Sciences	151	3***	Q1
Benchmarking	5	Business, Management, and Accounting	61	1*	Q1
Business Process Management Journal	5	Business, Management, and Accounting	87	2**	Q1

Source: Own elaboration (Scopus/Biblioshiny)

The symbol of significance is referred to those scientific papers that are published by Journals that are indexed by the Academic Journal Guide and produced by the Chartered Association of Business Schools (CABS). The journals are given a star rating from * to **** (the highest)

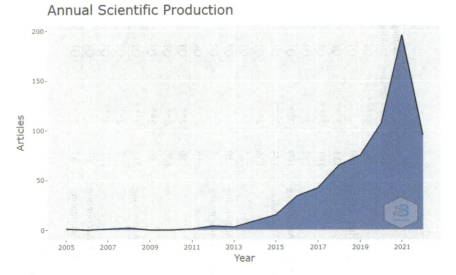

Fig. 1 Scientific production on the field of financial analytics and decision-making. Source: Scopus/Biblioshiny

3   Structural Levels of Financial Analytics

Financial analytics are structured in a series of overlapping levels, which form a pyramid (Fig. 2). At the base of the pyramid are the initial raw data, while at the top is the final decision-making. The transition from one level to another increases the ability to support business decisions.

At the base of the pyramid are the sources of the original data. This data comes mainly from transaction tracking systems, such as the Enterprise Resource Planning (ERP) systems, and corporate databases. Also, additional data sources can be businesses' web servers, internal documents, or external sources. The next level of the pyramid is that of data storage, which includes databases that contain the consolidated, aggregated, and health data. This data will be used to analyze and draw conclusions. The operations of exporting, transforming, and loading the data is also known as ETL (Extract, Transform, and Load) tasks and are performed at regular intervals. In the context of this work, the operational data that are relevant to the analysis to be performed are first selected. Data storage focuses on thematic areas, such as liabilities or company's assets. Based on that, relevant data should be included, and non-relevant data should be excluded. Moreover, data should be aggregated according to issues of interest to the financial expert. The third level of the pyramid includes the raw data that process the tasks. Within this stage, the user submits queries to the database, receives answers, and compiles reports. Reports include numerical values as well as tables and graphs. Graphs can convey information in a more vivid and enjoyable way. In general, visualization methods

Fig. 2 Pyramid of financial
analytics. Source: Own
elaboration

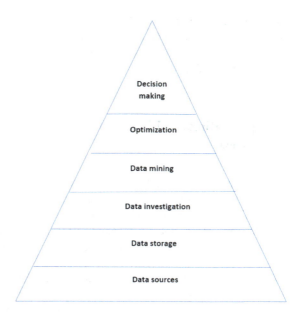

help to better present and understand the data. In addition, at this phase, an initial statistical processing of the data can be done. For example, averages, standard deviations, etc. can be calculated, while a characteristic of this level is that the user, according to his reasoning, develops hypotheses in advance and then uses the analysis tools to confirm that his hypotheses are supported by the data. In the fourth stage, a high level of data analysis is performed, using the most advanced techniques. Advanced statistical methods are used, as well methods that are derived from artificial intelligence and machine learning too. Classification methods allow the prediction of the category to which an object belongs based on its characteristics. Bankruptcy forecasting and credit rating are typical examples of application of categorization techniques. Also, cluster analysis methods are used and allow the identification of groups of similar objects. A characteristic feature that is found in these methods of this level is that the user does not need to make his own initial assumptions. Algorithms process data and extract information directly from it. Lastly, the output of the above process is a model. Optimization is the fourth level of the pyramid of financial analytics process. In this stage, experts search for the best solution among the alternative one. In terms of the number of the possible solutions, the problems are divided into two categories: dichotomous and multiple solution problems. In the case of dichotomous problems, decision-makers should decide among two possible solutions, while multiple solution problems can have a limited number of possible solutions.

At the top level of the pyramid is the decision-making process. At this point, it is important to emphasize that all the methods and systems that were mentioned above are intended to assist decision-makers in their decisions. These tools are essential for providing the appropriate data, analyzing data, and generating information. The final decision is made by the decision-maker, who will search for the best solution by integrating financial analytics techniques in combination with his own logic, knowledge, and skills.

4 Applications of Financial Analytics in Decision-Making Process

The main role of financial analytics is the planning and monitoring of financial flows with the use of data analytics techniques. Using this tool, experts in the field can monitor the course of both income and expenses of the company. Receivables, payables, and stock status are analyzed too. This way facilitates the preparation of the financial statements with current data, so that executives can assess the performance of the company. Also, a comparison is made with the size of the budget, so in the case that discrepancies may be found, necessary precautions can be taken. Specifically, financial analytics systems monitor the assets of the company throughout their life cycle from acquisition to depreciation. Also, these systems control profitability but also in particular by time period, region, customers, product category, etc. in order to identify trends, dynamics, and opportunities in this way. Monitoring accounts receivable and payable allows better working capital management and control of receivable risks. Current data are compared with historical data from previous years and target values to provide a more complete picture for the course of the business and its financial performance.

Financial analytics can find corresponding application possibilities in every activity of a business that requires decision-making. This section will present the applications of financial analytics in different parts of businesses (Andriosopoulos et al., 2019). Figure 3 is the thematic map which illustrates the research themes that are obtained from the conceptual structure of the documents included in the Bibliometrix analysis. The clusters in the graph indicate the themes of the research, while the size of the clusters highlights the proportionality to the number of the keywords. The quadrant in the upper-right position indicates the motor themes, which can be characterized by both high density and centrality, while the quadrant in the down-right position highlights the basic themes that are defined from high centrality but low density. Also, the quadrant in the upper-right position shows the niche themes of the studied field, and the quadrant in the down-left position is characterized as the emerging themes, with low centrality and density.

It is noteworthy that financial analytics systems have a strong connection with multiple criteria decision-making method (MCDM) (Zopounidis, 1999). MCDM is a subfield of operations research, dealing with decision-making problems, while a decision-making problem is characterized by the need to choose one or a few among several alternative solutions (Zopounidis & Doumpos, 2013). The field of MCDM assumes special importance in the era of Big Data and business analytics.

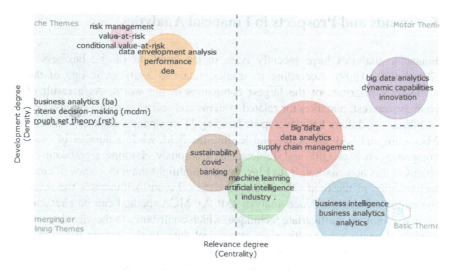

Fig. 3 Thematic map. Source: Scopus/Biblioshiny

However, findings show that MCDM can be applied in the field of financial analytics as well. This indicates that financial science has already started to review traditional principles and assessments regarding the empirical and theoretical study of financial issues like asset pricing theory (Kristoffersen et al., 2021). The rough set approach, which is included in the niche themes of the subject area of financial analytics, ends with a set of decision rules playing the role of a comprehensive preference model in MCDM (Lei et al., 2021; Yuan et al., 2021). It is more general than the classical functional or relational model, while its natural syntax makes it more understandable for the users (Omar et al., 2019).

In addition, as it is presented in the basic themes of the thematic map, supply chain management has integrated financial analytics in its process. The aim of the integration of financial analytics systems in supply chain contributes to a better management of it by producing and disseminating the appropriate information (Ramanathan & Ramanathan, 2021). There is an effective control of inventory levels, in combination with the needs for materials that are necessary for the production. So, this system can identify on time shortages, while delays in orders are treated, so as to secure that the production process will not be slowed down. In that way, product flow is better controlled, customer satisfaction with timely delivery is increased, and cancellations and returns are reduced. Moreover, financial analytics applies to suppliers too. The historical data of the suppliers, such as delivery times, consistency, pricing policies, discounts, and offers, are analyzed. Also, external data can be utilized about the potential suppliers regarding their business dynamics, financial situation, etc. (Emtehani et al., 2021; Nikulina & Wynstra, 2022).

5   Trends and Prospects in Financial Analytics

Financial analytics have recently been in the spotlight of the business world (Zopounidis, 1999). According to studies, financial analytics is one of the top technology priorities of the largest companies in the world. As a result of the business interest, a market for related systems and software with a turnover of tens of billions of dollars has developed. Leading IT companies such as Oracle, IBM, Microsoft, and SAP are active and leading the field, while a number of specialist companies such as Qlik and Tableau are vigorously claiming significant market shares in this new market. Both Figs. 4 and 5 highlight the importance of emerging technologies in the field of financial analytics. Figure 4 illustrates the results of the multiple correspondence analysis (MCA). MCA method can be characterized as an exploratory multivariate technique, which contributes to the visualization and numerical analysis of multivariate categorical data. In the current research work, MCA map presents two clusters, red and blue, which indicate the relationship between financial analytics, emerging technologies, and efficiency of businesses.

However, findings illustrate that traditional methods in decision-making are still being used. This is since companies face many obstacles in developing complicated performance measurement systems that measure the appropriate financial sizes. What is needed is a system that balances the historical accuracy of financial figures with critical elements of future performance while also assisting companies in implementing their differentiated strategies. The balanced scorecard method is the tool that answers to the above challenges. It was developed by Robert Kaplan,

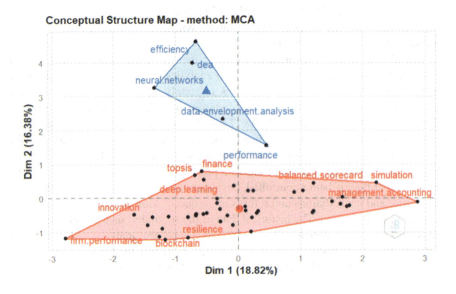

Fig. 4 Factorial analysis based on MCA method. Source: Scopus/Biblioshiny

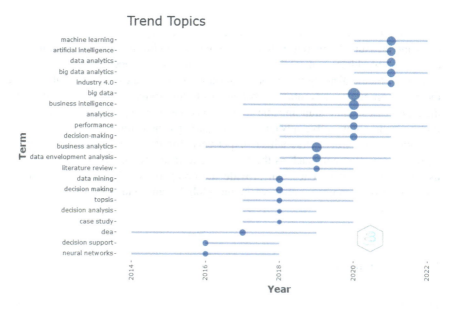

Fig. 5 Trending topics on the research field. Source: Scopus/Biblioshiny

a professor at Harvard University, and David Norton, also a consultant from the Boston area, in 1990 (Ahanin & Ismail, 2022). Over the next 4 years, several organizations will proceed to the adoption of this system, in order to achieve immediate results. Since then, the balanced scorecard has been adopted almost by the Fortune 1000 Bonds companies, and the process continues uninterrupted (Amaratunga et al., 2001; Taylor & Baines, 2012). The system has also been effectively implemented in non-profit organizations as well as in the public sector. The increased efficiency and widespread acceptance of the balanced scorecard have made it one of the 75 most important ideas of the twentieth century by the *Harvard Business Review*. The balanced scorecard system can be described as a carefully selected set of performance indicators derived from a company's strategy (Papenhausen & Einstein, 2006). The performance indicators selected for the scorecard represent a tool for managers to use in communicating with employees and external stakeholders to inform them of the results and performance guides through which the company will achieve its mission and its strategic objectives. However, this simple definition may not fully convey the meaning of the balanced scorecard. This tool is three things at the same time: a performance measurement system, a strategic control system, and a communication tool (Papenhausen & Einstein, 2006).

Moreover, emerging technologies will play a key role in the area and evolution of the domain of financial analytics. Especially, in the post-COVID environment, businesses are required to operate in a regime of increased volatility and uncertainty, at the level of macroeconomic trends but also geopolitics, among others. At the same time, customer expectations have reached an all-time high, while competition in every sector of the economy is constantly increasing, setting businesses under constant pressure to increase their efficiency. In addition, regulatory authorities around the world are constantly creating new rules for the operation of businesses. The use of financial analytics in combination with large-scale data (Big Data) can be the most competitive advantage of businesses in improving cost savings, redefining their processes, understanding the motivations and strategy of their competitors, finding their comparative advantage, and, perhaps most importantly, creating an exceptional and truly personalized experience for the customer. Particularly in regulated environments such as the banking and insurance industries, data and the use of artificial intelligence can provide the competitive edge that organizations seek to become more competitive in the global arena and achieve the required profitability.

6 Conclusions

In the past years, the process of decision-making was considered more as an art, based on the set of personal skills that executives had been developed through their experience over time (Neirotti et al., 2021). Today, this approach is not enough. Experts in the field, in addition to their personal skills, should take advantage of the opportunities offered by emerging technologies too. Information technologies, which have now been widely applied in business, provide unprecedented possibilities for retrieving information, as well as for processing it and drawing conclusions (Vidgen et al., 2020). Providing appropriate information is a key factor in receiving successful decisions. Proper information means that the right information is given to the right person at the right time. As mentioned before, the partiality of information is one of the main deterrents in making rational decisions. By providing the most complete information possible, this deterrent is reduced. Also, providing increased information leads to a better understanding of the problem and consequently to reducing uncertainty and reducing risk. In the modern business world, the pace of operation has accelerated. Business executives work under constant time pressure (Neirotti et al., 2021). So, they require quality information at the right time. Providing complete and timely information has the effect of improving decisions. Improved decisions and consequently improved management can increase a company's performance and give it a competitive edge.

Executives, to extract information and analyze data, use different information systems, such as business resource planning, supply chain management, and customer relationship management systems. All these systems record huge volumes of data related to the activities of the company daily in relational databases. In addition, systems that monitor financial information of businesses are used as well. Financial analytics give finance executives the ability to convert structured or unstructured data into information and facilitate decision-making process (Gu et al., 2021). Moreover, financial analytics helps funding teams gather the information they need to get a clear picture of key performance indicators (KPIs). In financial analytics, a set of tools has contributed to the transformation of financial departments and the expansion of the role and impact of human resources for the better. This is due to the technology that integrates the specific system of processing and analysis of financial information which helps in understanding the organizational performance, risk assessment, maximizing profits per customer or product, implementing business process improvement, predicting market fluctuations, the management of investment projects, and many others.

To sum up, the need of businesses to improve information and upgrade decision-making processes by integrating emerging technologies has been the springboard for the development of financial analytics (Kannagi et al., 2021; Selim & Eltarabily, 2022). Systems based on financial analytics are specialized information systems, which offer quality information, based on quality and aggregate data. The data is combined with software, which also implements data mining algorithms and can perform high-level analysis. The improvement in the quality of information is due to the capabilities of these systems, which provide quality data and allow faster access to information, easier system searches and reports, as well as advanced data analysis. Finally, the pandemic has pushed financial analytics systems to the forefront of the business world (Emtehani et al., 2021).

References

Abreu, J., Guimarães, T., Abelha, A., & Santos, M. F. (2021). Business analytics components for public health institution – Clinical decision area. *Procedia Computer Science, 198*, 335–340. https://doi.org/10.1016/J.PROCS.2021.12.250

Ahanin, Z., & Ismail, M. A. (2022). A multi-label emoji classification method using balanced pointwise mutual information-based feature selection. *Computer Speech & Language, 73*. https://doi.org/10.1016/J.CSL.2021.101330

Amaratunga, D., Baldry, D., & Sarshar, M. (2001). Process improvement through performance measurement: The balanced scorecard methodology. *Work Study, 50*(5), 179–189. https://doi.org/10.1108/EUM0000000005677/FULL/HTML

Anderson, I., & Thoma, V. (2021). The edge of reason: A thematic analysis of how professional financial traders understand analytical decision making. *European Management Journal, 39*(2), 304–314. https://doi.org/10.1016/J.EMJ.2020.08.006

Andriosopoulos, D., Doumpos, M., Pardalos, P. M., & Zopounidis, C. (2019). Computational approaches and data analytics in financial services: A literature review. *Journal of the Operational Research Society, 70*(10), 1581–1599. https://doi.org/10.1080/01605682.2019.1595193

Ashrafi, A., & Zareravasan, A. (2022). An ambidextrous approach on the business analytics-competitive advantage relationship: Exploring the moderating role of business analytics strategy. *Technological Forecasting and Social Change, 179*, 121665. https://doi.org/10.1016/J.TECHFORE.2022.121665

Bhatnagar, S., & Sharma, D. (2022). Evolution of green finance and its enablers: A bibliometric analysis. *Renewable and Sustainable Energy Reviews, 162*, 112405. https://doi.org/10.1016/J.RSER.2022.112405

Bleibtreu, C., Königsgruber, R., & Lanzi, T. (2021). Financial reporting and corporate political connections: An analytical model of interactions. *Journal of Accounting and Public Policy*. https://doi.org/10.1016/J.JACCPUBPOL.2021.106904

Emtehani, F., Nahavandi, N., & Rafiei, F. M. (2021). An operations-finance integrated model with financial constraints for a manufacturer in a multi-supplier multi-product supply chain. *Computers and Industrial Engineering, 153*. https://doi.org/10.1016/J.CIE.2021.107102

Escamilla-Solano, S., Paule-Vianez, J., & Blanco-González, A. (2022). Disclosure of gender policies: Do they affect business performance? *Heliyon, 8*(1). https://doi.org/10.1016/J.HELIYON.2022.E08791

Gu, X., Mamon, R., Duprey, T., & Xiong, H. (2021). Online estimation for a predictive analytics platform with a financial-stability-analysis application. *European Journal of Control, 57*, 205–221. https://doi.org/10.1016/J.EJCON.2020.05.008

Hayajneh, J. A. M., Elayan, M. B. H., Abdellatif, M. A. M., & Abubakar, A. M. (2022). Impact of business analytics and π-shaped skills on innovative performance: Findings from PLS-SEM and fsQCA. *Technology in Society, 68*. https://doi.org/10.1016/J.TECHSOC.2022.101914

Kannagi, A., Gori Mohammed, J., Sabari Giri Murugan, S., & Varsha, M. (2021). Intelligent mechanical systems and its applications on online fraud detection analysis using pattern recognition K-nearest neighbor algorithm for cloud security applications. *Materials Today: Proceedings*. https://doi.org/10.1016/J.MATPR.2021.04.228

Khan, M. A. (2022). ESG disclosure and firm performance: A bibliometric and meta analysis. *Research in International Business and Finance, 61*, 101668. https://doi.org/10.1016/J.RIBAF.2022.101668

Kristoffersen, E., Mikalef, P., Blomsma, F., & Li, J. (2021). The effects of business analytics capability on circular economy implementation, resource orchestration capability, and firm performance. *International Journal of Production Economics, 239*. https://doi.org/10.1016/J.IJPE.2021.108205

Lei, L., Chen, W., Wu, B., Chen, C., & Liu, W. (2021). A building energy consumption prediction model based on rough set theory and deep learning algorithms. *Energy and Buildings, 240*. https://doi.org/10.1016/J.ENBUILD.2021.110886

Neirotti, P., Pesce, D., & Battaglia, D. (2021). Algorithms for operational decision-making: An absorptive capacity perspective on the process of converting data into relevant knowledge. *Technological Forecasting and Social Change, 173*. https://doi.org/10.1016/J.TECHFORE.2021.121088

Nikulina, A., & Wynstra, F. (2022). Understanding supplier motivation to engage in multiparty performance-based contracts: The lens of expectancy theory. *Journal of Purchasing and Supply Management*. https://doi.org/10.1016/J.PURSUP.2022.100746

Omar, Y. M., Minoufekr, M., & Plapper, P. (2019). Business analytics in manufacturing: Current trends, challenges and pathway to market leadership. *Operations Research Perspectives, 6*. https://doi.org/10.1016/J.ORP.2019.100127

Papenhausen, C., & Einstein, W. (2006). Implementing the balanced scorecard at a college of business. *Measuring Business Excellence, 10*(3), 15–22. https://doi.org/10.1108/13683040610685757/FULL/HTML

Ramanathan, U., & Ramanathan, R. (2021). Information sharing and business analytics in global supply chains. *International Encyclopedia of Transportation*, 71–75. https://doi.org/10.1016/B978-0-08-102671-7.10222-2

Selim, T., & Eltarabily, M. G. (2022). Impact of COVID-19 lockdown on small-scale farming in Northeastern Nile Delta of Egypt and learned lessons for water conservation potentials. *Ain Shams Engineering Journal, 13*(4). https://doi.org/10.1016/J.ASEJ.2021.11.018

Shi, Y., Cui, T., & Liu, F. (2022). Disciplined autonomy: How business analytics complements customer involvement for digital innovation. *Journal of Strategic Information Systems, 31*(1). https://doi.org/10.1016/J.JSIS.2022.101706

Shrivastava, A., Nayak, C. K., Dilip, R., Samal, S. R., Rout, S., & Ashfaque, S. M. (2021). Automatic robotic system design and development for vertical hydroponic farming using IoT and big data analysis. *Materials Today: Proceedings*. https://doi.org/10.1016/J.MATPR.2021.07.294

Taylor, J., & Baines, C. (2012). Performance management in UK universities: Implementing the balanced scorecard. *Journal of Higher Education Policy and Management, 34*(2), 111–124. https://doi.org/10.1080/1360080X.2012.662737

Vidgen, R., Hindle, G., & Randolph, I. (2020). Exploring the ethical implications of business analytics with a business ethics canvas. *European Journal of Operational Research, 281*(3), 491–501. https://doi.org/10.1016/J.EJOR.2019.04.036

Yuan, Z., Chen, H., Xie, P., Zhang, P., Liu, J., & Li, T. (2021). Attribute reduction methods in fuzzy rough set theory: An overview, comparative experiments, and new directions. *Applied Soft Computing, 107*. https://doi.org/10.1016/J.ASOC.2021.107353

Zopounidis, C. (1999). Multicriteria decision aid in financial management. *European Journal of Operational Research, 119*(2), 404–415. https://doi.org/10.1016/S0377-2217(99)00142-3

Zopounidis, C., & Doumpos, M. (2013). Multicriteria decision systems for financial problems. *Top, 21*(2), 241–261. https://doi.org/10.1007/S11750-013-0279-7

IFRS 9 Financial Assets: Debt Instrument Classification and Management Under the New Accounting Standard—A Case Study of Greek Government Bonds in Banks' Investment Portfolios

Nikolaos Sachlas and Vasileios Giannopoulos

Abstract This study examines the effects, in financial statements, from different allocations of bonds, a characteristic type of debt instrument according to business models introduced by IFRS 9. Manager discretion in allocating bonds to their investment portfolios, and specifically bank managers, who invest significant amounts in those types of assets, can lead to significant differences in figures, for the same bonds, especially in periods of relative financial stability. The findings of this study suggest that excess "freedom" allowed by the new standard can lead to distortions for each period banks report under IFRS, in accordance with managers' decision for initial classification and subsequent measurement.

Keywords IFRS 9 · Business models · ECL model · Government bonds · Banks

1 Introduction

As many economists believed and later proved, among them Halevi et al. (2012), the huge economic growth during the period before 2008 was a huge bubble based on complex but toxic economic theories and models, many of which were later proved to be unable to explain, simultaneously, time and complexity of the capitalist economy. This was one of the most important factors that led to completely wrong assumptions about the real value or pricing of the financial assets linked to subprime mortgages, such as collateralized debt obligations (CDOs), mortgage-backed securities (MBSs), credit default swaps (CDSs), or even bonds, mostly

N. Sachlas (✉) · V. Giannopoulos
Department of Accounting and Finance, University of Peloponnese, Kalamata, Greece
e-mail: v.giannopoulos@accfin.edu.gr

© The Author(s), under exclusive license to Springer Nature Switzerland AG 2023
P. Alphonse et al. (eds.), *Essays on Financial Analytics*, Lecture Notes in Operations Research, https://doi.org/10.1007/978-3-031-29050-3_10

issued or included in investment portfolios, of investment, commercial banks, and insurance companies.

An accurate observation of Johannes et al. (2018) indicated that investors, on the one hand, were willing to invest in such assets because of the higher expected returns compared to US Treasury interest rates, while investment banks and insurance companies, on the other hand, were more than motivated to "sell" those assets, expecting high profits, from fees imposed on sale and safekeeping, of those securities (CDOs, MBSs, etc.).

Bear & Stearns, one of the most historic investment banks in the USA, announced on July 2007 that two major funds of the bank could not repay investors. The triggering point of the global financial panic, however, was the bankruptcy of Lehman Brothers on 15 September 2008, which unfolded the financial assets' bubble, with unpredictable (up to then) consequences for the modern global economy, not only for the USA.

In Europe, major banks were largely exposed to those products of US financial institutions, and as a natural consequence, this seemingly US financial crisis also shook Europe and the sovereign debts of European countries.

At the beginning of this period, only a few were concerned about sovereign debt, but the asymmetric effects in the European area were immediately felt during the late 2009 when a significant number of countries announced increases in deficit/GDP ratios and inability to lend, which was depicted in government bonds' value (Lane, 2012). Ireland was one of the first countries in Europe to react by insuring all deposits and bonds issued from banks active in the country of about 440 billion euros. Although the Irish government made efforts, on December 2010, the country didn't eventually avoid a bailout by the European Union.

Iceland asked for international monetary fund's (IMF) help, for an amount of 2.1 billion euros, while the US government rescued Citigroup by giving $20 billion, apart from the enormous amount of $800 billion injected into the financial system. In the European financial system, European Union responded with a total of 200 billion euros in a period of global investor hysteria.

Very soon, it became clear that this financial crisis was not limited to the banking sector but also spread to sovereign debts in the form of government bonds. This resulted in a huge demand fall and, consequently, significant spread rise.

In the case of Greece, as Angelopoulos (2019) highlights, banks and investors, although not exposed, broadly, to those highly toxic investments, faced the side effects of this credit crunch, as their participation in European and global markets consequently affected their liquidity and led to increased rates. Moreover, structural problems in the Greek economy worsened the problems faced by the banks, and in addition to three austerity programs followed, as a result of European Union and IMF bailouts, to keep the economy alive, three recapitalization programs (2012, 2014, and 2015) are needed for Greek banks, which formed the Greek banking system as of today.

The collapse of financial assets was a natural result in 2008. Many institutional and private investors, or even corporations with sufficient liquidity, invested huge capital, evaluating those investments as safe shelters proved wrong. The need for creating a new, stricter framework to reflect the objective and real value of those financial assets was important. The new framework, obligatory from 1 September 2018, is IFRS 9, and this paper mostly focuses on the evaluation and effects, of the classification of government bonds, in the asset side of banks' balance sheets, under the new standard relating to a management decision, for initial classification and subsequent measurement.

2 Literature Review

Globally, banks played an important role in this huge credit crunch, and their supervision committee, the Basel Committee on Banking Supervision, is needed to reform the rules of financial stability and compliance. Those rules were very briefly known as Basel I and the newly introduced (that year, 2008) Basel II, which were evaluated after the credit default as insufficient and no longer useful under these circumstances. On July 2009, the Basel Committee proposed a new set of rules, known as Basel III, keeping some basic concepts of the two previous versions (Basel I and II) and enhancing them with stricter ratios, including leverage ratios and capital buffers, and introducing the issue of liquidity in the calculation of minimum capital requirement (Pillar I). 2019 was the completion time limit for materializing those new rules of Basel III that banks must fulfill (BIS).

In brief, the most important ratio thresholds of Basel III (Pillar I, minimum capital requirements) are:

- Core Tier 1 ratio (including conservation buffer and countercyclical buffer) >7% up to 9.5%
- Tier 1 ratio (including conservation buffer and countercyclical buffer) >8.5% up to 10%
- Tier 1 + Tier 2 ratio (including conservation buffer and countercyclical buffer) >10.5% up to 12.5% (source: Angelopoulos, 2019)

Apart from the Basel Committee's actions to enhance banks' integrity and financial stability, the accounting framework for classification, valuation, and presentation of financial assets on financial statements needed reform. Strong criticism, mainly from the G20, but also from the EU, of delayed and inadequate recognition of credit losses under the precedent accounting model (IAS 39) led the International Accounting Standards Board (IASB) to implement the development plan of a new stricter framework as defined in IFRS 9 (Gebhardt, 2015).

The need to establish a framework for accounting and valuation of financial assets in order to enhance the information of investors, shareholders, and the general public through the financial statements has led the IASB to develop a new standard (IFRS 9), which replaced the previous one (IAS 39) and was developed gradually into four stages (KPMG, 2014):

- Definition, categorization, and initial measurement/recognition of financial assets (2009)

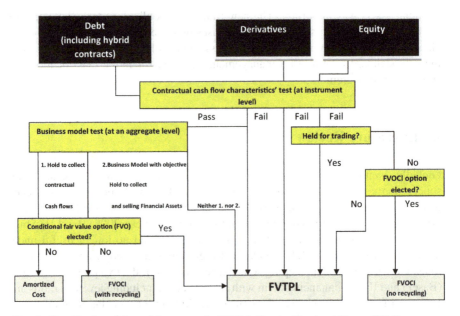

Fig. 1 Classification of financial assets under IFRS 9. Source: Ernst and Young (2016)

- Incorporation of IFRS 9 (2009) and addition of prerequisites for categorization and initial measurement/recognition (2010)
- Incorporation of IFRS 9 (2010), adjustments to the transition from the previous standard, as well as the addition of guidance on hedge accounting (2013)
- Incorporation of IFRS 9 (2013), with amendments to the requirements for the classification and measurement of financial assets, and addition on requirements for the new expected credit loss model for impairment (2014)

However, despite the considerable effort made by the IASB, the institutional body, to issue and monitor the implementation of IFRS worldwide, it remains unclear whether the new framework eliminates subjectivity or management discretion in illustrating the financial assets on the financial statements of companies listed on a regulated market and raising funds from investors.

This controversy is due to the fact that the application of IFRS 9 has become mandatory since 1 January 2018 for companies required to prepare financial statements in accordance with the International Financial Reporting Standards, so the study of the impact on both academic and real economy levels is still at an early stage.

Manager discretion in implementing IFRS 9 and decision for initial classification of financial assets is clear (requires management decision about the scope of each investment) as shown in Fig. 1.

Additionally, IFRS 9 introduced a new framework for recognizing credit losses different from that under the precedent accounting model (IAS 39).

Stage 1	Stage 2	Stage 3
Credit risk Initial recognition, or no significant increase in credit risk	**Credit risk** Significant increase in credit risk	**Credit risk** Objective evidence of impairment
Recognition of provision for expected losses Impairment amounting to 12-month expected credit losses	**Recognition of provision for expected losses** Impairment amounting to lifetime expected credit losses	**Recognition of provision for expected losses** Impairment amounting to lifetime expected credit losses
Interest revenue On basis of gross carrying value	**Interest revenue** On basis of gross carrying value	**Interest revenue** On basis of net carrying value

Fig. 2 General approach for impairment of financial assets under IFRS 9. Source: Ernst and Young (2016)

An entity shall recognize a loss allowance for expected credit losses on a financial asset, a lease receivable, a contract asset, or a loan commitment and a financial guarantee contract. An entity shall apply the impairment requirements for the recognition and measurement of a loss allowance for financial assets measured at fair value through other comprehensive income in accordance with paragraph 4.1.2A of IFRS 9. However, the loss allowance shall be recognized in other comprehensive income and shall not reduce the carrying amount of the financial asset in the statement of financial position (IASB, IFRS 9, par. 5.5.1 and 5.5.2).

At each reporting date, an entity shall measure the loss allowance for a financial instrument at an amount equal to the lifetime expected credit losses if the credit risk on that financial instrument has increased significantly since initial recognition. The objective of the impairment requirements is to recognize lifetime expected credit losses for all financial instruments for which there have been significant increases in credit risk since initial recognition—whether assessed on an individual or collective basis—considering all reasonable and supportable information, including that which is forward-looking (IASB, IFRS 9, par. 5.5.3 and 5.5.4).

If, at the reporting date, the credit risk of a financial instrument has not increased significantly since initial recognition, an entity shall measure the loss allowance for that financial instrument at an amount equal to 12-month expected credit losses (IASB, IFRS 9, par. 5.5.5).

A summary of the aforementioned is visualized in Fig. 2.

The study of Watts and Zimmerman (1990) on positive accounting, referring to manager discretion on accounting choices that maximize the value of the firm, is still food for thought about figures presented on financial statements, while manager discretion on bank provisioning is also highlighted in Ozili and Outa (2017) paper, where it warns regulators to pay attention on how much freedom must be given to managers in those calculations.

The initial reaction of shareholders of listed European companies to the announcement of the new framework introduced by IFRS 9 shows a positive level, first and foremost, of those in which the companies involved are based in countries where their regulatory framework was dictated either from local accounting standards or from the previous standard, IAS 39 (Onali & Ginesti, 2014).

But what about banks specifically, the predominantly affected institutions of this transition from IFRS 39 to IFRS 9, and also largely exposed from the 2008 credit crunch? A recent study from Ayariga (2020) on banks of Ghana suggests that the new standard is considered more reasonable while at the same time simplifying the task for preparers of financial statements and re-establishes prudence in impairment accounting.

Studies on the pre-adoption period, such as that of Zoltan Novotny-Farkas (2016), concluded that IFRS 9 and the new ECL model seem to mitigate the impact of pro-cyclicality on volatile financial markets as they emerged in 2008. However, the extent to which the ECL model will help eliminate pro-cyclicality depends on how it is implemented by management and its ability to detect significant changes in credit risk.

Gebhardt (2015) successfully, and in time, pointed out that the IFRS 9 approach focuses more on the synthesis of a theoretical model based entirely on management's expectations of the probability of credit default and expected cash flows; therefore, the results of these estimates have no directly observable financial impact. In addition to this, a critical question is: Is the financial result affected only by the subsequent valuation of financial assets and management's expectations about credit default or cash shortfall, or also by the initial classification of those assets, highly dependent on management decision and their business model? And if so, what is the financial impact of that decision?

As Brito and Judice (2020) suggest, if a financial asset is classified at fair value, it will allow a bank to realize potential gains that may occur from the acquisition date to maturity, whereas if classified as amortized cost (AC), this will not be possible, but will hide market fluctuations.

In many cases, though, those market fluctuations can reveal a lot about an asset's real value, as happened in the period prior to the 2008 credit crunch, where the real value of those instruments was not presented fairly in the banks' financial statements worldwide.

The framework for a financial asset to be classified as amortized cost, rather than fair value, that IFRS 9 sets, as presented previously, requires two conditions to be met: the objective one of the "solely payment of principal and interest (SPPI) criterion" and the subjective condition of business model decided in accordance with management's intentions or perceptions about the purpose of those investments. The second condition, business model designation, as highlighted by McKinsey & Co. (2017), will have a major consequence on the classification decision, and manipulation of P&L volatility, by hiding or revealing the market value of financial assets, according to management assessment.

PWC (2017) timely suggests that significant re-classifications are not expected under the new standard on banks' financial assets (as a whole). This observation was confirmed by Low et al. (2019) in a working paper for EBI, where the change from the previous regime, out of 78 European banks, is minor. After further investigation

Table 1 2017–2020 Greek
bond allocation (on the issue)
per investor type

	2017	2018	2019	2020
Real money	19.8%	45.6%	72.3%	69.4%
Banks	44.9%	22.9%	16.7%	22.6%
Hedge funds	35.3%	31.5%	11.0%	8.1%

Source: Public Debt Management Agency (pdma.gr)

on the issue of initial classification, Kounadeas (2020), in his recent study among 96 high-level employees of European banks responsible for IFRS 9 application, revealed that most investment assets are classified at amortized cost.

The above gives us a representative view of financial assets in general, but for government bonds, specifically, highly exposed to market fluctuations, as addressed in the introduction of this paper, academic research is limited, although critical.

Considering that banks make substantial investments in government bonds, either classified at amortized cost or fair value under IFRS 9, the decision on portfolio allocation by bank managers is critical. A study by Gennaioli et al. (2014) confirmed this significance, revealing that government bonds constitute, on average, 9% of the total assets in most banks' investment portfolios. In the case of Greek government bonds, it is obvious from Table 1 that a significant amount of the country's sovereign debt ends in bank investment portfolios in the period just before and shortly after the mandatory application of IFRS 9.

The amount of the above bonds issued by the Greek Government for this period (2017–2020) equals 50.8 billion euros (Public Debt Management Agency, a), emphasizing the significance of the banking sector's participation.

Trying to provide some answers to the above questions, this paper analyzes the impact of different classifications and subsequent measurement decisions on the allocation of bonds in banks' investment portfolios, following IFRS 9 guidelines, to fair value (fair value through profit & loss (FVTP&L) and fair value through other comprehensive income (FVTOCI)), or amortized cost, and the effect on total earnings from this decision.

Under the analysis of Greek government bonds' prices, we examine the fluctuation of profits presented in the statement of comprehensive income and values of those assets presented in financial statements to emphasize the effects of decisions made by bank managers in the allocation of investment portfolios.

3 Methodology

3.1 Data

This case study focuses on the exposure of Greek systemic banks to bonds, reporting under IFRS and, more specifically, under the newly established IFRS 9. Under the careful study of Greek systemic banks' financial statements, the extent of exposure to those types of investments is obvious. Alpha Bank presented an exposure of 7 and 8.6 billion euros of investments to bonds for the years 2018 and 2019, respectively, while the National Bank of Greece reported an exposure of 5.3 and 9.1 billion euros for the same period. The exposure on bonds is also high for the other two Greek systemic banks. Specifically, Eurobank presented an exposure of 7.7 billion euros for 2018 and 7.95 billion euros for 2019. Finally, the relative exposure of Piraeus Bank reached 2.7 and 3.2 billion euros in 2018 and 2019, respectively.

Sovereign bonds are issued with fixed and variable interest rate coupons. For the purpose of our study, we chose two Greek government bonds; the first was issued on August 2017 (ISIN: GR0114029540) with fixed annual coupon rate of 4.375% (7-year duration) and the second on February 2018 (ISIN: GR0118017657) with fixed annual coupon rate of 3.375% (5-year duration). For illustration purposes, the amounts reported in this study are on a nominal value of 1 million euro per bond.

The reason for choosing these two bonds, although different in duration, is that they were issued just before and after the mandatory implementation of IFRS 9 on 1 January 2018. The period covered by this study is the years 2018 and 2019 and the first two quarters of 2020. We try to analyze the effects of different bond allocations on banks' investment portfolios. During the studying period, the rating from Fitch regarding Greek government's credit standing has been stable and positive, as shown in Fig. 3. This is crucial to the whole study since we can clearly identify the effects of different allocations on investment portfolios, of those bonds, for a relatively stable period with a positive outlook, a factor that bank managers always keep in mind when they make substantial investments in sovereign debts.

As all four Greek systemic banks act as primary dealers (Public Debt Management Agency, b), they have the right to purchase those bonds at issue with a price lower than that of secondary markets and later keep or sell them according to their business models.

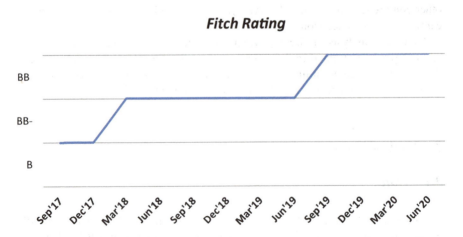

Fig. 3 Greece's credit standing for 2017–2020, according to Fitch rating agency. Source: Public Debt Management Agency (pdma.gr)

For bonds measured at fair value, it is very important to specify the prices to be used for those calculations. To increase consistency and comparability in fair value measurements and related disclosures, IFRS 13 (2011) establishes a fair value hierarchy that categorizes into three levels: Level 1 fair values are derived from unadjusted quoted prices from active markets for those assets. Level 2 inputs are inputs other than quoted prices included within Level 1 that are observable for the asset or liability, either directly or indirectly. Level 3 inputs are unobservable inputs for the asset or liability. IFRS 13 gives the highest priority (hierarchy) to quoted unadjusted prices in active markets for identical assets or liabilities (Level 1 inputs) and the lowest priority to unobservable inputs (Level 3 inputs). For Greek bonds tested in our study, Level 1 inputs are used since they are traded in active markets.

Issue prices of those bonds, and subsequent prices at the end of each reporting period, are derived from reliable sources (markets.businessinsider.com and finanzen.ch) to calculate amounts presented respectively on financial statements (Fig. 4).

Based on the nature of IFRS 9, the initial assessment on classification (IFRS 9.B4.1.1) is not binding. KPMG (2014) clearly points out that under the "hold to collect" business model, which leads to subsequent measurement at amortized cost, sales are typically lower in frequency and volume but not forbidden. In addition to the above, under the "both held to collect and sale" business model, sales are typically more in frequency and volume, but that does not mean that a sale of a financial asset must take place before maturity. Bonds are typical financial assets with contractual cash flows that give rise to payments on specified dates solely of principal and interest (SPPI test).Combining the above, it is obvious that bonds and instruments accounted for either amortized cost or FVTOCI, when initially categorized in each of these business models, do not include a clause of held until maturity or sell before maturity, at least a binding one.

Fig. 4 Bond prices. Source: Markets Insider-Business Insider and Finanzen

For this study, we assume that bank managers will not proceed with the sale of these bonds from the date of initial acquisition up to June 2020, consistent with the "freedom" given to managers from IFRS 9, as described in the previous paragraph.

Issue prices of the two bonds are quite close, and considering the role of Greek banks as primary dealers, it can be assumed that this was the price recognized for the first time in their books. The fact that the 5-year bond (ISIN: GR01104029540) was issued on August 2017, just a few months before the mandatory application of IFRS 9, which was, of course, a known factor for bank managers at that time, leads to the assumption that decision for classification and subsequent measurement would be reasonably based under IFRS 9 framework. Besides that, accounting under each category (fair value or amortized cost) of financial assets is the same as IAS 39 (PWC, 2017). A 7-year bond (ISIN: GR0118017657) was issued right after the mandatory implementation of IFRS 9 and classified and measured under this regime undoubtedly.

It is also important to mention that the whole study refers to a period (2017–2020) of positive credit standing for Greek sovereign debt with a stable outlook. This will help our study analyze the results in the statement of financial position and statement of comprehensive income, only from management discretion when determining the categorization of those bonds, in accordance with the business model introduced with IFRS 9.

For reporting periods, 31 March 2018, 30 June 2018, 30 September 2018, 31 December 2018, respective periods for 2019, and 31 March 2020 and June 2020, bonds have been measured as if classified either as FVTOCI or amortized cost. For the 5-year bond (ISIN: GR01104029540), issued on August 2017, the same calculations have been made for periods 30 September 2017 and 31 December 2017 for the bond to be comparable for 2018 and when IFRS 9 became mandatory. Calculations for bonds presented in this study also include expected credit losses according to impairment rules established under the new principle.

3.2   ECL Computation Approach

The objective of the impairment requirement under IFRS 9 is to recognize lifetime expected credit losses (ECL) for financial assets whose credit risk has increased since their acquisition. KPMG (2017) gives a detailed formula for ECL calculation under IFRS 9, consistent with the European Parliament and European Council Regulation (Regulation 575/2013) on prudential requirements that all European financial institutions must follow. This formula is defined as follows:

$$ECL = PD^*LGD^*EAD^*D$$

ECL is calculated based on the following components:

- Probability of default (PD)
- Loss given default (LGD)
- Exposure at default (EAD)
- Discount factor (D)

As Gebhardt (2015) reports, most banks have either developed their sophisticated internal model or assigned it to credit rating agencies in order to identify the amount of impairment for financial assets. It is also a fact that not all banks follow the same processes for calculating impairments, even for similar assets, resulting in different calculations.

Paragraph 9.5.5.17 of IFRS 9 refers to reasonable information available without undue cost or effort at the reporting date about past events, current conditions, and forecasts about future economic conditions when estimating the change in credit risk. In this part of IFRS 9, management discretion is also present since there is no consolidated framework for recognizing an increase in credit risk and subsequently calculating expected credit losses.

For computations of this study, elements of the ECL formula follow Regulation 575/2013 rules for financial institutions. Specifically, when calculating PD (probability of default), we assume that a bank follows Article 160 of the aforementioned regulation, referring to exposures to central governments, in our case, government bonds.

Probability of default rates are derived from Fitch cumulative default table as follows (Table 2):

The probability of default (PD factor) is calculated as at least 0.03% (Article 160 of Regulation 575/2013) when there is no such probability rate on Fitch's cumulative default rate table.

Loss given default (LGD factor) is valued at 45% for senior exposures without eligible collateral, according to Article 161 of 575/2013 Regulation. In practice, many financial institutions have received the permission of the competent authority to use their own LGD estimates for exposures to central governments, but for this study, it was assumed as 45%.

Article 166 of the 575/2013 Regulation, exposure value (EAD), mentions that "unless noted otherwise, the exposure value of on-balance sheet exposures shall be the accounting value measured without taking into account any credit risk adjustments made." This is the framework for calculating this factor of the ECL formula.

Discount factor (D) is the effective interest rate for these two bonds, taking into account the contractual interest rate of each bond and the gap between the issue price and face value, since bonds are considered to have been purchased at a discount from banks, who act as primary dealers. For the following calculations, regarding amortized cost measurements, we calculated the original effective interest rate at 4.6241% for the 5-year bond (ISIN: GR0114029540) and the respective rate for the 7-year bond (ISIN: GR0118017657), at 3.4992%, until maturity (Annex 1).

Table 2 Sovereign average cumulative default rate for 1995–2019

Fitch sovereign average cumulative default rates: 1995–2019

(%)	Year 1	Year 2	Year 3	Year 4	Year 5	Year 6	Year 7	Year 8	Year 9	Year 10
AAA	–	–	–	–	–	–	–	–	–	–
AA+	–	–	–	–	–	–	–	–	–	–
AA	–	–	–	–	–	–	–	–	–	–
AA-	–	–	–	–	–	–	–	–	–	–
A+	–	–	–	1.23	–	–	–	–	2.08	2.44
A	–	–	–	–	2.60	4.05	5.63	7.25	7.58	10.00
A-	–	–	–	–	–	–	–	–	–	–
BBB+	–	–	1.14	1.22	1.37	1.54	1.82	1.96	2.04	2.17
BBB	–	–	–	–	–	–	–	–	–	–
BBB-	–	1.23	1.95	2.84	3.94	5.17	5.66	6.32	7.23	7.04
BB+	–	–	–	–	–	–	0.91	1.96	2.13	2.35
BB	1.06	2.27	3.75	5.33	5.63	5.80	5.80	5.88	5.97	6.35
BB-	–	–	–	–	–	–	–	1.08	2.38	5.06
B+	0.66	2.11	4.58	6.72	7.55	7.14	6.59	7.23	8.11	7.81
B	1.92	3.47	5.30	8.26	10.00	12.12	14.44	14.63	13.89	12.90
B-	1.11	6.17	10.96	13.24	13.64	15.62	15.00	13.79	12.50	11.32
CCC to C	26.47	33.33	37.50	34.48	38.46	37.50	36.36	35.00	31.58	31.58
Investment grade	–	0.16	0.33	0.53	0.74	0.99	1.17	1.36	1.60	1.73
Speculative grade	1.81	3.35	4.96	6.06	6.67	7.16	7.51	7.91	7.94	8.24
All sovereigns	0.69	1.37	2.07	2.58	2.93	3.26	3.49	3.75	3.90	4.08

Source: Fitch ratings

4 Empirical Results

4.1 Calculations for 2018

2018 was the year of mandatory reporting under IFRS 9, and at that time, Greece's credit standing, according to Fitch, was three levels below the investment grade (BB-). For the 5-year bond, we can observe for the first half of 2018 a significant difference in the amount presented in the statement of financial position from different measurements (fair value or amortized cost). The same difference remains for the next two quarters, of 2018, with a minor convergence for the last quarter between the two measurement models. On the contrary, for the 7-year bond, the amounts presented under different classifications and measurements are quite similar and more conservative under FVTOCI calculations for all 2018 quarters (Table 3).

While ECL calculations for all quarters of 2018 under the two models do not seem to differ significantly, we cannot support the same for the amounts presented in the statement of comprehensive income. A significant difference can be observed for both bonds, which is somehow expected, because of the fair value measurements, under the FVTOCI model. While bonds at amortized cost give steady and increasingly positive results to the statement of comprehensive income, results vary significantly when the same bonds are measured at fair value. For the

Table 3 Calculations under AC and FVTOCI for 2018

Reporting period	ISIN: GR0114029540 (5-year bond)		ISIN: GR0118017657 (7-year bond)	
	AC	FVTOCI	AC	FVTOCI
Statement of financial position				
Mar 2018	990,301	1,045,359	992,384	972,869
Jun 2018	990,813	1,049,358	992,627	987,867
Sep 2018	991,330	1,048,658	992,874	985,567
Dec 2018	991,820	1,040,959	993,243	968,069
Statement of comprehensive income				
Mar 2018	11,160	15,947	4052	−15,463
Jun 2018	11,792	14,766	8642	23,281
Sep 2018	12,420	10,176	8980	6074
Dec 2018	12,919	3187	9350	−9124
ECL				
Mar 2018	134	141	134	131
Jun 2018	134	142	134	133
Sep 2018	134	142	134	133
Dec 2018	134	141	134	131

Source: author's table

5-year bond, results for the first half are greater than those measured under the "hold to collect" business model (amortized cost), but the results for the next two quarters are the opposite. For the 7-year bond, we observed a great difference in the second quarter of 2018 and even negative results for the last quarter of this year.

It is of great importance to mention that the effect on the statement of comprehensive income under FVTOCI refers to the result of the change in fair value for each period and is not realized until those bonds are sold. The cumulative amount from these changes in fair value under FVTOCI is presented in the statement of financial position's liability side, specifically in the reserves section. This reserve can be reclassified to P&L only when those bonds are sold. *In this study, the effect on the statement of comprehensive income under FVTOCI measurement refers to the change in the aforementioned reserve, which is debited or credited, respectively, to other comprehensive income, which is included in the total comprehensive income (Annex 2).*

An important observation from Table 3 is that for the fourth quarter of 2018, bond prices have slightly fallen, although there was no change (downgrade) in the credit rating from Fitch or any other agency. This can be explained by the silent postponement from the Greek government of the 10-year bond, issuance which was about to be executed at the end of 2018 (Financial Times, 2018).

4.2   Calculations for 2019

2019 was a year of stabilization and improvement for the Greek economy and its credit standing. This positive outlook was also expressed in credit agency ratings, in our case Fitch, where Greece's debt standing upgraded from BB- to BB for the year's second half. Based on Fitch cumulative default rates, ECL is higher for both bonds during quarters 3 and 4 since year 1 (since we have no indications of an increase in credit risk, but rather the opposite, we calculate ECL on a 12-month period), and the default rate for sovereign debt of this scale is shaped as 1.06% from 0.03%. This, of course, gives greater amounts of ECL for both categories, AC and FVTOCI.

On the contrary, for bonds measured at the fair value, this upgrade of Greece's credit rating gives significant positive results for the values presented in both statement of financial position and statement of comprehensive income as a result of an increase in market prices of Greek bonds, followed by this upgrade.

For bonds measured at amortized cost, changes in amounts presented from the previous year (2018) are minor, following a linear approach. Those differences according to different measurement models for the same bonds can be observed in Table 4.

Table 4 Calculations under AC and FVTOCI for 2019

Reporting period	ISIN: GR0114029540 (5-year bond)		ISIN: GR0118017657 (7-year bond)	
	AC	FVTOCI	AC	FVTOCI
Statement of financial position				
Mar 2019	992,350	1,081,854	993,492	1,023,062
Jun 2019	992,885	1,103,151	993,744	1,032,861
Sep 2019	988,822	1,112,667	989,388	1,126,202
Dec 2019	989,332	1,098,236	989,645	1,124,809
Statement of comprehensive income				
Mar 2019	11,184	51,542	8437	63,184
Jun 2019	11,839	32,059	8782	18,075
Sep 2019	7895	20,395	4518	101,709
Dec 2019	8405	8736	4775	1716
ECL				
Mar 2019	134	146	134	138
Jun 2019	134	149	134	139
Sep 2019	4739	5333	4742	5398
December 2019	4742	5264	4743	5391

Source: author's table

4.3 Calculations for 2020

Regarding the first half of 2020, it is more than obvious that the recent COVID-19 pandemic affected bond prices, at least for the first quarter of the year. DWS Investment (2020), in a recent study, confirmed the above while stating that contrary to the financial crisis of 2007/2008, where bonds were part of the problem, now they suffered from external shock. Central banks came out with gigantic rescue packages. The European Central Bank's Pandemic Emergency Program amounted to 750 billion euros (ECB, 2020). It led to a recovery in bond prices during the second quarter of 2020, giving steadily greater figures in both the statement of financial position and statement of comprehensive income for this period.

Despite the pandemic still being present, the above actions from central banks seem to bring back stability to global economy and financial system. The Greek economy, and, as a result, Greek sovereign debt's sustainability, was one of the biggest beneficiaries of this program, with the Greek bond yields recording the biggest drop since the ECB's announcement on March 2020.

When bond yields drop, prices of the bonds increase, and this is obvious from Table 5, where, when economic stabilization came back, amounts for both bonds under examination, reported at FVTOCI, were greater compared to those when measured at AC. This, of course, can improve amounts presented on banks' financial statements, for June 2020, but, on the contrary, it is important to mention that for

Table 5 Calculations under AC and FVTOCI for the first half of 2020

	ISIN: GR0114029540 (5-year bond)		ISIN: GR0118017657 (7-year bond)	
Reporting period	AC	FVTOCI	AC	FVTOCI
Statement of financial position				
Mar 2020	989,889	987,766	990,150	1,087,786
Jun 2020	990,447	1,082,611	990,409	1,107,193
Statement of comprehensive income				
Mar 2020	6724	−104,827	4176	−33,999
Jun 2020	7282	101,019	4436	22,608

Source: author's table

the first quarter of 2020 (March 2020), those bonds measured at AC hid market fluctuations, which, in many cases, are indicative of future malfunctions.

Since credit rating remained stable, there was no reason for banks or any other institution holding these bonds to calculate ECL for a period longer than 12 months since there was no evidence of credit increase according to IFRS 9 par. 9.5.5.10: "Credit Risk on a financial instrument has not increased significantly since initial recognition if the financial instrument is determined to have low credit risk at the reporting date." In this case, Greek bonds will continue to be allocated to Stage 1 for both quarters of 2020.

4.4 Summary

The difference in earnings and assets' values for the period covered by this study is clear when it is visualized using charts, which give a documentary approach.

Figures 5 and 6 (calculations from Annex 2) regarding the 5-year bond clearly depicted the positive effect on the asset side of the balance sheet under FVTOCI compared to AC measurement. As for the statement of comprehensive income effect, except for when the pandemic hit Europe, earnings are higher under FVTOCI measurement.

The 7-year bond (Figs. 7 and 8) helps us to understand what was mentioned before about the differences between the two allocation models. The increasing trend is clearer in figures under FVTOCI for a substantial period of financial stability, compared to AC. What is also evident in this case is the huge fall in respective figures in March 2020 under FVTOCI classification, which is not present when the same bond is measured at AC.

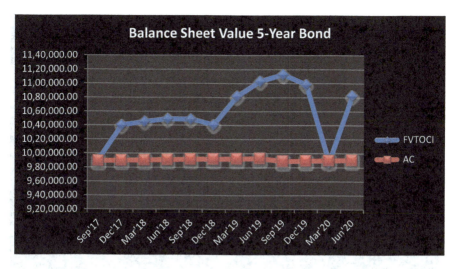

Fig. 5 Bond values presented in the statement of financial position. Source: author's figure

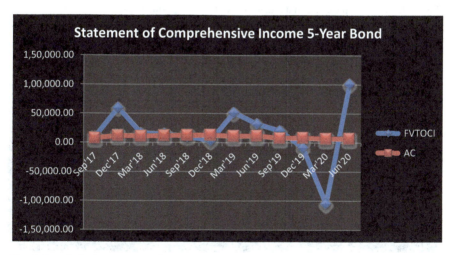

Fig. 6 Results in the statement of comprehensive income. Source: author's figure

5 Conclusion

From our analysis, it is evident that managers' discretion is crucial when determining the purpose of investment. This study highlights the effects of different measurement models of bonds in banks' investment portfolios, based on the flexibility given to managers from IFRS 9, not only when calculating ECL but

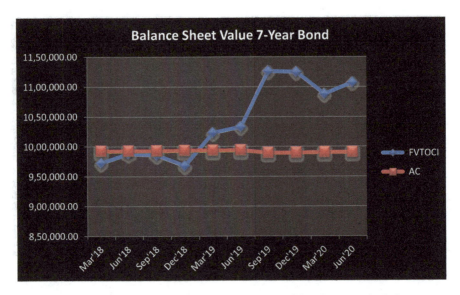

Fig. 7 Bond values presented in the statement of financial position. Source: author's figure

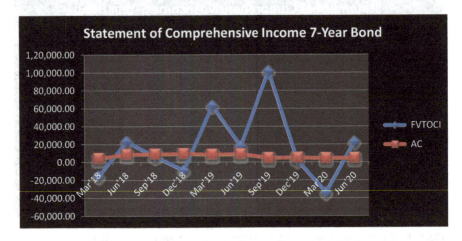

Fig. 8 Results in the statement of comprehensive income. Source: author's figure

also when initially allocating those bonds as "hold to collect" or "hold to collect and sale." Since there is no binding clause that has to be met (to hold or to sell according to initial classification), we tested the effect on financial statements when a bank holds those bonds, for a period relatively stable, without downgrades in a government's sovereign debt, under two different business models.

For both bonds measured at AC, it was clear that amounts reported on the statement of financial position and statement of comprehensive income were stable as expected, with no huge fluctuations during all the examined periods. This approach for both bonds, even if they eventually will not be held until maturity, gives a more conservative approach but, for a period rather unstable for the global financial system, as noticed on March 2020, hid market fluctuations, allowing banks to report positive figures, compared with FVTOCI measurement.

When those bonds, measured at FVTOCI, for a period of financial stability, with a positive or stable outlook, figures reported on financial statements were positively exceeding these, reporting under AC, and, respectively, were negatively exceeding when the financial system was under pressure. This is an important observation since pro-cyclicality in financial assets, which IAS 39 could not face, is the main reason for IFRS 9 appearance in 2018.

Based on the results of our study, we may conclude that when a period of financial stability or growth is expected, allocation of bonds as "hold to collect and sale," and subsequently gain from changes in fair values, could have a positive impact, in presented financial statements even if the initial purpose is not to sell them. Benefits will appear, in the form of higher earnings or higher values on the asset side of the balance sheet, on financial statements each quarter, which may also improve imposed Basel ratio thresholds for financial stability. On the other side, when a period of uncertainty is present, allocation of those bonds as "hold to collect" (which does not forbid later sales of those assets) could lead to hiding market fluctuations (falling prices) for the same reason mentioned above.

Finally, the results of this study must be interpreted carefully, considering the limitations and simplifications when executing different scenarios and calculations.

Our study can be a basis for further research about the impact of the different allocations of government bonds from countries like Portugal, Spain, or Italy, which faced the same problems as that of the Greek economy during the 2008 financial crisis but have recovered during recent years. The recent pandemic that hit Europe through 2020 can also be an interesting case for further investigation into the impact of the different allocations of European government bonds.

Annex 1: Calculation of IRR

This annex presents the calculation of the effective interest rate, under the assumption of holding until maturity, regarding both bonds tested under this study, using Microsoft Excel's formula internal rate of return (IRR) at the time of purchase, in order to calculate the amortization of the discount (revenue). Issue price is based on data collected from reliable sources, finanzen.ch and markets.businessinsider.com, for a nominal amount of 1 million euro.

Effective interest rate for a 7-year bond

Year 0	−992,400.00€
Year 1	33,750.00€
Year 2	33,750.00€
Year 3	33,750.00€
Year 4	33,750.00€
Year 5	33,750.00€
Year 6	33,750.00€
Year 7	1,033,750.00€
IRR->	*0.034992905*

Effective interest rate for a 5-year bond

Year 0	−989,100.00€
Year 1	43,750.00€
Year 2	43,750.00€
Year 3	43,750.00€
Year 4	43,750.00€
Year 5	1,043,750.00€
IRR->	*0.046241525*

Annex 2: Calculations for Bonds Under FVTOCI and AC for Each Quarter

Calculations under FVTOCI for a 7-year bond

Bond table	FVTOCI ISIN: GR0118017657	Days from issue or previous coupon	A Acquisition cost/prior valuation	B Accrued coupon	C Accrued coupon for the period	D Revenue recognition IRR 3.4992905%	Coupon receipt	15 February 2018 Nominal value receipt	3,375% E = A + D Value per books	1.000.000,00 € F Market price
Μαρ-18	Valuation	44.00	992,400.00	4068.49	4068.49	117.77			992,517.77	973,000.00
Ιουν-18	Valuation	91.00	973,000.00	8414.38	12,482.88	361.34			973,361.34	988,000.00
Σεπ-18	Valuation	92.00	988,000.00	8506.85	20,989.73	607.59			988,607.59	985,700.00
Δεκ-18	Valuation	92.00	985,700.00	8506.85	29,496.58	976.96			986,676.96	968,200.00
Φεβ-19	Coupon payment	46.00		4253.42	33,750.00	127.43	33,750.00			
Μαρ-19	Valuation	44.00	968,200.00	4068.49	4068.49	249.32			968,449.32	1,023,200.00
Ιουν-19	Valuation	91.00	1,023,200.00	8414.38	12,482.88	501.42			1,023,701.42	1,033,000.00
Σεπ-19	Valuation	92.00	1,033,000.00	8506.85	20,989.73	753.51			1,033,753.51	1,131,600.00
Δεκ-19	Valuation	92.00	1,131,600.00	8506.85	29,496.58	1011.15			1,132,611.15	1,130,200.00
Φεβ-20	Coupon payment	46.00		4253.42	33,750.00	131.89	33,750.00			
Μαρ-20	Valuation	45.00	1,130,200.00	4160.96	4160.96	507.18			1,130,707.18	1,093,000.00
Ιουν-20	Valuation	91.00	1,093,000.00	8414.38	12,575.34	768.10			1,093,768.10	1,112,500.00

G = E–F		H	I = F + H	J = B + D + G-H
Result to OCI	Cumulative OCI	ECL	Final value	Result to statement of comprehensive income
−19, 517.77	−19, 517.77	131.36	972,868.65	−15, 462.86
14, 638.66	−4879.11	133.38	987,866.62	23, 281.00
−2907.59	−7786.70	133.07	985,566.93	6073.78
−18, 476.96	−26, 263.66	130.71	968,069.29	−9123.86
54, 750.68	28, 487.02	138.13	1,023,061.87	63, 183.79
9298.58	37, 785.60	139.46	1,032,860.55	18, 074.93
97, 846.49	135, 632.09	5397.73	1,126,202.27	101, 709.12
−2411.15	133, 220.94	5391.05	1,124,808.95	1715.80
−37, 707.18	95, 513.76	5213.61	1,087,786.39	−33, 999.23
18, 731.90	114, 245.66	5306.63	1,107,193.38	22, 607.76

OCI, Other Comprehensive Income

Calculations under AC for a 7-year bond

Bond table		AC ISIN: GR0118017657						15 February 2018	3375%
			A	B	C	D	Coupon receipt	Nominal value receipt	E = A + D
		Days from issue or previous coupon	Acquisition cost/prior valuation	Accrued coupon	Accrued coupon for the period	Revenue recognition IRR 3.4992905%			Value per books
Mar 2018	Valuation	44.00	992,400.00	4068.49	4068.49	117.77			992,517.77
Jun 2018	Valuation	91.00	992,400.00	8414.38	12,482.88	361.34			992,761.34
Sep 2018	Valuation	92.00	992,400.00	8506.85	20,989.73	607.59			993,007.59
Dec 2018	Valuation	92.00	992,400.00	8506.85	29,496.58	976.96			993,376.96
Feb 2019	Coupon payment	46.00		4253.42	33,750.00	127.43	33,750.00		
Mar 2019	Valuation	44.00	993,376.96	4068.49	4068.49	249.32			993,626.28
Jun 2019	Valuation	91.00	993,376.96	8414.38	12,482.88	501.42			993,878.38
Sep 2019	Valuation	92.00	993,376.96	8506.85	20,989.73	753.51			994,130.47
Dec 2019	Valuation	92.00	993,376.96	8506.85	29,496.58	1011.15			994,388.11
Feb 2020	Coupon payment	46.00		4253.42	33,750.00	131.89	33,750.00		
Mar 2020	Valuation	45.00	994,388.11	4160.96	4160.96	507.18			994,895.29
Jun 2020	Valuation	91.00	994,388.11	8414.38	12,575.34	768.10			995,156.20

Bond table

| 1.000.000,00 € | | |
| F | G = E−F | H = B + D−F |
ECL	Final value	Result to statement of comprehensive income
133.99	992,383.78	4052.27
134.02	992,627.32	8641.70
134.06	992,873.53	8980.38
134.11	993,242.85	9349.70
134.14	993,492.14	8437.10
134.17	993,744.20	8781.63
4742.00	989,388.47	4518.36
4743.23	989,644.87	4774.76
4745.65	990,149.64	4175.92
4746.90	990,409.31	4435.59

Calculations under FVTOCI for a 5-year bond

Bond table		Days from issue or previous coupon	A Acquisition cost/prior valuation	B Accrued coupon	C Accrued coupon for the period	D Revenue recognition IRR 4.6241525%	Coupon receipt	1 August 2017 Nominal value receipt	4.375% E = A + D Value per books	1.000.000,00 € F Market price
FVTOCI ISIN: GR0114029540										
Σεπ-17	Valuation	60.00	989,100.00	7191.78	7191.78	138.02			989,238.02	991,400.00
Δεκ-17	Valuation	92.00	991,400.00	11,037.39	18,229.17	828.12			992,228.12	1,040,200.00
Μαρ-18	Valuation	90.00	1,040,200.00	10,787.67	29,016.84	506.45			1,040,706.45	1,045,500.00
Ιουν-18	Valuation	91.00	1,045,500.00	10,907.53	39,924.37	1018.52			1,046,518.52	1,049,500.00
Αυγ-18	Coupon payment	32.00		3825.63	43,750.00		43,750.00			
Σεπ-18	Valuation	60.00	1,049,500.00	7191.78	7191.78	1536.22			1,051,036.22	1,048,800.00
Δεκ-18	Valuation	92.00	1,048,800.00	11,027.40	18,219.18	2025.79			1,050,825.79	1,041,100.00
Μαρ-19	Valuation	90.00	1,041,100.00	10,787.67	29,006.85	529.87			1,041,629.87	1,082,000.00
Ιουν-19	Valuation	91.00	1,082,000.00	10,907.53	39,914.38	1065.62			1,083,065.62	1,103,300.00
Αυγ-19	Coupon payment	32.00		3835.62	43,750.00		43,750.00			
Σεπ-19	Valuation	60.00	1,103,300.00	7191.78	7191.78	1607.26			1,104,907.26	1,118,000.00
Δεκ-19	Valuation	92.00	1,118,000.00	11,027.40	18,219.18	2119.46			1,120,119.46	1,103,500.00
Μαρ-20	Valuation	91.00	1,103,500.00	10,907.53	29,126.71	560.53			1,104,060.53	992,500.00
Ιουν-20	Valuation	91.00	992,500.00	10,907.53	40,034.25	1121.05			993,621.05	1,087,800.00

$G = E-F$		H	$I = F+H$	$J = B+D+G-H$
Result to OCI	Cumulative OCI	ECL	Final value	Result to statement of comprehensive income
2161.98	2161.98		991,400.00	9491.78
47,971.88	50,133.86		1,040,200.00	59,837.39
4793.55	54,927.41	141.14	1,045,358.86	15,946.53
2981.48	57,908.89	141.68	1,049,358.32	14,765.85
−2236.22	55,672.67	141.59	1,048,658.41	10,175.82
−9725.79	45,946.88	140.55	1,040,959.45	3186.85
40,370.13	86,317.02	146.07	1,081,853.93	51,541.60
20,234.38	106,551.40	148.95	1,103,151.05	32,058.59
13,092.74	119,644.14	5332.86	1,112,667.14	20,394.54
−16,619.46	103,024.68	5263.70	1,098,236.31	−8736.30
−111,560.53	−8535.85	4734.23	987,765.78	−104,826.69
94,178.95	85,643.10	5188.81	1,082,611.19	101,018.73

Calculations under AC for a 5-year bond

Bond table	AC ISIN: GR0114029540	Days from issue or previous coupon	A Acquisition cost/prior valuation	B Accrued coupon	C Accrued coupon for the period	D Revenue recognition IRR 4.624152%	Coupon receipt	1 August 2017 Nominal value receipt	4.375% E = A + D Value per books
Sep 2017	Valuation	60.00	989,100.00	7191.78	7191.78	138.02			989,238.02
Dec 2017	Valuation	92.00	989,100.00	11,037.39	18,229.17	828.12			989,928.12
Mar 2018	Valuation	90.00	989,928.12	10,787.67	29,016.84	506.45			990,434.57
Jun 2018	Valuation	91.00	989,928.12	10,907.53	39,924.37	1018.52			990,946.64
Aug 2018	Coupon payment	32.00		3825.63	43,750.00		43,750.00		
Sep 2018	Valuation	60.00	989,928.12	7191.78	7191.78	1536.22			991,464.34
Dec 2018	Valuation	92.00	989,928.12	11,027.40	18,219.18	2025.79			991,953.91
Mar 2019	Valuation	90.00	991,953.91	10,787.67	29,006.85	529.87			992,483.77
Jun 2019	Valuation	91.00	991,953.91	10,907.53	39,914.38	1,065.62			993,019.53
Aug 2019	Coupon payment	32.00		3835.62	43,750.00		43,750.00		
Sep 2019	Valuation	60.00	991,953.91	7191.78	7191.78	1607.26			993,561.17
Dec 2019	Valuation	92.00	991,953.91	11,027.40	18,219.18	2119.46			994,073.37
Mar 2020	Valuation	91.00	994,073.37	10,907.53	29,126.71	560.53			994,633.90
Jun 2020	Valuation	91.00	994,073.37	10,907.53	40,034.25	1121.05			995,194.42

1.000.000,00 €		
F	G = E−F	H = B + D−F
ECL	Final value	Result to statement of comprehensive income
	989, 238.02	7329.80
	989, 928.12	11, 865.51
133.71	990, 300.86	11, 160.41
133.78	990, 812.86	11, 792.28
133.85	991, 330.50	12, 419.78
133.91	991, 819.99	12, 919.27
133.99	992, 349.79	11, 183.55
134.06	992, 885.47	11, 839.09
4739.29	988, 821.88	7895.37
4741.73	989, 331.64	8405.13
4744.40	989, 889.49	6723.66
4747.08	990, 447.35	7281.51

Bibliography

International

Ayariga, C. (2020). IAS39 and IFRS9: Effects of changing accounting standards for financial instruments on the financial asset management of commercial banks in the Sekondi-Takoradi metropolis of Ghana. *International Journal of Accounting and Financial Reporting*. https://doi.org/10.5296/ijafr.v10i1.16085

Brito, R., & Judice, P. (2020). *Asset classification under the IFRS 9 framework for the construction of a banking investment portfolio*. CeBER working paper no. (2020).

DWS Investment GmbH. (2020, April 16). *Coronavirus reshuffles the bond markets*. https://www.dws.com/en-kr/insights/cio-view/cio-view-quarterly/q1-2020/coronavirus-reshuffles-bonds-markets/

ECB (European Central Bank). *Press release 18 March 2020: ECB announces €750 billion pandemic emergency purchase programme (PEPP)*. https://www.ecb.europa.eu/press/pr/date/2020/html/ecb.pr200318_1~3949d6f266.en.html

Edgar, L., Emma, S. L., & Franz, T. L. *Accounting for financial instruments under IFRS 9 −First time application effects on European Banks' balance sheets*. Working paper for EBI 2019-no 48.

Ernst & Young. (2016). *Applying IFRS /IFRS 9 for non-financial entities*. https://www.ey.com/Publication/vwLUAssets/Applying_IFRS_%E2%80%93_IFRS_9_for_non-financial_entities/\protect\T1\textdollarFILE/Applying-FI-Mar2016.pdf

European Parliament. (2013). *Regulation (E.U.) No 575/2013 of the European Parliament and of the Council on prudential requirements for credit institutions and investment firms and amending regulation (E.U.) no 648/2012*.

Gennaioli, N., Martin, A., & Rossi, S. (2014). *Banks, government bonds, and default: What do the data say?* IMF working paper (2014).

Gunther, G. (2015). *Impairments of Greek Government Bonds under IAS 39 and IFRS 9*. Study for the ECON Committee, European Parliament.

Halevi, J., Varoufakis, Y., & Theocarakis, N. (2012). *Modern political economics making sense of the post-2008 world*. Routledge. https://doi.org/10.4324/9780203829356

IASB. (2011). *IFRS 13 fair value measurement*. IFRS Foundation. https://www.ifrs.org/issued-standards/list-of-standards/ifrs-13-fair-value-measurement/

IASB. (2019). *IFRS 9 financial instruments*. IFRS Foundation. https://www.ifrs.org/issued-standards/list-of-standards/ifrs-9-financial-instruments/

Johannes, R., Dedy, D., & Muksin, A. (2018). The preparation of banking industry in implementing IFRS 9 financial instruments (A case study of HSBC holdings Plc listed on London stock exchange of Year 2015–2017). *International Journal of Economics and Financial Issues, 8*(6), 124–136. https://doi.org/10.32479/ijefi.7280

KPMG. (2014). *First impressions: IFRS 9 – Hedge accounting and transition*. https://home.kpmg/content/dam/kpmg/pdf/2014/09/first-impressions-IFRS9.pdf

KPMG. (2017). *Demystifying expected credit losses*. https://assets.kpmg/content/dam/kpmg/in/pdf/2017/07/Demystifying-Expected-Credit-Loss.pdf

McKinsey & Company. (2017). *IFRS 9: A silent revolution in banks' business models*. https://www.mckinsey.com/business-functions/risk/our-insights/ifrs-9-a-silent-revolution-in-banks-business-models

Onali, E., & Ginesti, G. (2014). Pre-adoption market reaction to IFRS 9: A cross-country event-study. *Journal of Accounting and Public Policy, 33*, 628–637.

Peterson, O. K., & Erick, O. (2017). Bank loan loss provisions research: A review. *Borsa Istanbul Review, 17*(3), 144–163.

Philip, L. R. (2012). The European sovereign debt crisis. *Journal of Economic Perspectives, 26*(3), 49–68. https://doi.org/10.1257/jep.26.3.49

PwC. (2017). *IFRS 9 financial instruments – Understanding the basics*. https://www.pwc.com/gx/en/audit-services/ifrs/publications/ifrs-9/ifrs-9-understanding-the-basics.pdf

Watts, R. L., & Zimmerman, J. L. (1990). Positive accounting theory: A ten year perspective. *The Accounting Review*.

Zoltan, N.-F. (2016). The interaction of the IFRS 9 expected loss approach with supervisory rules and implications for financial stability. *Accounting in Europe, 13*(2), 197–227. https://doi.org/10.1080/17449480.2016.1210180

Greek

ΑγγελόπουλοςΧρ. Παναγιώτης "Τράπεζες και Χρηματοπιστωτικό Σύστημα" Εκδόσεις Unibooks,'Ε Έκδοση2019

Κουναδέας Θεόδωρος, Διδακτορική Διατριβή: "Η εφαρμογή των Διεθνών Λογιστικών Προτύπων / Διεθνών Προτύπων Χρηματοοικονομικής Αναφοράς (ΔΛΠ/ΔΠΧΑ) στον ευρωπαϊκό τραπεζικό κλάδο: η συνεισφορά της υιοθέτησης του ΔΠΧΑ 9 στην ποιότητα της παρεχόμενης λογιστικής πληροφόρησης" Εθνικό και Καποδιστριακό Πανεπιστήμιο Αθηνών (ΕΚΠΑ), Σχολή Νομικών, Οικονομικών και Πολιτικών Επιστημών, Τμήμα Οικονομικών Επιστημών (2020)

Websites

BIS. (n.d.). http://www.bis.org/bcbs

Finanzen. (n.d.). https://www.finanzen.ch/obligationen/historisch/griechenlandeo-notes_201825-obligation-2025gr0118017657;   https://www.finanzen.ch/obligationen/historisch/griechenlandeo-bonds_201722-obligation-2022-gr0114029540

Fitch Ratings. (n.d.). https://www.fitchratings.com/research/corporate-finance/2019-transition-default-studies-27-03-2020

Markets   Insider-Business   Insider.   (n.d.).   https://markets.businessinsider.com/bonds/griechenlandeo-notes_201825-bond-2025-gr0118017657;   https://markets.businessinsider.com/bonds/griechenlandeo-bonds_201722-bond-2022-gr0114029540

Public Debt Management Agency, a. (n.d.). http://www.pdma.gr/en/debt-instruments-greek-government-bonds/ggb-allocation/ggb-allocation-2018

Public Debt Management Agency, b. (n.d.). http://www.pdma.gr/en/debt-instruments-greek-government-bonds/primary-dealers

Part IV
Portfolio Management and Fintech

Geographic Dispersion and IPO Underpricing

Dimitrios Gounopoulos

Abstract This study provides empirical evidence that underpricing is larger for more geographically dispersed firms when using a measure that captures the number of states in which firms have economic interests. The findings show that the average underpricing for local firms is 4.85% less than for dispersed firms (firms that have economic interests in more than three states in the USA). The hypothesis that underpricing is larger for more geographically dispersed firms is confirmed, and the evidence is robust for alternative measures of geographic dispersion. Results reveal that the likelihood of a firm committing accounting fraud increases the more geographically dispersed a firm's economic interests become.

Keywords Geographical location · Home bias · IPOs · First-day returns · Underwriter reputation

JEL Classifications: G10, G14, G39

1 Introduction

When Twitter had an initial public offering (IPO) in the USA in November 2013, 70 million shares were sold at $26 a share. At the end of the first trading day, the stocks traded at $44.94 each, up to 72.84%. Twitter could therefore have sold 70 million shares at $44.94 and could have raised more than $3 billion, a billion dollar more than what they did raise. Hence, the issuing firm left $1 billion on the table. Early investors can thus make capital gains on their investments when IPOs are underpriced.

D. Gounopoulos (✉)
School of Management, University of Bath, Bath, UK
e-mail: d.gounopoulos@bath.ac.uk

© The Author(s), under exclusive license to Springer Nature Switzerland AG 2023
P. Alphonse et al. (eds.), *Essays on Financial Analytics*, Lecture Notes in Operations Research, https://doi.org/10.1007/978-3-031-29050-3_11

A substantial body of work regarding the IPO of common stock examines various theories that explain underpricing. These theories come under four broad categories, namely, asymmetric information, institutional reasons, control considerations and behavioural approaches. Beatty and Ritter (1986) and Welch (1989) document strong evidence that information asymmetry contributes significantly to increased underpricing. Cliff and Denis (2004) and Lowry and Murphy (2006) reveal a significant positive relation between underwriter reputation and underpricing. Bradley and Jordan (2002) investigate the effects that revision, overhang, venture capital (VC) backing and hot markets have on underpricing, indicating that all four determinants significantly increase underpricing.

The literature on corporate geography suggests that geographically dispersed information on company earnings and cash flows contributes to increased asymmetric information (García & Norli, 2012; Platikanova & Mattei, 2016). The geographic dispersion of business activities across multiple states in the USA is making it more difficult to achieve efficient and informed investment decisions. Gao et al. (2008) reveal that as a firm's operations become more geographically dispersed, the valuation discount grows. García and Norli (2012) show that monthly returns on common stock for local firms are more than for geographically dispersed firms. Platikanova and Mattei (2016) highlight that analysts' forecasts become less accurate for more geographically dispersed firms due to information asymmetry.

In an important departure from prior evidence, this study focuses on the degree to which geographic dispersion across states in the USA affects underpricing. Prior studies state that there may not be relevant information about company performance and future sales trends for geographically dispersed firms due to inefficiencies in aggregating this information across business activities in multiple states. They further reveal that a firm that has economic activities across multiple states in the USA sees an increase in management discretion, such as shifting profits to different states, which increases information asymmetry.

Heider and Ljungqvist (2015) mention that tax code variation across states in the USA further contributes to the complexity of efficiently aggregating relevant information across states and increases information asymmetry. Therefore, an investigation is conducted here using a measure for geographic dispersion to see if there is empirical evidence consistent with Platikanova and Mattei (2016) that geographically dispersed information contributes to increased levels of information asymmetry and ultimately increases underpricing.

Using publicly listed companies in the USA that file annual 10-K reports with the Securities and Exchange Commission (SEC) and that went public between 1995 and 2015, a measure for geographic dispersion is developed here based on the work by García and Norli (2012), capturing all the economic ties between a firm's economic interests and its headquarters. Using the measure for geographic dispersion and controlling for several determinants for underpricing, the study reveals that the IPOs of firms with business activities in more than three states in the USA are more underpriced than firms that have economic interests in three or fewer states.

The study is robust to using Platikanova and Mattei (2016) measure for geographic dispersion, i.e. concentration, and shows that geographic dispersion is a determinant of underpricing. The study further shows that as the number of states in which a firm has economic interest increases, the likelihood of that firm committing fraud also increases. The study contributes to the body of knowledge on the geography of corporations and how it affects the efficiency of aggregating relevant information across multiple states in the USA and the impact it has on underpricing.

The study is structured as follows. Section 2 entails a literature review of relevant studies that were curried to investigate the determinants of underpricing and that have examined the role that geographic dispersion plays in information asymmetry and stock returns, valuation, accuracy of analysts' forecasts and earnings quality. Section 3 provides the hypothesis development, related to the effect that geographic dispersion has on underpricing. Section 4 showcases the empirical link between geographic dispersion, underpricing and accounting fraud, while Sect. 5 concludes the manuscript.

2 Literature Review

This literature review looks at the meaning of and provides evidence of underpricing. Firm characteristics that are positively and negatively associated with underpricing are examined, and a further investigation into the theories proposed to explain the causes of underpricing is carried out. The literature on geographic dispersion and its effects on various firm attributes, such as operating efficiency, trading performance, stock returns, forecasting and firm valuation, is explored, and a discussion is started on whether geographic dispersion could be significantly associated with underpricing.

Logue (1973) states that investors who buy common stock IPOs during the offer price period quickly realise substantial systematic profits. This is because the shares that companies sell when they go public are underpriced as there is a substantial jump in price on the first day of trading. Underpricing is defined as the percentage difference between the offer price, the price at which the investors bought the IPO shares and the price that the shares trade at on the market. In advanced capital markets such as in the USA and the UK, the full extent of underpricing is visible quickly, normally by the end of the first trading day.

2.1 Underpricing Theories

2.1.1 Asymmetric Information

Underpricing is to some extent explained through the notion that one of the parties involved in an IPO has privy to more information than other parties. The principal-agent problem thus arises, and these frictions of information lead to underpricing.

The principal-agent problem can be examined through three lenses, i.e. when either the investment bank, the issuing firm or the new investors know more.

Baron (1982) theory assumes that the investment bank knows more than the issuing firm when it comes to demand conditions and thus uses underpricing as a method to drive high-selling efforts. Beatty and Ritter (1986) find that investment banks persuade unwilling issuing companies to purposefully underprice IPO shares to encourage uninformed investors to not leave the IPO market.

The theory by Welch (1989) reveals that the issuing firm has more information about the true value of the firm and uses underpricing as a method to signal to investors. According to Welch (1989), there are two types of firms, namely, good firms (high-quality firms) and bad firms (low-quality firms), and these firms look indistinguishable to outside investors.

A good firm can signal to investors that it is of high quality by underpricing its shares and deliberately leaving money on the table as it will be able to recover it later through a seasoned equity offering. However, this gives low-quality firms the incentive to mimic the actions of good firms, i.e. underprice their shares during the IPO, yet low-quality firms typically refrain from signalling that they are good firms because the risk of detection means that they will be unable to recoup the money left on the table at the post-IPO financing stage.

Rock (1986) with his winner's curse provides an explanation for underpricing from an asymmetric information perspective. He assumes that the investors know more and are able to avoid participating in overpriced IPOs, bidding only for those that are attractively priced. Rock (1986), meanwhile, report that uninformed investors bid indiscriminately for attractive/unattractive IPO offerings. Thus, uninformed investors buy all the unattractively priced shares, and their demand for the attractively priced shares is crowded out by informed investors. Rock (1986), therefore, documents that uninformed investors need to underprice on purpose to prevent informed investors from not participating in the IPO. Lastly, Benveniste and Spindt (1989) make the assumption that as better-informed investors honestly reveal the information they have before the issuing price is finalised, they reduce the amount of money left on the table.

2.1.2 Institutional Reasons

Lowry and Shu (2002) find that in the USA, almost 6% of companies listed between 1988 and 1995 were sued for IPO-related violations. Tiniç (1988) states that underpricing could be intentional as an insurance against such lawsuits. Logue (1973) and Ibbotson (1975) findings indicate that there are institutional explanations for underpricing. They state that the issuing firms deliberately offer their shares at a discount for litigation purposes.

Issuing firms indicate that the likelihood of future lawsuits reduces when the likelihood of shareholders being disappointed with the performance of their shares post-IPO decreases. However, this explanation is mostly significant in the USA, and the risk of being sued is not significant in countries such as Finland, Australia,

Germany, Japan, the UK and Switzerland. Lowry and Shu (2002) reveal contradicting evidence: underpricing decreases when companies are sued. According to Tiniç (1988), Logue (1973) and Ibbotson (1975), underpricing increases when companies are sued.

Another institutional reason is price stabilisation. Ruud (1993) states that companies do not underprice deliberately but rather that IPOs are priced at the expected market value, and those offerings that appear they will fall under the offer price are stabilised in the aftermarket. Ruud (1993) mentions that price stabilisation gives the picture of a positive increase in price. Asquith et al. (1998) state that if Ruud (1993) analysis that underpricing is the consequence of price support is correct, then the underpricing distribution of unsupported offerings should have a mean of zero. Asquith et al. (1998) do not provide any evidence and state that underpricing is caused by other factors rather than price support.

2.1.3   Ownership and Control Considerations

Brennan and Franks (1997) state that managers of firms deliberately underprice to generate excess demand. They mention that the excess demand equips managers to ration investors so that they end up owning a smaller amount of the business. This method of allocating shares strategically enables managers to protect their private benefits and avoid more scrutiny regarding non-value maximising behaviour. Brennan and Franks (1997) therefore consider underpricing as a method to retain control of the business.

Stoughton and Zechner (1998) report that underpricing is a method to reduce agency costs. They state that it might be beneficial to allocate shares to a large institutional investor for monitoring purposes. They assert that while monitoring benefits all shareholders, it has its limits as shareholders will only monitor up to the point where it is no longer optimal for the size of their stake in the company. Stoughton and Zechner (1998) therefore find that to encourage better monitoring, managers should allocate a larger stake to an individual investor with an incentive in the form of underpricing.

2.1.4   Behavioural Approaches and Other Theories

Welch (1992) finds that informational cascades can develop in IPOs when investment decisions are made sequentially through later investors basing their positioning on earlier bids, thereby disregarding their own beliefs and the information they are privy to. Therefore, when initial sales are very successful, later investors believe that earlier bidders held favourable information and choose to invest regardless of the information they possess, and thus demand grows substantially.

In contrast, when initial sales are unsuccessful, later investors may be dissuaded from buying and demand merely remains low over time. Therefore, information cascades give early investors market power and put them in a position to demand underpricing from the issuing firm in return for committing to the IPO (Welch, 1992).

Bradley and Jordan (2002) investigate the extent to which underpricing can be predicted based on information that are publicly available before the offer date. They examined four variables, namely, overhang and file range amendments; venture capitalist (VC) backing, which had been studied before and for which contradictory results are available; and the hot market issue, which states that there is a cyclical pattern that underpricing is larger when firms go public in hot market years. Bradley and Jordan (2002) define file range amendments (revision) as the percentage difference between the initial file ranges and the final IPO offer prices. They document that revision has a statistically significant effect on underpricing. They highlight that when all things are kept equal, upward revisions are related to more underpricing, and downward revisions are related to less underpricing, compared to issues with no revisions. This supports the findings of Cliff and Denis (2004) that underpricing and revision are positively related.

The third variable of interest in is the effect of VC backing on underpricing. Megginson and Weiss (1991) research on the matter suggests that issues by VC-backed firms are significantly less underpriced compared to non-VC-backed firms. However, Bradley and Jordan (2002) find that the opposite is true in more recent years. The fourth variable of interest, hot market issue, significantly affects underpriced. Their findings are in agreement with Ibbotson and Jaffe (1975), Ritter (1984), Loughran and Ritter (2002) and Goergen et al. (2021) that underpricing is positively correlated with hot market issues.

Carter and Manaster (1990) study on IPOs and underwriter reputation states that it is very costly to the issuing firm to leave money on the table (underpricing), and therefore low-risk firms tend to attempt to reveal their low-risk characteristics to the market. According to Carter and Manaster (1990), low-risk firms do this by selecting highly ranked or prestigious underwriters. They find empirical evidence that underwriters that are highly ranked are typically associated with less risky offerings. This finding supports Rock (1986) study that underpricing is greater for more risky IPOs as investor capital migrates toward them for information purposes. Habib and Ljungqvist (2015) report similar evidence for auditors that firm will try to reveal their low-risk characteristics by selecting a Big 4 auditor; hence, Big 4 auditors should be associated with less underpricing.

Lowry and Murphy (2006) document that underpricing is larger for better-ranked underwriters, and this provides support to Loughran and Ritter (2004), Gounopoulos et al. (2017), Colak et al. (2021a), Economidou et al. (2022a, b) and Gounopoulos and Huang (2022) who state that underpricing is larger for highly ranked underwriters. These underwriters typically have more leverage to underprice the IPO shares, which creates valuable currency which can be allocated to investment banking clients. Cliff and Denis (2004) reveal that more highly ranked underwriters are associated with more underpricing and that increasing an underwriter's rank from 7 to 9 will increase underpricing by 4.5%.

Habib and Ljungqvist (2015) study on underpricing and entrepreneurial wealth losses reveals that leverage significantly affects underpricing. They find that underpricing is less when a firm's leverage is larger. This supports the finding by James and Wier (1990) that underpricing is affected by leverage. Both Carter and Manaster (1990) and Cliff and Denis (2004) document weak evidence that offer size (proceeds) is related to underpricing. Both indicate that the coefficient for the natural log of IPO proceeds is not statistically different from zero.

2.2 Geographic Dispersion

Underpricing theories are mainly grouped under four broad categories. This study focuses on geographic dispersion as a variable to explain underpricing. The rationale has come about through various research on the relationship between industry and geographically concentrated firms and factors such as profitability, corporate decision-making, stock returns, firm valuation, earnings quality and accuracy of analysts' forecasts.

Previous research by Grullon et al. (2019) examine whether firms are becoming more industry-concentrated. They define industry-concentrated firms as those that own a large market share in an industry and document that US firms in industries with the biggest increase in product market concentration have larger profit margins and experience more lucrative horizontal merger and acquisition deals. Grullon et al. (2019) identify that the increase in profitability in more concentrated industries can be attributed to lower levels of contestability resulting from increased barriers to entry to the industry. Therefore, lower numbers of competitors allow industry market shareholders to gain wider profits through higher prices and lower production costs. Firms, therefore, seem to benefit from a profitability perspective when they are industry-concentrated.

Gao et al. (2008) state that corporations are ever-expanding their business operations far beyond their headquarters to tap into assets found in those locations, such as larger consumer bases, skilled workforces, proximity to certain natural resources, lower taxes and/or certain corporate tax breaks. However, Gao et al. (2008) reveal that geographic dispersion does affect firm valuation. Specifically, they document that firms that are geographically dispersed, meaning firms that have subsidiaries located in different regions in the USA, experience a valuation discount of 6.2% after controlling for global and industrial diversifications. The results show that as firms become more geographically dispersed by expanding their operations to different regions, the valuation discount increases and, therefore, geographic locations have significant implications for firm valuation.

Landier et al. (2009) suggest that the geographical dispersion of firms, which they define as companies that have a distance between their respective divisions and their headquarters, has an effect on corporate decision-making. Landier et al. (2009) report that geographically dispersed firms are less employee-friendly and those divisions of firms that are geographically closer to their headquarters are less likely to face layoffs. Divisions near headquarters perform significantly worse financially before managers consider divesting or restructuring them.

García and Norli (2012) define geographic dispersion as the number of US states mentioned in the 10-K annual reports that are filed with the SEC. They relate the number of states mentioned in these filing to the number of states that these firms operate in (have business/economic activities in). They create stock return portfolios by geographic dispersion, whereby the local portfolio includes firms that operate in a number of states below the 20th percentile number of states and the dispersed portfolio includes firms that operate in a number of states above the 80th percentile number of states.

Shi et al. (2015) analyse how the earnings management choice between real activities management and accrual-based management is affected by the geographic dispersion of a firm's operations. They define geographic dispersion as the count of the states that are mentioned in the 10-K annual reports filed with the SEC, which is based on the same measure for geographic dispersion that García and Norli (2012) constructed. They reveal that compared with geographically concentrated firms, geographically dispersed firms have higher real earnings management and lower accrual-based management; therefore, dispersed firms prefer real activities management, while concentrated firms tend to prefer accrual-based management. They indicate this effect is due to geographically dispersed firms being in possession of a much wider investor base. These firms typically receive more attention from the media, analysts and financial institutions because if dispersed firms engaged in more accrual-based management, they are exposed to more outside scrutiny.

Platikanova and Mattei (2016) create a normalised measure for geographic dispersion, namely, concentration. They then use concentration as the independent variable and the accuracy of financial analysts' forecasts as the dependent variable. The authors find that for geographically dispersed firms, financial analysts issue less reliable and more biased earnings forecasts, while geographically concentrated firms have more reliable earnings forecasts due to the cost of information gathering being lower.

3 Hypothesis Development

Platikanova and Mattei (2016) state that local and dispersed firms may have varying degrees of information asymmetry due to diversification-related information problems. Thomas (2002) declares that the aggregation of financial information is this type of problem for dispersed firms. Abarbanell and Lehavy (2003) find that asymmetric information exists because, for geographically dispersed firms, managers are privy to more information than outside investors because they can observe cash flows in each state that the company has operations in, while outside investors can only observe noisy estimates of these cash flows.

Prior studies find empirical evidence that more geographically dispersed firms are more likely to issue yearly and quarterly filings with delay, can restate information segments related to sales and have more discretionary managed earnings. They mention that all these factors contribute to information asymmetry. Welch (1989) finds that when managers have more information, it typically leads to underpricing. The hypothesis is presented as follows: Underpricing is more (less) for firms with more (less) geographically dispersed economic activities.

3.1 Geographic Dispersion Sample Selection and Data Sources

The US Securities and Exchange Commission (SEC) requires an annual 10-K report that gives a comprehensive summary of a public company's performance and operations. Public companies must file such 10-K reports with the SEC within 90 days after the end of their fiscal year. The 10-K statement provides information about the evolution of a company in a fiscal year and reports its financial data (García & Norli, 2012).

Four sections of the 10-K statements filed with the SEC from 1995 to 2015 are collected, namely, "Item 1: Business", "Item 2: Properties", "Item 6: Selected Financial Data" and "Item 7: Management's Discussion and Analysis" (García & Norli, 2012). States mentioned in the collected four sections of the 10-K annual reports are counted and used to identify the number of states in which the firms operate.

In some cases, there are sections missing within the 10-K annual reports, and to address this issue, 10-K/A reports, known as amended filings, are employed whereby the missing sections are added. There are instances where there are no 10-K filings available, and the same procedure, i.e. counting mentioned state names, is repeated for the 10-K405, 10-KSB, 10-KT, 10KSB and 10KT405 filings and the amendments to these filings. Only state names in one filing are counted per year (García & Norli, 2012).

Two measures of geographic dispersion are then constructed, namely, the number of states basis and the concentration basis. Firstly, firms that have operations in a small number of states in the USA are classified as local firms, and firms that have operations in many states across the USA are classified as dispersed. Secondly, firms that have high levels of concentration are classified as local firms, while firms with low levels of concentration are classified as dispersed firms.

3.1.1 Number of States as a Measure of Geographic Dispersion

The degree of geographic dispersion is determined based on the number of US state names that are explored within the four sections of the filed 10-K annual reports. Therefore, firm i based on the fiscal year t has a geographic dispersion that is an integer between 1 and 50, as there are 50 states in the USA. Hence, the geographic dispersion for firm i in year t is the count from the last annual report filed prior to December of year t (García & Norli, 2012).

Desai et al. (2017) shows the number of companies that filed 10-K reports with the SEC and went public each year for the period of 1995–2015, the cross-sectional

Fig. 1 Cross-sectional average number of US states per year

Table 1 Summary statistics on geographic dispersion (number of states)

	Number of firms	Geographic dispersion (number of states)							
		Mean	Std.	Min	Max	20%	40%	60%	80%
Average	195	7.57	6.84	1	50	2.89	4.58	6.70	10.59
Median	147	7.81	6.67	1	50	3.00	5.00	6.00	10.00
Minimum	21	5.32	4.31	1	50	2.00	3.00	5.00	7.00
Maximum	676	9.47	9.23	1	50	4.00	6.00	9.00	14.80

average number of states that these companies operate in and the standard deviation. Hence, of the 440 companies that filed 10-K annual reports with the SEC and went public in 1995, on average each company operates in 6.49 states, with a standard deviation of 6.63 states.

Figure 1 illustrates the yearly cross-sectional average number of states for the period of 1995–2015. The mean number of states that firms operate in is close to being stable over time between 1995 and 1999, with firms operating in six to seven states on average. A small decline is observed in the year 2000 when, on average, firms operate in 5.32 states, most probably due to the crash of the dot.com bubble causing firms to concentrate their operations. From the year 2001 to 2015, firms have operations in seven to ten states in the USA on average.

Table 1 shows the summary statistics for geographic dispersion. A substantial variation in the geographic dispersion measure (number of US states that firms operate in) is observed with an average of 6.84 states. The cross-sectional variation varies between a minimum of 4.31 states and a maximum of 9.23 states. The average number of (i.e. see Fig. 2), which is calculated as the average of the cross-sectional average time series for the period of 1995–2015. The median number of states that firms operate in, which is calculated as the median of the cross-sectional average time series, is 7.81 states. The minimum average of states that firms operate in is 5.32 states, and the maximum average of states that firms operate in is 9.47 states. Table 1, Panel B, shows the mean, standard deviation and median of the firm characteristics. The mean underpricing for the data set is 24.69%. Underpricing experiences large standard deviations from the mean of up to 62.50%. The median underpricing is 9.39% (Figs. 2 and 3).

Figure 3 reveals the number of Local and Dispersed firms in the United States. We observe that across our sample the dispersed firms are the majority while over

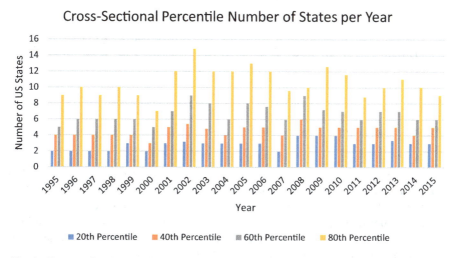

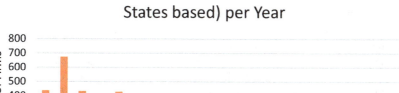

Fig. 2 Cross-sectional percentile number of states per year

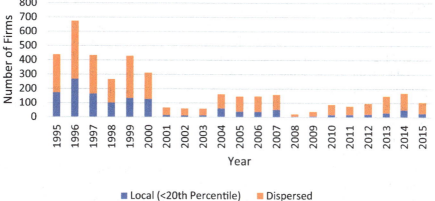

Fig. 3 Number of local and dispersed firms (number of states based) per year

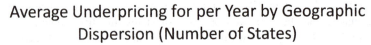

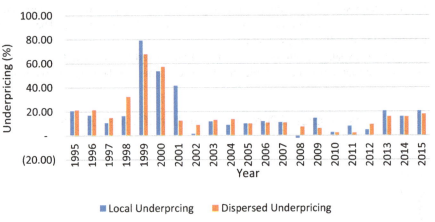

Fig. 4 Average underpricing per year by geographic dispersion (number of states)

the last ten years there are very few local companies. This is a general trend as enterprises diversity their operations.

Figure 4 shows the average cross-sectional underpricing for the local and dispersed portfolios per year for the time period 1995–2015. As discussed, a local firm is defined as a firm that operates in three or fewer states, and dispersed firms are defined as firms that operate in more than three states. Large underpricing is observed in the late 1990s and early 2000s.

Figure 5 also shows the same for leverage, revision, natural log of IPO proceeds, overhang, natural log of total assets and natural log of firm age. The median underpricing for dispersed firms is therefore 12.93%, and for local firms, it is 11.83%, indicating that geographic dispersion could potentially help to explain underpricing. Thus, the hypothesis that underpricing is higher for more geographically dispersed firms may hold true. The median revision for local firms is 0.60% and for dispersed firms it is −0.85%. The medians for leverage, natural log of IPO proceeds, overhang, natural log of total assets and natural log of firm age are higher for dispersed firms.

Table 2 shows the summary statistics on concentration as a measure of geographic dispersion. The average and the median for the cross-sectional average concentration time series is 0.39, the minimum is 0.26 and the maximum is 0.47. A significant variation in concentration is observed with an average variation of 0.23, a median variation of 0.24, and fluctuates between 0.17 and 0.28. On average 195 firms filed annual reports with the SEC and went public each year for the time period 1995 to 2015. The median number of firms that went public each year is 147 firms. The minimum number of firms that went public in a year is 21 firms and the maximum is 676 firms. The minimum is 0.36 and the maximum is 0.74. Firms that have a concentration of more than 0.56 are classified as local firms.

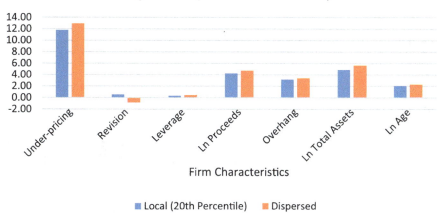

Fig. 5 Median firm characteristics by geographic dispersion (number of states)

Table 2 Summary statistics on geographic dispersion (concentration)

	Number of firms	Geographic dispersion (concentration)							
		Mean	Std.	Min	Max	20%	40%	60%	80%
Average	195	0.39	0.23	1	50	0.19	0.29	0.41	0.56
Median	147	0.39	0.24	1	50	0.19	0.30	0.40	0.56
Minimum	21	0.26	0.17	1	50	0.12	0.18	0.27	0.36
Maximum	676	0.47	0.28	1	50	0.25	0.35	0.49	0.74

3.1.2 Concentration as a Measure of Geographic Dispersion

Building on the number of states measured for geographic dispersion, concentration as a measure for geographic dispersion is constructed. The number of states measured captures the economic ties between a company's headquarters and its geographically dispersed operations, such as plants and equipment, store locations, office locations and acquisition activities, which are reported in the 10-K reports (Platikanova & Mattei, 2016).

The concentration measure is constructed by computing a normalised Herfindahl-Hirschman Index (HHI) of state activities (Platikanova & Mattei, 2016). Firstly, the sum of the squared relative state counts for firm i in year t ($SS_{i,t}$) is calculated as follows:

$$SS_{i,t} = \left(\frac{\#\text{Texas}_{i,t}}{\#\text{Total US States}_{i,t}}\right)^2 + \cdots + \left(\frac{\#\text{Washington}_{i,t}}{\#\text{Total US States}_{i,t}}\right)^2 + \cdots + \left(\frac{\#\text{Florida}_{i,t}}{\#\text{Total US States}_{i,t}}\right)^2$$

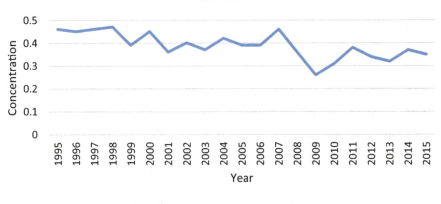

Fig. 6 Cross-sectional average concentration per year

Once $SS_{i,t}$ is calculated, the concentration measure can be calculated as follows:

$$\text{Concentration}_{i,t} = \frac{SS_{i,t} - (1/50)}{1 - (1/50)}$$

Therefore, if a firm has operations that are concentrated in only one state, the concentration measure will be equal to 1. If a firm has operations that are equally concentrated across every 50 US states, the concentration measure will be equal to zero. Therefore, a higher concentration value indicates that a firm's business activities are concentrated in a smaller number of states.

The study shows the cross-sectional average of concentration and the standard deviation per year for companies that filed 10-K annual reports with the SEC that went public in the 1995–2015 period. Therefore, the 440 companies that filed annual reports with the SEC and went public in 1995 have a concentration of 0.46 on average, with a standard deviation of 0.26 from the mean.

Figure 6 shows the yearly cross-sectional average concentration for the 1995–2015 period. Concentration is observed to be stable over time from 1995 to 1998, with a decrease in concentration (geographic expansion) being observed in 1999 due to the Internet boom and the excessive growth that took place at the time. In the year 2000, concentration increases, potentially indicating the crash of the dot.com bubble. From 2007 to 2009, concentration decreases, but it rises again thereafter as the effects of the financial crisis come into play. From 2011 to 2015, the cross-sectional average concentration fluctuates between 0.35 and 0.38.

Figure 7 shows the yearly cross-sectional 20th, 40th, 60th and 80th percentile concentrations for the time period 1995–2015. The 80th percentile concentration

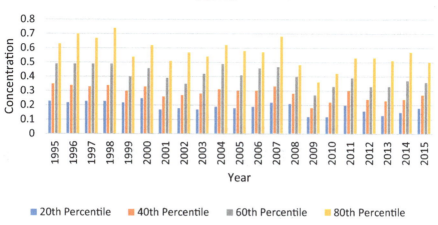

Fig. 7 Cross-sectional percentile of concentration time series

for the year 1995 is 0.63. The highest 80th percentile concentration is 0.74 in 1998. The lowest 80th percentile concentration is 0.36 in 2009. Figure 8 shows the number of firms classified as local and dispersed by concentration for the 1995–2015 period. The median for the cross-sectional 80th percentile time series is 0.56 and is employed to create local and dispersed portfolios. Of the 440 companies that filed 10-K annual reports with the SEC and went public in 1995, 116 companies are classified as local, while 324 are classified as dispersed.

3.1.3 Concentration and Other Firm Characteristics

Figure 9 shows the medians for underpricing, revision, leverage, natural log of IPO proceeds, overhang, natural log of total assets and natural log of firm age for local and dispersed firms for the time period 1995–2015. The median underpricing for local firms is 9.30%, and the median underpricing for dispersed firms is 9.44%, indicating that geographic dispersion could help to explain underpricing and thus the hypothesis that underpricing is more evident for more geographically dispersed firms could hold true. The median revision is 0% for both the local and dispersed portfolios. The medians for leverage, natural log of IPO proceeds, overhang, natural log of total assets and the natural log of firm age are all larger for dispersed firms.

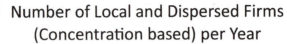

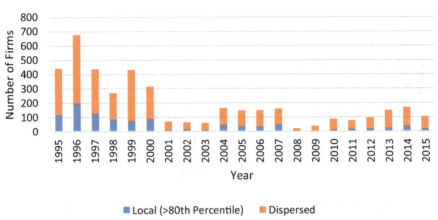

Fig. 8 Number of local and dispersed firms (concentration based) per year

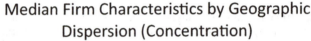

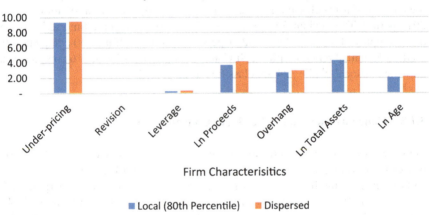

Fig. 9 Median firm characteristics by geographic dispersion (concentration based)

3.2 Litigation (Accounting Fraud)

Based on the finding that more geographically dispersed firms potentially experience more underpricing, it is interesting to see if geographic dispersion could also increase the likelihood of a firm committing accounting fraud, as accounting compliance can be harder to monitor and enforce when a firm's operations are highly dispersed across the USA. Data on accounting fraud are therefore collected through the *Stanford Law School Securities Class Action Clearinghouse*. This resource provides a detailed case summary and the full class action complaint form for any litigation issues associated with a public company. The case summary is investigated for the possible mentioning of accounting fraud, and if not found, the full class action is investigated for the potential mentioning thereof.

Accounting fraud involves intentionally misrepresenting or altering financial records to manipulate the financial health of a company. This includes overstating revenue/sales, underrepresenting or hiding costs and purposefully misstating assets and liabilities. It also involves inflating the value of a company's stock, illegally obtaining better financing and avoiding paying back debt.

Having already collected data on geographic dispersion and other firm characteristics, a litigation dummy variable can now be created that receives the value of 1 if a company has been identified as having committed accounting fraud, and 0 otherwise. The litigation dummy variable makes it possible to investigate through logistic regression models if geographic dispersion could increase the likelihood of a firm committing accounting fraud while controlling for other firm characteristics.

3.3   Explanatory Variables for Underpricing and Litigation

The median underpricing for dispersed firms is higher than for local firms, and it gives the rationale for a deeper dive into underpricing and geographic dispersion. The phenomenon of underpricing is complex, and comparing underpricing between local and dispersed portfolios is insufficient to make inferences.

Control variables, such as the other firm characteristics discussed, are required to potentially help explain underpricing. These firm characteristics are also suitable as control variables for investigating whether more geographically dispersed firms are more likely to commit accounting fraud.

4   Empirical Results

4.1   Introduction

In this section, regression analysis is conducted to investigate the relationship between geographic dispersion and underpricing while controlling for leverage, revision, IPO proceeds, overhang and total firm assets. The hypothesis states that there is no statistically significant relationship between geographic dispersion and underpricing in a large sample of US publicly listed firms spanning 1995–2015.

Year and industry fixed effects are controlled for to determine if the fixed effects explain the significance of geographic dispersion as a determinant of underpricing.

Robustness tests are conducted using different measures for geographic dispersion to test if the assumptions made are true. Logistic models are developed to investigate if more geographically dispersed firms are more likely to commit accounting fraud while controlling for firm characteristics similar to those used in the underpricing models. The empirical results are reported and discussed within the framework of relevant literature in the field.

4.2 Main Findings/Results

4.2.1 Underpricing and Geographic Dispersion (Local Firm 20) Regressions

After developing the geographic dispersion measures (number of states and concentration) and collecting the data, the next step involves running regression models with underpricing as the dependent variable and geographic dispersion as the independent variable while controlling for the other firm characteristics. The first step in running regression models is to set up the and alternative hypotheses. The hypothesis is defined as follows:

H1: There is no relationship between the independent variable (geographic dispersion and other control variables) and the dependent variable (underpricing). The opposite is true for the alternative hypothesis (Table 2).

Regression models are developed by adding a control variable for each consecutive model to investigate if geographic dispersion loses its significance as a determinant of underpricing when adding a specific control variable. The effects that geographic dispersion has on underpricing, as presented in Tables 3 and 4, are estimated with the model:

$$
\begin{aligned}
\text{Underpricing}_{i,t} = {} & \beta_0 + \beta_1 \text{Local Firm } 20_{i,t} + \beta_2 \text{Leverage}_{i,t} + \beta_3 \text{VC}_{i,t} \\
& + \beta_4 \text{Revision}_{i,t} + \beta_5 \text{Ln Total Assets}_{i,t} + \beta_6 \text{Overhang}_{i,t} \\
& + \beta_7 \text{Prestigious Underwriter}_{i,t} + \beta_8 \text{New York}_{i,t} \\
& + \beta_9 \text{Hot Market}_{i,t} + \beta_{10} \text{Auditor04}_{i,t} + \varepsilon_{i,t}
\end{aligned}
$$

$$(1)$$

In model, controlling for firm leverage, the null hypothesis that geographic dispersion does not have a statistically significant effect on underpricing is not rejected at the 10% significance level. Leverage has a statistically significant effect on underpricing at the 1% significance level. All else remaining equal, if the firm's leverage increases by 1%, the average underpricing will be reduced by 0.2479%. The finding that leverage is significantly negatively associated with underpricing supports the findings of Habib and Ljungqvist (2015).

It also controls for leverage and whether the firm was backed by a venture capitalist; the coefficient for geographic dispersion is negative and significant at the 10% significance level. Hence, if a firm is classified as a local firm, and all

Table 3 Underpricing and geographic dispersion (local firm 20)

Underpricing	1	2	3	4	5
Panel A. Dependent variable: underpricing					
Intercept	35.313**** (12.76)	26.580**** (8.65)	25.341**** (8.03)	20.813**** (5.90)	19.221**** (5.34)
Local firm 20	−2.103 (−1.06)	−3.291* (−1.73)	−3.557* (−1.95)	−3.656* (−1.95)	−3.832** (−2.02)
Leverage	−24.799**** (−5.07)	−19.156**** (−4.51)	−14.843**** (−3.32)	−19.025*** (−2.76)	−20.004*** (−2.83)
VC		16.011**** (7.07)	13.457**** (6.07)	13.566**** (5.56)	11.701**** (4.64)
Revision			1.264**** (20.08)	1.264**** (20.72)	1.244**** (19.63)
Ln total assets				1.217* (1.73)	0.925 (1.25)
Overhang					1.177** (2.15)
Year FE	No	No	No	No	No
Industry FE	No	No	No	No	No
Adjusted R^2	0.0212	0.0361	0.1064	0.1098	0.1171
Number of observations	3982	3982	3934	3804	3724
Panel B. Dependent variable: underpricing					
Intercept	31.560**** (19.73)	26.496**** (13.76)	25.919**** (13.63)	16.159**** (3.94)	15.079**** (3.60)
Local firm 20	−4.077** (−1.99)	−4.503** (−2.20)	−4.832** (−2.40)	−4.721** (−2.27)	−4.745** (−2.25)
Leverage	−13.769**** (−5.14)	−11.822**** (−4.37)	−8.788*** (−3.29)	−12.438*** (−3.55)	−13.740*** (−3.79)
VC		10.316**** (4.69)	7.802**** (3.59)	8.168**** (3.67)	7.220*** (3.19)
Revision			1.044**** (14.32)	1.020**** (13.26)	1.012**** (12.91)
Ln total assets				2.232*** (2.82)	2.099** (2.53)
Overhang					0.779*** (3.74)
Year FE	Yes	Yes	Yes	Yes	Yes
Industry FE	Yes	Yes	Yes	Yes	Yes
Adjusted R^2	0.1121	0.1168	0.1606	0.1629	0.1657
Number of observations	3982	3982	3934	3804	3724

Notes: This table reports the effect a firm's geographic dispersion has on underpricing. The dependent variable is underpricing, and the independent variables include geographic dispersion (local firm 20 dummy variable) and a variety of controls that have been identified in other literature. The coefficient, standard error and statistical significance for the intercept and each independent variable are given. ***, ** and * denote statistically significant coefficients at the 1, 5 and 10% levels, respectively. **** denotes a p-value of less than 0.1%

Table 4 Underpricing and geographic dispersion (local firm 20) models (6–10)

Underpricing	6	7	8	9	10
Panel A. Dependent variable: underpricing					
Intercept	23.136****(5.82)	17.022****(4.61)	−0.025(−0.01)	−1.244(−0.30)	2.308(0.44)
Local firm 20	−4.056**(−2.13)	−4.307**(−2.26)	−4.683**(−2.45)	−4.676**(−2.45)	−4.451**(−2.31)
Leverage	−18.816***(−2.81)	−18.486***(−2.75)	−19.153***(−2.69)	−18.893***(−2.67)	−13.555***(−3.16)
VC	10.231****(3.93)	8.130***(2.98)	9.988****(3.67)	9.389****(3.25)	9.282****(3.54)
Revision	1.209****(19.26)	1.189****(19.06)	1.089****(17.32)	1.090****(17.38)	1.087****(18.02)
Ln total assets	−0.696(−0.91)	1.308(1.62)	2.997***(3.21)	2.804***(2.99)	
Overhang	1.064**(2.08)	1.082**(2.18)	1.023**(2.18)	1.024**(2.18)	0.749**(2.26)
Prestigious underwriter	12.445****(4.66)	13.461****(4.87)	11.858****(4.44)	11.524****(4.43)	12.457****(4.47)
New York		−16.807****(−7.00)	−14.572****(−6.48)	−14.664****(−6.47)	−13.415****(−6.54)
Hot market			14.368****(7.71)	14.645****(7.69)	14.348****(7.92)
Auditor4				3.321*(1.68)	3.639*(1.76)
Ln proceeds					2.103*(1.96)
Year FE	No	No	No	No	No
Industry FE	No	No	No	No	No
Adjusted R^2	0.1242	0.1314	0.1411	0.1414	0.1350
Number of observations	3724	3724	3724	3724	3852

Panel B. Dependent variable: underpricing. Controlling for year and industry fixed effects

Intercept	17.775****(4.16)	14.276***(3.25)	11.549**(2.17)	11.090**(2.07)	17.763***(3.06)
Local firm 20	−4.860**(−2.31)	−4.887**(−2.32)	−4.861**(−2.31)	−4.852**(−2.30)	−4.682**(−2.28)
Leverage	−13.254****(−3.66)	−13.274****(−3.67)	−13.309****(−3.68)	−13.227****(−3.66)	−9.618****(−3.50)
VC	6.675***(2.94)	5.711**(2.50)	5.729**(2.51)	5.511**(2.39)	5.494**(2.44)
Revision	1.000****(12.75)	0.996****(12.72)	0.992****(12.63)	0.993****(12.64)	1.000****(13.00)
Ln total assets	1.053(1.18)	2.180**(2.29)	2.183**(2.29)	2.092**(2.17)	
Overhang	0.732****(3.50)	0.750****(3.59)	0.750****(3.60)	0.753****(3.61)	0.555***(3.20)
Prestigious underwriter	7.080***(3.15)	7.931****(3.51)	7.937****(3.51)	7.813****(3.44)	8.999****(4.03)
New York		−10.160****(−3.31)	−10.179****(−3.31)	−10.245****(−3.33)	−8.305***(−2.72)
Hot market			4.376(0.91)	4.375(0.91)	4.346(0.92)
Auditor4				1.465(0.66)	2.060(0.95)
Ln proceeds					0.408(0.32)
Year FE	Yes	Yes	Yes	Yes	Yes
Industry FE	Yes	Yes	Yes	Yes	Yes
Adjusted R^2	0.1677	0.1700	0.1699	0.1698	0.1669
Number of observations	3724	3724	3724	3724	3852

Notes: This table builds on Table 5 and shows another four regression models continuing to add a control variable with each model. Ln total assets in model 9 is switched with Ln IPO proceeds, creating model 10. Panel B estimates are obtained with controlling for year and industry fixed effects. ***, ** and * denote statistically significant coefficients at the 1, 5 and 10% levels, respectively. **** denotes a p-value of less than 0.1%

else remains equal, the average underpricing will be reduced by 3.29%. Leverage provides similar results. The VC-backed firm dummy variable's coefficient is positive and statistically significant at the 1% level of significance. Therefore, if a firm is backed by a venture capitalist, and all else is kept equal, the average underpricing will be increased by 16.01%. The finding that VC backing is associated with higher underpricing is consistent with Hamao et al. (2001) and Georgakopoulos et al. (2022).

We further control for leverage, VC-backed firms and revision, and the coefficient for geographic dispersion is negative and significant at the 10% significance level. Therefore, ceteris paribus, if a firm is classified as local, the average underpricing will be reduced by 3.56%. The coefficient for leverage is negative and significant at the 1% significance level. Ceteris paribus, a 1% increase in leverage will lead to a 0.148% reduction in the average underpricing. The VC-backed variable delivers similar results to model 2. The coefficient for revision is positive and statistically significant at the 1% significance level. Thus, if IPO revision increases by 1%, average underpricing will increase by 0.012%. The finding that an increase in revision is associated with higher underpricing is consistent with the findings of Ljungqvist and Wilhelm (2002).

We continue by controlling for leverage, VC, revision and natural log of total assets; the null hypothesis that geographic dispersion does not have a significant effect on underpricing is rejected at the 10% significance level. Ceteris paribus, if a firm is classified as local, average underpricing will be reduced by 3.66%. Leverage, VC and revision deliver similar results to previous models. The natural log of total assets coefficient is positive and significant at the 10% significance level. Therefore, ceteris paribus, if the log of total assets increases by one unit, the average underpricing will increase by 1.217%. The finding that a larger total asset value is associated with higher underpricing is in contrast to Lowry and Murphy (2006) hypothesis that larger firms with greater assets have less underpricing. The finding is consistent with the results regarding geographic dispersion, as larger firms with greater assets are dispersed and are associated with higher underpricing.

Then we control for the same variables as previously and add the overhang variable; the coefficient for geographic dispersion is negative and significant at the 5% significance level. Therefore, ceteris paribus, if a firm is classified as a local firm, average underpricing will be reduced by 3.83%. Leverage, VC and revision deliver similar results. The coefficient for overhang is positive and significant at the 5% significance level. Ceteris paribus, a 1% increase in overhang leads to a 1.177% increase in average underpricing. The finding that greater overhang is associated with more underpricing is consistent with the findings of Bradley and Jordan (2002) and Lowry and Murphy (2006). When firms issue a smaller number of shares relative to the existing shares, the dilution cost is low, which suggests that underpricing is high.

García and Norli (2012) indicate that measures of geographic dispersion could have a strong correlation with industry groups or with the year the IPO occurred; therefore, the findings discussed above can be caused by IPO year or industry fixed effects rather than geographic dispersion. This concern is addressed in the Panel

B regression models. By running the same models while controlling for industry and year fixed effects, the null hypothesis that geographic dispersion does not have a statistically significant effect on underpricing is rejected at the 5% level of significance for all five models. Therefore, the industry and year fixed effects do not explain the significance of geographic dispersion as a determinant of underpricing. Depending on the model, when controlling for fixed effects, ceteris paribus, if a firm is local, average underpricing will be reduced between 4.08 and 4.75%. All other control variables are also statistically significant and affect underpricing.

We continue by controlling for the same variables as previously and add a prestigious underwriter rank dummy variable that is 1 if the underwriter has a rank of 9; the coefficient for geographic dispersion is negative and significant at the 5% significance level. All else being equal, if a company is classified as a local firm, average underpricing will be reduced by 4.056%. The coefficient for prestigious underwriter is positive and significant at the 1% significance level. All else being equal, if the underwriter's rank is 9, average underpricing will increase by 12.45%. The other control variables deliver similar results. The finding that a high underwriter rank is associated with more underpricing is consistent with the findings of Loughran and Ritter (2004), who state that this is due to highly respected and high performing analysts having the leverage to underprice IPO shares.

Further testings take place by adding the New York dummy variable, which is 1 if a firm is listed on the NYSE and 0 otherwise; the coefficient for geographic dispersion is negative and significant at the 5% level of significance. Ceteris paribus, if a firm is classified as a local firm, the average underpricing will be reduced by 4.31%. The coefficient for the NYSE listing variable is negative and significant at the 1% significance level. Therefore, if a firm is listed on the NYSE, average underpricing will reduce by 16.81%.

We continue by including the *Hot Market* dummy variable, which is 1 in years of a bullish market and 0 otherwise; the coefficient for geographic dispersion is negative and significant at the 5% significance level. If else is kept equal, if a firm is classified as local, average underpricing will be reduced by 4.68%. Controlling for the hot market dummy variable, the constant loses its statistical significance. The natural log of total assets becomes statistically significant at the 5% significance level again. Ceteris paribus, a one-unit change in the natural log of total assets will increase average underpricing by 2.99%. The hot dummy variable is statistically significant with effect on underpricing at the 1% significance level. If a firm issues in a hot market year, underpricing increases by 14.37%. This finding is consistent with Ritter (1984), Bradley and Jordan (2002), Loughran and Ritter (2004), Gounopoulos and Pham (2017), Gounopoulos and Pham (2018), Colak et al. (2021b) and Gounopoulos et al. (2022). When controlling for year and industry fixed effects, the hot market dummy variable is no longer significantly associated with underpricing.

We make a step forward by adding the *Auditor4* dummy variable, which is 1 if a firm was audited by one of the Big 4 auditors and 0 otherwise; the coefficient for geographic dispersion is negative and significant at the 5% significance level. This means that if a firm is classified as a local firm, average underpricing will be reduced by 4.68%. The coefficient for the Auditor4 variable is positive and significant at the 10% significance level, and, all else being equal, if a firm is audited by a Big 4 firm, the average underpricing will be increased by 3.32%. The finding that a Big 4 auditor is associated with more underpricing contradicts Habib and Ljungqvist (2015); however, when controlling for year and industry fixed effects, the Big 4 auditor dummy variable is no longer significantly associated with underpricing.

Next, we control for the same variables as previously but switch the natural log of total assets variable with the natural log of IPO proceeds variable:

$$\begin{aligned} \text{Underpricing}_{i,t} = \ & \beta_0 + \beta_1 \text{Local Firm } 20_{i,t} + \beta_2 \text{Leverage}_{i,t} + \beta_3 \text{VC}_{i,t} \\ & + \beta_4 \text{Revision}_{i,t} + \beta_6 \text{Overhang}_{i,t} + \beta_7 \text{Prestigious Underwriter}_{i,t} \\ & + \beta_8 \text{New York}_{i,t} + \beta_9 \text{Hot Market}_{i,t} + \beta_{10} \text{Auditor04}_{i,t} \\ & + \beta_{11} \text{Ln Proceeds}_{i,t} + \varepsilon_{i,t} \end{aligned}$$

$$(2)$$

This is due to the variables being strongly correlated. The model delivers similar results to model 9; however, the adjusted R^2 is reduced from 0.141 to 0.135. IPO proceeds are significantly positively related to underpricing at the 10% significance level but lose significance when controlling for year and industry fixed effects. This supports the findings by Carter and Manaster (1990) and Cliff and Denis (2004) that proceeds do not significantly help to explain underpricing.

Panel B gives the coefficients and standard error for the variables of the same models that were run in Panel A, but controlling for industry and year fixed effects to investigate if these fixed effects explain the significance of geographic dispersion as a determinant of underpricing. The coefficient for geographic dispersion is negative and significant at the 5% significance level. Thus, industry and year fixed effects do not explain the significance of geographic dispersion as a determinant of underpricing. Depending on the model, ceteris paribus, if a firm is classified as a local firm, the average underpricing will be reduced by 4.68–4.89%.

4.2.2 Robustness Test with Concentration as a Measure of Geographic Dispersion

Table 5 investigates if there is a relationship between concentration and underpricing. When controlling for firm leverage at the time of IPO, the results show that the hypothesis cannot be rejected at the 10% level of significance and that geographic dispersion (concentration) does not have a statistically significant effect on underpricing. This is the same result reported in baseline model. The results indicates that there is a statistically significant relationship between concentration and underpricing. Thus, if a firm has high concentration, average underpricing will be reduced between 6.66–6.904%, depending on the model. The robustness tests support the finding that geographic dispersion has a statistically significant effect on underpricing and initial returns are lower for firms with less geographically dispersed economic activities.

Table 5 Underpricing and geographic dispersion (concentration) models (11–15)

Underpricing	11	12	13	14	15
Intercept	36.700****(11.36)	27.014*****(7.64)	27.014*****(7.64)	22.527****(5.74)	20.762****(5.20)
Concentration	−4.989(−1.58)	−6.904**(−2.38)	−6.904**(−2.38)	−6.754**(−2.26)	−6.657**(−2.23)
Leverage	−24.821****(−5.09)	−14.788*****(−3.33)	−14.788*****(−3.33)	−18.896***(−2.73)	−19.846***(−2.80)
VC		13.456****(6.05)	13.456****(6.05)	13.541****(5.53)	11.668****(4.61)
Revision			1.263****(20.14)	1.263****(20.73)	1.243****(19.63)
Ln total assets				1.185*(1.68)	0.912(1.23)
Overhang					1.171**(2.15)
Year FE	No	No	No	No	No
Industry FE	No	No	No	No	No
Adjusted R^2	0.0214	0.1064	0.1064	0.1097	0.1170
Number of observations	3982	3934	3934	3804	3724

Notes: This table tabulates additional empirical tests using concentration as the measure for geographic dispersion as a robustness check. The estimates are obtained without controlling for fixed effects. ***, ** and * denote statistically significant coefficients at the 1, 5 and 10% levels, respectively. **** denotes a p-value of less than 0.1%

Table 6 uses concentration as the measure for geographic dispersion instead of the local firm 20 dummy variable. The hypothesis that geographic dispersion does not have an effect on underpricing is rejected at the 5% level of significance. Ceteris paribus, if a firm has a concentration of 1, average underpricing will be reduced by 6.43%. There is thus a 99% confidence level that concentration has a statistically significant relationship with underpricing. If an enterprise has a complete concentration, average underpricing will be reduced by 8.23%. The robustness test supports that geographic dispersion does have a statistically significant effect on underpricing and that underpricing is less for firms with less geographically dispersed economic activities.

4.2.3 Robustness Test with Local Firm 80 as Measure of Geographic Dispersion

Table 7 shows results using the local firm 80 dummy variable as the measure for geographic dispersion. The hypothesis that geographic dispersion does not have a statistically significant effect on underpricing is rejected at a 1% level of significance for all five models. Therefore, depending on the model, if a firm is classified as a local firm (has a concentration larger than 0.56), average underpricing will be reduced by 4.67–5.73%. The robustness tests support the findings that geographic dispersion does have a statistically significant effect on underpricing and that underpricing is less for low geographically dispersed firm's economic activities.

The results of Table 8 reveal that if a firm is classified as a 'local', the mean underpricing will be 4.77–5.07% less than for 'dispersed' characterised firms. The results indicate that underpricing is lower for firms with less geographically dispersed economic activities.

4.2.4 Geographic Dispersion and Litigation (Accounting Fraud) Regressions

Logistic regression models are developed to investigate whether firms that have more geographically dispersed economic activities are more likely to commit accounting fraud compared to more geographically concentrated firms. The likelihood of committing accounting fraud as a function of geographic dispersion is estimated by running logistic regression models, starting with controlling for one variable and adding a control variable for every model thereafter, to investigate if geographic dispersion loses its significance as a determinant of the increased likelihood of accounting fraud when controlling for a specific variable:

$$
\begin{aligned}
\text{Accounting Fraud}_{i,t} = {} & \beta_0 + \beta_1 \text{Number of States}_{i,t} + \beta_2 \text{VC}_{i,t} + \beta_3 \text{Leverage}_{i,t} \\
& + \beta_4 \text{Revision}_{i,t} + \beta_5 \text{Overhang}_{i,t} \\
& + \beta_6 \text{Prestigious Underwriter}_{i,t} + \beta_7 \text{New York}_{i,t} \\
& + \beta_8 \text{Hot Market}_{i,t} + \beta_9 \text{Auditor04}_{i,t} + \varepsilon_{i,t}
\end{aligned}
$$

$$(3)$$

Table 6 Underpricing and geographic dispersion (concentration) models (16–20)

Underpricing	16	17	18	19	20
Intercept	24.365****(5.65)	19.025****(4.72)	2.197(0.49)	0.928(0.21)	4.800(0.85)
Concentration	−6.426**(−2.17)	−8.231***(−2.69)	−9.082***(−2.94)	−8.873***(−2.91)	−8.241***(−2.63)
Leverage	−18.649***(−2.78)	−18.326***(−2.71)	−18.981***(−2.66)	−18.732***(−2.63)	−13.378***(−3.16)
VC	10.195****(3.90)	8.082****(2.95)	9.941****(3.64)	9.369****(3.23)	9.249****(3.52)
Revision	1.207****(19.25)	1.188****(19.05)	1.088****(17.29)	1.089****(17.35)	1.088****(18.07)
Ln total assets	−0.672(−0.88)	1.327*(1.65)	3.017***(3.22)	2.838***(3.03)	
Overhang	1.059**(2.08)	1.077**(2.17)	1.017**(2.17)	1.018**(2.18)	0.746**(2.25)
Prestigious underwriter	12.327****(4.64)	13.349****(4.86)	11.733****(4.42)	11.416****(4.41)	12.450****(4.47)
New York		−17.159****(−7.00)	−14.958****(−6.51)	−15.034****(−6.49)	−13.601****(−6.58)
Hot market			14.395****(7.73)	14.654****(7.70)	14.253****(7.92)
Auditor4				3.154(1.60)	3.516*(1.71)
Ln proceeds					2.006*(1.86)
Year FE	No	No	No	No	No
Industry FE	No	No	No	No	No
Adjusted R^2	0.1240	0.1314	0.1411	0.1413	0.1350
Number of observations	3724	3724	3724	3724	3852

Notes: This table tabulates additional empirical tests using concentration as the measure for geographic dispersion as a robustness check. The estimates are obtained without controlling for year and industry fixed effects. ***, ** and * denote statistically significant coefficients at the 1, 5 and 10% levels, respectively. **** denotes a p-value of less than 0.1%

Table 7 Underpricing and geographic dispersion (local firm 80) models (21–25)

Underpricing	21	22	23	24	25
Intercept	35.734**** (13.98)	26.750**** (9.23)	25.343**** (8.41)	20.670**** (6.30)	18.875**** (5.58)
Local firm 80	−4.900*** (−2.60)	−5.734*** (−3.09)	−5.334*** (−3.01)	−4.891*** (−2.73)	−4.669*** (−2.62)
Leverage	−24.728**** (−5.14)	−18.954**** (−4.56)	−14.617**** (−3.33)	−18.680*** (−2.70)	−19.619*** (−2.77)
VC		16.012**** (7.02)	13.414**** (6.00)	13.510**** (5.50)	11.644**** (4.59)
Revision			1.261**** (20.11)	1.261**** (20.67)	1.241**** (19.58)
Ln total assets				1.211* (1.72)	0.943 (1.28)
Overhang					1.167** (2.15)
Year FE	No	No	No	No	No
Industry FE	No	No	No	No	No
Adjusted R^2	0.0221	0.0370	0.1070	0.1101	0.1173
Number of observations	3982	3982	3934	3804	3724

Notes: This table tabulates additional empirical tests using the local firm 80 dummy variable as a measure for geographic dispersion as a robustness check. The estimates are obtained without controlling for fixed effects. ***, ** and * denote statistically significant coefficients at the 1, 5 and 10% levels, respectively. **** denotes a p-value of less than 0.1%

Table 8 Underpricing and geographic dispersion (local firm 80) models (26–30)

Underpricing	26	27	28	29	30
Intercept	22.434****(6.07)	16.326****(4.73)	−0.785(−0.19)	−1.994(−0.49)	2.298(0.45)
Local firm 80	−4.313**(−2.46)	−4.774****(−2.69)	−4.952***(−2.79)	−4.857***(−2.76)	−5.076***(−2.82)
Leverage	−18.443***(−2.75)	−18.084***(−2.68)	−18.718***(−2.63)	−18.471***(−2.61)	−13.197****(−3.15)
VC	10.175****(3.88)	8.066***(2.94)	9.902****(3.62)	9.323***(3.21)	9.191****(3.48)
Revision	1.206****(19.20)	1.186****(18.99)	1.086****(17.23)	1.087****(17.29)	1.086****(18.01)
Ln total assets	−0.623(−0.83)	1.389*(1.73)	3.084***(3.29)	2.901***(3.10)	
Overhang	1.057**(2.08)	1.074**(2.18)	1.015*(2.18)	1.016**(2.18)	0.747**(2.26)
Prestigious underwriter	12.247****(4.62)	13.251****(4.84)	11.644****(4.40)	11.325****(4.39)	12.351****(4.45)
New York		−16.897****(−7.02)	−14.671****(−6.50)	−14.756****(−6.49)	−13.360****(−6.56)
Hot market			14.290****(7.71)	14.555****(7.70)	14.175****(7.90)
Auditor4				3.197(1.62)	3.545*(1.72)
Ln proceeds					2.063*(1.95)
Year FE	No	No	No	No	No
Industry FE	No	No	No	No	No
Adjusted R^2	0.1242	0.1314	0.1410	0.1412	0.1351
Number of observations	3724	3724	3724	3724	3852

Notes: This table tabulates additional empirical tests using the local firm 80 dummy variable as the measure for geographic dispersion as a robustness check. The estimates are obtained without controlling for year and industry fixed effects. ***, ** and * denote statistically significant coefficients at the 1, 5 and 10% levels, respectively. **** denotes a p-value of less than 0.1%

Table 9 shows the logistic regression model estimates for all the variables. The models deliver similar results for the control variables that overlap between models, with the pseudo R^2 increasing with each extra control variable that is added. The number of states variable's coefficient is positive, indicating that as the number of states increases, the likelihood of a firm committing accounting fraud also increases, and as the number of states that firms operate in decreases, the likelihood of committing accounting fraud also decreases. The coefficient is statistically significant at the 5% level of significance.

Table 10 shows the logistic regression model estimates. The coefficients are positive for all four models, indicating that firms with more geographically dispersed economic activities are more likely to commit accounting fraud and that firms with less geographically dispersed economic activities are less likely to commit accounting fraud. The number of states coefficient is statistically significant at the 5% level of significance. Therefore, even when controlling for eight other variables, geographic dispersion still has a statistically significant effect on the likelihood of committing accounting fraud.

5 Conclusion

This study examines the association between underpricing, geographic dispersion and the likelihood of accounting fraud. The findings indicate that the geographic dispersion of a firm's operations, measured by the number of states mentioned in its 10-K annual report filed with the SEC, is related to underpricing. Results show a significant negative relationship between underpricing and local firms. The negative association is robust to controls for other significant determinants of underpricing examined in the previous literature, year and industry fixed effects and alternative measures of geographic dispersion. These findings are consistent with the hypothesis that underpricing is more likely among more geographically dispersed firms. Firms that are more geographically dispersed face larger information asymmetry problems, such as the aggregation of financial data across firms.

The study further provides evidence that more geographically dispersed firms are likely to commit accounting fraud than their local counterparts. The finding remains robust for other firm attributes that have been examined in the previous literature. More geographically dispersed firms face larger obstacles in monitoring accounting compliance across states, which may explain this finding.

Managers should be aware that information asymmetries and accounting fraud stem from the geographic dispersion of a firm's operations and economic activities. Managers should thus develop controls and put systems in place to ensure that relevant information can be efficiently aggregated across multiple states and shared with outside investors. Managers should invest in appropriate monitoring and control systems to ensure accounting compliance across states.

Table 9 Geographic dispersion and litigation regression models (31–34)

Accounting fraud	31	32	33	34
Intercept	−4.913**** (19.60)	−4.776**** (−16.19)	−4.798**** (−16.23)	−4.862**** (−15.78)
Number of states	0.029** (2.13)	0.032** (2.39)	0.032** (2.33)	0.031** (2.21)
VC	1.969**** (8.17)	1.881**** (7.49)	1.846**** (7.33)	1.871**** (7.17)
Leverage		−0.291 (−0.76)	−0.205 (−0.54)	−0.332 (−0.81)
Revision			0.013** (2.01)	0.012* (1.79)
Overhang				0.018** (2.18)
Pseudo R^2	0.0809	0.0791	0.0824	0.0880
Number of observations	4104	3982	3934	3852

Notes: This table shows the empirical link between geographic dispersion and accounting fraud while controlling for up to four variables which include other firm. The variables are defined in Table A1. The estimates are obtained without controlling for year and industry fixed effects. ***, ** and * denote statistically significant coefficients at the 1, 5 and 10% levels, respectively. **** denotes a p-value of less than 0.1%

Table 10 Geographic dispersion and litigation regression models (35–38)

Accounting fraud	35	36	37	38
Intercept	−5.025**** (−15.76)	−5.016**** (−15.70)	−5.107**** (−14.23)	−5.043**** (−12.99)
Number of states	0.029** (2.04)	0.029** (2.05)	0.029** (2.05)	0.029** (2.06)
VC	1.812**** (6.89)	1.796**** (6.70)	1.809**** (6.72)	1.823**** (6.73)
Leverage	−0.400 (−0.95)	−0.379 (−0.89)	−0.370 (−0.87)	−0.373 (−0.88)
Revision	0.009 (1.33)	0.009 (1.33)	0.008 (1.19)	0.008 (1.20)
Overhang	0.015* (1.75)	0.015* (1.77)	0.015* (1.76)	0.015* (1.76)
Prestigious underwriter	0.564*** (2.91)	0.572*** (2.92)	0.570*** (2.91)	0.582*** (2.94)
New York		−0.089 (−0.29)	−0.040 (−0.13)	−0.037 (−0.12)
Hot market			0.119 (0.56)	0.105 (0.49)
Auditor4				−0.096 (−0.42)
Pseudo R^2	0.0960	0.0961	0.0963	0.0965
Number of observations	3852	3852	3852	3852

This table shows the empirical link between geographic dispersion and accounting fraud while controlling for up to eight variables. The variables are defined in Table A1. The estimates are obtained without controlling for year and industry fixed effects. ***, ** and * denote statistically significant coefficients at the 1, 5 and 10% levels, respectively. **** denotes a p-value of less than 0.1%

Appendix

Table A.1 Variable definitions

Firm characteristic	Description	Data sources
Underpricing	Percentage IPO return = 100 * ((closing price on the first day of trading/offer price)−1) (Cliff & Denis, 2004)	SDC Platinum New Issues Database, CRSP
Revision	100 * (offer price/[0.5 * (P_{High} + P_{Low})]−1), where P_{High} and P_{Low} are defined as the upper and lower bounds of the indicative price range that is filed with the IPO issuer's regulator (Ljungqvist & Wilhelm, 2002)	SDC Platinum New Issues Database
Leverage	Debt/(debt + equity) (Habib & Ljungqvist, 2015)	SDC Platinum New Issues Database
Ln proceeds	Natural log of the proceeds of the offering in millions of dollars = Ln (offer price * number of shares sold) (Aggarwal et al., 2002).	SDC Platinum New Issues Database
Overhang	100 * (pre-IPO shares being retained by pre-IPO shareholders/shares issued in the IPO) (Lowry & Murphy, 2006)	SDC Platinum New Issues Database
Ln total assets	Natural log of total assets in millions of dollars (Butler et al., 2014)	Compustat
Ln age	Natural log of 1 + IPO firm age, where firm age = IPO issue year—the year the firm was founded (Butler et al., 2014)	Jay Ritter Web Site
VC	Dummy is 1 if firm is backed by a venture capitalist and 0 otherwise (Butler et al., 2014)	SDC Platinum New Issues Database
Prestigious underwriter	Dummy is 1 if underwriter reputation is ranked 9 and 0 otherwise (Butler et al., 2014)	SDC Platinum New Issued Database, Jay Ritter Web Site
New York	Dummy is 1 if the IPO listed on the NYSE and 0 otherwise (Butler et al., 2014)	CRSP
Hot market	Dummy is 1 if offering occurred in hot/bullish market and 0 otherwise (Derrien, 2005)	Hot market years include 1995–2000, 2004 and 2006
Auditor4	Dummy is 1 if IPOs use Big 4 auditors (Deloitte, KPMG, EY, PWC) and 0 otherwise (Smart & Zutter, 2003)	SDC Platinum New Issued Database
Local firm 20	Dummy is 1 if firm operates in three or fewer states (<= 20th percentile number of states) and 0 otherwise	EDGAR Database
Local firm 80	Dummy is 1 if firm has a concentration of more than 0.56 (>80th percentile of concentration) and 0 otherwise	EDGAR Database

References

Abarbanell, J., & Lehavy, R. (2003). Biased forecasts or biased earnings? The role of reported earnings in explaining apparent bias and over/underreaction in analysts' earnings forecasts. *Journal of Accounting and Economics, 36*, 105–146.

Aggarwal, R., Krigman, L., & Womack, K. (2002). Strategic IPO underpricing, information momentum, and lockup expiration selling. *Journal of Financial Economics, 66*, 105–137.

Asquith, D., Jones, J. D., & Kieschnick, R. (1998). Evidence on price stabilization and underpricing in early IPO returns. *The Journal of Finance, 53*, 1759–1773.

Baron, D. P. (1982). A model of the demand for investment banking advising and distribution services for new issues. *The Journal of Finance, 37*, 955–976.

Beatty, R. P., & Ritter, J. R. (1986). Investment banking, reputation, and the underpricing of initial public offerings. *Journal of Financial Economics, 15*, 213–232.

Benveniste, L. M., & Spindt, P. A. (1989). How investment bankers determine the offer price and allocation of new issues. *Journal of Financial Economics, 24*, 343–361.

Bradley, D. J., & Jordan, B. D. (2002). Partial adjustment to public information and IPO underpricing. *The Journal of Financial and Quantitative Analysis, 37*, 595–616.

Brennan, M., & Franks, J. (1997). Underpricing, ownership and control in initial public offerings of equity securities in the UK. *Journal of Financial Economics, 45*, 391–413.

Butler, A. W., Keefe, M. O. C., & Kieschnick, R. (2014). Robust determinants of IPO underpricing and their implications for IPO research. *Journal of Corporate Finance, 27*, 367–383.

Carter, R. B., & Manaster, S. (1990). Initial public offerings and underwriter reputation. *Journal of Finance, 45*, 1045–1067.

Cliff, M. T., & Denis, D. J. (2004). Do initial public offering firms purchase analyst coverage with underpricing? *The Journal of Finance, 59*, 2871–2901.

Colak, G., Gounopoulos, D., Loukopoulos, P., & Loukopoulos, G. (2021a). Political power, local policy uncertainty and IPO pricing. *Journal of Corporate Finance, 67*, 101907.

Colak, G., Gounopoulos, D., Loukopoulos, P., & Loukopoulos, G. (2021b). Tournament incentives and IPO failure risk. *Journal of Banking & Finance, 130*, 106193.

Derrien, F. (2005). IPO pricing in "hot" market conditions: Who leaves money on the table? *The Journal of Finance, 60*, 487–521.

Desai, V., Kim, J. W., Srivastava, R. P., & Desai, R. V. (2017). A study of the relationship between a going concern opinion and its financial distress metrics. *Journal of Emerging Technologies in Accounting., 14*, 17–28.

Economidou, C., Gounopoulos, D., Drivas K., Konstantios D., & Tsiritakis M. (2022a). *Trademarks, patents and performance of IPOs*. Working paper.

Economidou, C., Gounopoulos, D., Konstantios, D., & Tsiritakis, E. (2022b). Is sustainability rating material to the market? *Financial Management*.

Gao, W., Ng, L., & Wang, Q. (2008). Does geographic dispersion affect firm valuation? *Journal of Corporate Finance, 14*, 674–687.

García, D., & Norli, Ø. (2012). Geographic dispersion and stock returns. *Journal of Financial Economics, 106*, 547–565.

Georgakopoulos, G., Gounopoulos, D., Huang, C., & Patsika, V. (2022). The impact of IFRS adoption on IPOs management earnings forecasts in Australia. *Journal of International Accounting, Auditing and Taxation, 48*, 100490.

Goergen, M., Gounopoulos, D., & Koutroumpis, P. (2021). Do multiple credit ratings reduce money left on the table? Evidence from U.S. IPOs. *Journal of Corporate Finance, 67*, 101898.

Gounopoulos, D., & Huang, C. (2022). *Stay concentrate to survive*. Working paper, University of Bath.

Gounopoulos, D., & Pham, H. (2017). Credit rating effect on earnings management in U.S. IPOs. *Journal of Business Finance and Accounting, 44*, 154–195.

Gounopoulos, D., & Pham, H. (2018). Specialist CEOs and IPO survival. *Journal of Corporate Finance, 48*, 217–243.

Gounopoulos, D., Kallias, A., Kallias, K., & Tzeremes, P. (2017). Political money contributions of U.S. IPOs. *Journal of Corporate Finance, 43*, 19–38.

Gounopoulos, D., Loukopoulos, G., Loukopoulos, P., & Wood, G. (2022). Corporate political activities and the SEC's oversight role in the IPO process. *Journal of Management Studies.*

Grullon, G., Larkin, Y., & Michaely, R. (2019). Are US industries becoming more concentrated?*. *Review of Finance, 23*, 697–743.

Habib, M. A., & Ljungqvist, A. P. (2015). Underpricing and entrepreneurial wealth losses in IPOs: Theory and evidence. *The Review of Financial Studies, 14*, 433–458.

Hamao, Y., Packer, F., & Ritter, J. (2001). Institutional affiliation and the role of venture capital: Evidence from initial public offerings in Japan. *Pacific-Basin Finance Journal, 8*, 529–558.

Heider, F., & Ljungqvist, A. (2015). As certain as debt and taxes: Estimating the tax sensitivity of leverage from state tax changes. *Journal of Financial Economics, 118*, 684–712.

Ibbotson, R. G. (1975). Price performance of common stock new issues. *Journal of Financial Economics, 2*, 235–272.

Ibbotson, R. G., & Jaffe, J. F. (1975). "HOT ISSUE" MARKETS. *The Journal of Finance, 30*, 1027–1042.

James, C., & Wier, P. (1990). Borrowing relationships, intermediation, and the cost of issuing public securities. *Journal of Financial Economics, 28*, 149–171.

Landier, A., Nair, V. B., & Wulf, J. (2009). Trade-offs in staying close: Corporate decision making and geographic dispersion. *The Review of Financial Studies, 22*, 1119–1148.

Ljungqvist, A. P., & Wilhelm, W. J. (2002). IPO allocations: Discriminatory or discretionary? *Journal of Financial Economics, 65*, 167–201.

Logue, D. E. (1973). On the pricing of unseasoned equity issues: 1965–1969. *The Journal of Financial and Quantitative Analysis, 8*, 91–103.

Loughran, T., & Ritter, J. R. (2002). Why don't issuers get upset about leaving money on the table in IPOs? *The Review of Financial Studies, 15*, 413–443.

Loughran, T., & Ritter, J. (2004). Why has IPO underpricing changed over time? *Financial Management, 33*, 5–37.

Lowry, M., & Murphy, K. (2006). Executive stock options and IPO underpricing. *Journal of Financial Economics, 85*, 39–65.

Lowry, M., & Shu, S. (2002). Litigation risk and IPO underpricing. *Journal of Financial Economics, 65*, 309–335.

Megginson, W. L., & Weiss, K. A. (1991). Venture capitalist certification in initial public offerings. *Journal of Finance, 46*, 879–903.

Platikanova, P., & Mattei, M. M. (2016). Firm geographic dispersion and financial analysts' forecasts. *Journal of Banking & Finance, 64*, 71–89.

Ritter, J. R. (1984). The "hot issue" market of 1980. *The Journal of Business, 57*, 215–240.

Rock, K. (1986). Why new issues are underpriced. *Journal of Financial Economics, 15*, 187–212.

Ruud, J. S. (1993). Underwriter price support and the IPO underpricing puzzle. *Journal of Financial Economics, 34*, 135–151.

Shi, G., Sun, J., & Luo, R. (2015). Geographic dispersion and earnings management. *Journal of Accounting and Public Policy, 34*, 490–508.

Smart, S. B., & Zutter, C. J. (2003). Control as a motivation for underpricing: A comparison of dual and single-class IPOs. *Journal of Financial Economics, 69*, 85–110.

Stoughton, N. M., & Zechner, J. (1998). IPO-mechanisms, monitoring and ownership structure. *Journal of Financial Economics, 49*, 45–77.

Thomas, S. (2002). Firm diversification and asymmetric information: Evidence from analysts' forecasts and earnings announcements. *Journal of Financial Economics, 64*, 373–396.

Tiniç, S. M. (1988). Anatomy of initial public offerings of common stock. *The Journal of Finance, 43*, 789–822.

Welch, I. (1989). Seasoned offerings, imitation costs, and the underpricing of initial public offerings. *The Journal of Finance, 44*, 421–449.

Welch, I. (1992). Sequential sales, learning, and cascades. *The Journal of Finance, 47*, 695–732.

An Advanced Approach to Algorithmic Portfolio Management

Z. N. P. Margaronis, R. B. Nath, G. S. Metallinos, Menelaos Karanasos, and Stavroula Yfanti

Abstract Algorithm output profit profiles from the Nixon algorithm (RGZ Ltd.) are used to analyse the benefits of diversification within many commodity and asset class sectors in order to generate a superior portfolio profile. The metrics developed are the algorithm optimisation metric (AOM) and the parameter sensitivity index (PSI). The former accounts for noise and stability in profit profiles and optimises algorithms and portfolios, yielding superior return-risk characteristics. The latter measures the stability of a given algorithm's parameters and proportional changes in profits with respect to each parameter. Comparing these portfolio profits with those of more standard portfolios, we demonstrate the superiority of the developed metrics. The alignment of data is found to be a significant factor. Optimising a portfolio with unaligned data outputs leads to incorrect portfolio weightings and an erroneous profit profile on back-tested data. Correlations of prices and algorithmic returns are analysed showing the resultant dilution of correlation due to the effect of the strategy and the trading of security spreads.

Keywords Algorithmic trading · Commodity spreads · Crude oil benchmarks · AOM · RAP · PSI · Portfolio management

1 Introduction

This study investigates the superior performance of trading security spreads, primarily inter-commodity spreads, using a commercially developed trading algorithm

Z. N. P. Margaronis · R. B. Nath · G. S. Metallinos
RGZ Ltd., Buckinghamshire, UK

M. Karanasos (✉)
Brunel University, London, UK
e-mail: Menelaos.Karanasos@brunel.ac.uk

S. Yfanti
Queen Mary University of London, London, UK

© The Author(s), under exclusive license to Springer Nature Switzerland AG 2023
P. Alphonse et al. (eds.), *Essays on Financial Analytics*, Lecture Notes in Operations Research, https://doi.org/10.1007/978-3-031-29050-3_12

of RGZ Ltd., a research company specialising in algorithmic trading.[1] The chief characteristic of security spreads, such as the spread of the crude oil benchmarks WTI and Brent, is that they are more stable and predictable than individual commodities. This leads to a superior risk-return characteristic upon which the algorithm can capitalise. The algorithms themselves are multi-parameter models which are coupled with a trading rule. The algorithms use back-tested daily futures data of settlement prices (over several years) to build a time series on which the model parameters are optimised. Typically, trades are of very low duration, lasting a number of days and in some cases weeks. The optimisation of the algorithms is subject to the metrics presented in this study, and the diversification benefits of optimising long/short trading systems or portfolios using these metrics are explored.

Given the 2008 turmoil in financial markets, commodities must play a key role in standard investment portfolios consisting of stocks, bonds, and cash deposits. This is because there are very low yields on fixed term deposits, stock market returns are very risky, and there are significant default risks associated with bonds, particularly those of the Portugal Italy Greece Spain (PIGS) economies during the European Sovereign Debt Crisis (ESDC), which succeeded the 2008 Global Financial Crisis (GFC). The concerns regarding the PIGS have become an increasingly important issue as elections in these countries brought in new political parties, as seen in Greece. These events have knock-on effects on many economies due to various degrees of exposure with respect to currency, trade, and other factors. The commercial importance of trading security spreads together with single commodities cannot be understated, given the trading yields of the algorithm.

Crude oil, precious metals, and other soft commodities such as cocoa and coffee, although fundamentally volatile if considered on their own, can be used in cointegrated pairs and as single securities hedging each other, where they are significantly more stable and predictable (see, e.g. Clegg & Krauss, 2018). Any price changes in the security due to structural, market, or supply and demand factors do not significantly impact the spread of security pairs. An exception to this is the front-second month basis spread, where the price structure of the market is considered, depending on whether it is in flat, backwardation, or contango. They exhibit trends that can be exploited by trading algorithms based on such commodity prices and their spreads. The developed strategy can also be extended to other securities, including foreign exchange, bonds, and equity indices. In practice, there are periods of upward and downward trends where the 'noise' component or volatility is low. The strategy is also applied to single securities, which can be shown to hedge each other.

A successful algorithm should be able to generate consistent profits in the key regimes of trends and stationary oscillations (Davey, 2014; Lee & Sabbaghi, 2020; Han et al., 2021). The current RGZ algorithm is able to do this with Sharpe ratios (Sharpe, 1994) in excess of 4.2 (annualised) and annualised returns in excess of

---

[1] The Nixon algorithm is the intellectual property of the company and cannot be disclosed.

140%. The algorithm is a seven-non-linear parameter model back-tested on daily closing price data over 5 years throughout the GFC. This contrasts with Chatrath et al. (2002), who show commodity prices to be chaotic to a certain degree. Of course, this study only considers the prices of four agricultural commodities that tend to 'spike' more often, usually due to demand and supply shocks. Chatrath et al. (2002) use ARCH models to explain the non-linearity in data (see also Karanasos et al., 2018). However, given the stability of trading algorithms in terms of their returns, the extra volatility obtained in specific seasons exists but is not significant for a trading system that trades at a low frequency. This is because the optimisation of the algorithm considers any extra volatility obtained, even if it is seasonal.

Vivian and Wohar (2012) demonstrate that the volatility obtained by commodities in the GFC is not significant and that there are no real volatility breaks. This is, however, not true for other financial crises where the volatility breaks are more obvious. For this study, the GFC is more of interest as the optimisations are carried out over 5 years of data (see also Karanasos et al. (2018) for a comprehensive analysis of breaks in the volatility of commodity futures). The fact that Vivian and Wohar (2012) findings show no real evidence of volatility breaks despite the financial crisis is important. This is because the profits obtained from the trading algorithms also show no structural break in volatility even during the financial crisis. This may be supported by viewing the homoskedasticity of the profit profiles.

Current algorithmic trading systems utilise simple 'channel trade' systems available, where the user is required to view current prices continually, ensuring the trade occurs at the correct instant. These types of models take advantage of volatility during certain times of the day where fluctuations may occur perpetually. They allow for consistent trades to be made and give multiple trades of a similar value, while they sometimes incorporate degrees of sentimental trading. Of course, more advanced systems exist where models are used for trading various securities that incorporate Bollinger bands and other established methods. Most models are top secret and therefore remain the intellectual property of the investment bank, hedge fund, or other financial institution which developed or purchased them. More advanced models try to capture volatility and trends and usually have a detailed econometric study supporting them. The key is to develop a model that captures trends and spikes and can deal with the volatility between trends and spikes.

Cheung and Miu (2010) agree that diversification benefits can be gained by investing in commodities and that the diversification benefit of commodities is far more complex than generally perceived in finance. The view that commodity regimes change is also interesting as we observe a vast amount of heteroskedasticity throughout our analysis. However, diversifying into portfolios with commodities yielding a positive risk-return relationship compared to international equities is in line with what we believe. The RGZ Research (2010, 2011) algorithms have proved that being correctly diversified can lead to a superior portfolio performance even in times of a bearish commodity environment. The reason is the existence of spreads and that algorithms, despite correlations in prices, do not display these correlations in their profits since different algorithms are in different buy/sell positions, constantly hedging themselves with respect to historical back-testing.

Karali and Power (2009) support the view of diversification through the inclusion of different instruments in different sectors, especially within commodities, to balance a portfolio, given the increased volatility during crises in commodity markets. Macroeconomic variables impact commodity prices but affect each sector in different ways. This supports the idea that diversification is crucial, even within a single market with various sectors.

The remainder of the paper is structured as follows. Section 2 details the development of the algorithm optimisation metric (AOM) and the risk-adjusted profits (RAP) metric. Section 3 presents the parameter sensitivity index (PSI). In Sect. 4, we demonstrate the significance of our metrics for portfolio management. Finally, Sect. 5 concludes the analysis.

2   AOM and RAP Metrics Development

2.1   *Spreads*

Trading spreads allows for a more stable and less risky strategy because one does not expose themselves to intraday or daily volatility of a single security (see, among others, Liu & Chou, 2003; Hammoudeh et al., 2008; Clegg & Krauss, 2018). For example, when trading equity indices, it may be wise to try and capture trends in spreads between similar economies such as the French (Cac) and German (Dax) rather than play a single equity index. This is because if there is a financial shock, such as in 2008, the spread of two indices will not be affected as much as a single equity index. Figure 1 shows how the spread is far more stable than the absolute price. This can be seen clearly by comparing the two vertical axes and their scales and is a phenomenon characterising many cointegrated pairs.

Trading two securities as a spread is particularly interesting. For example, the prices of WTI and Brent crude oils are highly cointegrated, with WTI leading the price of Brent, as proved in the cointegration analysis of the two major crude oil benchmarks (Hammoudeh et al., 2008). The present study analyses the results of a newly engineered and revolutionary trading algorithm created and owned by RGZ Ltd. The Nixon algorithm remains the property of the company; however, the results of the profit profiles and other outputs are analysed here in order to obtain a new portfolio optimising metric and investigate the algorithmic portfolio behaviour. The algorithm was designed to trade commodity spreads, but after applying it to various securities, it is clear it can be utilised and adapted in other markets and single (outright) securities.

Fig. 1 Dax and Cac daily closing PX-last (Bloomberg)

2.2 Diversification and Algorithm Optimisation Metric (AOM)

It is important to apply the Nixon algorithm to various securities as it allows for diversification within a portfolio which is imperative for day-to-day stability. The types of diversification are crucial; for example, not all trading systems should be identical across the constituent instruments. Further, different types of securities should be included, such as grains, energy, equity indices, metals, foreign exchange, softs, and bonds. This is significant because the various sectors behave differently, as observed by their pairwise correlations. The way in which the margin is apportioned is meaningful because over-margining in energy, for instance, will make the portfolio unbalanced and lead to unnecessary exposure to this sector. Finally, it is imperative that both spreads and single securities are used since both behave differently in different phases of the business cycle. As a result, such diversification with a suitable trading system can generate consistent profits, even in times of financial turmoil.

Ji and Fan (2012) have found that the impact of the oil market spills over into other commodity markets. This may indeed be true in terms of price; however, it is clear that after applying a trading strategy with many instruments, the way in which the algorithm trades and is optimised for different securities varies. It is important to remember the significance of diversification along with the idea of trading spreads which reduces the exposure to a single commodity. This is linked to the correlation analysis where the prices may be correlated, but the returns of the algorithms are not; even if prices are correlated, the algorithms are not necessarily in the same buy/sell position.

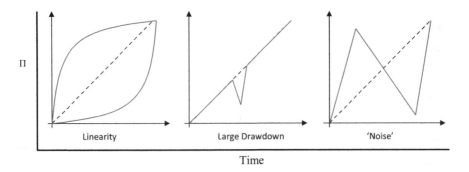

Fig. 2 Representation of limiting cases for undesirable portfolio performance with regimes of poor linearity, large drawdown, and large noise

Looking at a profit profile of various trading histories, it is clear that a metric can be developed to minimise the aspects that would make a portfolio undesirable. It is found that such a metric is more powerful in this respect than the Sharpe ratio. The algorithm optimisation metric (AOM) looks at three aspects of portfolio performance. It optimises the performance by minimising the noise in a back-tested P&L (profit) profile, rewarding linearity, and penalising drops of P&L, known as maximum drawdown. The maximum drawdown of a profile is measured as the largest drop in P&L, including successive negative trades, as well as small increases resulting from positive trades. Proof that the AOM is a better way to measure stability is investigated with a series of graphs depicting several extreme scenarios of profit profile and explaining why these might be undesirable. The three undesirable regimes are shown and include profiles that draw down, have poor positive to negative or 'noise' ratios, and are not linear. Also, the graphs show why the AOM's three components minimise the undesirable aspects wealth managers and other stakeholders desire in a profit profile.

The profits plotted against time profiles in Fig. 2 represent extreme departures from a desirable linear P&L profile (dashed) that stakeholders and wealth managers would find undesirable in a portfolio's performance. These represent limiting cases for which the AOM should be penalised. The idea is for the metric developed to minimise the three scenarios where essentially linearity is critical, assuming no reinvestment. It is imperative for the noise, as seen in the last graph, to be minimised and for sudden drops, in the second graph, to be penalised.

The AOM is defined as follows:

$$\text{AOM} = \text{NR} \bullet \text{DC} \bullet R^2, \tag{1}$$

where R^2 is the coefficient of determination and NR is the noise ratio defined as:

$$\text{NR} = \frac{\sum \Delta^+ \pi}{\sum \Delta^+ \pi + \left| \sum \Delta^- \pi \right|}, \tag{2}$$

with π the P&L (profit and loss), Δ^+ the positive daily change, Δ^- the negative daily change, and DC the drawdown coefficient defined as:

$$DC = 1 - \frac{MD}{MD + \frac{252\pi_{max}}{N}}, \tag{3}$$

where MD is the maximum drawdown, N is the number of trading days in sample, and 252 is the number of trading days in a year.

2.3   Risk-Adjusted Profits (RAP)

Risk-adjusted profits (RAP) is a term used for the product of the profit of an algorithm for its entire back-tested history and the AOM associated with it. This is because, in reality, a trading system is utilised to generate profits. Maximising stability through the AOM can therefore be combined with the P&L generated to form the RAP of an algorithm. The RAP is a standardised way to distinguish between optimal and non-optimal parameters, as is the AOM, while also weighting performance on profit. It is an efficient measure of allowing balancing between securities or security pairs when considering the degrees of diversification.

The optimisation and trading algorithms were developed using Fortran 95 programming language, where each security or pair has its own designated program. The outputs of the optimisation programs include a list of algorithm parameters and all combinations thereof as well as the AOM and RAP associated with each set of parameter combinations. The combination of parameters that give the highest RAP is chosen as the optimal parameters for that particular algorithm. A brute strength approach is used in optimising the algorithm parameters as every possible combination of parameters is tried and tested against the data.

2.4   Data

The data used throughout is daily PX_LAST future prices obtained from Bloomberg. Specifically, this study considers the front month contract of the various futures, and this is typical because the front month tends to have the highest volumes and hence liquidity, making it the prime candidate contract for trading by speculators. PX_LAST is the price at the close of business, while the prices themselves are procured over approximately a 5-year period from 2007 onwards during the GFC and the beginning of economic recovery. The number of prices (or days since daily prices are considered) varies from instrument to instrument due to different markets following different holiday conventions. The raw data are mapped using a mapping procedure developed by RGZ Ltd. (RGZ Research, 2011), while the mapping procedure itself is detailed in Karanasos et al. (2019).

The data considered in this study include ten raw datasets. From these ten sets, two spreads are considered, and the rest are taken as outright positions resulting in a total of eight separately tradable futures.

Three equity indices are tested: Nasdaq-100 (Nasdaq), Dax 30 (Dax), and Cac 40 (Cac). Dax and Cac are incorporated as a spread, i.e. Dax-Cac. The metals are represented by copper. The agriculturals considered are cocoa and oats, while the energies, typically the most prominent sector in commodities, are natural gas, WTI crude, and Brent crude. In this study, the crude oils are included in a spread commonly known as the WTI-Brent spread. The construction of spreads within the energy sector allows for hedging and lower exposure to the famously highly volatile crude oil markets. Finally, EURUSD is considered to represent the foreign exchange future sector. It is clear that there is a good degree of diversification with respect to the markets and the sectors. Our analysis shows how the portfolio construction in algorithmic trading may benefit by applying spreads, diversifying markets, and utilising bespoke and revolutionary metrics.

3 PSI Metric Development

The parameter sensitivity index (PSI) we develop allows for the stability of the constituent parts of the trading system to be measured by applying it to each security or security pair. The PSI program works by varying a single parameter (100% plus or minus its optimised value) while keeping all the others constant and carrying this out for all parameters. The PSI is then evaluated as the ratio of actual versus maximal (optimised) profits. This allows the user to see how changing a single parameter changes the level of RAP, AOM, and profit generated. A matrix is then generated whereby the sensitivities are plotted for the two primary parameters, and a surface plot can then be used to visualise the stability of each security. This can be used to judge whether an algorithm is too parameter-sensitive (unstable) or not. Also, it helps to show if there are multiple regions of higher levels of RAP and AOM. More importantly, it can allow for a region of lower AOM and RAP to be selected because of its superior stability. Examples of PSI outputs are shown in Fig. 4.

The actual PSI is evaluated by looping through a series of values of single parameters (100% plus or minus its value) by keeping all other parameters constant and then repeating this process for all parameters. In order to be able to create a surface that may be visualised and because it is found that two of the parameters are the most sensitive (primary parameters), the graphs for AOM or RAP are plotted for the primary parameters. The way in which a value of PSI is then generated is by

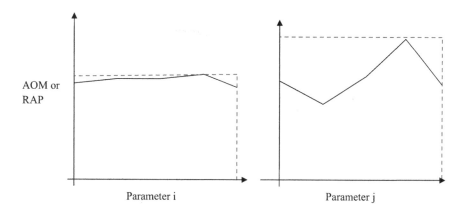

Fig. 3 RAP/AOM variations with (**a**) insensitive parameter and (**b**) sensitive parameter

considering the area under the graph of the parameter in question and comparing it to the maximum possible area. This is once again seen more clearly on the graph in Fig. 3.

The two profiles of Fig. 3 depict what the output from a PSI file may look like (a) depicting an insensitive parameter since the AOM and RAP values do not vary much with the parameter value. On the other hand, (b) shows a relatively sensitive parameter where the values of AOM and RAP seem to change dramatically as parameter value is changed. The dashed lines represent the maximum possible values of AOM or RAP obtainable by the parameter value. The ratio of positive areas under the actual and maximal profiles provides a reasonable measure of parameter sensitivity. Actual outputs of PSI are shown in Fig. 4, where surfaces are presented as they are a plot of two-parameter sensitivities. A total PSI can then be calculated by computing the product of all security sensitivities across all parameters.

From the two surfaces of Fig. 4, it is clear that the Nasdaq algorithm is far more sensitive with respect to parameter A than the Dax-Cac algorithm. The PSI values for Nasdaq and Dax-Cac are 14.2 and 27.1%, respectively. As a result, the Dax-Cac algorithm is far more stable because changing these parameters does not translate into a significant drop in the RAP, meaning the algorithm will still perform near its peak performance. This is not the case for the Nasdaq algorithm, where small changes in parameter A result in significant decreases in RAP, which suggests the algorithm may not perform well and may make losses with small deviations in behaviour.

It is clear that this analysis is useful in real-life trading situations and does not aim to simply optimise a theoretical tool by maximising a single outcome. Some profit profiles for various algorithms are presented in Fig. 5. The profiles shown in Fig. 5

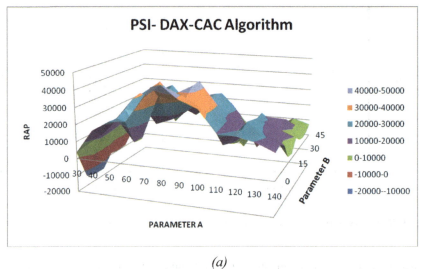

(a)

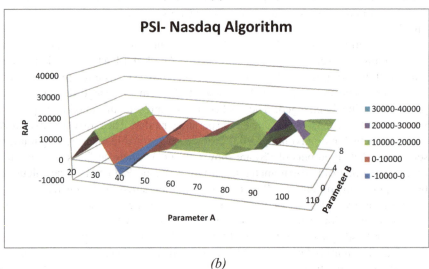

(b)

Fig. 4 PSI plot for sensitive and insensitive instruments

are outputs from the algorithms developed and owned by RGZ Ltd. (RGZ Research, 2010, 2011). The outputs from other instruments are presented in the Appendix. The post analysis is what we are interested in for managing a portfolio and maximising its performance.

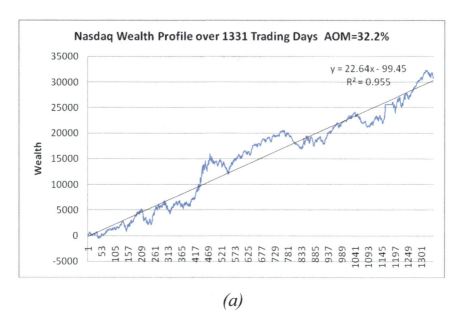

(a)

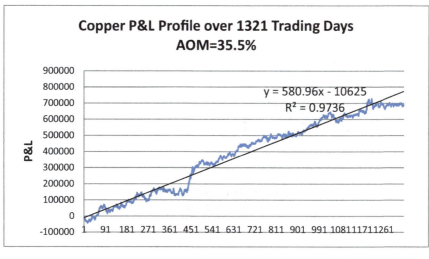

(b)

Fig. 5 Profit profiles from algorithm outputs for various instruments

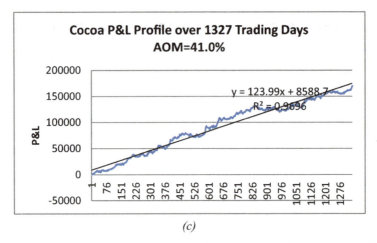

(c)

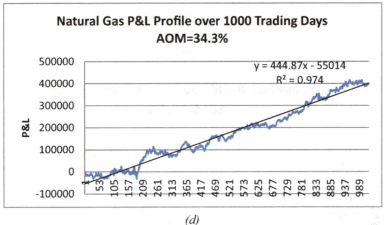

(d)

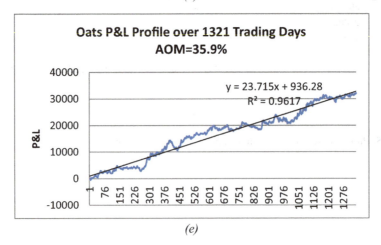

(e)

Fig. 5 (continued)

4 Significance in Portfolio Management

4.1 Portfolios

The individual instrument profiles will now be added with certain weightings in order to obtain a diversified portfolio where the noise component (Eq. 2) and drawdown (Eq. 3) are minimised and linearity is maximised given a specific margin investable. Hence, the overall AOM (Eq. 1) and RAP of the portfolio are maximised.

The final profit profiles of the diversified portfolios are shown in Fig. 6. Figure 6a represents a portfolio containing all the securities considered in this study. Figure 6b shows the portfolio accumulated when only certain securities are included. The reason for showing both is to show the effects of diversification and how important it is in minimising the volatility in a portfolio. Both profiles have been chosen based on RAP and a margin of $100,000, assuming a nominal level of leveraging of 10:1.

From the two profiles shown in Fig. 6, the latter (b) has a larger component of noise in the P&L profile. The volatility of the second portfolio, whose margin is the same, is far greater. Hence, we conclude that diversification is imperative, even in algorithmic trading. It is a requirement for stability and consistency of returns in such a portfolio.

4.2 Alignment

In order for an accurate portfolio AOM and RAP to be generated, the output profit data has to be aligned by date. The actual performance of a portfolio can only be generated if the dates are known for each particular level of P&L for each security or pair. This is an imperative but tedious process as it involves aligning the daily outputs of a range of securities that have different trading days since they are traded on different exchanges. This is again automated in order to account for non-trading days of specific securities. The automated alignment gives correct correlation matrices for the securities to be generated (discussed below) and therefore achieves a correct diversification. The weightings are obtained by a program that uses the aligned data to find the optimal portfolio. The date is the reference point. Using a nominal portfolio value and individual security margins based on 10:1 leveraging level, the program generates possible combinations of weightings for each security. This program then selects the optimal combination of weightings based on the maximisation of the RAP metric for the entire set representing the real-time daily behaviour of the portfolio. The program is able to apportion an initial margin to each security or pair and give a superior outcome of performance regarding RAP. The margins themselves are determined by and procured from (through Bloomberg and Thomson Reuters) the main exchanges used to trade commodities futures (CME and ICE). Computational time is minimised by only creating combinations for portfolio margins within a certain range since the

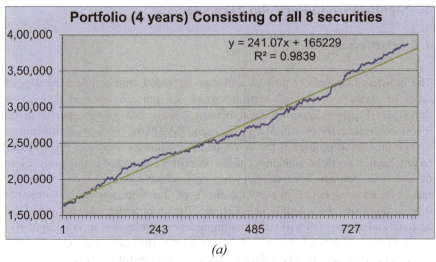

(a)

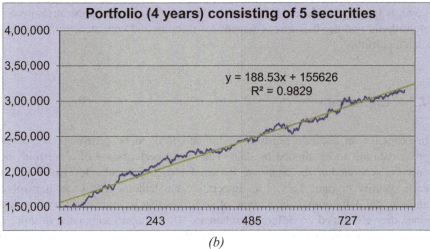

(b)

Fig. 6 Portfolios (**a**) consisting of all eight securities and (**b**) consisting of five securities representing the impact on the performance of successful diversification

optimisation approach is brute strength. The AOMs generated from this program are substantially superior to any of the individual securities or pairs. In this way, by combining the real-time date, margin, and optimised profits of each algorithm, the actual historical performance of a portfolio can be seen and then traded with confidence due to its accuracy.

In selecting the correct combination of securities to trade, it is imperative that the program has the true behaviour of algorithms with respect to time in order to minimise the noise component of the portfolio. This can therefore result in a true

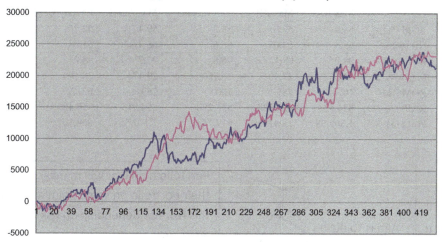

Fig. 7 Portfolio performance over 400 days showing alignment error between aligned (blue) and unaligned (pink) profits

maximised portfolio RAP. A profile of aligned profit profiles and non-aligned profit profiles will be compared to show how significant this error can be. This is also very important because the program needs to have accurate daily behaviours for all traded instruments in order to make a correct selection for a noise-minimising portfolio. An example of how the misalignment can mislead someone when taking positions is shown in Fig. 7: we present a simple portfolio profit profile containing only copper and three positions of the crude oil spread (WTI-Brent) shown for 400 days. There are two profiles where one is the actual aligned profits with respect to dates and the other is not. It is important to remember that the misalignment in the second profile is up to about 10 days, which is realistic given the time span. Real portfolio drops are underestimated, and gains can be overestimated. Also, the noise component is 'ironed out' or smoothed. Therefore, it is clear that incorporating the incorrect graph into an optimisation program that maximises the RAP (the noise, drawdown, and linearity of a misaligned dataset) will be erroneous and ultimately incorrect, resulting in incorrect weightings and exposure to risk due to this.

To prove that the maximum RAP is indeed the most effective method for optimising a portfolio, it must be compared to other more conventional methods such as the return-risk ratio (RR), minimum variance, and even perhaps comparing the maximum AOM to maximum RAP combinations to see possible differences in portfolio performance with respect to consistent and stable profits.

In order to show this, a number of essential characteristics need to be considered because the differences will not be clear from a profit profile. A table is created showing the measures of optimising portfolio performance and the characteristics of those portfolios. The characteristics used include the negative ratio (NR), which

Table 1 Portfolio characteristics for various optimisation metrics

	Max RAP	Max RR	Min variance	Max AOM	Equally weighted
AOM (%)	58.9	59.6	58.2	59.4	52.7
NR (%)	65.3	67.0	66.6	66.4	61.8
R^2 (%)	98.0	97.1	96.8	97.7	98.2
Max loss ($)	34,662	27,401	28,750	29,474	38,144
ROM (%)	1054	755	700	769	621
RAP	824,533	620,588	535,290	654,915	457,489
Profit ($)	1,399,887	1,041,255	919,742	1,102,551	868,101

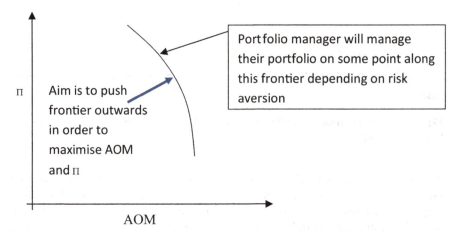

Fig. 8 Profit against AOM plot showing the existence of frontier of trading and where portfolio operates

is a measure of downward movements in profit of the profile; the coefficient of determination (R^2); the maximum loss, which is simply the value (in USD) of the largest drop in profit over the trading history; and the return on margin (ROM), which is the returns generated in relation to the amount of capital margined out initially in the portfolio. The RR is calculated by the ratio of the mean to standard deviation of the daily returns. The equally weighted portfolio is simply a combination of weightings whose margin is equal. We assume all these portfolios have a nominal margin of $50,000 and trade for a 4-year period.

In Table 1, we observe that the portfolios' performance across the metrics is fairly similar; however, the maximum RAP combination is superior in the amount of profit generated and its ROM. Across the table, all other characteristics seem similar, and therefore, we conclude that the maximum RAP combination is most desirable mainly due to its significantly larger return (Fig. 8).

Another tool to show portfolio diversification is the correlation matrix of daily price changes for all the component securities and a correlation of all the daily profit changes. This allows a direct comparison between these two correlation matrices.

The reason price returns are not used is due to the CFD (contracts for difference) nature of trading, where profits are a function of price differences. Comparing these two correlations will allow any portfolio manager to understand the degree of diversification and which securities are correlated. In addition, it can show the effectiveness of using long-short strategies to diversify portfolios. For example, a portfolio can be highly exposed to equity indices because they are indeed correlated. The European economies, for example, find themselves in turmoil during the ESDC, affecting the US and Asian markets because many banks and companies share funding and collaborate through trade, meaning they are exposed to each other in one way or another. In Table 2, the correlations of the profits generated show how using the selected combination of securities (defined by the maximum RAP from the program) reduces the correlations even more. Despite prices being highly correlated, the algorithm output for the two instruments is not since instruments' positions are not necessarily in the same long/short position during the trading history. Thus, this approach may be viewed as a black box that decouples the structural correlation between the securities by using back-testing and taking long or short positions accordingly to maximise the diversification effects and hence the portfolio performance. It should be noted that the Dax-Cac spread is considered in the post-correlation as the program runs the spread. The pre-correlation, however, considers the two indices separately in order to give a better understanding of how the two are related to each other. On the other hand, the WTI-Brent spread is a price that is procured as such. This means the price of the spread is constructed by the exchange. In Table 2, the emboldened correlations represent levels above 15%, the threshold chosen to differentiate significant and insignificant correlations in this study.

4.3   Correlations

From the correlations carried out on the absolute price changes, it is clear there is a significant amount of correlation between many of the securities. For example, EURUSD seems to be correlated to all the securities considered. Reasons for this relationship with respect to the agriculturals may arise from the significance of the import and export markets of these commodities and their consumption by the European Union. EURUSD is also expected to have a certain degree of correlation with its primary economic indices, and this will in turn spill over to some degree to the agricultural commodities. Copper prices tend to be an economic indicator since copper is a primary base metal used in most electronic equipment and wiring. Its relationships with the oil spread and the indices may therefore be justified. The indices themselves are expected to have a certain degree of correlation among them, given the structure of financial systems worldwide where countries share debt and trade, and this is remarkable in the significant correlations between Dax, Cac, and Nasdaq.

From the final correlation reported above, it is clear that the correlations of the price returns become insignificant once they have been processed by the trading system (see Table 2b). The correlations are insignificant across the table with a

Table 2 Correlation matrices for (**a**) absolute price changes and (**b**) algorithm profit changes. Correlations are chosen to be significant at the 15% level (emboldened)

Pre	Copper	Oats	Cocoa	Dax	Cac	Nasdaq	EurUsd	Natural Gas	WTI-Brent
Copper	100.00%								
Oats	29.10%	100.00%							
Cocoa	29.40%	14.30%	100.00%						
Dax	52.10%	21.60%	23.30%	100.00%					
Cac	53.60%	25.50%	24.30%	92.80%	100.00%				
Nasdaq	32.50%	16.60%	15.80%	59.50%	56.50%	100.00%			
EurUsd	34.50%	22.90%	28.10%	33.60%	33.50%	31.40%	100.00%		
Natural Gas	14.40%	15.90%	10.90%	11.90%	11.40%	9.80%	13.90%	100.00%	
WTI-Brent	50.50%	28.00%	26.20%	39.90%	41.10%	33.50%	32.30%	23.30%	100.00%

Post	Copper	WTI-Brent	Natural Gas	Dax-Cac	Nasdaq	Oats	Cocoa	EurUsd
Copper	100.00%							
WTI-Brent	-1.00%	100.00%						
Natural Gas	-0.10%	-10.10%	100.00%					
Dax-Cac	-5.80%	0.30%	-1.20%	100.00%				
Nasdaq	6.50%	-0.90%	-1.80%	6.30%	100.00%			
Oats	-3.70%	0.50%	-2.20%	-0.40%	-14.80%	100.00%		
Cocoa	27.80%	2.50%	-3.60%	-26.70%	21.10%	-2.10%	100.00%	
EurUsd	20.50%	0.40%	-0.20%	-9.40%	12.40%	-4.60%	13.30%	100.00%

few exceptions as there are far fewer pairs with correlation magnitudes higher than 15%. This demonstrates an important effect of correlation dilution that exists by virtue of the trading strategy. The fact that trading allows one to take long/short positions means that profits can be achieved on both increases and decreases in the price of a security. Even though the prices for various securities are linked (correlated), the algorithm is not necessarily in the same position across these securities, and historical back-testing is utilised to offset and hence smooth portfolio profit profiles taking into account historical scenarios of their behaviour. Therefore, we can conclude that the diversification impact in such a portfolio in algorithmic trading has a substantial impact on the portfolio performance.

5 Conclusions

In conclusion, this study shows that a portfolio containing both spreads and single securities reduces exposure to certain markets by reducing 'noise', smoothing portfolio performance, and dealing with spillovers among markets (Ji & Fan, 2012). At the same time, the PSI can be instrumental in establishing how stable an algorithm will be in generating consistent profits. Other findings show that a truly diversified portfolio over many different asset classes yields superior performance, and this can include both securities and security pairs, which in turn can diversify risk by hedging against holding outright positions in securities, in line with previous studies supporting spreads trading strategies (Liu & Chou, 2003; Clegg & Krauss, 2018).

Moreover, the alignment of data with respect to date is shown to be vital in establishing true portfolio weightings and meaningful correlation matrices. We further conclude that correlations of daily price returns are significantly different from those of the output profit changes due to the effect of correlation dilution under the trading strategy or algorithm. This is because there are differences in the long/short positions across component instruments over time. Our significant contribution to algorithmic trading literature (Davey, 2014; Lee & Sabbaghi, 2020; Han et al., 2021) consists in demonstrating that a portfolio optimisation according to the maximum RAP and AOM criteria leads to superior performance, particularly when compared to that of other criteria such as a maximum RR and minimum variance. Utilising the RAP and AOM in this instance (as well as other algorithmic systems governing portfolios or more simple portfolios comprised of a basket of stocks) can result in more profit generated and yield a far more desirable P&L profile.

Finally, as part of future research, we intend to implement our optimisation approach to different trading algorithms used in financial markets and compare their performance with the Nixon algorithm optimisation. A further line of research could focus on applying our metrics to portfolio data covering the recent pandemic-induced crisis.

A.1   Appendix

Fig. A.1 EURUSD wealth profile

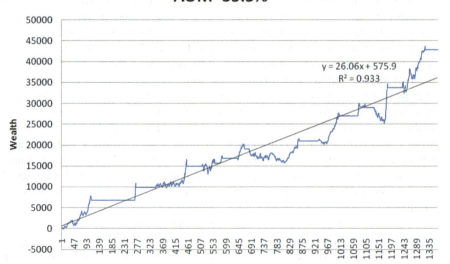

Fig. A.2 Dax-Cac wealth profile

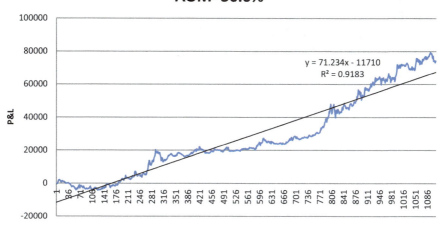

Fig. A.3 WTI-Brent wealth profile

References

Chatrath, A., Adrangi, B., & Dhanda, K. K. (2002). Are commodity prices chaotic? *Agricultural Economics, 27,* 123–137.

Cheung, C. S., & Miu, P. (2010). Diversification benefits of commodity futures. *Journal of International Financial Markets Institutions and Money, 20,* 451–474.

Clegg, M., & Krauss, C. (2018). Pairs trading with partial cointegration. *Quantitative Finance, 18,* 121–138.

Davey, K. J. (2014). *Building winning algorithmic trading systems: A trader's journey from data mining to Monte Carlo simulation to live trading.* Wiley.

Hammoudeh, S. M., Ewing, B. T., & Thompson, M. A. (2008). Threshold cointegration analysis of crude oil benchmarks. *The Energy Journal, 29,* 79–95.

Han, H., Teng, J., Xia, J., Wang, Y., Guo, Z., & Li, D. (2021). Predict high-frequency trading marker via manifold learning. *Knowledge-Based Systems, 213,* 106662.

Ji, Q., & Fan, Y. (2012). How does oil price volatility affect non-energy commodity markets? *Applied Energy, 89,* 273–280.

Karali, B., & Power, G. J. (2009). *What explains high commodity price volatility? Estimating a unified model of common and commodity-specific, high-and low-frequency factors.* Agricultural & Applied Economics Association, working paper no. 319-2016-9765.

Karanasos, M., Ali, F. M., Margaronis, Z., & Nath, R. (2018). Modelling time varying volatility spillovers and conditional correlations across commodity metal futures. *International Review of Financial Analysis, 57,* 246–256.

Karanasos, M., Koutroumpis, P., Margaronis, Z., & Nath, R. (2019). The importance of rollover in commodity returns using PARCH models. In *Financial mathematics, volatility and covariance modelling* (pp. 59–92). Routledge.

Lee, J., & Sabbaghi, N. (2020). Multi-objective optimization case study for algorithmic trading strategies in foreign exchange markets. *Digital Finance, 2,* 15–37.

Liu, S. M., & Chou, C. H. (2003). Parities and spread trading in gold and silver markets: A fractional cointegration analysis. *Applied Financial Economics, 13,* 899–911.

RGZ Research. (2010). *Econometric analysis of precious metals and crude oils commodity pairs.* Internal document. RGZ Ltd.

RGZ Research. (2011). *Mapping crude oil futures contract data for use in algorithmic processing.* Internal document. RGZ Ltd.

Sharpe, W. F. (1994). The Sharpe ratio. *Journal of Portfolio Management*, (Fall), 49–58.

Vivian, A., & Wohar, M. E. (2012). Commodity volatility breaks. *Journal of International Financial Markets Institutions and Money, 22*, 395–422.

The Rise of Fintech and Healthcare SPACs

Victoria Patsika

Abstract This study examines the level acquisition companies (SPACs). The results demonstrate low underpricing for both types of SPAC, with unit and share prices of around $10 from 2010 to 2021. Leverage, market capitalisation, the size measured by total assets, and management teams with finance experience have a statistically significant impact on underpricing. Interestingly, the management team affected the share price (closing price) when the SPACs merged with the target companies on the first trading day. SPACs appear to be an alternative in comparison with IPOs. Furthermore, the relevance of agency theory, information asymmetry theory, signalling theory, and the winner's curse is confirmed. The results provide practical implications for private target companies and investors that are interested in SPACs.

Keywords Fintech and healthcare SPACs · Underpricing · Management team

1 Introduction

Special purpose acquisition company (SPAC)[1] IPO investors have earned annualised returns of 15.9%, while investors for the merged companies have earned −8.1% in the first year on common shares but 68.0% on warrants (Gahng et al., 2021). From 2010, there was a trend towards an increasing number of SPACs. However, SPACs experienced an especially abrupt increase towards 2019–2021, rising from 59 SPACs in 2019 to 248 SPACs in 2020. In 2020, SPACs accounted for more

---

[1] A SPAC, a blank check company created by a sponsor, goes public to raise capital and then find a non-listed operating company to merge with, in the process taking the company public.

V. Patsika (✉)
Cardiff Business School, Cardiff University, Cardiff, UK

Department of Accounting and Finance, University of Macedonia, Thessaloniki, Greece
e-mail: patsikav@cardiff.ac.uk

© The Author(s), under exclusive license to Springer Nature Switzerland AG 2023
P. Alphonse et al. (eds.), *Essays on Financial Analytics*, Lecture Notes in Operations Research, https://doi.org/10.1007/978-3-031-29050-3_13

than 50% of new publicly listed US companies (Bazerman & Patel, 2021). Lin et al. (2021) and Gahng et al. (2021) also document that 248 SPACs raised $83.4 billion— far more than the money raised by traditional initial public offerings (IPOs). SPACs have already raised as much cash in their IPOs in 2020 as they did over the past 10 years (Klausner et al., 2022). Moreover, most of the SPACs increasingly targeted the fintech and healthcare industries in 2020 (Hung et al., 2021). Thus, investigating this abrupt increase in interest in SPACs in 2020 is worthwhile.

The recent rise of the SPAC market has resulted in a heated debate about SPACs among both practitioners and academics. Proponents of SPACs argue that, by giving an additional option for raising capital and listing for private companies, SPACs benefit both investors and issuers. Critics, citing poor post-merger returns, raise an incentive misalignment issue between SPAC sponsors and investors created by the fact that a sponsor receives no payoff if a merger is not completed. Furthermore, the 20% sponsor promote and 5.5% underwriting commission result in a high expense level per dollar of cash delivered, especially if many shareholders redeem their shares.

Chong et al. (2021) asserted that the sudden increase of SPACs in 2020 can be explained from the perspectives of the economic environment, management, private companies' owners, and investors. From an economic environment perspective, Passador (2021) provides evidence that SPACs' volume increased more than fourfold due to the COVID-19 pandemic in 2020. Interestingly, a high volume of SPACs appeared in 2008 due to the global financial crisis (Dimitrova, 2017; Passador, 2021). An uncertain environment thus increases the volume of SPACs. Cizmovic et al. (2013) report that the largest SPACs, in terms of the dollar amount collected at the IPO, happened in 2007 and 2008, with a significant decline in size thereafter.

From a management perspective, the technology industry is the dominant sector for SPAC investment, and an increasing number of SPACs are formed worldwide to combine with target companies in the fintech sector. The rise of technology has widely spread in the financial service industry, thereby ensuring operational efficiency, improving customer-centric services, and favouring information technology (Gomber et al., 2017; Lee & Shin, 2018; Junger & Mietzner, 2020). Moreover, fintech SPAC transactions are increasing in the US and European ecosystems (Cardenes, 2021). Passador (2021) report that in 2020, information technology and healthcare industries were more popular for SPACs—an interesting insight regarding the level of constant innovation, dynamism, and capital required by those sectors.

Furthermore, in the SEC S-1 forms, many SPACs mention that they believe that the fintech and healthcare sectors have many opportunities, resulting in shifts in the global trends and technology disruptions in the financial service and healthcare sectors. The management teams also believe that fintech or digital services sectors are the "new economy sectors", especially in Southeast Asia and Australia. Moreover, as the pandemic caused in-person healthcare visits to plummet in 2020, healthcare companies need capital to pursue new opportunities in digital health insurance and technology. Finally, most SPACs focus on companies in biotechnology markets, making this a good opportunity for healthcare companies to raise funds from SPACs (Bazerman & Patel, 2021).

From the perspective of target fintech companies, they also have advantages in going public via SPACs over traditional IPOs. They can benefit from faster listing processes, certainty overvaluation, and contractual flexibility by directly negotiating SPAC merger agreement terms with SPAC sponsors and going public with experienced SPAC management teams (Cardenes, 2021). Salerno et al. (2022) concluded that fintech IPO firms have underpricing issues because fintech ventures are young start-ups and thus need funding from external investors to further expand their activities (Haddad & Hornuf, 2019; Sheng, 2021). Secondly, there is difficulty in evaluating the fair value of fintech companies. They have few tangible assets, possessing mainly intangible assets and bounded earnings in the early life cycle. Next, the uncertainty also makes it difficult to evaluate fintech companies due to the rapidly increasing amount of new technologies and regulations within the industry. Lastly, historical information about fintech companies is scarce. Underpricing them is thus necessary to increase investor demand, and as fintech firms need capital funds, they accept a lower price to go public earlier (Salerno et al., 2022).

From the investor's perspective, SPACs provide public investors access to private equity investment, which was previously only available to institutional clients such as investment banks and hedge funds (Boyer & Baigent, 2008). Furthermore, SPACs provide only limited disadvantages to investors as the money invested by the shareholders is held in trust. They also have the right to vote to either accept or reject the merger acquisition proposed by the management team (Boyer & Baigent, 2008). The amount held in trust will also return to the shareholders if the acquisition is not accomplished within 18 months. Some studies have referred to SPAC investment as a risk-free investment (Jenkinson & Sousa, 2011). Gahng et al. (2021) document that the SPAC structures evolve and become more investor-friendly.

Moreover, Salerno et al. (2022) conclude that fintech IPOs experience more underpricing than similar non-fintech IPOs. There are arguments that SPACs could be a cheaper way to go public than IPOs (Klausner et al., 2022). The difference between IPOs and SPACs is the valuation and structure in this context. Further, IPOs have more price uncertainty compared to SPACs (Klausner et al., 2022). The results from Salerno et al. (2022) show a positive relationship between fintech IPO firms and the level of underpricing compared to non-fintech IPO firms.

Therefore, this study extends the work of Salerno et al. (2022) by analysing the underpricing of fintech SPACs. Moreover, an analysis compares traditional IPOs and non-traditional IPOs (SPACs) in fintech and healthcare. The aim hereby is to evaluate whether SPAC acquisitions are viable alternatives to IPOs for private fintech and healthcare firms. Jog and Sun (2007) concludes that SPACs exhibit a very low level of underpricing. Berger (2008) states that SPACs provide many features that traditional IPOs are incapable of providing, such as readily available cash, valuation benchmarks, and exit opportunities.

Most of the existing SPAC literature has focused on excess returns and approval probability. Moreover, it documents inconclusive results regarding underpricing. It is thus interesting to study underpricing in SPACs to examine whether they could be a better alternative than traditional IPOs. This study aims to add another perspective by examining whether the SPAC management team impacts underpricing because of the unique structure of SPACs and the unavoidable conflict of interest between shareholders and the management team.

This manuscript hereby attempts to answer the following questions to evaluate the relationship between fintech and healthcare SPACs and underpricing: What effect do the management teams have on the share price of fintech and healthcare SPACs? Do they have an impact on underpricing? The aim hereby is to use the findings to examine whether SPACs could be an alternative compared to traditional IPOs.

This study relates to the work of Cizmovic et al. (2013), Shachmurove and Vulanovic (2018), Hung et al. (2021), and Salerno et al. (2022) which report that fintech IPOs have a considerable level of underpricing. The author reports that fintech IPOs lead on average to an increase of 11.11% in the level of underpricing compared to non-fintech IPOs. This work updates the authors' findings by investigating the level of underpricing in fintech and healthcare SPACs. The management team is the focus here to investigate whether it affects underpricing as well as abnormal returns. Hung et al. (2021) also mention the need for a further investigation into the relationship between the management team and returns, especially for fintech SPACs. The authors only had 22 observations for fintech SPACs, and this research expands the number of observations to 237. The majority of the SPAC literature has focused on observing abnormal returns at significant announcement dates and acquisition announcement returns. Also, only a few studies address the performance of SPAC subsamples with either a geographical or an industrial focus (Shachmurove & Vulanovic, 2018). The only study to do so focused on the shipping industry, which raises funds through SPACs and accesses US financial capital markets (Shachmurove & Vulanovic, 2015). Thus, this is the first study to focus on fintech and healthcare SPACs.

The rest of the manuscript is organised as follows. Section 2 presents the literature review and the theoretical framework related to the current literature on SPACs and their management teams. Section 3 explains the source of the data and the models suggested by the literature to determine whether underpricing exists in fintech and healthcare SPACs and to explore whether any variables affect underpricing. Section 4 includes the empirical analysis and results, and Sec. 5 presents the discussion and the conclusion, summarising the main findings and limitations.

2 Literature Review

2.1 SPACs

Blomkvist and Vulanovic (2020) define SPACs as shell companies that go public through issuing units that consist of one common share and a fraction of warrants. The main purpose of SPACs is to use the IPO proceeds raised from the public to fund and merge with unspecified private target companies going public within 2 years. The IPO proceeds are deposited in an escrow account and are only employed for deal financing if the investors approve of the acquisition target. The authors focused on the wave pattern of SPAC listings that arose in 2020.

A SPAC, a blank check company created by a sponsor, goes public to raise capital and then find a non-listed operating company to merge with, in the process taking the company public. For almost all SPACs created from 2010, units priced at $10 each are issued in the IPO. A typical unit is composed of a common share and one or more derivative securities, usually a fraction of a warrant (a call option issued by the company) entitling the holder to buy a share at an exercise price of $11.50 with a maturity date that is 5 years after the completion of a merger. Importantly, the money raised in the IPO is placed in an escrow (trust) account where it earns interest. The units later become unbundled, allowing the shares and warrants to trade separately.

SPACs usually pay 5.5% of the proceeds as underwriting commissions, with 2% paid at the time of the IPO and the rest deferred—payable only upon the completion of a merger (business combination). Sponsors are typically compensated by retaining 20% of the SPAC shares, but these sponsor shares (known as the "promote") have no access to the trust account. Sponsors also usually purchase private placement warrants or units at the time of the IPO for approximately their fair market value, with the millions of dollars paid for the securities going to cover the up-front underwriting fees and future expenses as the SPAC searches for an operating company to merge with. This purchase allows the public investors to start with $10 per share in the trust account, rather than the $9.80 in net proceeds from the IPO. All of the sponsors' compensation (payoffs on their shares and warrants) and more than half of the underwriters' fees are thus contingent upon the consummation of a business combination.

SPACs are not allowed to have pre-identified target companies and usually set 18–24 months as a deadline to complete a merger. If a SPAC cannot consummate a merger within this timeline, it must liquidate, distributing the IPO proceeds and the accrued interest in the trust account to its investors. Once a SPAC identifies a target company and reaches an agreement for a merger, public shareholders of the SPAC vote whether to approve the proposed business combination or not. Separately, at this time, each public shareholder decides whether to redeem their shares or not. The redemption option means that there is a money-back guaranty for SPAC IPO investors. Unit holders are allowed to keep (or sell) their warrants even when they redeem their shares.

2.2   The Economic Role of SPAC Investors

Klausner et al. (2022) and Gahng et al. (2021) examined the claims regarding the advantages of going public through SPACs rather than IPOs, especially given the recent rise of SPACs. They report that the claim is overstated in terms of cost, namely, the implicit cost built into SPACs is significantly higher than with traditional IPOs due to the dilution of the discounted shareholders' shares as compensation fees for the management to find good-quality companies to merge. Thus, the authors concluded that merging with SPACs is more expensive than pursuing a traditional IPO due to the implicit cost. However, the authors argue that companies with high underpricing tend to choose SPACs over IPO. Alternatively, the companies experience withdrawn deals as they chose traditional IPOs. Therefore, the authors stated that SPACs are still an alternative for private companies to go public, considering that the companies have difficulties going public through traditional IPOs. Bai et al. (2021) agreed that riskier firms tend to merge through SPACs.

From 2007 to 2008, the literature has focused on the legal overview of SPACs and the description of SPACs' structure. Hale (2007) affirmed that the introduction of SPACs exhibits a productive development in the financial markets. Modern SPACs provide sufficiently high protection for investors, and following the introduction of Rule 419 by the Securities and Exchange Commission (SEC), SPACs have a more efficient corporate structure (Riemer, 2007).

Some authors state that the structure of SPACs provides many features that traditional IPOs are incapable of providing (Boyer & Baigent, 2008; Floros, 2008; Berger, 2008; Rodriguez & Stegemoller, 2021). For example, foreign companies with high levels of debt, low levels of protection of shareholders' rights, and legal efficiency in their home countries (Floros, 2008) have difficulties raising funds through a traditional IPO and, instead, have the option to raise funds by going public through SPACs. SPACs can provide readily available cash and valuation benchmarks and offer exit opportunities (Berger, 2008). For instance, Shachmurove and Vulanovic (2015) affirmed that Chinese private companies use SPACs as an exit strategy to go public in the US market, as they have difficulties going public in the US market through traditional IPOs. Lastly, SPACs also provide a less costly and faster path to public financing (Boyer & Baigent, 2008). Therefore, from the private companies' perspectives, SPAC structures are a valid alternative to traditional IPOs that are complementary with the advantages of cash injection, shared liquidity, and vested-in underwriters.

Lewellen (2009) contributed by emphasising that SPACs should be treated as a separate asset class because they are different from common stocks and can be seen as risk-free assets because of their unique structure. The author broke down the SPAC life cycle into the stages of no target stage, target found, and acquisition completed or withdrawal. The framework provides highly predictable returns, and it is applied by most of the SPAC literature. The author also reveals that investors treat the sponsor's risk capital as a signal of managerial quality. Thus, investors perceive an increasing trend in sponsors' risk capital as a proxy for the quality of the SPAC management team.

Gahng et al. (2021) demonstrate that even the worst-performing SPAC has provided a positive return of 0.51% per year from 2010. The structure of the SPAC market has adjusted towards a more sustainable equilibrium by making SPAC units less attractive to SPAC investors and more attractive to post-merger shareholders, thus encouraging shareholders to keep the shares when the merger is announced. The shareholders have the right to either keep or sell the shares regardless of their approval of the merger decision. In contrast, Dimitrova (2017) concluded that SPACs illustrate poor performances across the board. Ignatyeva et al. (2013) also report that European SPACs are value-destroying post-acquisition, with −11.4% semi-annual and −14.2% annual returns, while European SPACs have several structural characteristics in common with US SPACs.

Stulz (2020) points to the growing importance of SPACs, especially for young companies with intangible assets, who can find it expensive to go public through traditional IPOs due to the high uncertainty and the fact that they are difficult to evaluate. Thus, SPACs could be a better alternative for them to go public to raise funds, and they can also enjoy the benefit of the expertise of the management team. However, the author indicates that when a business combination is completed under time pressure, especially near the end of the SPAC life cycle, it can experience underpricing. Degeorge et al. (2016) show the same pattern in the private equity market.

Lin et al. (2021) concluded that its management team affects a SPAC's value, which is responsible for the process of deal sourcing and target picking until post-merger management. Thus, because of this specific structure of SPACs, the quality and ability of SPAC management teams are critical factors to the eventual success of SPAC IPO. For illustration, a high-quality management team reveals more information content about their targets by increasing the length of the Form S-4 prospectus to signal to the investors that they are confident about the acquisition; this, in turn, potentially leads to a higher probability of a successful merger and superior performance after a business combination (Keys et al., 2010). Lakicevic and Vulanovic (2011) also asserted that investors interpret the SPAC merger proposal as a signal of the quality of the management team. Thus, the management team has become a critical factor to be considered as it can enhance or destroy a SPAC's value for investors.

Lowry et al. (2010) proved that when companies are difficult to measure, small, young, and focused on technology, their IPO initial return variability is higher. Moreover, due to the same attributes, there is a high likelihood that they will experience higher underpricing on average at the IPO.

Chatterjee et al. (2016) concluded that the level of underpricing may be predetermined by the level of equity, referring to the shares provided to the SPAC management team as compensation for their service. Common shares are given to the management team as an incentive to obtain information about firm characteristics and to accept high-quality companies for acquisition. The purpose of the warrant is to dilute the equity holdings and motivation for founders to choose companies with lower risk. The level of the free shares given to the SPAC management team could represent the level of underpricing before SPAC investors pre-commit. Thus, the nature of SPAC underpricing is different from that of traditional IPOs.

Since there is a predetermined reasonable level of underpricing, SPACs' targeted companies have the certainty of knowing the amount of capital that will be raised compared to traditional IPOs. However, the authors also mentioned that changes in the economic conditions impact the probability of SPACs completing the merger acquisition successfully. Thus, it can sometimes be difficult to examine whether a SPAC liquidation is due to a bad economic environment or to the quality of the management team, particularly as the management team can claim that they liquidated the SPAC to avoid bad acquisition deals. Therefore, there is no certain benchmark for investors to measure the performance of a SPAC management team.

2.3 Theoretical Framework

2.3.1 Signalling Theory

Signalling theory examines IPO underpricing from the theoretical perspective (Ross, 1977; Bhattacharya, 1979; Certo et al., 2001). Deeds et al. (1997) asserted that signalling theory could be used to resolve the information asymmetry issue as it is consistent with the perspective that the management team has more knowledge about the targeted companies' quality and more insider information compared to investors (Keasey & Short, 1997; Lawless et al., 1998; Gounopoulos et al., 2017; Gounopoulos & Pham, 2017, 2018; Goergen et al., 2021; Colak et al., 2021a, b). Thus, in order to decrease the possibility of discounting the share price, managers will find ways to convey companies' qualities to attract less informed investors (Beatty, 1989; Carter & Manaster, 1990). The authors suggest that particular variables send signals to potential investors regarding the abilities and future value of the companies (Deeds et al., 1997). This implies that the SPAC management team will find a way to signal the firm's quality to investors to mitigate the agency problem (Daily et al., 2003).

Furthermore, many SPAC studies have used signalling theory to explain the purpose of the management team purchasing the warrant, namely, to signal the quality of SPACs. The SPAC management team can credibly signal their quality by increasing the "skin in the game" (Newman & Trautman, 2021; Blomkvist & Vulanovic, 2020). In other words, this refers to the management team's purchase of additional warrants in the SPAC investment, which investors could interpret as a sign that the SPAC management teams are confident with the targeted companies as they are willing to invest more by purchasing additional warrants in that acquisition. Purchasing additional warrants could serve to mitigate the asymmetry information issue between the management team and shareholders.

Chatterjee et al. (2016) also demonstrate that requiring the SPAC management team to purchase additional warrants can successfully prevent an incapable management team from setting up a SPAC as the management teams are required to make a substantial initial investment by investing 1–3% of the total amounts of funds raised beforehand. Furthermore, the pricing of warrants in financial markets is also one of the signalling methods to attract investors.

Besides purchasing additional warrants, the SPACs' managerial experience is a signal of firm quality, according to Kim (2009). The author stated that the experience of the SPAC management team positively increases the possibility of an acquisition. However, these results are based on the Korean context, rather than the US, and Korea has different regulations. Moreover, the reputation of the management team also signals its quality. Authors have affirmed that SPACs have private equity and hedge fund manager teams with a successful proven track record to signal to investors that they are good-quality sponsors (Rodrigues & Stegemoller, 2011; Klausner et al., 2022). However, the potential risk is that most SPACs are one-time transactions, and the same management team rarely executes several SPACs. Thus, the failure of a single SPAC transaction does not result in a high reputational loss.

The deferred underwriters' fee could act as a signal to investors regarding the quality of the SPAC beyond the SPAC management team. According to Lakicevic and Vulanovic (2013), the average underwriters' fee is 7% of the gross proceeds. The fees are separated into 3.95% to pay the underwriters at the IPO, and the remaining 3.06% is only paid if the merger is successful. Thus, investors could perceive the signal as the underwriters' confidence regarding the SPAC's merger acquisition and demonstrate their commitment towards the final acquisition and, also, to align the motivation of both management teams and underwriters to consummate the deal.

Furthermore, according to several studies, companies choose prestigious underwriters to signal the quality of the firm to investors (Carter & Manaster, 1990; Michaely & Shaw, 1994). These authors argued that prestigious underwriters only choose high-quality firms by practising extensive due diligence to maintain their reputations.

To conclude, regarding the possibility that SPACs will experience underpricing, the management team and underwriters find ways to signal that their interests are aligned with those of the shareholders to mitigate the agency problem. Management teams thus purchase more warrants to signal that there is a high probability that they will consummate the deal. For the underwriters, the deferred underwriters' fees are the signal to mitigate the agency problem as they will only be paid if the merger is successful. Therefore, investors perceive the positive signs from both the management team and the underwriters that they have the commitment and confidence in consummating the deal, considering the amount of the capital invested by both parties in the acquisition.

2.3.2 Agency Theory

Agency theory is used to explain IPO underpricing. According to Jensen and Meckling (1976), agency theory refers to managers who maximise their own wealth rather than maximising shareholders' wealth. Based on Boyer and Baigent (2008), in theory, the contractual relationship motivates the SPAC management team to find the best target company within the time available. Therefore, this will maximise shareholder value and enhance the approval probability.

To ensure that the management's incentives are aligned with the shareholders' interests, the management team is required to purchase 20% of the companies' equity and warrants, which is also called the "skin in the game", "sponsor promotion", or "at-risk investment" (Lewellen, 2009; Chatterjee et al., 2016; Layne et al., 2018; Chong et al., 2021). Consequently, if the acquisition is incomplete or is not approved by the investors, the shares and warrants invested by the management will be worthless. Therefore, sponsors have extremely strong economic incentives to complete the acquisition.

The management team has 18–24 months to find target companies to merge with, and they do not receive a salary until the deal is completed (Cumming et al., 2014; Agarwal, 2021). Thus, to ensure that the managers' interests are aligned with those of the shareholders and to ensure a good acquisition, the management team's final payoffs are highly dependent on the shareholders' approval: If the shareholders disapprove of an acquisition, the SPAC will be liquidated, making both the sponsors' promotions and warrants worthless. Therefore, the management team consummates the acquisition to avoid their common shares and warrants becoming worthless.

However, according to Jog and Sun (2007), the SPAC management team can receive very high compensation. They document that the median annual return is 1900% for the management team. This could be explained by their having a strong incentive to complete the deal even if it could be value-destroying (Lin et al., 2021). Thus, although conflicts of interest exist, the management team will still complete the acquisition as it may otherwise lose its entire at-risk investment, in addition to the opportunity costs of the time invested in managing the SPAC.

Summarising, the research indicates that when the end of the specified time is approaching, the management team will suggest low-quality deals as potential acquisitions (Dimitrova, 2017; Gahng et al., 2021). The authors reveal that business combinations that are announced 6 months before the deadline or during an extended period are strongly associated with negative returns due to the agency problem. Therefore, this could prove that the SPAC management team has an extremely strong economic incentive to complete an acquisition, especially before the expiration date.

To conclude, although the SPAC structure is designed to align the interests between the management team and investors, there is still a strong economic interest for the management team to consummate the deal as it does not want to forego 20% of the firm equity and warrants. Thus, it is forced to complete the deal under time pressure. With other private equity investments, the management team has 3–5 years to complete the acquisition, but SPAC management teams only have 18–24 months to do the same (Dimitrova, 2017). As a result, the management team might consummate the deal with low-quality target companies. Alternatively, they may pay the target companies a higher fund as SEC requires SPACs to spend 80% of the gross IPO proceeds on that particular acquisition.

2.3.3 Information Asymmetry

According to Rock (1986), the foundation of underpricing is explained by information asymmetry (Beatty & Ritter, 1986; Loughran & Ritter, 2002; Ritter & Welch, 2002). Specifically, uninformed investors recognise that they will generally earn below-average returns. Thus, to attract uninformed investors as well as to increase demand, the underwriters will make the effort to underprice the newly issued shares (Daily et al., 2003; Colak et al., 2021a, b; Thomadakis et al., 2012, 2017; Wei & Marsidi, 2019; Gounopoulos et al., 2021, 2022).

The literature has used information asymmetry theory to explain IPO underpricing. Kim et al. (2008) stated that the majority of the finance literature suggests that IPO underpricing originates from asymmetric information. Information asymmetry theory refers to the information imbalance that exists between insiders (executives) and outsiders. In this context, information asymmetry refers to the unbalanced information between the SPAC management team and investors. Based on Cizmovic et al., the degree of information asymmetry impacts the issued securities' pricing at the IPO. When the companies potentially have the highest degree of information asymmetry, they illustrate higher underpricing.

Beatty and Ritter (1986) extended Rock's (1986) model and illustrate that companies with higher information asymmetry experience higher underpricing on average. Chatterjee et al. (2016) explained that underpricing is positively related to firm risk. Due to the nature of SPACs, which have neither historical performance nor assets, there is only limited available information to investors (Lin et al., 2021). Therefore, investors only have little information regarding potential SPAC acquisition targets until the final target is announced through the SEC 8-k form (Gosen, 2021). This could affirm that information asymmetry exists between the management team and investors. Consequently, uncertainty is generated for investors and this results in underpricing.

Moreover, Jog and Sun (2007) mentioned that investors only have information regarding the management team at the announcement of SPACs. Investors can only make judgments based on the previous track record and their belief in the management team. Thus, the process of setting the share price will highly depend on the information gap between the management team and shareholders. However, in their sample for recent SPACs, Cizmovic et al. evidenced that the degree of information asymmetry insignificantly affects the pricing on the IPO day.

Fintech IPOs have a higher chance of experiencing underpricing, as shown by numerous studies (Aboody & Lev, 2000; Chan et al., 2001; Eberhart et al., 2004; Salerno et al., 2022). The authors have proposed that research and development (R&D) is the main contribution to the underpricing of fintech IPOs as investors believe that company insiders have higher quality information regarding R&D projects. Moreover, fintech IPOs are young, meaning that investors have neither adequate time-series data nor high-quality information to evaluate the feasibility of R&D projects (Cho & Lee, 2013). High-tech companies also compound R&D investments with intangible assets, making it difficult for investors to evaluate the true value of an R&D project. Therefore, for investors, R&D is expected to induce more information asymmetry compared to non-high-tech IPO companies.

The structure of SPACs has been uniquely designed to resolve the information asymmetry problem, especially as SPACs are perceived as risky investments by investors (Shachmurove and Vulanovic, 2017; Chatterjee et al., 2016). SPACs' units can further dilute into shares at a future date and warrant strike price, allowing investors to justify the companies' true value in the future (Chemmanur & Fulghieri, 1997; Schultz, 1993). Cizmovic et al. also observe that sponsors purchase more warrants to demonstrate commitment and mitigate the potential information asymmetry problem.

Klausner et al. (2022) suggested that for companies that have difficulties resolving information asymmetries with potential investors, SPACs give them the freedom to provide and explain the details in the prospectus with the protection of "safe harbour" principles. It means that companies are encouraged to disclose all available financial information even if it is uncertain. They are also not liable for any misstatements or false information.

In conclusion, when there is uncertainty and the belief that information asymmetry exists among investors, companies have a higher chance of experiencing underpricing. Thus, to reduce the information asymmetry problem, SPACs try to issue units that can dilute into shares and warrants in the future as a signal to investors of the true value of the potential acquisition. Further, companies that have difficulties conveying the information can now provide all available information to shareholders under protection from misstatement, thereby reducing the probability of underpricing.

2.3.4 Winner's Curse

Many studies emphasise that uncertainty causes some IPOs to experience underpricing (Beatty & Ritter, 1986; Rock, 1986; Salerno et al., 2022). Rock's (1986) winner's curse is under the asymmetric information model, which is an application of Akerlof's (1978) lemons problem. This refers to the fact that only bad-quality companies remain in the market as the good firms will be valued as underpriced, and thus they will not raise capital through equity (Akerlof, 1978).

Jenkinson and Sousa (2011) suggested that SPACs are not value-creating entities in general. The financial market can identify bad SPACs before the acquisition date, but many acquisitions are approved despite expected post-merger negative returns. The authors also document that investors who agree to SPAC sponsors' proposals, rather than listening to the market, suffer average cumulative returns of -39% within 6 months, rising to -79% after a year. In addition, although a good voting mechanism protects the shareholders, they still tend to approve acquisitions that might be value-reducing. This suggests that the management team will consummate the deal based on their own strong economic incentives, even if they know that the acquisition is of low quality.

Ritter and Welch (2002) explain that high-quality issuers distinguish themselves from low-quality issuers. In the Akerlof model, as rational investors are worried about a lemons problem, only issuers with below-average quality are willing to sell their shares at the average price. Thus, some believe that the SPAC bubble involves too much money potentially flowing to lower-quality companies that perhaps should not be publicly held (Klausner et al., 2022; Passador, 2021). Moreover, Bai et al. (2021) reveal that lower-quality SPACs offer more warrants and rights.

Furthermore, Lamont and Thaler (2003) stated that explaining underpricing security requires irrational investors who are willing to hold overpriced securities. Especially for SPACs, the authors believe that the future exchange value at the DeSPAC is predetermined (Saengchote, 2021). Then, the investors would know the value of the share price in advance, making it difficult to justify the reasoning of shareholders who hold underpriced shares. For illustration, when the merger is announced, the rule of thumb for investors who do not redeem the share is that they must believe that they will receive approximately $10 per share (Klausner et al., 2022). Otherwise, they will disapprove of the acquisition, and their money will be returned to them from the escrow trust account. Therefore, evidence of SPAC overpayment suggests that investors may not fully understand SPACs, resulting in a higher probability that bad acquisitions are suggested for approval by the management team.

Overall, investors may suffer a loss from a bad acquisition even though they had the opportunity to disapprove of the acquisition. Instead, they merely follow the management team rather than the market. This is explained by irrational human behaviour rather than bad SPACs in the market. This also leads to the hypothesis that the management team affects underpricing since investors heavily depend on the management team to search for the target companies.

2.4   Hypotheses Development

With the rise of SPACs, particularly in the fintech and healthcare industries, it is crucial to investigate if there is underpricing. Findings on the factors affecting underpricing are inconclusive in the previous literature. Most of the SPAC researchers focus on investigating abnormal returns and the approval probability. Furthermore, for IPOs, the offering price is only set until the day before the IPO. However, a SPAC merger agreement tends to set the price before the merger's closing (Gosen, 2021). As a result, there are arguments that there is more price certainty for SPACs, which ensures that SPACs go public to raise funds with less underpricing than IPOs (Chatterjee et al., 2016). The abovementioned studies build the foundation to examine the following hypothesis:

H1: Fintech and healthcare SPACs experience underpricing.

Chatterjee et al. (2016) discuss that the structure of SPACs needs to be carefully designed to ensure that the interests of investors and the management team are aligned. There are also arguments from the literature suggesting that investors can only rely on the management team's ability to find value-creating target companies to merge with because SPACs are shell companies without an operating history (Cumming et al., 2014; Hung et al., 2021). Also, so-called founder shares are given to the management team in exchange for their effort in consummating a deal. Thus, it is crucial to investigate whether the attributes of the management team affect underpricing within the model. There are strong economic incentives for the management team to consummate the deal, leading to some conflict of interest. In turn, investors might suffer a loss because of a bad acquisition proposed by the management team. This leads to the question of whether the management team will propose a bad acquisition to investors.

H2: The management team has an impact on underpricing in fintech and healthcare SPACs.

Based on the above hypotheses, we conduct an analysis to examine whether SPACs could be a better alternative in the fintech and healthcare sectors than traditional IPOs. It is a common claim that SPACs offer greater price and deal certainty compared to IPOs, and this opportunity might be strongly attractive to companies with high information asymmetries (Gosen, 2021).

3   Data and Methodology

This study extracted the details of 848 SPACs from the US Securities and Exchange Commission (SEC) EDGAR filings from 2010 to 2021. These are registered with SEC under the industrial code SIC 6770 "blank check companies", which refers to shell companies that have no operating assets and no operating history (Jog & Sun,

2007). We also cross-check the number of SPACs with the number given by SPAC Analytics and found a match.

After obtaining the list of SPACs, we examined the 848 SPACs to identify those that particularly targeted the fintech and healthcare industries. The information are from the S-1 prospectuses under the "target business" section. On the S-1 form, most SPACs include which industries they are targeting in combining businesses. We document 237 SPACs targeting the fintech and healthcare industries from 2010 to 2021.

Most of the data, including syndicate size, size of the management team, average age of the management team, and unit offer price, were then hand-collected from the SEC EDGAR S-1 form. Agarwal (2021) stated that the prospectuses of SPACs focus on the management team, and thus it is reasonable to collect information related to the management team from these. Total assets, total liabilities, and the status of SPAC IPOs were collected from the 8-K and 10-K forms.

Furthermore, to complete the database, Refinitiv Eikon Thomson Reuters, SPAC Track, Nasdaq, and Stock Market MBA were used to collect additional information, such as IPO date, unit open and close price, share price, share price when the merger takes place on the first trading day, and market capitalisation. This is consistent with other existing SPAC literature, in which most of the data were hand-collected from SEC EDGAR, and then Refinitiv Eikon and SPAC Track were used to collect additional information and to cross-check the data with SEC EDGAR to ensure that the data were comprehensive (Saengchote, 2021). Regarding the data of non-fintech and healthcare SPACs, we obtain them from Stock Market MBA in terms of the unit price on the last closing day.

3.1 Methodology

This study investigates whether there is underpricing among fintech and healthcare SPACs. While Salerno et al. (2022) indicate that there is underpricing for fintech IPOs, Cizmovic et al. (2013) did not report that healthcare industry experience significantly leads to underpricing. This further seeks to examine whether SPACs could be an alternative to IPOs for private companies to go public.

The SPAC IPO is structured as a sale of units consisting of both common stock and warrants, which cannot be exercised until the SPAC completes an acquisition (Dimitrova, 2017). As not all fintech and healthcare SPACs have the unit closing price on the first trading day, we use 134 observations. We checked for the relevant data from NASDAQ, Thomson Reuters Refinitiv Eikon, and SPAC Track, but no data were available for those SPACs, either because the SPACs were not successful after filing with the SEC or they had been delisted.

After collecting both the unit closing price at the end of the first trading day and the original unit price as stated in the prospectus, we find that there is marginal underpricing (0.0251) with statistical significance at the 1% level for fintech and healthcare SPACs on the sample of 134 observations from 2010 to 2021.

Jog and Sun (2007) document that SPACs experience low level of underpricing with a mean of 0.019. The results are aligned with our hypothesis that SPACs could be either marginally underpriced or overpriced because SPACs do not have an operating history, the merger may not receive approval from shareholders, and there are unavoidable fees involved in finding the target companies to merge, such as underwriting fees and operating fees (Jog & Sun, 2007). Furthermore, the management team receives "sponsor shares" at a large discount, which will affect the market price as well.

Furthermore, the result of underpricing may be explained by agency theory and information asymmetry theory. Investors believe that there is an information misbalance between them and the SPAC management team. Moreover, the existence of potential risk and for a conflict of interest between management and shareholders are stated in the SEC prospectus (Agarwal, 2021). Specifically, SPAC management teams are allowed to work in other businesses while searching for potential target companies with which to merge.

As a result, after applying the model suggested by Jog and Sun (2007), we document that fintech and healthcare SPACs experience marginal underpricing (0.0251). There is only marginal underpricing if the targeted private companies choose to go public through SPACs, considering that they can take advantage of a faster listing process in going public and experience certainty in terms of valuation.

3.1.1 SPAC Pricing

Regarding SPAC pricing, most special purpose acquisition companies had a unit offer price of $10 since 2010 (Cumming et al., 2014; Lin et al., 2021; Saengchote, 2021). The purchase price per unit of a SPAC IPO is usually $10 (Cumming et al., 2014).

In total, 103 fintech and healthcare SPACs did not make it to the IPO because they were either delisted or removed. Thus, there is no unit price for all of the identified 237 fintech and healthcare SPACs. Klausner et al. (2022) demonstrate that most SPACs trade at $10 per unit until the mergers are completed. The results in Table 1 provide confirmation. For non-fintech and healthcare SPACs, the average last unit closing price before the completion of merger is $10.06, which is above

Table 1 Unit closing price at the last day before the actual mergers

	Non-fintech and healthcare SPACs	Fintech and healthcare SPACs
Observations	556	172
Mean	$10.06	$10.03
Median	$9.99	$9.95
Minimum	$0	$2.73
Maximum	$19.47	$17
P-value	0.0000	0.0000

$10. Regarding fintech and healthcare SPACs, the last unit closing price is $10.25, which is above $10. Thus, the results match those of Klausner et al. (2022).

Next, the reason for using the share price is because common shares and callable warrants are normally decoupled from the units approximately 1 month after the IPO (Lewellen, 2009; Cumming et al., 2014; Dimitrova, 2017). When the merger is completed, the "de-SPAC" process is when the target merges with the SPAC to become a listed company (Saengchote, 2021). The SPAC IPO is traded under a new name and symbol. Due to the unique structure of SPACs, most special purpose acquisition companies trade at $10 per unit. Thus, when a business merger happens, the share price tends to be around $10 per share as well (Cumming et al., 2014; Saengchote, 2021). Therefore, it is crucial to identify if the share price trades either above or below $10 per share after merging.

Klausner et al. (2022) illustrate that many SPACs trade at approximately $10 per share after being combined with a new business. Furthermore, when a SPAC merges, its value is fixed at $10. As most SPAC IPOs occurred in 2020 and 2021, there are more available data over this period. As mentioned, only 172 fintech and healthcare SPAC observations are included to avoid misleading results. Our findings are in line with Klausner et al. (2022) for both non-fintech and healthcare SPACs and fintech and healthcare SPACs.

Many studies in the SPAC literature applied the OLS model to test hypotheses related to stock market performance in terms of abnormal returns (Rodrigues & Stegemoller, 2014; Dimitrova, 2017). Mezhoud and Boubaker (2011) suggest that investors perceive market capitalisation as the quality of the target companies. Wei and Marsidi (2019) report that the higher the market capitalisation, the lower the uncertainty and, in turn, the lower the level of underpricing. Furthermore, Bansal and Khanna (2012) document that there is a significantly positive link between market capitalisation and underpricing. Baker and Wurgler (2007) also concluded that investors do not prefer companies with low capitalisation as they assume that they demonstrate poor profitability and a lower growth rate. This will result in low demand for their shares (Bansal & Khanna, 2012). According to Wei and Marsidi (2019), signalling theory can be used to explain the impact of market capitalisation on the degree of underpricing. As investors consider market capitalisation as one of the signals of firm quality, market capitalisation is one of the factors that will affect the performance of SPACs on the first trading day.

Salerno et al. (2022) used total assets as a proxy for firm size. Moreover, prior evidence indicates that the size of the firm affects the level of underpricing. Syndicate size is the number of underwriters involved in the SPACs. Chen and Mohan (2002) highlight that the higher the number of underwriters involved, the greater the underpricing. Furthermore, team size is the number of members on the SPAC management team. Hung et al. (2021) concluded that team size has a positive effect on the success of a SPAC merger.

"Days" is the *number of days* between the company filing the S-1 registration statement and the IPO date. The reason to include days in the model is that according to Saengchote (2021), the median time to announce a merger has declined from nearly 2 years in 2018 to approximately 2 months in the last quarter of 2020. There is a belief that as the number of SPAC IPOs has continued to increase, management teams are hurrying to consummate deals (Saengchote, 2021). Furthermore, Gahng et al. (2021) suggest that speed is an important factor when private companies go public by merging with SPACs in 2020. Therefore, it is crucial to investigate if speed causes underpricing for fintech and healthcare SPACs.

"Average team age" is the *average age of the management team's members* and is calculated by dividing the cumulative age of the team members by the number of team members. It is the proxy for the SPAC management team's experience level (Lin et al., 2021). According to Hogan and McPheters, age is positively correlated with experience: The greater the experience, the more likely it is that the management team can find high-quality acquisition targets. Furthermore, Hung et al. (2021) report that there is a positive relationship between the average age of the management team and experience in the finance industry, with a p-value of 0.013 for SPACs' returns. As the authors explained, a management team with successful experience in finance will result in more efficient operations.

The dummy variables include PhD and MBA. Hung et al. (2021) stated that education level is an extension factor that possibly affects the performance of SPACs. For illustration, according to Lakicevic et al. (2014), SPAC managers who have experience in finance can generate positive value for shareholders. Moreover, for target companies, the proportion of experienced managers in finance is also a reflection of a professional background, which is relevant when deciding to merge with SPACs. A study by Tran proved that a manager's previous experience in finance positively impacts the performance of a SPAC in terms of merger probability.

Regarding experience in the financial industry, Hung et al. document that there is a positive relationship between SPAC returns and the average financial experience of the management team. This study extends this by examining whether experience in the finance industry has an impact on underpricing.

Furthermore, Chong et al. (2021) report that the average percentage of management team members holding a PhD in the healthcare sector is significantly higher than for other sectors. SPACs in the healthcare industry invite more experts with PhD degrees to join the management team as evaluating the value of potential private healthcare companies requires highly specialised professional knowledge. Hung et al. (2021) also proved that experience in other industries, except the finance industry, has a positive impact on SPACs' returns.

4 Empirical Analysis

Descriptive analysis can serve as a data cleaning process in order to remove unreasonable data. Also, it allows the assumptions mentioned in the previous section to be checked (Gosen, 2021). If the assumptions are not met, then the data can be adjusted by either taking logarithms for the variables or removing outliers.

Table 2 presents the descriptive analysis of the independent variables, namely, days, leverage, total assets, team size, average age of the management team, syndicate size, market capitalisation, MBA, PhD, finance experience, and healthcare experience for 176 fintech and healthcare SPACs from 2010 to 2021. The results show that days, leverage, syndicate size, total assets, market capitalisation, average age, and healthcare experience are statistically significant at the 1% level, while MBA and finance experience are statistically significant at the 5% level.

The average number of days between the SPACs filing with the SEC and the IPO date is 63. This is aligned with Saengchote (2021), who stated that the time taken for SPACs to merge has decreased to approximately 2 months. The mean leverage is 0.22, compared to fintech IPOs, with mean leverage of 0.52 (Salerno et al., 2022). Malerno (2020) states that leverage of 0.5 or below is good. Thus, fintech and healthcare SPACs have a better leverage ratio and more assets than liabilities, which, in turn, lowers the financial risk. This is because the higher the firm risk, the higher the probability of underpricing (Chatterjee et al., 2016).

The syndicate size, with a mean of two underwriters involved in the SPAC, is statistically significant at the 1% level. This is aligned with the literature that the number of underwriters involved in SPACs has decreased. Moreover, if more underwriters are involved, investors would perceive that the SPAC acquisition is more complicated and riskier. Lin et al. (2021) also report that if the syndicate size increases, the probability of the deal being approved decreases. The team size has a mean of 6.39. Hung et al. (2021) document that the average team size in fintech and healthcare SPACs is 7.7 and 7.1, respectively.

As for the total assets, which are an indicator of firm size, it is statistically significant at the 1% level with a mean of $205 million. Thus, firm size is crucial. Furthermore, the market capitalisation, with a mean of $381 million, is statistically significant at the 1% level. The previous literature mentions that the higher the market capitalisation, the lower the uncertainty. The average age of the management team is a proxy for experience level (Lin et al., 2021). We find that the average age of 51 years is statistically significant at the 1% level. This is aligned with the prior literature suggesting that age is positively related to experience (Hung et al., 2021). This will affect the quality of the acquisition targets. Hung et al. (2021) also indicate that the average age of the management team members involved in SPACs is approximately 53 years old. Therefore, it is crucial to investigate if these variables that are statistically significant have a significant impact on underpricing for fintech and healthcare SPACs.

4.1   Regression Analysis

Before applying the multivariate regression, we examine if each variable has an impact on underpricing, respectively. Considering the endogeneity problem, it is important to accurately test if the variables have a significant impact on underpricing to avoid biased results. From the results in Table 3, leverage and logarithm of

Table 2 Descriptive statistic for fintech and healthcare SPACs

	Days	Leverage	Syndicate size	Team size	Total assets ($)	Market capitalisation ($)	Age	MBA	PhD	Finance experience	Healthcare experience
Number	176	176	176	176	176	176	176	176	176	176	176
Mean	62.53	0.22	1.65	6.39	229,000,000	464,000,000	51.31	2426	0.5284	4.82	2.45
Median	53	0.09	1	6	109,000,000	312,000,000	53	2	0	5	1
Max	73	1.54	5	12	1,380,000,000	5,320,000,000	73	6	4	11	9
Prob	0.000***	0.000***	0.000***	0.623	0.000***	0.000***	0.000***	0.020**	0.000***	0.021**	0.000***

Table 3 SPAC returns

	Underpricing
Constant	−0.2056 (0.1156)
Leverage	−2.3513 (0.0198)***
Days	0.2653 (0.7911)
Log (total assets)	3.2080 (0.0016)***
Syndicate size	0.4724 (0.6372)
Team size	−0.0588 (0.2912)
Age	0.0689 (0.9451)
MBA	−1.988 (0.0483)**
PhD	1.2400 (0.2168)
Financial experience	−1.6789 (0.0950)*
Healthcare experience	1.2375 (0.2176)
Heteroskedasticity	Yes (0.0294 < 0.05)
N	176
R^2	0.1154
Adjusted R^2	0.1031
P-value	0.041**

total assets are statistically significant at the 1% level. Salerno et al. (2022) also report that leverage and total assets have an impact on underpricing for fintech IPOs, with statistical significance at the 10 and 1% levels. We extend their by adding variables related to the management team; only MBA and management team with finance experience are statistically significant at the 5 and 10%, respectively, levels. The independent variables, including leverage, total assets, MBA, and finance experience, are statistically significant at the 10, 5, and 1% levels, respectively. It appears that they have an impact on underpricing.

Table 4 shows that after adding the dummy variables including PhD and MBA into the model, it is statistically significant at the 10% level (column 2 of Table 4). The model R increases from 0.0548 to 0.0817. Within the model, the logarithm of total assets is statistically significant at the 5% level. After running the White test, only model (2) does not have heteroscedasticity (p-value of 0.4502 > 0.10). If the model has heteroscedasticity, it will still exist if the sample size grows larger as the error term is not constant in the model. Also, the assumption of the model will be incorrect.

4.2 Robustness Checks

The relationship between the variables can vary between +1 and −1. From the results in Table 6, we conclude that most of the variables are not strongly correlated, with a range of 0.000 to 0.200, i.e. no relationship to an extremely weak relationship. However, there is a moderate correlation between team size and fintech, at 0.690. Based on the descriptive analysis, the team size is not statistically significant.

Table 4 SPAC additional tests

	Underpricing	Underpricing	Underpricing
Constant	−0.2056 (0.1156)	−0.2216 (0.1290)	−0.1923 (0.1330)
Leverage	−0.0111 (0.0562)	0.0138 (0.0588)	0.0078 90.0602)
Market capitalisation	1.3000 (1.9700)	1.2100 (2.0400)	1.2000 (2.0500)
Lot (total assets)	0.0110* (0.0060)	0.0133** (0.0062)	0.0132*** (0.0062)
Days^2	2.8700 (5.8800)	1.8800 (5.9500)	1.6100 (5.9600)
Syndicate size		0.0071 (0.0154)	0.062 (0.015)
Age		−0.0003 (0.0012)	−0.0002 (0.0013)
MBA		−0.0133 (0.0073)	−0.0095 (0.0079)
PhD		0.0167 (0.0154)	0.0150 (0.0157)
Financial experience			−0.0081 (0.0063)
Healthcare experience			0.0065 (0.0052
Heteroskedasticity	Yes (0.0294 < 0.05)	No (0.4502 > 0.10)	Yes (0.0000 < 0.01)
N	176	176	176
R^2	0.0548	0.0817	0.0908
Adjusted R^2	0.0323	0.0369	0.0347
P-value	0.049**	0.0758*	0.1056

Thus, we exclude team size from the regression. PhD and the management team having healthcare experience show a moderate correlation at 0.496, which results in underpricing model (3) having insignificant results (column 3 of Table 4).

4.2.1 The Effect of the Management Team on the Share Price

Interestingly, we find that the management team impacts the share price (closing price) when SPACs merge with target companies and go public on the first IPO day. To perform a robustness check using alternative estimation specifications, we include dummy variables (MBA and PhD); Table 5b shows that the model (8) has the highest * "value, with 0.2705 and adjusted *" with 0.2445, with statistical significance at the 1% level. Surprisingly, we find that when MBA and PhD are both included in the model, MBA is statistically significant at the 10% level, but PhD is not statistically significant. However, we can conclude that the educational level affects the share price (Hung et al., 2021).

In the share price model (9), we include extra variable by adding the experience in fintech and healthcare, respectively, and find that the model is statistically significant at the 1% level (column 4 of Table 5b). It has the highest R^2 with 0.2839 and the adjusted R^2 is 0.2518. Having experience in relevant industries thus affects the share price, and consequently, we can conclude that the management team has an impact on the share price.

Table 5 (a) Impact of SPAC share price, (b) SPAC share price additional results

(a)

	Share price	Share price	Share price	Share price	Share price
Leverage	−0.9159**** (0.2107)	−0.8416*** (0.2054)	−0.4573*** (0.2004)	−0.4604** (0.2004)	−0.4427** (0.2035)
Market capitalisation		1.7500*** (4.8600)	1.2400*** (4.5800)	1.1500** (4.6600)	1.1200** (4.7200)
Log (total assets)			0.4883*** (0.0789)	0.4961*** (0.0792)	0.4990*** (0.0795)
Days^2				1.6200 (1.5000)	1.5600 (1.5100)
Syndicate size					0.1560 (0.2968)
N	176	176	176	176	176
R^2	0.0744	0.1249	0.2498	0.2537	0.2545
Adjusted R^2	0.0705	0.1173	0.2400	0.2406	0.2381
P-value	0.00002***	0.000000***	0.00000***	0.00000***	0.000000***

(b)

	Share price	Share price	Share price	Share price
Leverage	−0.4359** (0.2040)	−0.4327** (0.2032)	−0.4442** (0.2031)	−0.4506** (0.2070)
Market capitalisation	1.1100** (4.7200)	1.1500** (4.7100)	1.1800** (4.100)	1.1900*** (4.7100)
Log (total assets)	0.5063*** (0.0804)	0.4966*** (0.0803)	0.4917*** (0.0803)	0.4824*** (0.0801)
Days^2	1.6200 (1.5000)	1.6600 (1.5100)	1.5200 (1.5100)	1.5100 (1.5000)
Syndicate size	0.1654 (0.2975)	−0.0961 (0.2993)	0.1561 (0.3023)	0.1629 (0.3010)
Age	−0.0177 (0.0266)	−0.0235 (0.0266)	−0.0246 (0.0267)	−0.0201 (0.0267)
MBA		0.2628 (0.1594)	0.2632* (0.1592)	0.3261* (0.1747)
PhD			0.3987 (0.3026)	0.1187 (0.3418)
Experience in fintech				0.1519 (0.1035)
Experience healthcare				−0.1819 (0.1433)
N	176	176	176	176
R^2	0.2560	0.2648	0.2705	
Adjusted R^2	0.2363	0.2421	0.2445	
P-value	0.00002***	0.000000***	0.00000***	0.00000***

Table 6 SPAC logit model
results

	Share price
Leverage	1.4591 (0.8919)
Market capitalisation	−0.0601* (0.0332)
Log (total assets)	0.1624* (0.0932)
Syndicate size	0.1628 (0.2121)
Age	0.0292 (0.019)
MBA	0.1505 (0.1115)
PhD	−0.1837 (0.1915)
Finance experience	−0.0112 (0.0865)
Prob (LR statistics)	0.0303**

Notes: The dependent variable is underpricing which takes a value of 1 if the fintech and healthcare SPACs experience underpricing and otherwise is 0

4.3 Logit Model

The application of the logit model examines whether the factors will affect the probability of underpricing. Salerno et al. (2022) use a logit model. Most SPAC studies, besides using the OLS regression, apply the logit model to examine the deal approval probability (Floros & Sapp, 2011; Lakicevic et al., 2014; Vulanovic, 2017).

However, in this study, we mainly focus on investigating whether fintech and healthcare SPACs experience underpricing. Thus, we set the dependent variable as underpricing—a binary variable equal to 1 if the fintech and healthcare SPACs experience underpricing, and 0 otherwise. The logit model of the equation can also be extended to the multivariate case. The advantage of the logit model is that it does not presume equal covariance matrixes and multivariate normality.

In Table 6, the probability (LR statistic) is $0.0303 < 0.05$. Thus, the model is statistically significant at the 5% level. For the logit model, we interpret the sign of coefficients, which indicates either a positive or a negative influence on underpricing. Only market capitalisation and logarithm of total assets are statistically significant at the 10% level. Both of the variables have a positive influence on the possibility of underpricing. Overall, the results suggest that the variables have the possibility to cause underpricing.

4.4 Probit Model

From the SPAC literature, the probit regression model can be applied as the robustness check for the logistic regression model (Cumming et al., 2014; Lakicevic et al., 2014). Table 7 reveals that the logarithms of total assets and market capitalisation are statistically significant at the 10% level, respectively. Additionally, leverage is statistically significant at the 10% level. The LR statistic has slightly

Table 7 SPAC probit regression model results

	Share price	Share price
Leverage	1.4591 (0.8919)	0.8648* (0.5219)
Market capitalisation	−0.0601* (0.0332)	−0.0580 (0.0834)
Log (total assets)	0.1624* (0.0932)	0.0956* (0.0540
Syndicate size	0.1628 (0.2121)	0.1020 (0.1278)
Age	0.0292 (0.019)	0.0165 (0.0105)
MBA	0.1505 (0.1115)	0.0923 (0.0679)
PhD	−0.1837 (0.1915)	−0.1123 (0.1175)
Finance experience	−0.0112 (0.0865)	−0.0051 (0.0522)
Days		−0.0580 (0.0834)
Prob (LR statistics)	0.0303**	0.0315**

The dependent variable is underpricing which takes a value of 1 if the fintech and healthcare SPACs experience underpricing and otherwise is 0. All 173 fintech and healthcare SPACs analysed have all information on the characteristics

increased from 0.0303 to 0.0315. However, the whole model is still statistically significant at the 5% level.

5 Conclusion

This study investigated if fintech and healthcare SPACs experience underpricing. From the theoretical perspective, there are a few reasons why underpricing may exist in this case. Firstly, due to the structure of SPACs, agency theory may explain that the management team has a strong economic incentive to consummate the deal as their "sponsor shares" and warrants become worthless once the SPAC is liquidated or the shareholders disapprove of the deal. Therefore, although the management team will complete the deal, the merger might involve a low-quality company.

Furthermore, signalling theory also explains underpricing. The SPAC management team finds a way to signal the firm's quality to shareholders to mitigate the information asymmetry and increase the demand, thereby lowering the probability of underpricing. The information asymmetry theory explains that companies with higher information asymmetry have a higher probability of experiencing underpricing, especially high-tech companies. Moreover, the winner's curse theory explains that only irrational shareholders approve of a low-quality acquisition. With bad SPACs, shareholders have the right to disapprove of the acquisition and prevent themselves from suffering a loss.

In response to the questions raised in the introduction, the findings of this study imply that fintech and healthcare SPACs from 2010 to 2021 experienced moderate underpricing. Applying Jog and Sun's (2007) method, the results show there is moderate underpricing, with a mean of 0.0251 and statistical significance at the 1% level. The result is consistent, with the mean of 0.019. This work claims that one could expect SPACs to have moderate underpricing due to the nature of SPACs, i.e. without an operating history. Thus, there is a lack of information for investors to analyse. The only information provided comprises the details of the management team, including its average age, team size, experience, and education level, in the S-1 prospectus. Furthermore, after applying Cizmovic et al.'s (2013) method, we find a moderate underpricing of −0.0742 that is statistically significant at the 1% level for fintech and healthcare SPACs on the first day of trading.

This study has meaningful implications for fintech and healthcare private companies that intend to go public through SPACs and for the investors who intend to invest in SPACs. Various forms of regression models were applied to examine if the attributes of the management team impact underpricing in this study. The results illustrate that the underpricing is significant. The evidence shows that the management team attributes impact on fintech and healthcare SPACs' underpricing. The team size is not significant, which might suggest that the quantity of the management team is trivial compared to its quality. The logarithm of total assets is consistent and shows a significant impact on underpricing in all three regression models, while leverage, MBA, management with finance experience, and market capitalisation are statistically significant. However, the existence of endogeneity is also demonstrated. In addition, interestingly, the results illustrate that the management team has an impact on the share price, with the variables of leverage, market capitalisation, the logarithm of total assets, and MBA. Here, agency theory could explain underpricing in that the management teams have a strong economic incentive to consummate deals. This is a critical factor to be considered by shareholders when investing in SPACs. Furthermore, information asymmetry exists because there is no basis with which public investors can evaluate the company's abilities (Agarwal, 2021). Therefore, shareholders must rely on the management team.

Overall, based on our findings, SPACs could be a better alternative to IPO, especially when a company is young and has a high information asymmetry, particularly as SPACs provide the opportunity to convey important information to potential shareholders through an S-1 prospectus and are protected under the "safe harbour provision" (Daily et al., 2003). Another advantage is that the standard process, with SEC registrations, prospectuses, and investor roadshows, allows SPAC investors to determine the ability and quality of the SPAC management team to reduce information asymmetry. Thus, SPACs could be a viable alternative to traditional IPOs. However, there are contradictory views on whether SPACs are better than traditional IPO in terms of hidden costs and price certainty (Klausner et al., 2022; Gahng et al., 2021). Therefore, future research on SPAC underpricing is called for to provide more accurate and comprehensive views. Figure 1 provide the number of SPACs for the period of our study. We see the drammatic increase of SPACs over the period 2019–2021 which indicates the future trend. Figure 2 shows the SPACs count on target industries. It is not of surprise that Tech (Fintech, Biotech and Proptech) dominates the arena.

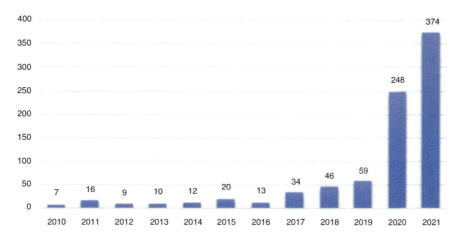

Fig. 1 Number of SPACs from 2010 to 2021

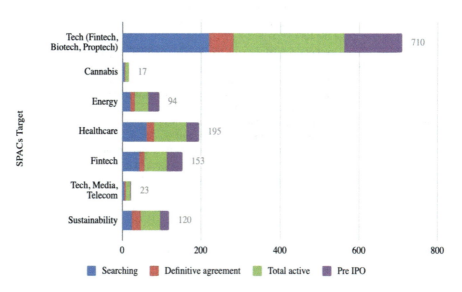

Fig. 2 SPAC count on targeted industries and stages in 2020 and 2021

A.1 Appendix

Variable definition. This table provides detailed description of the data gathering process and the calculation method for all variables.

Variables	Definition
IPO pricing	
Fill_IPO_Date	Number of the dates from filing S-1 registration statement until IPO date
Underpricing	The difference between the first day trading closing price on the secondary market and the offer price
Leverage	The ratio of total liabilities to total assets
TA	Natural logarithm of total assets
EV	The multiple of enterprise value to EBITA
ROA	Management effectiveness
Price/book	The multiple of market value of equity to book value of equity
SPAC structure	
No. of managers	Number of active, equity-holding members of the management team
SPAC size	Market capitalisation of the SPAC at the time of the IPO; gross proceeds of the IPO
Deferred underwriting fees	Level of deferred fee until the outcome of SPAC acquisition
Syndicate size/number of underwriters	The number of investment banks that comprise the underwriting syndicate. Number of all syndicate members that have underwritten stakes of the offering amount
Threshold	Maximum % of SPAC shareholders that are allowed to redeem shares without rejecting the proposed acquisition. (SEC S-1/F-1 form) Indirect measure of management team quality (Cumming et al., 2014, b)
Trust value	Percentage of the net IPO proceeds transferred to the escrow account
Fintech	Dummy variable which is set to 1 if firms belong to fintech industry and 0 otherwise
Healthcare	Dummy variable which is set to 1 if firms belong to healthcare industry and 0 otherwise
Management team	
Average team age	Average team age of the respective SPAC team as stated in the latest 424/425 SEC filing
Years of financial service background	Number of average management team years worked in financial service industry as defined for the variable financial service background
Years of healthcare background	Number of average management team years worked in financial service industry as defined for the variable healthcare background
MBA	Sum of dummy variables of a master of business administration degree
PHD	Sum of dummy variables of a PhD or comparable academic degree

References

Aboody, D., & Lev, B. (2000). Information asymmetry, R&D, and insider gains. *The Journal of Finance, 55*(6), 2747–2766.

Agarwal, R. (2021). *An insight into SPACs and their valuation conundrum.* Working paper, University of California at Los Angeles.

Akerlof, G. A. (1978). The market for "lemons": Quality uncertainty and the market mechanism. In *Uncertainty in economics* (pp. 235–251). Academic Press.

Bai, J., Ma, A., & Zheng, M. (2021). *Reaching for yield in the going-public market: Evidence from SPACs.* Working Paper.

Baker, M., & Wurgler, J. (2007). Investor sentiment in the stock market. *Journal of Economic Perspectives, 21*(2), 129–152.

Bansal, R., & Khanna, A. (2012). Determinants of IPOs initial return: Extreme analysis of indian market. *Journal of Financial Risk Management, 1*(04), 68.

Bazerman, M. H., & Patel, P. (2021). SPACs: What you need to know. *Harvard Business Review, 99*(4), 102–112.

Beatty, R. P. (1989). Auditor reputation and the pricing of initial public offerings. *Accounting Review*, 693–709.

Beatty, R. P., & Ritter, J. R. (1986). Investment banking, reputation, and the underpricing of initial public offerings. *Journal of Financial Economics, 15*(1–2), 213–232.

Berger, R. (2008). SPACs: An alternative way to access the public markets. *Journal of Applied Corporate Finance, 20*(3), 68–75.

Bhattacharya, S. (1979). Imperfect information, dividend policy, and the bird in the hand fallacy. *The Bell Journal of Economics*, 259–270.

Blomkvist, M., & Vulanovic, M. (2020). SPAC IPO waves. *Economics Letters, 197*, 109645. Booth and Smith, 1986.

Boyer, C. M., & Baigent, G. G. (2008). SPACs as alternative investments: An examination of performance and factors that drive prices. *The Journal of Private Equity, 11*(3), 8–15.

Cardenes, J. (2021). *Fintech SPAC transactions in Europe and the United States: Fintech laws and regulations.* ICLG.

Carter, R., & Manaster, S. (1990). Initial public offerings and underwriter reputation. *The Journal of Finance, 45*(4), 1045–1067.

Certo, S. T., Daily, C. M., & Dalton, D. R. (2001). Signaling firm value through board structure: An investigation of initial public offerings. *Entrepreneurship Theory and Practice, 26*(2), 33–50.

Chan, L. K., Lakonishok, J., & Sougiannis, T. (2001). The stock market valuation of research and development expenditures. *The Journal of Finance, 56*(6), 2431–2456.

Chatterjee, S., Chidambaran, N. K., & Goswami, G. (2016). Security design for a non-standard IPO: The case of SPACs. *Journal of International Money and Finance, 69*, 151–178.

Chemmanur, T. J., & Fulghieri, P. (1997). Why include warrants in new equity issues? A theory of unit IPOs. *Journal of Financial and Quantitative Analysis, 32*(1), 1–24.

Chen, C. R., & Mohan, N. J. (2002). Underwriter spread, underwriter reputation, and IPO underpricing: A simultaneous equation analysis. *Journal of Business Finance & Accounting, 29*(3–4), 521–540.

Cho, J., & Lee, J. (2013). The venture capital certification role in R&D: Evidence from IPO underpricing in Korea. *Pacific-Basin Finance Journal, 23*, 83–108.

Chong, E., Zhong, E., Li, F., Li, Q., Agrawal, S., & Zhang, T. (2021). *Comprehensive study of special purpose acquisition company (SPAC): An investment perspective.* Working paper, University of Illinois at Urbana-Champaign.

Cizmovic, M., Lakicevic, M., & Vulanovic, M. (2013). *Unit IPOs: A case of specified purpose acquisition companies (SPACs).* Working paper, Mediterranean University.

Colak, G., Gounopoulos, D., Loukopoulos, G., & Loukopoulos, P. (2021a). Political power, local policy uncertainty and IPO underpricing. *Journal of Corporate Finance, 67*, 1–32.

Colak, G., Gounopoulos, D., Loukopoulos, P., & Loukopoulos, G. (2021b). Tournament incentives and IPO failure risk. *Journal of Banking & Finance, 130*, 106193.

Cumming, D., Haß, L. H., & Schweizer, D. (2014). The fast track IPO–success factors for taking firms public with SPACs. *Journal of Banking & Finance, 47*, 198–213.

Daily, C. M., Certo, S. T., Dalton, D. R., & Roengpitya, R. (2003). IPO underpricing: A meta–analysis and research synthesis. *Entrepreneurship Theory and Practice, 27*(3), 271–295.

Deeds, D. L., Decarolis, D., & Coombs, J. E. (1997). The impact of firm specific capabilities on the amount of capital raised in an initial public offering: Evidence from the biotechnology industry. *Journal of Business Venturing, 12*(1), 31–46.

Degeorge, F., Martin, J., & Phalippou, L. (2016). On secondary buyouts. *Journal of Financial Economics, 120*(1), 124–145.

Dimitrova, L. (2017). Perverse incentives of special purpose acquisition companies, the "poor man's private equity funds". *Journal of Accounting and Economics, 63*, 99–120.

Eberhart, A. C., Maxwell, W. F., & Siddique, A. R. (2004). An examination of long-term abnormal stock returns and operating performance following R&D increases. *The Journal of Finance, 59*(2), 623–650.

Floros, I.V. (2008). *Two essays on alternative mechanisms to going public.* PhD thesis, University of Pittsburgh, Pittsburgh, PA.

Floros, I. V., & Sapp, T. R. (2011). Shell games: On the value of shell companies. *Journal of Corporate Finance, 17*(4), 850–867.

Gahng, M., Ritter, J., & Zhang, D. (2021). *SPACs.* Working paper, University of Florida.

Goergen, M., Gounopoulos, D., & Koutroumpis, P. (2021). Do multiple credit ratings reduce money left on the table? Evidence from U.S. IPOs. *Journal of Corporate Finance, 67*, 1–32.

Gomber, P., Koch, J. A., & Siering, M. (2017). Digital finance and fintech: Current research and future research directions. *Journal of Business Economics, 87*(5), 537–580.

Gosen, N., (2021). The influence of experienced intermediaries on the performance of SPACs. University of Twente.

Gounopoulos, D., & Pham, H. (2017). Credit rating effect on earnings management in U.S. IPOs. *Journal of Business Finance and Accounting, 44*, 154–195.

Gounopoulos, D., & Pham, H. (2018). Specialist CEOs and IPO survival. *Journal of Corporate Finance, 48*, 217–243.

Gounopoulos, D., Kallias, A., Kallias, K., & Tzeremes, P. (2017). Political money contributions of US IPOs. *Journal of Corporate Finance, 43*, 19–38.

Gounopoulos, D., Mazouz, K., & Wood, G. (2021). The consequences of political donations for IPO premium and performance. *Journal of Corporate Finance, 67*, 101888.

Gounopoulos, D., Loukopoulos, G., Loukopoulos, P., & Wood, G. (2022). Corporate political activities and the SEC's oversight role in the IPO process. *Journal of Management Studies.*

Haddad, C., & Hornuf, L. (2019). The emergence of the global fintech market: Economic and technological determinants. *Small Business Economics, 53*(1), 81–105.

Hale, L. M. (2007). SPAC: A financing tool with something for everyone. *Journal of Corporate Accounting & Finance, 18*(2), 67–74.

Hung, H., Liu, J., Yao, X., Zhang, H., Zhumabayev, M., & Zhang, T. (2021). *Factor analysis of SPACs: Impact on SPACs performance by management factors.* Working paper, University of Illinois at Urbana Champaign.

Ignatyeva, E., Rauch, C., & Wahrenburg, M. (2013). Analyzing European SPACs. *The Journal of Private Equity, 17*(1), 64–79.

Jenkinson, T., & Sousa, M. (2011). Why SPAC investors should listen to the market. *Journal of Applied Finance, 21.*

Jensen, M. C., & Meckling, W. H. (1976). Theory of the firm: Managerial behavior, agency costs and ownership structure. *Journal of Financial Economics, 3*(4), 305–360.

Jog, V. M., & Sun, C. (2007). *Blank check IPOs: A home run for management.*

Junger, M., & Mietzner, M. (2020). Banking goes digital: The adoption of fintech services by German households. *Finance Research Letters, 34*, 101260.

Keasey, K., & Short, H. (1997). Equity retention and initial public offerings: The influence of signalling and entrenchment effects. *Applied Financial Economics, 7*(1), 75–85.

Keys, B. J., Mukherjee, T., Seru, A., & Vig, V. (2010). Did securitization lead to lax screening? Evidence from subprime loans. *Quarterly Journal of Economics, 125*(1), 307–362.

Kim, H. (2009). *Essays on management quality, IPO characteristics and the success of business combinations*. Doctoral Thesis, Louisianna State University.

Kim, J., Pukthuanthong-Le, K., & Walker, T. (2008). Leverage and IPO underpricing: High-tech versus low-tech IPOs. *Management Decision, 46*(1).

Klausner, M., Ohlrogge, M., & Ruan, E. (2022). *A sober look at SPACs*.

Lakicevic, M., & Vulanovic, M. (2011). Determinants of mergers: A case of specified purpose acquisition companies (SPACs). *Investment Management and Financial Innovations, 8*(3), 114–120.

Lakicevic, M., & Vulanovic, M. (2013). A story on SPACs. *Managerial Finance, 39*(4).

Lakicevic, M., Shachmurove, Y., & Vulanovic, M. (2014). Institutional changes of specified purpose acquisition companies (SPACs). *The North American Journal of Economics and Finance, 28*, 149–169.

Lamont, O. A., & Thaler, R. H. (2003). Anomalies: The law of one price in financial markets. *Journal of Economic Perspectives, 17*(4), 191–202.

Lawless, R. M., Ferris, S. P., & Bacon, B. (1998). The influence of legal liability on corporate financial signaling. *Journal of Corporate Law, 23*, 209.

Layne, R., Lenahan, B. V., & Eikkins, L. L. P. (2018). *Special purpose acquisition companies: An introduction*. Harvard Law School Forum on Corporate Governance.

Loughran, T., Ritter, J. (2002). Why don't issuers get upset about leaving money on the table of IPOs? *Review of Financial Studies 15*, 413–443

Lee, I., & Shin, Y. J. (2018). Fintech: Ecosystem, business models, investment decisions, and challenges. *Business Horizons, 61*(1), 35–46.

Lewellen, S. M. (2009). *SPACs as an asset class*. Working paper, Pennsylvania State University.

Lin, C., Lu, F., Michaely, R., & Qin, S. (2021). *SPAC IPOs and sponsor network centrality*. Harvard Law School Forum on Corporate Governance.

Lowry, M., Officer, M. S., & Schwert, G. W. (2010). The variability of IPO initial returns. *The Journal of Finance, 65*(2), 425–465.

Mezhoud, M., & Boubaker, A. (2011). Determinants of the components of IPO initial returns: Paris stock exchange. *International Journal of Accounting and Financial Reporting, 1*(1), 190.

Michaely, R., & Shaw, W. H. (1994). The pricing of initial public offerings: Tests of adverse-selection and signaling theories. *The Review of Financial Studies, 7*(2), 279–319.

Newman, N., & Trautman, L. J. (2021). *Special purpose acquisition companies (SPACs) and the SEC*. Working paper, Texas AM University.

Passador, M. L. (2021). *In vogue again: The re-rise of SPACs in the IPO market*. Available at SSRN 3820957.

Riemer, D. S. (2007). Special purpose acquisition companies: SPAC and SPAN, or blank check redux. *Washington University Law Review, 85*, 931.

Ritter, J. R., & Welch, I. (2002). A review of IPO activity, pricing, and allocations. *The Journal of Finance, 57*(4), 1795–1828.

Rock, K. (1986). Why new issues are underpriced. *Journal of Financial Economics, 15*(1–2), 187–212.

Rodrigues, U., & Stegemoller, M. (2011). *Special purpose acquisition corporations: A public view of private equity*. UGA legal studies research paper, (11–12).

Rodrigues, U., & Stegemoller, M. (2014). What all-cash companies tell us about IPOs and acquisitions. *Journal of Corporate Finance, 29*, 111–121.

Rodriguez, U., & Stegemoller, M. (2021). *Redeeming SPACs*. Working Paper University of Georgia.

Ross, S. A. (1977). The determination of financial structure: The incentive-signalling approach. *The Bell Journal of Economics*, 23–40.

Saengchote, K. (2021). *The Tesla effect and the mispricing of special purpose acquisition companies (SPACs)*. Working paper, Chulalongkorn Business School.

Salerno, D., Sampagnaro, G., & Verdoliva, V. (2022). Fintech and IPO underpricing: An explorative study. *Finance Research Letters*, 1–10.

Schultz, P. (1993). Unit initial public offerings: A form of staged financing. *Journal of Financial Economics, 34*(2), 199–229.

Shachmurove, Y., & Vulanovic, M. (2015). Specified purpose acquisition companies in shipping. *Global Finance Journal, 26*, 64–79.

Shachmurove, Y., & Vulanovic, M. (2018). *Specified purpose acquisition company IPOs* (p. 301). The Oxford Handbook of IPOs.

Sheng, T. (2021). The effect of fintech on banks' credit provision to SMEs: Evidence from China. *Finance Research Letters, 39*, 101558.

Stulz, R. M. (2020). Public versus private equity. *Oxford Review of Economic Policy, 36*(2), 275–290.

Thomadakis, S., Gounopoulos, D., & Nounis, C. (2012). Long term performance of Greek IPOs. *European Financial Management, 17*, 117–141.

Thomadakis, S., Gounopoulos, D., Nounis, C., & Riginos, M. (2017). Innovation and upheaval: Early growth in the Greek capital market listing and IPOs from 1880 to world war II in the Athens stock exchange. *Economic History Review, 70*, 859–889.

Vulanovic, M. (2017). SPACs: Post-merger survival. *Managerial Finance, 43*(6).

Wei, F. J., & Marsidi, A. (2019). Determinants of initial public offering (IPO) underpricing in Malaysian stock market. *International Journal of Academic Research in Business and Social Sciences, 9*(11).

An Answer to Roll's Critique (1977) 45 Years Later

Marc Desban, Erkin Diyarbakirlioglu, Souad Lajili Jarjir, and Mehmet Hakan Satman

Abstract We implement a new framework to mitigate the errors-in-variables (EIV) problem in the estimation of asset pricing models. Considering an international data of portfolio stock returns from 1990 to 2021 widely used in empirical studies, we highlight the importance of the estimation method in time-series regressions. We compare the traditional ordinary-least squares (OLS) method to an alternative estimator based on a compact genetic algorithm (CGA) in the case of the CAPM. Based on intercepts, betas, adjusted R2, and the Gibbons et al. (1989) test, we find that the CGA-based method outperforms overall the OLS method. In particular, we obtain less statistically significant intercepts, smoother R2 across different portfolios, and lower GRS test statistics.

Specifically, in line with Roll's critique (1977) on the unobservability of the market portfolio, we reduce the attenuation bias in market risk premium estimates. Moreover, our results are robust to alternative methods such as instrumental variables estimated with generalized-method of moments (GMM). Our findings have several empirical and managerial implications related to the estimation of asset

---

Some results in this chapter are published in *Asset pricing models with measurement error problems: A new framework with Compact Genetic Algorithms*, Finance, 2022. https://doi.org/10.3917/fina.432.0001

M. Desban
Université Paris Est Creteil, IRG, Creteil, France

Université Gustave Eiffel, IRG, Marne-la-Vallée, France

E. Diyarbakirlioglu
Université Paris Est Creteil, IRG, Creteil, France

Université Gustave Eiffel, IRG, Marne-la-Vallée, France

S. Lajili Jarjir (✉)
Université de Lorraine, CEREFIGE, Nancy, France
e-mail: souad.lajili@univ-lorraine.fr

M. H. Satman
Department of Econometrics, Istanbul University, Istanbul, Turkey

pricing models as well as their interpretation as a popular tool in terms of corporate financial decision-making.

Keywords Asset pricing · CAPM · Market portfolio · Time-series regressions · Ordinary-least squares (OLS) · Errors-in-variables (EIV) · GMM with instrumental variables · Compact genetic algorithms (CGAs)

1 Introduction

The traditional Sharpe-Lintner-Mossin factor modeling framework (Sharpe, 1964; Lintner, 1965; Mossin, 1966), which, later, has been substantially tuned by several authors including, among others, Fama and French (1992, 1993, 1995, 2015) or Carhart (1997), constitutes the backbone of modeling asset prices in finance. These models give the researcher a systematic analysis framework to break down the risk-return trade-off of a particular set of assets by means of testable relationships between the asset returns and a set of common risk factors. An extensive body of research discusses both the theoretical and empirical issues related to these models of the risk-expected return trade-off; see, among others, Huang and Litzenberger (1988), Cochrane (2005) or, more recently, Ferson (2019).

In this chapter, we contribute to the empirical literature by addressing the errors-in-variables (EIV) problem in the estimation of asset pricing models with a focus on the market risk factor that is still at the heart of most modeling efforts despite numerous theoretical and empirical advances made insofar. In line with the earlier remarks initially pinpointed by Fama & MacBeth (1973) and Roll (1977), the latter being subsequently came to be known as "Roll's critique," the measurement error problem is *endemic* in any factor model setup that employs the "market risk" in the spirit of the Sharpe-Lintner-Mossin CAPM paradigm.[1] Defined as the incremental return on a hypothetical market portfolio over the yield on a risk-free asset, the market risk factor relies on the observability of a market portfolio, which Fama and French (1997) consider as the "fundamental input to achieve market clearing conditions under complete agreement among investors."

We thus focus on the *market portfolio M^** as the main right-hand-side variable predicting the variation in asset returns and consider it subject to EIV by its very definition. The true market portfolio is an artifact, one that can never be truly observed, so is the true market risk premium. We then speculate, fairly reasonably, that any proxy used in the existing body of empirical work can at best be seen as a representation of the true variable but is likely to include some measurement error u, which we define as the difference between the true and observed values as $u = M - M^*$. The implications of ignoring the measurement error are not neutral. To start with the simplest case of the market model framework first, all fitted

---

[1] See Huang and Litzenberger (1988, ch. 10) for a complete discussion of the conceptual and econometric issues involved in testing the CAPM.

coefficients that ignore the error in the observed values of the proxy will be biased downward under some mild assumptions; see Hausman (2001), Racicot (2015b), or Greene (2018), among others, for a thorough discussion of this attenuation effect. This implies that any output or indicator related to the market risk premium will be erroneous. That a market beta estimate is systematically less than its true value simply means that the market risk itself is also underestimated. Second, the downward bias in β also induces an upward bias of the opposite sign in the model intercept α as long as the mean of the market risk premium is positive, a condition one naturally expects to hold given the definition of the market portfolio. It then turns out that negative alphas happen to appear "less negative" than they truly are while those positive in reality tend to materialize lower than their true levels. It can be readily seen that the implications of such a behavior of the fitted intercepts can be quite pervasive from the perspective of financial management industry.

To implement our study, we employ a dataset widely used in the empirical asset pricing literature. Specifically, we use portfolio return data from Kenneth French's library broken down into five geographic regions: World, North America, Europe, Asia-Pacific, and Japan. Time series are in monthly frequencies and span the period from 1990 to 2021. We then fit time-series regressions by the traditional OLS that ignore the potential measurement error in the market portfolio first, and then by a new estimator based on a compact genetic algorithm devised in Satman and Diyarbakirlioglu (2015) to mitigate the impact of EIV. We compare the results obtained from these two methods by reporting the fitted intercepts, market betas, adjusted R^2 values, and the Gibbons et al. (1989) (GRS) test statistics.

Our results shed light on several issues not only on empirical asset pricing but also corporate financial decision-making. First, we show that naive OLS estimations ignoring the EIV in market risk premium are unsatisfactory as a tool to run time-series regressions of stock returns. We observe substantial downward bias in fitted slope coefficients as predicted by the classical EIV model. On average, OLS without EIV correction underestimates the market beta by 25% as much as lower than the CGA-based estimations, implying substantial measurement error in the market risk premium. Second, by cutting down the bias in the fitted betas, we also show the extent to which the model intercepts can be inflated due to the contamination effect. We capture this observation by GRS tests. Specifically, we observe significant drop in GRS test statistics regardless of the portfolio type and geography. Almost all $\mathcal{F}$-values whereby we jointly test the significance of model intercepts exhibit substantial drawdown. We conjecture that our findings lead to several managerial implications in connection with portfolio management, asset pricing, and corporate financial as well as capital-budgeting decisions.

The chapter is organized as follows: Sect. 2 reviews the main literature on the two fields of our interest: asset pricing on one hand and EIV on the other. Section 3 presents a brief overview of the econometric treatment of classical EIV model. Section 4 indicates the methodology used and the data. Sections 5 and 1 present the results of the empirical analyses. Finally, Sect. 6 concludes the chapter and outlines the main issues for future research.

2 Literature Review

2.1 Asset Pricing Framework

The positive and linear relation between the expected return on an asset and the systematic risk to which the asset is exposed is probably the most tested hypothesis in the field of asset pricing. This relationship is the main state given by the capital asset pricing model (henceforth CAPM) (Sharpe, 1964; Lintner, 1965; Mossin, 1966; Black, 1972). Originally, the CAPM is consistent with the mean-variance optimization framework proposed by Markowitz (1952) and extended by Tobin (1958). However, despite the popularity of the CAPM, a large body of theoretical and empirical work puts into perspective a number of failures in explaining the risk vs. expected return trade-off.

Among the earliest and well-known critics is Roll's critique (Roll, 1977) about the unobservability of the market portfolio. In empirical studies, we commonly talk about "anomalies." Among the rich collection of these anomalies highlighted in the empirical work on the CAPM, some are more popular than others. For example, Basu (1977) observes significant abnormal returns for portfolios sorted by the book-to-market ratio and controlled for market betas. Other empirical studies confirm this observation named "value effect" (Rosenberg et al., 1985; De Bondt and Thaler, 1985; Chan et al., 1991). However, the main issue that remains is how to explain these anomalies and how to settle between the lack of market efficiency and the misspecification of the asset pricing model.

On the other hand, many other studies report that the beta weakly explains the returns of small stocks (Reinganum, 1981; Breeden et al., 1989; Fama and French, 1992). This "size effect" is introduced the first time by Banz (1981). Some empirical studies show that the size effect tends to disappear after the publication of Banz's article. For example, Amihud (2002) does not detect an additional risk premium regarding the size on the US market after 1980. Dimson and Marsh (1999) report a size effect only on the period earlier than 1983. The same result about the size and the book-to-market ratio in explaining the cross-sectional difference of average stock returns is reported about the profitability ratio (measured by the gross profits to assets) by Novy-Marx (2013). Cochrane (2011) speaks of a "zoo" of explanatory factors. Recently, Hou et al. (2015) identify 437 anomalies.

On the basis of these empirical observations, Fama and French (1992, 1993) develop the three-factor model. They demonstrate empirically that adding size and value effects to the market beta explains better the time-series variation in the returns, in the US market first and with an international data after. The beginning of the 1990s marks the start of a huge literature about factor models: three-, four-, and five-factor models; see Carhart (1997), Fama and French (1993, 2012, 2015, 2016, 2018b,a,c, 2020).

Even if some of these factors are subject of debate because of different reasons (weak historical records, vary significantly over time, weaken after discovery, concentrated among micro-cap stocks, weak internationally, lack of theoretical explanation, etc.), researchers' and practitioners' interest on this issue does not stop.

2.2 Errors-in-Variables Framework

Despite the early acknowledgment as well as the persistent presence of the EIV in financial economics (Fama & MacBeth, 1973; Shanken, 1992), the efforts to address, if not definitely solve, this challenge have attracted less attention compared to other issues related to the estimation of asset pricing models. At first sight, it may be argued that the consequences of ignoring the EIV are mostly mild for there is no change of sign in the coefficients and the attenuation effect is rather limited in high R^2 models. This argument is likely to hold when it comes to several regression-based modeling efforts in finance once we have good reasons to believe that the linear relationship between the left- and right-hand-side variables are strong, such as the link between a tracker and its benchmark. Second, coping with the undesirable effects of the EIV is a notoriously difficult endeavor, especially once we pass from one predictor case to the next stage with multiple regressors. As clearly set forth by Cragg (1994, 1997), the results that are shown to hold for the one variable no longer apply to the multiple regressions. Greene (2018, p. 283–284) shows that even with a single badly measured variable, it is not possible to derive expressions that indicate the magnitude and/or the sign of the bias in the slope. In addition, other coefficient estimates are also biased with unknown directions unless we have extra information about the true data generating process (Carmichael & Coën, 2008, p. 779).

Measurement error models are typically treated with instrumental variable techniques as EIV arises after all as an endogeneity issue given the nonzero correlation between the error terms and the regressors. The econometric literature on the IV estimation of EIV models is extensive; see, among others, Hausman and Watson (1985), Fuller (1987), Leamer (1987), or Greene (2018). Consistent estimates of model parameters can be obtained as long as we come up with valid instruments correlated with the true but unobserved values of the predictor *and* uncorrelated with the measurement error. Ashenfelter and Krueger (1994) who examine the return to schooling is a classic example of IV-based treatment of EIV problem. "Education" is, like many other socio-economic variables, intrinsically not measurable, and any attempt to parameterize the benefits of education has no other choice but using a proxy for "measuring" it, like "years of schooling." The authors' solution consists in contrasting the wage rates of identical twins with different schooling levels by isolating the outcome from the individual's own traits. Andersson and Møen (2016, p. 114) note that the popularity of IV estimators in applied work is probably due to the fact this method is intuitive and easy to implement. From a practical viewpoint, however, the key difficulty associated with the IV estimation of EIV models lies in finding such valid instruments simultaneously correlated with the true regressor *and* uncorrelated with the measurement error (Durbin, 1954; Carroll et al., 2006; Carmichael & Coën, 2008). In particular, when the set of instruments is only weakly correlated with the original regressors, the problems due to EIV can even be exacerbated (Racicot & Theoret, 2015). IV estimates not only turn out to exhibit much larger standard errors than their least-squares counterparts, but they are also asymptotically biased (Wooldridge, 2015; Stock et al., 2002), and consistent estimation of model parameters turns out to be even more difficult as the orthogonality assumption of the instruments also requires additional instruments for which the assumption should hold (Iwata, 1992).

As long as we consider the common ground between the two strands of literature on EIV and asset pricing models, an influential approach based on which numerous subsequent studies have been published is the method developed by Dagenais and Dagenais (DD) (1997). Loosely speaking, the DD estimation consists of a matrix-like combination of Durbin and Pal's estimators (Durbin, 1954; Pal, 1980).

DD suggest various combinations of the left- and right-hand-side variables' own higher and cross-moments as a set of valid instruments. Unlike other IV-based approaches in the literature, the DD estimator requires no extraneous information as the proposed instruments are derived from sample moments of order higher than two (Dagenais & Dagenais (1997, p. 193)). Carmichael and Coën (2008, p. 781) underline that an important feature of the DD estimator is that it is likely to be particularly suitable to financial time series given the frequently observed non-normality and significant third and fourth moments of such data. As one potential downside related to the DD estimation, however, Cragg (1997) notes that the number of parameters that must be estimated to mitigate the EIV increases much faster than the number of model parameters because of the number of significant higher cross-moments between different right-hand-side variables (Cragg, 1997, p. 89–90).

To paraphrase Carmichael and Coën (2008, p. 779), the DD approach turns out to be promising in financial economics as long as the non-normality of the true unobserved variables is verified. This is in turn quite a plausible assumption given the omnipresent non-Gaussianity in asset returns. Accordingly, several studies have so far addressed the EIV in asset pricing models by constructing instruments from the higher moments of the original data (Coën & Racicot, 2007; Carmichael & Coën, 2008; Coen et al., 2010). Implementing the higher-moment estimator for the CAPM, Fama-French three- and four-factor models, Coën and Racicot (2007, p. 449) note that the IV estimation improves significantly the performance of the fitted models, so that the use of higher-moment techniques should be warranted for interpreting Jensen's (1968) α and β coefficients frequently used in applied work. Using Fama and French (1992) monthly returns on 25 value-weighted portfolios from January 1963 to February 2006, Carmichael and Coën (2008) argue that estimates of the Jensen's α differ substantially between OLS and DD higher-moment approach. More recently, the higher-moment instrumental variables approach to tackle the EIV issue in linear asset pricing models has been extended by Racicot (2015a) who developed an estimation methodology that enables to deal with the weak instrument problem. Several subsequent papers have then used this new "GMMd" estimation method in the context of some mainstream asset pricing models (Racicot & Theoret, 2015, 2016; Racicot et al., 2018; Racicot et al., 2019). Racicot and Theoret (2015) apply the GMMd approach to address the EIV problem in Pastor and Stambaugh's model Pástor and Stambaugh (2003), which is basically an augmented version of the Fama-French five-factor model by an additional risk factor that incorporates a liquidity premium. The authors note that the "liquidity variable at best contains significant measurement errors or at worst is ill-conceived" Racicot and Theoret (2015) [p. 338]. In a related work, Racicot and Theoret (2016) emphasize that the effect of all systematic risk factors tend to vanish when controlled for measurement errors except the traditional market factor (p. 447). Collectively, the results set forth by Racicot and Theoret (2015), (2016) are consistent with Harvey et al. (2016) or Cochrane (2011), who warn against the "potential unreliability" of the extra risk factors developed by Fama and French or Pastor and Stambaugh, which greatly shaped the financial literature over the last decades (Racicot & Theoret, 2015, p.338).

3 Errors-in-Variables

3.1 Consequences of EIV

In this section, we provide an outline of the classical errors-in-variables (EIV) framework and demonstrate the downward bias in the slope coefficient in the presence of EIV. Our presentation is limited to the single-variable case for both sake of simplicity and the fact that the attenuation bias constitutes the central result of EIV. The central message carried out by the treatment of the single-variable case covers to a large extent how EIV leads to puzzling consequences. That is said, it must be noted that some results derived from the single predictor model do not necessarily generalize to the multiple case when more than one variable is subject to measurement error. For detailed treatments of the issue, see, among others, Cragg (1994), Carroll et al. (2006), Buonaccorsi (2010), or Racicot (2015b).

To start, consider the following population regression model:

$$Y_t^* = \alpha + \beta X_t^* + \epsilon_t \tag{1}$$

for $t = 1, ..., T$, where Y^* and X^* are two series of dependent and independent variables, $\epsilon \sim iid(0, \sigma_\epsilon^2)$ the disturbance term assumed to be serially uncorrelated with homogeneous variance, and α and β, the parameters to estimate. The (classical) measurement error framework is typically introduced using the following additive relationship:

$$Y_t = Y_t^* + v_t$$
$$X_t = X_t^* + u_t$$

that can be read as "observation is the sum of the true value plus measurement error." In what follows, we delimit the scope to the measurement error to the right-hand-side variable as it can be easily shown that the impact of the error on Y is limited to a lower goodness-of-the-fit without a cost on parameter estimates.[2]

We set $Y = Y^*$ and $X = X^* + u$ with the additional assumptions $E(u) = 0$, $E(uX^*) = 0$ and $E(uY^*) = 0$. The measurement error in X is thus uncorrelated with the true values X^* as well as with those of the dependent variable. These assumptions define collectively the *classical errors-in-variables* model. We can then rewrite the Eq. (1) as

$$Y_t = \alpha + \beta X_t + (\epsilon_t - \beta_1 u_t) \tag{2}$$

Consider the least-squares estimate of the slope coefficient:

$$\widehat{\beta}_1^{LS} = \beta_1 + \frac{\sum_t \left(X_t^* - \bar{X}^* \right) \epsilon_t}{\sum_t \left(X_t^* - \bar{X}^* \right)^2} \tag{3}$$

which states the estimate is the sum of the true parameter plus a bias. Introducing EIV by $X_t^* = X_t - u_t$ and the compound error term of the model $\epsilon_t - \beta_1 u_t$, we obtain:

$$\widehat{\beta}_1^{LS} = \beta_1 + \frac{\sum_t \left(X_t - \bar{X} \right) \left(\epsilon_t - \beta_1 u_t \right)}{\sum_t \left(X_t - \bar{X} \right)^2} \tag{4}$$

Because $\bar{X} = \bar{X}^* + \bar{u}$ and $E(u) = 0$ by definition, the last expression can be rewritten as

$$
\begin{aligned}
\widehat{\beta}_1^{LS} &= \beta_1 + \frac{\sum \left(X_t - \bar{X}^* \right) \left(\epsilon_t - \beta_1 u_t \right)}{\sum \left(X_t - \bar{X}^* \right)^2} \\
&= \beta_1 + \frac{\sum \left(X_t^* + u_t - \bar{X}^* \right) \left(\epsilon_t - \beta_1 u_t \right)}{\sum \left(X_t^* + u_t - \bar{X}^* \right)^2} \\
&= \beta_1 + \frac{\sum X_t^* \epsilon_t - \beta_1 \sum X_t^* u_t + \sum u_t \epsilon_t - \beta_1 \sum u_t^2 - \bar{X}^* \sum \epsilon_t + \beta_1 \bar{X}^* \sum u_t}{\sum X_t^{*2} + \sum u_t^2 + T \bar{X}^{*2} + 2 \sum X_t^* u_t - 2 \bar{X}^* \sum X_t^* - 2 \bar{X}^* \sum u_t}
\end{aligned} \tag{5}
$$

Noting that the term $-2\bar{X}^* \sum X_t^*$ is equivalent to $-2T\bar{X}^{*2}$ and making use of the classical EIV assumptions, the last line collapses to,[3]

$$\widehat{\beta}_1^{LS} = \beta_1 + \frac{-\beta_1 \sum u_t^2}{\sum X_t^{*2} - T \bar{X}^{*2} + \sum u_t^2} \tag{6}$$

---

[2] The cost of a badly measured Y is that the variance of ϵ is equal to $Var(\epsilon) + Var(v)$.

[3] The trick is $-2\bar{X}^* \sum X_t^* \times \frac{T}{T} = -2T\bar{X}^{*2}$.

Multiplying both the numerator and the denominator of the term capturing the bias by $1/T$, we obtain $\frac{1}{T}\sum u_t^2 = \sigma_u^2$ and $\frac{1}{T}\left(\sum X_t^{*2} - T\bar{X}^{*2}\right) = \sigma_{X*}^2$. This yields to

$$\hat{\beta}_1^{LS} = \beta_1 - \frac{\beta_1 \sigma_u^2}{\sigma_{X*}^2 + \sigma_u^2}$$

$$= \beta_1 \left(\frac{\sigma_{X*}^2}{\sigma_{X*}^2 + \sigma_u^2}\right) \tag{7}$$

Thus, due to the nonzero correlation between the slope and the error term as $Cov(X,(\epsilon - \beta u)) = Cov((X^* + u),(\epsilon - \beta u)) = -\beta\sigma_u^2$, the last term in parenthesis will be between 0 and 1. The result is that the slope is biased downward even in large samples.

Two important observations come out of the previous analysis: First, and foremost, the least-squares estimate of the slope $\hat{\beta}^{LS}$ is biased downward given that the inequality $Var(X^*) + Var(u) > Var(X^*)$ will hold as long as the right-hand-side variable contains an additive measurement error. In addition, Eq. (7) implies that the bias in β gets worse as the variance of the measurement error $Var(u)$ increases relative to $Var(X^*)$. Hausman (2001) calls this simple yet fundamental result as the *iron law of econometrics*—the magnitude of the estimate is usually smaller than expected. Second, the attenuation effect on β generates a bias of the opposite sign on the intercept α if the mean of the predictor X^* is positive (Cragg, 1994, p. 780). In other words, negative intercepts will be estimated higher than their true values, while positive ones will be estimated lower than they truly are.[4]

When the predictor is subject to such measurement error, consistent estimation of the model parameters usually requires additional data or information. As discussed previously, there exists an extensive literature regarding the techniques devised to address the EIV; see, among others, Fuller (1987), Cheng and Van Ness (1999), Buonaccorsi (2010), or Racicot (2015b). Theoretically, one would get such a consistent estimate of the slope via *method of moments* if the value of the ratio $\lambda = Var(X^*)/(Var(X^*) + Var(u))$, also called the *reliability ratio*, is known (Fuller, 1987). In this case, a generalized-least-squares estimator can be readily obtained by dividing the fitted slope to the reliability ratio. However, as pointed out by Buonaccorsi (2010), the true value of the reliability ratio is never known in practice so that it must also be replaced by its sample counterpart, $\hat{\lambda} = \left(\hat{\sigma}_X^2 - \hat{\sigma}_u^2\right)/\hat{\sigma}_X^2$.[5]

---

[4] This is a key result when it comes to the relationship between the measurement error and the regression-based estimation of asset pricing models in finance. Consider, for simplicity, the single-factor model where the right-hand-side variable is the market risk premium. By construction, it is positive. It turns out that under errors-in-variables, positive alphas will tend to be underestimated while negative alphas will be overestimated than their true levels. Recognizing this effect and putting it into context would have profound impacts on the fund management industry. We will later turn to this discussion in this paper.

[5] The algebra of $\hat{\lambda}$ follows from the fact that $Var(X^*) = Var(X - u)$.

Matters get worse when there are k predictors subject to measurement error like $X_{i,t} = X_{i,t}^* + u_{i,t}, i = 1, ..., k$. In this case, even when there is only one X measured with error, the EIV effect spills over not just on the intercept and the slope of the variable of interest but also on other slope coefficients. In addition, it is not possible to derive exact formulas to express neither the sign nor the magnitude of the bias in each slope β_i because the error in X_i does not only affect the corresponding coefficient but also other coefficients in the model (Greene, 2018, p. 281–285), raising a further issue known as the *contamination effect* (Cragg, 1994). There are several methods that have been so far developed in the literature to deal with the multiple case, yet no solution insofar has proved reliable enough to put full faith on to eradicate the undesirable consequences of EIV.[6]

3.2 CGA-Based Estimation of EIV Model

In this section, we describe the CGA-based estimation of the EIV model developed by Satman and Diyarbakirlioglu (2015). We start by rewriting the one-variable EIV model given in Eq. (2):

$$Y_t = \alpha + \beta X_t + (\epsilon_t - \beta u_t) \tag{8}$$

where $\epsilon - \beta u$ is the compound error term given $X_t = X_t^* + u_t$. It has been previously stressed that ignoring the measurement error u yields biased and inconsistent estimates of the slope even in large samples. Our approach consists in using predictive regressions in order to obtain a *filtered* version of the observed values X and then plug it back to the original model to mitigate the EIV problem.

The central piece of the method is the following auxiliary regression of the badly measured variable on $i = 1, \ldots, d$ dummy variables D_i:

$$X_t = \phi_0 + \phi_1 D_1 + \cdots + \phi_d D_d + \eta_t \tag{9}$$

where $\eta_t \sim iid(0, \sigma_\eta^2)$ is the disturbance series and ϕ_i are model parameters to be estimated. The fitted model is

$$X_t^{CGA} = \widehat{\phi}_0 + \widehat{\phi}_1 D_1 + \cdots + \widehat{\phi}_d D_d \tag{10}$$

such that $X_t = X_t^{CGA} + \widehat{\eta}_t$.[7] We can read this as "observed values are equal to corrected ones plus error." The intuition behind this auxiliary regression model is to break down the observed values X, assumed to be subject to measurement error,

---

[6] This is maybe the main reason why textbook treatments of measurement error models are mostly limited to the one-variable model.

[7] We deliberately drop the "hat" over the fitted series for ease of exposition.

into two components, one deterministic X^{CGA} and the other stochastic $\widehat{\eta}$. In other words, we consider X^{CGA} and $\widehat{\eta}$ as the *fitted equivalents* of the true values of the predictor X^* and its measurement error u, respectively.[8] Plugging the values X^{CGA} back into the original regression model, we get:

$$Y_t = \alpha + \beta X_t^{CGA} + \epsilon_t \tag{11}$$

The estimated coefficients $\widehat{\alpha}^{CGA}$ and $\widehat{\beta}^{CGA}$ are solutions to the following discrete optimization problem:

$$\underset{D_1,\dots,D_d,\widehat{\alpha}^{CGA},\widehat{\beta}^{CGA}}{\text{argmin}} \sum_{t=1}^{T} \left(Y_t - \left(\widehat{\alpha}^{CGA} + \widehat{\beta}^{CGA} X_t^{CGA} \right) \right)^2 \tag{12}$$

so that we perform a joint estimation of the auxiliary regression and the baseline model by substituting the corrected values back into the original regression.[9] Using Monte Carlo simulations, Satman and Diyarbakirlioglu (2015) showed that the CGA-based intercept and slope coefficients have smaller biases with respect to their initial error-prone LS estimates. This comes with some cost in loss of efficiency because $\widehat{\alpha}^{CGA}$ and $\widehat{\beta}^{CGA}$ have also higher variances, which is due to the fact the estimator seeks maximizing the R-square of the regression. The increase in the variance of the estimate is however offset by the bias correction, and, overall, the mean-square-error of the CGA-based estimate is smaller than that of the least-squares as

$$\left(bias \left(\widehat{\beta}^{CGA} \right) \right)^2 + Var \left(\widehat{\beta}^{CGA} \right) = MSE \left(\widehat{\beta}^{CGA} \right) \leq MSE \left(\widehat{\beta}^{LS} \right) \tag{13}$$

There are a number of noticeable features associated with the CGA-based approach. We discuss these in some depth. We also provide in the appendix a pseudo-code of the estimation procedure to accompany our discussion.

Broadly speaking, the goal of EIV-CGA estimation is to extract from an initial population the *best solution* among all *possible combinations* that could be conceived by the algorithm. The best solution corresponds to the state where the algorithm converges and extracts the filtered values X^{CGA}, which we later plug back into the original model.

We initialize the procedure by setting two parameters, namely, (1) the number of dummy variables d that will enter the auxiliary regressions and (2) the *population*

---

[8] Constructing such *error-free* estimates of the regressors has been previously suggested within the IV-based methods of EIV models in the literature; see, for example, Dagenais and Dagenais (1997) or Coën and Racicot (2007).

[9] The appendix gives a detailed exposition of the pseudo-code of the algorithm.

size.[10] d is a user-defined parameter to estimate the regression specified in Eq. 9. Under the current setup, there are no specific guidelines concerning the value d that must be chosen. That is said, Satman and Diyarbakirlioglu (2015, p. 3224–3225) show using simulations involving various configurations that the mean-square-error of the estimator $MSE\left(\widehat{\beta}^{CGA}\right)$ tends to stabilize in the neighborhood of $d = 10$. We also choose this value in our estimations. The *population size* is used to update iteratively the probability vector of the search space until the stability condition for the auxiliary dummy-variables regressions is reached. We set the population size by taking into a consideration the trade-off between the speed with which the algorithm converges and the risk of local optimum trap. Satman and Diyarbakirlioglu (2015) suggest using simulations that for values equal to 20 or above, the population size has negligible effect on the results, with too large values coming at a cost of slowing down the time it takes the CGA to converge.

We turn to the auxiliary dummy-variables regression. First, fitting the model (9) involves several computational problems because of the lack of a closed-form solution, so numerical methods must be used. Genetic algorithms (GAs) provide a handy toolkit for optimizing the objective function (12) and derive the dummies D_i. In a nutshell, GAs are a family of optimization techniques that mimic the natural selection process, whose mechanics and vocabulary borrow extensively, and unsurprisingly, from the theory of evolution. GAs perform a parallel search by screening the entire population by randomizing candidates in different areas of the search space. A potential issue associated with GAs is that the optimization of the objective function is likely to consume too much computational memory. Compact genetic algorithms (CGAs) are primarily designed to overcome this issue. While it cannot be asserted that CGAs are superior to classical GAs in reaching the global optimum, they represent a number of advantages. Specifically, in a CGA, chromosomes, e.g., candidate solutions, are sampled using a probability vector, and the number of iterations is defined with respect to the population size. Therefore, CGAs consume much less computational memory compared to classical GAs. As noted by Baluja and Caruana (1995), CGAs remove "genetics" from GAs by replacing the term "crossing over" by "sampling."[11]

Second, the decomposition of the observed X's as proposed in Eq. (9) considers the residuals η_t as the measurement error on X and the remaining portion $\phi_0 + \phi_1 D_1 + \cdots + \phi_d D_d$ as a "clean" version of the true values of the variable. The approach thus requires solving for the appropriate *linear combination* of the dummy variables to construct the estimate X^{CGA}. This is a genuine component of the approach we adopt and constitutes the central block of the algorithm we describe in the appendix. Given d, the iterations starts off with a probability vector whose elements are all equal to 0.5, and iterations continue until all elements of the vector

---

[10] The setup also requires a third parameter n, which is simply the sample size of the mismeasured variable X.

[11] Pioneering studies include, among others, Holland (1973, 1975, 1987) and Goldberg (1989). For a review of CGAs, see, among others, Baluja and Caruana (1995) or Harik et al. (1999, 2006).

take either the value of 1 or 0. As a simple illustration, consider the following initial state probability vector from which samples, e.g., "chromosomes" of 4-d length will be generated:[12]

$$P = [0.8, 0.1, 0.7, 0.2]$$

which tells that the probability of obtaining $D_1 = 1$ is 0.8, the probability of obtaining $D_2 = 1$ is 0.1, and so on for $P(D_3 = 1)$ and $P(D_4 = 1)$. Given P, sampling a chromosome like $C_1 = [1, 0, 1, 0]$ is much more likely than sampling $C_2 = [0, 1, 0, 1]$. Then, the algorithm initiates by sampling two parents, say C_1 and C_2 using the initial P. The winner is the one who takes the lowest cost function, which is, in our case, the C for which the sum of squared residuals of the dummy regression is lowest. Once C^{winner} is determined, the vector P is updated using the formula:

$$P_i = \begin{cases} P_i + \frac{1}{popSize} & \text{if } C_i^{winner} = 1 \\ P_i - \frac{1}{popSize} & \text{if } C_i^{winner} = 0 \end{cases}$$

With the new P_i obtained, the process moves onward by sampling new parents, generating new offsprings, and updating P_i until each element takes either the value of 1 or 0. The final state yields the new series X^{CGA}, which is then plugged back into the baseline model.

3.3   GMM-Based Estimation of EIV Model

In this subsection, we introduce estimations based on an instrumental variables method. Specifically, we adopt the GMM$_d$ approach developed by Racicot (2015a) and subsequently implemented by, among others, Racicot and Theoret (2015, 2016) or Racicot et al. (2017, 2019). The GMM$_d$ estimator is basically a robust instruments variables-based extension of Hansen's generalized method of moment estimator (Hansen, 1982) and is characterized by the following equation:

$$\arg\min_{\widehat{\beta}} = \left\{ T^{-1} \left[D^\top (Y - X\widehat{\beta}) \right]^\top W T^{-1} \left[D^\top (Y - X\widehat{\beta}) \right] \right\} \tag{14}$$

to estimate the $K \times 1$ vector of population parameters in the linear model $Y = X\beta + \epsilon$. T is the sample size and W is the heteroskedasticity and autocorrelation consistent weighting matrix. X is the $T \times K$ matrix of right-hand-side variables. The

---

[12] The term "probability vector" employed here does not correspond to a conventional vector whose elements sum up to 1 but instead refers to a list where each element shows the probability that the given element takes a specific value.

matrix D has elements $d_{i,t} = x_{i,t} - \widehat{x}_{i,t}$ and is viewed as a "filtered version" of the endogenous variables that should potentially attenuate the measurement errors. $x_{i,t}$ is the mean-centered values of the ith regressor. $\widehat{x}_{i,t}$ in turn are fitted values of the linear model $\widehat{x}_{i,t} = \widehat{\gamma}_0 + z\widehat{\phi}$. The vector of z instruments include $z_0 = i_T$, $z_1 = x \bullet x$, and $z_2 = x \bullet x \bullet x - 3x \, \text{diag} \left(\frac{x^\top x}{T} \right)$ where "$\bullet$" is the Hadamard element-wise product operator. Thus, we estimate for all test portfolios the following equation:

$$r_{i,t} - r_{f,t} = \alpha_i + \beta_i (i \, v_{r_{M,t} - r_{f,t}}) + \epsilon_{i,t} \tag{15}$$

that is the GMM$_d$ equivalent of the CAPM specified in Eq. 15. Given our main focus on the collective significance of intercepts (Jensen's alpha), we collect $\alpha_i^{GMM_d}$ for all test portfolios for every region. Results show that estimations based on GMM$_d$ outperform, on average, OLS but still generate a higher number of significant α than CGA does.

We also follow Montiel-Olea and Pflueger (2013) to verify the robustness as well as the exogeneity of the instruments. We proceed by running the regressions of each explanatory variable in the models to the set of instruments described above. According to Olea and Pflueger, if at least one of the $\mathcal{F}$-statistics in the regressions of "filtered" x to the instrument set z is above 24, then this is a signal against the potential problem of weak instruments. Finally, we control for the exogeneity of the instruments z by running the following regressions of fitted residuals $\widehat{\epsilon}_{i,t}$ from Eq. 15, to the instrument set:

$$\widehat{\epsilon}_{i,t} = c + z\delta + \eta_{i,t} \tag{16}$$

As pointed out by Racicot and Theoret (2015, p. 335), the coefficients vector δ are analogous to the partial correlation coefficients between the regressors and the instruments. Exogeneity requires these coefficients not to be significantly different from 0 as well as a negligible goodness-of-the-fit measure. We estimate a total of 500 regressions from (16) for the CAPM across the 5 geographies and 4 panels of portfolios, each containing 25 series. Given the t-statistics, we conclude that the fitted coefficients are mostly not significantly different from 0. In addition, the goodness-of-the-fit measures, overall, are very low. We obtain an average R^2 by only 0.0181 with a maximum equal to 0.1084 across all of the 500 estimations. The numbers are consistent across different geographies and specifications under considerations. Thus, the results suggest that the instruments are exogenous.[13]

---

[13] Detailed results are available upon request.

4   Data and Methodology

We consider equity portfolio returns sorted by five equity characteristics: size, book-to-market, operating profitability, investment, and momentum.[14] The time series of monthly excess returns run from November 1990 to February 2021. For presentation purposes, we split our portfolios into four panels as Panel A (size vs. book-to-market); Panel B (size vs. operating profitability); Panel C (size vs. investment); and Panel D (size vs. momentum).

As we consider portfolios sorted by quintiles on each pair of dimensions, we obtain $5 \times 5 = 25$ portfolios under each panel. Therefore, we obtain $25 \times 4 = 100$ portfolios for 5 different geographic regions, namely, World, North America, Europe, Asia-Pacific, and Japan. To sum up, we work with 500 different test portfolios broken down by 5 geographies and 4 pairs of equity characteristics.

For each time series of test portfolios, we fit the standard CAPM asset pricing model:

$$r_{i,t} - r_{f,t} = \alpha_i + \beta_i (r_{M,t} - r_{f,t}) + \epsilon_{i,t} \qquad (17)$$

where $(r_{M,t} - r_{f,t})$ is the market risk factor. The coefficients α_i and β_i are model parameters of interest, and ϵ_i are regression errors assumed to be serially uncorrelated with constant variance.

As emphasized above, we speculate that the true market risk premium is only observed with error because the *market portfolio* as defined in the underlying theory is simply not observable. The observed market risk premium series contains an additive measurement error such that $M = M^* + u$, where M^* represents the true market portfolio. Without any further knowledge about the variance of the measurement error in M^*, nor that of the true market portfolio returns, it is not possible to act as if we know the reliability ratio and obtain consistent estimates by generalized least-squares on time-series data.

We suggest comparing the traditional OLS outputs with those one will get by bringing in the EIV correction to the market risk premium through our CGA-based method. We report for each geographic region and test portfolio one set of fitted coefficients and regression output via least-squares and another set of coefficients and output derived from the CGA-based method.

Besides some elementary output from the fitted models, we also report the GRS test statistic devised by Gibbons et al. (1989). The objective of the GRS test is to check the central proposition of the CAPM which holds that if expected returns are linearly related to the market risk factor, then model intercepts should not be systematically different from zero.

---

[14] All data are extracted from Kenneth French's website: https://mba.tuck.dartmouth.edu/pages/faculty/ken.french/data_library.html.

Specifically, we calculate the following test statistic separately for OLS and CGA outputs for each panel and each region:

$$GRS = \frac{T - N - K}{N} \times \left(1 + \widehat{\mu}_f^\top \widehat{\Omega}_f^{-1} \widehat{\mu}_f\right)^{-1} \times \left(\widehat{\alpha}^\top \widehat{\Sigma}_\epsilon^{-1} \widehat{\alpha}\right) \sim F_{N,T-N-K} \qquad (18)$$

where T is the sample size, N the total number of test assets, K the number of explanatory variables (i.e., systematic risk factors), $\widehat{\mu}_f$ the $K \times 1$ mean vector of explanatory variables, $\widehat{\Omega}_f$ the $K \times K$ covariance matrix of explanatory variables, $\widehat{\alpha}$ the $N \times 1$ vector of fitted intercepts, and $\widehat{\Sigma}_\epsilon$ the $N \times N$ covariance matrix of fitted residuals. If the null hypothesis is true, then all intercepts are jointly equal to zero $\mathcal{H}_0 : \alpha_i = 0$, for all test assets $i = 1, ..., N$, and the GRS statistic follows an $\mathcal{F}$ distribution with N and $T - N - K$ degrees of freedom. As long as we analyze the economic significance of a given asset pricing model, comparing the GRS statistics across two competing estimation methods makes sense as one expects a lower value of the statistic as less significant pricing errors among the portfolios' returns.

5 Time-Series Regressions' Results

We discuss the results of our estimations. As mentioned above, we run CAPM time-series regressions using two methods (OLS and CGA) for five different regions (World, North America, Europe, Asia-Pacific, and Japan). Doing so, we fit a total of 1000 regressions. To set the stage for the discussion of the results, we focus primarily on essential time-series outputs, namely, the fitted intercepts $\widehat{\alpha}$ and market risk loadings $\widehat{\beta}_M$ as well as the models' adjusted R^2 scores. We also report the GRS statistics for each pair of "portfolio & geography" and compare the output across OLS and CGA estimations.

5.1 Intercepts (α)

We start the discussion by reporting the intercepts fitted by OLS vs. CGA across Tables 1, 2, 3, 4, and 5. Each table shows the intercepts (in percentage values) of CAPM regressions divided into four panels of test portfolios as defined above. The t statistics are shown below each coefficient, and their significance levels are marked by an asterisk * next to the coefficients. We expect a lower number of significant intercepts with the CGA estimation as, by construction, it is designed to curb the attenuation bias in market risk coefficients $\widehat{\beta}_M$ and, consequently, the bias in the fitted intercepts $\widehat{\alpha}$ too.

A simple count of the significant intercepts between the OLS and CGA methods is practical. In Table 1, we see that the number of significant intercepts is 77 for the OLS estimations and 72 for the CGA estimations. In the case of North America

Table 1 WORLD: Fitted intercepts from CAPM regressions. The table presents, for each portfolio, the intercept in percentage (bold figures) and the corresponding t-statistics. Statistical significance at 1, 5, and 10% is shown by a *, **, and ***, respectively. Portfolios are sorted by firm characteristics: Size-Book to market (Panel A); Size-Operating profitability (Panel B); Size-Investment (Panel C), and Size-Momentum (Panel D). Time-series regressions of monthly excess returns run from November 1990 to February 2021 using ordinary-least-squares (top part) and compact genetic algorithm (bottom part)

Intercepts based on Ordinary-Least-Square method (in%)

	Panel A: Book-to-Market					Panel B: Operating Profitability				
	BM1	BM2	BM3	BM4	BM5	OP1	OP2	OP3	OP4	OP5
Size 1	**-0.16**	**0.14**	**0.38** ***	**0.42** ***	**0.72** ***	**0.24**	**0.64** ***	**0.59** ***	**0.62** ***	**0.62** ***
	0.91	1.00	2.75	3.70	5.72	1.62	5.98	5.28	5.39	5.07
Size 2	**-0.09**	**0.18** *	**0.25** ***	**0.34** ***	**0.40** ***	**-0.05**	**0.34** ***	**0.35** ***	**0.40** ***	**0.52** ***
	0.61	1.64	2.59	3.64	3.45	0.38	3.71	3.48	3.86	4.77
Size 3	**0.02**	**0.12**	**0.23** ***	**0.29** ***	**0.37** ***	**-0.04**	**0.23** ***	**0.36** ***	**0.36** ***	**0.37** ***
	0.1	1.21	2.83	3.30	3.39	0.41	2.82	4.52	4.17	3.95
Size 4	**0.18**	**0.21** ***	**0.20** ***	**0.28** ***	**0.26** **	**-0.06**	**0.26** ***	**0.33** ***	**0.33** ***	**0.31** ***
	1.52	3.01	3.16	3.37	2.55	0.60	4.05	4.94	4.60	4.30
Size 5	**0.25** ***	**0.24** ***	**0.19** ***	**0.19** ***	**0.11**	**-0.35** ***	**0.05**	**0.22** ***	**0.29** ***	**0.36** ***
	2.73	4.55	3.85	2.84	0.99	4.12	0.86	4.09	5.39	5.64

	Panel C: Investment					Panel D: Momentum				
	Inv1	Inv2	Inv3	Inv4	Inv5	MoM1	MoM2	MoM3	MoM4	MoM5
Size 1	**0.54** ***	**0.67** ***	**0.63** ***	**0.56** ***	**0.06**	**-0.34** *	**0.36** ***	**0.61** ***	**0.82** ***	**1.10** ***
	3.73	6.31	5.94	5.06	0.40	1.93	3.36	6.01	7.28	6.72
Size 2	**0.27** **	**0.46** ***	**0.40** ***	**0.35** ***	**-0.06**	**-0.27**	**0.23** **	**0.36** ***	**0.55** ***	**0.73** ***
	2.41	4.55	4.46	3.55	0.46	1.62	2.26	3.95	5.58	4.64
Size 3	**0.29** ***	**0.34** ***	**0.39** ***	**0.27** ***	**-0.12**	**-0.19**	**0.19** *	**0.31** ***	**0.38** ***	**0.53** ***
	3.02	3.96	4.80	3.41	0.99	1.21	1.90	3.73	4.48	3.65
Size 4	**0.25** ***	**0.37** ***	**0.32** ***	**0.28** ***	**0.00**	**-0.21**	**0.17** *	**0.32** ***	**0.32** ***	**0.54** ***
	3.08	4.89	5.03	4.33	0.04	1.31	1.91	4.87	4.52	3.78
Size 5	**0.30** ***	**0.22** ***	**0.21** ***	**0.17** ***	**0.09**	**-0.25** ***	**0.11**	**0.24** ***	**0.36** ***	**0.42** ***
	4.60	3.72	4.13	2.67	1.03	1.62	1.35	3.96	4.86	2.85

(continued)

Table 1 (continued)

Intercepts based on Compact Genetic Algorithm (in %)

Panel A: Book-to-Market

	BM1		BM2	BM3		BM4		BM5	
Size 1	-0.45	***	-0.06	0.21	*	0.27	***	0.51	***
	3.64		0.55	1.81		2.86		5.09	
Size 2	-0.29	**	0.06	0.15		0.25	**	0.24	**
	2.46		0.55	1.50		2.45		2.45	
Size 3	-0.13		0.03	0.17		0.21	**	0.24	**
	1.21		0.28	1.54		2.18		2.08	
Size 4	0.06		0.16	0.16		0.21	**	0.16	
	0.56		1.36	1.55		2.02		1.51	
Size 5	0.16	*	0.21 **	0.16		0.15		0.02	
	1.71		2.25	1.64		1.44		0.13	

Panel B: Operating Profitability

	OP1		OP2		OP3		OP4		OP5	
Size 1	0.01		0.49	***	0.42	***	0.47	***	0.45	***
	0.05		5.28		4.42		4.64		4.46	
Size 2	-0.17		0.24	**	0.24	**	0.29	***	0.40	***
	1.51		2.55		2.56		2.74		3.83	
Size 3	-0.15		0.16	*	0.29	***	0.29	***	0.28	***
	1.39		1.67		2.92		2.63		2.72	
Size 4	-0.13		0.22	**	0.29	**	0.28	***	0.26	***
	1.03		2.38		3.00		2.78		2.60	
Size 5	-0.42	***	0.02		0.18	*	0.26	***	0.31	***
	3.29		0.15		1.92		2.98		3.92	

Panel C: Investment

	Inv1		Inv2		Inv3		Inv4		Inv5	
Size 1	0.30	***	0.51	***	0.49	***	0.40	***	-0.16	
	2.69		5.97		6.38		3.60		1.34	
Size 2	0.13		0.32	***	0.29	***	0.25	**	-0.20	
	1.39		3.65		3.21		2.36		1.62	
Size 3	0.20	*	0.27	***	0.31	***	0.22	**	-0.23	*
	1.88		2.90		3.14		2.10		1.79	
Size 4	0.19	*	0.32	***	0.27	***	0.25	**	-0.10	
	1.68		3.43		3.06		2.42		0.83	
Size 5	0.25	***	0.17	**	0.18	**	0.12		0.02	
	2.77		2.29		2.08		1.28		0.18	

Panel D: Momentum

	MoM1		MoM2		MoM3		MoM4		MoM5	
Size 1	-0.57	***	0.23	**	0.48	***	0.65	***	0.82	***
	3.98		2.36		5.43		7.78		7.37	
Size 2	-0.49	***	0.13		0.27	***	0.43	***	0.48	***
	3.40		1.33		2.93		4.67		4.47	
Size 3	-0.38	***	0.10		0.23	**	0.30	***	0.32	***
	2.82		1.06		2.55		3.50		2.90	
Size 4	-0.41	***	0.10		0.27	***	0.27	***	0.34	***
	2.78		0.90		2.63		2.98		3.02	
Size 5	-0.46	***	0.04		0.19	**	0.30	**	0.22	**
	3.51		0.44		2.48		3.11		1.96	

Table 2 NORTH AMERICA: Fitted intercepts from CAPM regressions. The table presents, for each portfolio, the intercept in percentage (bold figures) and the corresponding *t*-statistics. Statistical significance at 1, 5, and 10% is shown by a *, **, and ***, respectively. Portfolios are sorted by firm characteristics: Size-Book to market (Panel A); Size-Operating profitability (Panel B); Size-Investment (Panel C); and Size-Momentum (Panel D). Time-series regressions of monthly excess returns run from November 1990 to February 2021 using ordinary-least-squares (top part) and compact genetic algorithm (bottom part)

Intercepts based on Ordinary-Least-Square method (in%)

Panel A: Book-to-Market

	BM1		BM2		BM3		BM4		BM5	
Size 1	-0.29		0.01		0.37	*	0.31	*	0.59	***
	1.00		0.06		1.81		1.88		3.31	
Size 2	-0.20		0.02		0.26	*	0.27	**	0.29	*
	0.87		0.11		1.81		2.12		1.79	
Size 3	0.16		0.12		0.24	**	0.25	**	0.37	***
	0.79		0.83		2.26		2.13		2.61	
Size 4	0.26	*	0.17		0.35	***	0.26	**	0.26	*
	1.39		1.79		3.83		2.34		1.95	
Size 5	0.28	***	0.24	***	0.18	**	0.18	**	0.05	
	2.71		3.50		2.33		2.01		0.35	

Panel B: Operating Profitability

	OP1		OP2		OP3		OP4		OP5	
Size 1	0.18		0.60	***	0.47	***	0.51	***	0.44	**
	0.78		3.72		2.97		2.97		2.33	
Size 2	-0.23		0.33	**	0.40	***	0.54	***	0.49	***
	1.19		2.45		2.88		3.52		2.95	
Size 3	-0.09		0.26	**	0.34	**	0.41	***	0.40	***
	0.53		2.29		2.88		3.31		2.92	
Size 4	-0.11		0.31	***	0.40	***	0.34	***	0.47	***
	0.72		3.64		4.23		3.31		4.26	
Size 5	-0.32	***	-0.01		0.12		0.35	***	0.35	***
	2.79		0.10		1.61		5.19		4.10	

Panel C: Investment

	Inv1		Inv2		Inv3		Inv4		Inv5	
Size 1	0.57	**	0.61	***	0.52	***	0.41	***	-0.20	
	2.51		3.59		3.27		2.65		0.92	
Size 2	0.25		0.48	***	0.38	***	0.28	**	-0.33	*
	1.60		3.29		2.68		1.96		1.72	
Size 3	0.31	**	0.40	***	0.41	***	0.21	*	-0.15	
	2.54		3.42		3.60		1.83		0.76	
Size 4	0.36	***	0.48	***	0.38	***	0.33	***	-0.10	
	3.44		4.84		4.14		3.53		0.56	
Size 5	0.31	***	0.25	***	0.22	***	0.17	*	-0.02	
	4.13		3.19		3.25		1.94		0.15	

Panel D: Momentum

	MoM1		MoM2		MoM3		MoM4		MoM5	
Size 1	-0.48	**	0.34	**	0.62	***	0.81	***	0.94	***
	2.02		2.28		4.11		4.70		3.87	
Size 2	-0.39	*	0.32	**	0.35	***	0.49	***	0.60	**
	1.82		2.29		2.62		3.42		2.53	
Size 3	-0.36	*	0.21	*	0.35	***	0.40	***	0.53	**
	1.79		1.72		3.17		3.21		2.45	
Size 4	-0.27		0.25	**	0.37	***	0.41	***	0.56	***
	1.35		2.28		4.29		4.44		2.69	
Size 5	-0.21		0.17	*	0.21	***	0.34	***	0.48	**
	1.14		1.68		2.58		3.78		2.53	

(continued)

Table 2 (continued)

Intercepts based on Compact Genetic Algorithm (in %)

	BM1	BM2	BM3	BM4	BM5	OP1	OP2	OP3	OP4	OP5
	Panel A: Book-to-Market					**Panel B: Operating Profitability**				
Size 1	**−1.03** ***	**−0.52** ***	**−0.10**	**−0.03**	**0.16**	**−0.34** **	**0.20**	**0.13**	**0.13**	**0.03**
	6.01	3.00	0.61	0.25	1.16	2.01	1.64	1.26	0.95	0.23
Size 2	**−0.72** ***	**−0.39** ***	**−0.02**	**0.03**	**−0.06**	**−0.59** ***	**0.09**	**0.15**	**0.23** **	**0.18**
	4.10	2.73	0.14	0.22	0.50	3.93	0.75	1.25	2.02	1.32
Size 3	**−0.26**	**−0.10**	**0.10**	**0.04**	**0.12**	**−0.43** ***	**0.10**	**0.15**	**0.19** *	**0.16**
	1.63	0.79	0.83	0.40	1.09	3.08	0.87	1.38	1.68	1.37
Size 4	**−0.04**	**0.05**	**0.25** **	**0.09**	**0.05**	**−0.33** **	**0.22** **	**0.29** **	**0.18** *	**0.28** **
	0.23	0.45	2.39	0.89	0.41	2.26	2.16	2.51	1.71	2.35
Size 5	**0.13**	**0.17** *	**0.08**	**0.05** **	**−0.24** **	**−0.46** ***	**−0.09**	**0.04**	**0.28** ***	**0.23** ***
	1.30	1.83	0.80	0.58	2.04	3.18	0.86	0.42	3.38	2.35

	Inv1	Inv2	Inv3	Inv4	Inv5	MoM1	MoM2	MoM3	MoM4	MoM5
	Panel C: Investment					**Panel D: Momentum**				
Size 1	**0.04**	**0.22**	**0.19**	**0.07**	**−0.67** ***	**−1.02** ***	**0.04**	**0.28** **	**0.42** ***	**0.29** *
	0.24	1.54	1.59	0.57	4.40	6.00	0.32	2.36	3.35	1.65
Size 2	**−0.06**	**0.15**	**0.06**	**0.04**	**−0.68** ***	**−0.82** ***	**0.08**	**0.10**	**0.19**	**0.07**
	0.46	1.16	0.49	0.30	4.52	4.41	0.70	0.84	1.56	0.44
Size 3	**0.12**	**0.23** **	**0.22** **	**0.04**	**−0.53** ***	**−0.71** ***	**0.03**	**0.18**	**0.19** *	**0.00**
	0.93	2.06	2.03	0.32	3.68	4.17	0.24	1.49	1.67	0.01
Size 4	**0.22** **	**0.32** ***	**0.27** ***	**0.23** **	**−0.36** **	**−0.65** ***	**0.11**	**0.25** ***	**0.29** ***	**0.04**
	2.63	3.22	2.84	2.25	1.85	4.59	1.13	2.59	2.81	0.28

Table 3 EUROPE: Fitted intercepts from CAPM regressions. The table presents, for each portfolio, the intercept in percentage (bold figures) and the corresponding t-statistics. Statistical significance at 1, 5, and 10% is shown by a *, **, and ***, respectively. Portfolios are sorted by firm characteristics: Size-Book to market (Panel A); Size-Operating profitability (Panel B); Size-Investment (Panel C), and Size-Momentum (Panel D). Time-series regressions of monthly excess returns run from November 1990 to February 2021 using ordinary-least-squares (top part) and compact genetic algorithm (bottom part)

Intercepts based on Ordinary-Least-Square method (in%)

Panel A: Book-to-Market

	BM1		BM2		BM3		BM4		BM5	
Size 1	**-0.18**		**0.15**		**0.24**	*	**0.36**	***	**0.51**	***
	1.11		1.08		1.86		3.00		3.96	
Size 2	**0.05**		**0.26**	**	**0.26**	**	**0.40**	***	**0.45**	***
	0.33		2.09		2.26		3.36		3.43	
Size 3	**0.14**		**0.34**	***	**0.26**	**	**0.27**	**	**0.37**	***
	0.94		3.17		2.52		2.54		3.01	
Size 4	**0.28**	**	**0.30**	***	**0.25**	***	**0.24**	**	**0.26**	**
	2.55		3.40		3.22		2.48		2.10	
Size 5	**0.18**	*	**0.29**	***	**0.22**	***	**0.27**	***	**0.06**	
	1.71		3.92		3.55		3.30		0.44	

Panel B: Operating Profitability

	OP1		OP2		OP3		OP4		OP5	
Size 1	**-0.07**		**0.45**	***	**0.52**	***	**0.65**	***	**0.53**	***
	0.49		3.80		4.18		5.47		4.12	
Size 2	**-0.05**		**0.33**	***	**0.35**	***	**0.50**	***	**0.69**	***
	0.39		2.89		2.94		4.29		5.45	
Size 3	**-0.03**		**0.31**	***	**0.44**	***	**0.33**	***	**0.51**	***
	0.30		3.30		4.38		3.24		4.61	
Size 4	**-0.06**		**0.26**	**	**0.34**	***	**0.44**	***	**0.42**	***
	0.61		2.95		3.99		5.20		4.93	
Size 5	**-0.24**	**	**0.18**	**	**0.22**	***	**0.18**		**0.39**	***
	1.99		2.34		3.08		2.68		4.66	

Panel C: Investment

	Inv1		Inv2		Inv3		Inv4		Inv5	
Size 1	**0.31**	**	**0.48**	***	**0.49**	***	**0.43**	***	**-0.03**	
	2.36		4.29		4.23		3.58		0.21	
Size 2	**0.28**	**	**0.47**	***	**0.48**	***	**0.36**	***	**0.10**	
	2.18		4.12		4.27		3.15		0.76	
Size 3	**0.31**	***	**0.35**	***	**0.41**	***	**0.23**	**	**0.07**	
	2.80		3.27		4.17		2.34		0.55	
Size 4	**0.29**	***	**0.26**	***	**0.39**	***	**0.34**	***	**0.08**	
	2.95		2.95		4.99		4.31		0.74	
Size 5	**0.20**	**	**0.31**	***	**0.17**	***	**0.12**		**0.17**	*
	2.42		4.35		2.87		1.58		1.95	

Panel D: Momentum

	MoM1		MoM2		MoM3		MoM4		MoM5	
Size 1	**-0.66**	***	**0.13**		**0.43**	***	**0.76**	***	**1.37**	***
	3.74		1.12		3.79		6.46		8.02	
Size 2	**-0.53**	***	**0.11**		**0.42**	***	**0.72**	***	**1.09**	***
	2.95		0.87		3.83		6.34		6.91	
Size 3	**-0.33**	**	**0.14**		**0.33**	***	**0.59**	***	**0.83**	***
	1.97		1.30		3.33		5.60		5.42	
Size 4	**-0.27**		**0.20**	**	**0.34**	***	**0.47**	***	**0.75**	***
	1.54		2.20		3.92		4.98		5.48	
Size 5	**-0.33**	*	**0.09**		**0.30**	***	**0.38**	***	**0.45**	***
	1.86		0.88		4.34		4.25		2.97	

(continued)

Table 3 (continued)

Intercepts based on Compact Genetic Algorithm (in %)

Panel A: Book-to-Market

	BM1	BM2	BM3	BM4	BM5
Size 1	-0.40 ***	-0.03	0.10	0.24 **	0.36 ***
	3.39	0.23	0.82	2.20	3.58
Size 2	-0.12	0.13	0.15	0.30 **	0.32 **
	1.06	1.22	1.34	2.52	2.52
Size 3	-0.01	0.25 **	0.18	0.18	0.26 **
	0.07	2.20	1.54	1.39	2.06
Size 4	0.18 *	0.23 **	0.20 *	0.18	0.15
	1.75	2.18	1.76	1.56	1.23
Size 5	0.09	0.24 **	0.20 *	0.21 *	-0.05
	0.87	2.48	1.74	1.71	0.39

Panel B: Operating Profitability

	OP1	OP2	OP3	OP4	OP5
Size 1	-0.21 *	0.34 ***	0.38 ***	0.53 ***	0.39 ***
	1.75	2.96	3.62	4.31	3.71
Size 2	-0.17	0.22 *	0.24 *	0.39 ***	0.57 ***
	1.38	1.87	1.94	3.19	4.60
Size 3	-0.11	0.24 **	0.37 ***	0.24 **	0.43 ***
	0.94	2.25	2.87	2.14	3.47
Size 4	-0.15	0.19 *	0.29 ***	0.39 ***	0.36 ***
	1.24	1.74	2.81	3.33	3.69
Size 5	-0.34 ***	0.14	0.19 *	0.14	0.32 ***
	2.70	1.15	1.68	1.41	3.33

Panel C: Investment

	Inv1	Inv2	Inv3	Inv4	Inv5
Size 1	0.16	0.37 ***	0.37 ***	0.29 ***	-0.24 *
	1.38	3.39	3.72	2.76	1.95
Size 2	0.14	0.37 ***	0.38 ***	0.26 **	-0.04
	1.19	3.15	3.69	2.27	0.27
Size 3	0.22 *	0.26 **	0.33 ***	0.15	-0.04
	1.83	2.51	3.10	1.39	0.27
Size 4	0.20 *	0.21 *	0.34 ***	0.29 ***	0.00
	1.78	1.73	3.24	2.60	0.01
Size 5	0.15	0.27 ***	0.14	0.07	0.11
	1.40	2.58	1.42	0.63	0.97

Panel D: Momentum

	MoM1	MoM2	MoM3	MoM4	MoM5
Size 1	-0.86 ***	0.03	0.31 ***	0.63 ***	1.12 ***
	5.79	0.25	2.88	6.64	10.72
Size 2	-0.71 ***	-0.01	0.32 ***	0.60 ***	0.88 ***
	4.16	0.07	3.13	5.71	6.75
Size 3	-0.49 ***	0.07	0.25 *	0.50 *	0.63 ***
	3.06	0.53	1.87	4.59	5.28
Size 4	-0.44 **	0.15	0.27 **	0.40 **	0.60 ***
	2.37	1.08	2.51	3.78	5.56
Size 5	-0.49 ***	0.03	0.25 **	0.30 **	0.27 **
	3.30	0.21	2.36	3.01	2.47

Table 4 ASIA-PACIFIC: Fitted intercepts from CAPM regressions. The table presents, for each portfolio, the intercept in percentage (bold figures) and the corresponding *t*-statistics. Statistical significance at 1, 5, and 10% is shown by a *, **, and ***, respectively. Portfolios are sorted by firm characteristics: Size-Book to market (Panel A); Size-Operating profitability (Panel B); Size-Investment (Panel C), and Size-Momentum (Panel D). Time-series regressions of monthly excess returns run from November 1990 to February 2021 using ordinary-least-squares (top part) and compact genetic algorithm (bottom part)

Intercepts based on Ordinary-Least-Square method (in%)

	Panel A: Book-to-Market					Panel B: Operating Profitability				
	BM1	BM2	BM3	BM4	BM5	OP1	OP2	OP3	OP4	OP5
Size 1	**-0.05**	**-0.13**	**0.16**	**0.46** **	**0.86** ***	**0.20**	**0.80** ***	**0.65** ***	**0.69** ***	**0.65** ***
	0.19	0.59	0.82	2.31	3.84	0.81	3.82	3.46	3.58	3.66
Size 2	**-0.53** ***	**-0.25**	**-0.24**	**0.07**	**0.24**	**-0.40** *	**-0.06**	**0.20**	**0.24**	**0.25**
	2.88	1.44	1.54	0.46	1.17	1.83	0.33	1.31	1.40	1.58
Size 3	**-0.36** *	**-0.11**	**0.10**	**0.15**	**0.17**	**-0.45** **	**0.19**	**0.02**	**0.38** ***	**0.30**
	1.95	0.69	0.68	0.98	0.90	2.55	1.14	0.15	2.82	1.98
Size 4	**0.19**	**0.28** **	**0.10**	**0.39** ***	**0.26**	**-0.22**	**0.28** **	**0.27** *	**0.39** ***	**0.46** ***
	1.22	2.03	0.79	3.17	1.54	1.33	2.08	1.81	3.07	3.25
Size 5	**0.15**	**0.28** ***	**0.27** ***	**0.23** *	**0.29**	**-0.08**	**0.21**	**0.27** ***	**0.40** ***	**0.27** **
	1.12	3.13	2.80	1.84	1.42	0.47	1.49	2.77	3.68	2.13

	Panel C: Investment					Panel D: Momentum				
	Inv1	Inv2	Inv3	Inv4	Inv5	MoM1	MoM2	MoM3	MoM4	MoM5
Size 1	**0.58** **	**0.72** ***	**0.77** ***	**0.54** ***	**-0.02**	**-0.34**	**0.29**	**0.74** ***	**1.17** ***	**1.11** ***
	2.49	3.89	3.56	2.69	0.10	1.47	1.53	4.28	5.73	4.58
Size 2	**-0.01**	**0.33** **	**0.13**	**0.03**	**-0.53** ***	**-1.17** ***	**0.05**	**0.26** *	**0.53** ***	**0.63** ***
	0.05	2.03	0.84	0.16	2.69	5.42	0.27	1.76	3.29	2.74
Size 3	**0.01**	**0.46** ***	**0.10**	**0.17**	**-0.42** **	**-0.85** ***	**0.03**	**0.23** *	**0.59** ***	**0.44** **
	0.09	3.12	0.71	1.16	2.39	4.04	0.25	1.72	4.31	2.06
Size 4	**0.11**	**0.30** **	**0.43** ***	**0.32** **	**-0.05**	**-0.39** *	**0.05**	**0.30** **	**0.46** ***	**0.39** *
	0.89	2.37	3.47	2.08	0.31	1.91	0.36	2.47	3.86	1.92
Size 5	**0.46** ***	**0.21** *	**0.24** **	**0.23** **	**0.01**	**0.18**	**0.07**	**0.34** ***	**0.37** ***	**0.53** ***
	3.36	1.82	2.57	1.99	0.05	0.77	0.44	3.32	3.11	2.64

(continued)

320   M. Desban et al.

Table 4 (continued)

Intercepts based on Compact Genetic Algorithm (in %)

Panel A: Book-to-Market

	BM1		BM2		BM3		BM4		BM5	
Size 1	-0.59	***	-0.44	***	-0.12		0.13		0.47	***
	2.96		2.79		0.74		0.85		3.07	
Size 2	-0.80	***	-0.48	***	-0.43	***	-0.11		-0.05	
	5.49		2.75		2.94		0.83		0.27	
Size 3	-0.64	***	-0.30	**	-0.07		-0.02		-0.04	
	4.16		1.97		0.47		0.15		0.24	
Size 4	0.01		0.15		-0.03		0.28	**	0.11	
	0.06		1.02		0.22		2.01		0.66	
Size 5	0.00		0.20	*	0.20		0.12		0.02	
	0.03		1.77		1.51		0.81		0.11	

Panel B: Operating Profitability

	OP1		OP2		OP3		OP4		OP5	
Size 1	-0.22		0.43	***	0.38	***	0.38	***	0.40	***
	1.35		3.05		2.57		2.66		2.97	
Size 2	-0.77	***	-0.30	*	0.02		0.03		0.06	
	4.31		1.92		0.15		0.17		0.46	
Size 3	-0.69	***	0.00		-0.11		0.23	*	0.14	
	4.25		0.02		0.76		1.81		1.00	
Size 4	-0.39	**	0.18	**	0.09		0.26	*	0.29	**
	2.49		1.08		0.72		1.83		2.01	
Size 5	-0.22		0.06		0.21	*	0.30	**	0.13	
	1.36		0.36		1.65		2.36		1.08	

Panel C: Investment

	Inv1		Inv2		Inv3		Inv4		Inv5	
Size 1	0.15		0.41	***	0.41	***	0.21		-0.39	**
	0.97		3.04		2.70		1.42		2.35	
Size 2	-0.24		0.13		-0.07		-0.23		-0.79	***
	1.59		1.04		0.49		1.30		4.59	
Size 3	-0.20		0.27	**	-0.05		0.03		-0.62	***
	1.38		2.01		0.29		0.20		3.97	
Size 4	0.00		0.18		0.34	**	0.17		-0.22	
	0.02		1.31		2.19		1.05		1.38	
Size 5	0.30	**	0.10		0.17		0.13		-0.17	
	2.24		0.81		1.32		0.82		1.14	

Panel D: Momentum

	MoM1		MoM2		MoM3		MoM4		MoM5	
Size 1	-0.68	***	0.00		0.46	***	0.83	***	0.69	***
	3.92		0.02		3.36		5.83		3.78	
Size 2	-1.43	***	-0.14		0.08		0.33	**	0.25	
	7.19		0.92		0.61		2.46		1.48	
Size 3	-1.06	***	-0.10		0.08		0.44	***	0.14	
	5.57		0.74		0.69		3.16		0.77	
Size 4	-0.58	***	-0.07		0.17		0.34	***	0.12	
	2.77		0.48		1.29		2.60		0.71	
Size 5	-0.05		-0.05		0.25	**	0.26	**	0.24	
	0.26		0.32		2.10		2.06		1.53	

Table 5 JAPAN: Fitted intercepts from CAPM regressions. The table presents, for each portfolio, the intercept in percentage (bold figures) and the corresponding t-statistics. Statistical significance at 1, 5, and 10% is shown by a *, **, and ***, respectively. Portfolios are sorted by firm characteristics: Size-Book to market (Panel A); Size-Operating profitability (Panel B); Size-Investment (Panel C), and Size-Momentum (Panel D). Time-series regressions of monthly excess returns run from November 1990 to February 2021 using ordinary-least-squares (top part) and compact genetic algorithm (bottom part)

Intercepts based on Ordinary-Least-Square method (in%)

Panel A: Book-to-Market

	BM1	BM2	BM3	BM4	BM5
Size 1	**0.31**	**0.43** *	**0.48** **	**0.45** **	**0.56** ***
	1.12	1.93	2.36	2.53	3.00
Size 2	**0.26**	**0.06**	**0.21**	**0.36** **	**0.27**
	1.02	0.31	1.17	2.28	1.61
Size 3	**0.01**	**0.08**	**0.16**	**0.19**	**0.33** **
	0.07	0.53	1.13	1.37	2.14
Size 4	**-0.02**	**0.16**	**0.22** **	**0.27** **	**0.26** *
	0.13	1.48	2.06	2.32	1.79
Size 5	**0.13**	**0.22** **	**0.22** **	**0.33** ***	**0.47** ***
	1.06	2.28	2.38	3.02	2.69

Panel B: Operating Profitability

	OP1	OP2	OP3	OP4	OP5
Size 1	**0.36** *	**0.52** ***	**0.47** **	**0.46** **	**0.73** ***
	1.76	2.85	2.53	2.40	3.21
Size 2	**0.11**	**0.26** *	**0.31** *	**0.32** *	**0.34** *
	0.60	1.65	1.82	1.84	1.75
Size 3	**0.12**	**0.17**	**0.22** *	**0.22**	**0.26**
	0.70	1.18	1.67	1.60	1.55
Size 4	**-0.01**	**0.18**	**0.32** ***	**0.32** ***	**0.17**
	0.10	1.54	3.01	2.97	1.45
Size 5	**0.06**	**0.17**	**0.32** ***	**0.22** **	**0.27** ***
	0.39	1.55	3.61	2.34	2.73

Panel C: Investment

	Inv1	Inv2	Inv3	Inv4	Inv5
Size 1	**0.42** **	**0.43** **	**0.55** ***	**0.45** **	**0.53** **
	1.98	2.34	2.87	2.26	2.39
Size 2	**0.27**	**0.25**	**0.28** *	**0.34** *	**0.15**
	1.40	1.48	1.72	1.93	0.82
Size 3	**0.21**	**0.23**	**0.19**	**0.15**	**0.16**
	1.29	1.53	1.37	0.96	1.00
Size 4	**0.20**	**0.20**	**0.30** ***	**0.11**	**0.19**
	1.51	1.63	2.76	1.05	1.56
Size 5	**0.21** *	**0.14**	**0.11**	**0.26** ***	**0.18**
	1.67	1.33	1.24	2.57	1.46

Panel D: Momentum

	MoM1	MoM2	MoM3	MoM4	MoM5
Size 1	**0.47** *	**0.57** ***	**0.54** ***	**0.62** ***	**0.42** *
	1.94	3.08	3.10	3.42	1.76
Size 2	**0.18**	**0.25**	**0.32** **	**0.30** *	**0.31**
	0.80	1.50	1.97	1.82	1.56
Size 3	**0.25**	**0.13**	**0.21**	**0.28** **	**0.24**
	1.30	0.86	1.53	2.03	1.29
Size 4	**0.26**	**0.25** *	**0.19** *	**0.12**	**0.30** *
	1.40	1.93	1.69	1.08	1.76
Size 5	**0.18**	**0.07**	**0.03**	**0.26** **	**0.26**
	0.90	0.60	0.35	2.55	1.51

(continued)

Table 5 (continued)

Intercepts based on Compact Genetic Algorithm (in %)

Panel A: Book-to-Market

	BM1	BM2	BM3	BM4	BM5
Size 1	0.21	0.36 **	0.42 **	0.40 ***	0.50 ***
	1.16	2.47	2.50	2.94	3.70
Size 2	0.17	0.01	0.16	0.32 **	0.23
	0.94	0.07	1.01	2.43	1.62
Size 3	-0.04	0.05	0.12	0.15	0.29 **
	0.28	0.36	0.96	1.33	2.45
Size 4	-0.06	0.14	0.20 *	0.24 **	0.23 *
	0.39	1.15	1.77	2.12	1.75
Size 5	0.11	0.20 *	0.21 *	0.31 ***	0.42 ***
	0.89	1.86	1.92	2.93	2.83

Panel B: Operating Profitability

	OP1	OP2	OP3	OP4	OP5
Size 1	0.29 *	0.46 ***	0.42 ***	0.39 ***	0.65 ***
	1.94	3.44	3.27	2.79	4.18
Size 2	0.06	0.22 *	0.26 **	0.27 **	0.28 **
	0.40	1.79	2.04	2.15	2.17
Size 3	0.07	0.13	0.19	0.19	0.22
	0.54	1.04	1.35	1.57	1.36
Size 4	-0.04	0.15	0.30 ***	0.31 **	0.15
	0.29	1.18	2.86	2.38	1.26
Size 5	0.03	0.15	0.31 ***	0.21 ***	0.26 **
	0.22	1.06	2.89	1.89	2.34

Panel C: Investment

	Inv1	Inv2	Inv3	Inv4	Inv5
Size 1	0.35 **	0.38 ***	0.50 ***	0.39 ***	0.46 ***
	2.18	3.14	3.46	2.68	3.12
Size 2	0.21	0.20	0.24 *	0.29 *	0.10
	1.47	1.64	1.91	1.86	0.64
Size 3	0.17	0.20	0.16	0.11	0.12
	1.29	1.48	1.27	0.98	0.82
Size 4	0.17	0.17 *	0.28 **	0.09	0.17
	1.25	1.72	2.54	0.76	1.40
Size 5	0.18	0.12	0.10	0.24 **	0.16
	1.45	0.94	0.88	2.14	1.28

Panel D: Momentum

	MoM1	MoM2	MoM3	MoM4	MoM5
Size 1	0.39 **	0.51 ***	0.48 ***	0.57 ***	0.34 *
	2.19	4.13	4.17	4.29	1.88
Size 2	0.11	0.20 *	0.27 **	0.25 **	0.24 *
	0.67	1.66	2.12	2.15	1.72
Size 3	0.19	0.09	0.17	0.25 **	0.18
	1.20	0.70	1.61	2.15	1.33
Size 4	0.21	0.22 **	0.17	0.10	0.25 *
	1.43	1.96	1.41	0.85	1.96
Size 5	0.13	0.05	0.02	0.24 ***	0.21
	0.78	0.36	0.18	2.62	1.61

(Table 2), the improvement is more pronounced with only 46 significant intercepts with CGA versus 79 with OLS. For Europe (Table 3), CGA estimations cut the number of significant intercepts from 80 (OLS) to 67 (CGA). In Table 4 with Asia-Pacific markets, CGA method gives the lowest number of significant intercepts with only 43 (compared to 57 with OLS). Finally, in the case of Japan (Table 5), the results of the two methods are similar. The half of the intercepts are not significantly different from zero of all regressions. For comparison and robustness, we give the intercepts with GMM in Tables 6, 7, 8, 9, and 10.

5.2   Market Risk Premium and β_M

We now outline the results about market risk loadings. Box plots Figs. 1, 2, 3, 4, and 5 compare the OLS vs. CGA market betas for the five geographic regions. Each figure displays the fitted coefficients for our four panels (A, B, C, and D) of test portfolios. In each figure, the blue color refers to the OLS betas and the red color to the CGA betas. The graphics convey collectively one major observation.

The attenuation bias is once more corroborated in our dataset regardless of the specification to describe asset prices or the geography: All OLS market betas are lower than their CGA-driven counterparts. Looking at the market beta estimates, the average of the fitted coefficients across the 500 portfolios (all panels and all regions) is 1.02, while this rises to 1.28 for the CGA-driven market betas. For example, while the average market beta estimate for the North America portfolios is 1.09 when one ignores the EIV, the same average goes up to 1.44 for the same geography as long as we assume that the CAPM is the true specification. Put another way, the measurement error in the market portfolio yields seriously underestimated risk factor loadings in line with the expected consequences of EIV. The systematically lower market betas are thus likely to systematically underestimate the true "market risk" which a given portfolio is exposed to Figs. 1, 2, 3, 4, and 5.

In Figs. 1, 2, 3, 4, and 5, we show the market beta obtained for all regions (World, North America, Europe, Asia-Pacific, and Japan) all panels (A, B, C, and D) with the three approaches (OLS with blue color, GMM_d with green color, and CGA with red color). In each region and each panel, the CGA method corrects the downward bias of $\beta^{r_M - r_f}$. For each region, each panel, the average beta given with the CGA method is higher than the mean betas obtained with the OLS and the GMM_d methods. Moreover, we conduct the GRS test to compare the three methods. In Fig. 7, we draw the GRS results for all regions and all panels in the case of the CAPM (OLS with blue color, GMM_d with green color, and CGA with red color). We observe that the CGA results give the lowest values (closer to the center zero). Overall, the CGA estimators outperform the OLS and the GMM_d estimators.

Table 6 WORLD: Time-series regressions intercepts in percentage of the monthly excess returns of panels A, B, C, and D with the CAPM estimated with GMM_d: November 1990 to February 2021

Market model intercepts estimated with GMM_d (in%)

	BM1	BM2	BM3	BM4	BM5	OP1	OP2	OP3	OP4	OP5
Size 1	−0.15	0.17	0.40**	0.44***	0.74***	0.55***	0.68***	0.65***	0.58***	0.08
	0.70	0.97	2.50	3.01	4.29	2.98	5.15	4.86	4.13	0.43
Size 2	−0.08	0.19*	0.26***	0.35***	0.42***	0.28**	0.46***	0.42***	0.37***	−0.04
	0.53	1.66	2.68	3.32	3.00	2.31	4.22	4.18	3.67	0.31
Size 3	0.02	0.13	0.24***	0.30***	0.38***	0.29***	0.35***	0.40***	0.29***	−0.11
	0.13	1.36	2.93	3.09	2.65	2.70	3.45	4.46	3.22	0.78
Size 4	0.18	0.21***	0.21***	0.29***	0.28**	0.25**	0.38***	0.33***	0.29***	0.02
	1.36	3.19	2.65	2.64	2.00	2.44	3.76	4.36	4.23	0.12
Size 5	0.24**	0.23***	0.20***	0.20**	0.13	0.30***	0.22***	0.21***	0.17***	0.09
	2.13	4.30	3.47	2.56	0.93	4.02	3.17	3.77	2.55	0.76

	Inv1	Inv2	Inv3	Inv4	Inv5	MoM1	MoM2	MoM3	MoM4	MoM5
Size 1	−0.33*	0.39***	0.63***	0.84***	1.12***	0.26	0.65***	0.61***	0.64***	0.64***
	1.85	2.94	4.83	5.70	4.94	1.37	4.68	4.27	4.47	4.43
Size 2	−0.28*	0.24**	0.37***	0.56***	0.75***	−0.04	0.35***	0.37***	0.42***	0.53***
	1.66	2.16	3.58	4.98	4.24	0.34	3.45	3.32	3.66	4.27
Size 3	−0.20	0.20*	0.32***	0.39***	0.54***	−0.04	0.24**	0.38***	0.37***	0.38***
	1.23	1.77	3.36	4.31	3.55	0.43	2.56	4.37	3.70	3.91
Size 4	−0.22	0.17	0.33***	0.33***	0.55***	−0.06	0.26***	0.35***	0.34***	0.32***
	1.30	1.67	4.42	4.27	3.76	0.62	3.59	4.12	3.86	4.16
Size 5	−0.26*	0.11	0.24***	0.36***	0.41***	−0.35***	0.05	0.22***	0.29***	0.36***
	1.67	1.20	4.42	5.30	2.73	3.62	0.84	3.97	5.21	5.02

Table 7 NORTH AMERICA: Time-series regressions intercepts in percentage of the monthly excess returns of panels A, B, C, and D with the CAPM estimated with GMM_d: November 1990 to February 2021

Market model intercepts estimated with GMM_d (in%)

	BM1		BM2		BM3		BM4		BM5		OP1		OP2		OP3		OP4		OP5	
Size 1	-0.26		0.03		0.39	*	0.34	*	0.62	***	0.60	**	0.63	***	0.55	***	0.44	**	-0.16	
	0.81		0.14		1.82		1.94		2.95		2.44		3.41		3.20		2.57		0.69	
Size 2	-0.19		0.03		0.27	**	0.28	**	0.31	*	0.27	*	0.49	***	0.40	***	0.30	**	-0.32	**
	0.81		0.17		2.12		2.25		1.71		1.86		3.49		2.91		2.27		1.55	
Size 3	0.16		0.13		0.25	**	0.26	*	0.39	**	0.31	**	0.41	***	0.42	***	0.24	*	-0.13	
	0.80		1.00		2.28		1.89		2.36		2.24		2.99		3.32		1.93		0.61	
Size 4	0.25	**	0.18	*	0.37	***	0.29	**	0.28	*	0.36	***	0.49	***	0.40	***	0.35	***	-0.08	
	1.10		1.91		3.52		2.10		1.70		2.98		4.20		3.61		3.92		0.41	
Size 5	0.27	**	0.23	***	0.19	***	0.19	**	0.06		0.30	***	0.25	***	0.22	***	0.16		-0.03	
	2.00		3.60		2.56		2.00		0.37		3.41		2.66		3.21		1.87		0.17	

	Inv1		Inv2		Inv3		Inv4		Inv5		MoM1		MoM2		MoM3		MoM4		MoM5	
Size 1	-0.46	**	0.39	**	0.66	***	0.84	***	0.98	***	0.21		0.63	***	0.49	***	0.55	***	0.46	**
	2.15		2.39		3.85		4.20		3.33		0.84		3.45		2.77		2.93		2.25	
Size 2	-0.40	**	0.34	**	0.36	**	0.51	***	0.62	***	-0.21		0.34	***	0.42	***	0.56	***	0.51	***
	2.05		2.32		2.78		3.70		2.72		1.16		2.66		3.21		3.33		2.73	
Size 3	-0.36	**	0.22	*	0.38	***	0.42	***	0.55	***	-0.09		0.27	**	0.36	***	0.41	***	0.43	***
	2.01		1.68		3.31		3.19		2.84		0.49		2.19		2.72		2.82		2.73	
Size 4	-0.27		0.27	**	0.38	***	0.43	***	0.57	***	-0.11		0.33	***	0.42	***	0.35	**	0.47	***
	1.39		1.99		3.78		4.62		2.94		0.60		3.84		3.73		2.41		3.68	
Size 5	-0.22		0.17		0.22	***	0.33	***	0.47	**	-0.31	**	0.00		0.12	*	0.34	***	0.34	***
	1.28		1.81		2.88		4.07		2.48		2.10		0.03		1.64		5.23		3.88	

Table 8 EUROPE: Time-series regressions intercepts in percentage of the monthly excess returns of panels A, B, C, and D with the CAPM estimated with GMM_d: November 1990 to February 2021

Market model intercepts estimated with GMM_d (in%)

	BM1	BM2	BM3	BM4	BM5	OP1	OP2	OP3	OP4	OP5
Size 1	−0.18	0.17	0.26 *	0.38 ***	0.54 ***	0.33 **	0.50 ***	0.51 ***	0.44 ***	−0.02
	0.88	0.99	1.77	2.67	3.27	2.04	3.72	3.73	3.17	0.08
Size 2	0.06	0.27 **	0.28 **	0.42 ***	0.47 ***	0.29 **	0.49 ***	0.50 ***	0.38 ***	0.12
	0.32	2.06	2.38	2.99	3.10	2.03	3.98	4.56	3.25	0.77
Size 3	0.14	0.35 ***	0.28 ***	0.28 ***	0.38 **	0.32 ***	0.36 ***	0.43 ***	0.24 ***	0.09
	0.83	3.16	2.72	2.62	2.52	2.60	3.16	4.17	2.49	0.59
Size 4	0.29 **	0.31 ***	0.25 ***	0.25 **	0.27 **	0.29 ***	0.27 ***	0.39 **	0.34 ***	0.10
	2.37	3.61	2.98	2.30	1.97	2.65	2.57	5.31	4.32	0.78
Size 5	0.18	0.28 ***	0.22 ***	0.27 ***	0.07	0.20 **	0.30 **	0.17 ***	0.12	0.17
	1.44	3.99	3.26	2.88	0.51	2.38	4.15	2.84	1.41	1.62
	Inv1	Inv2	Inv3	Inv4	Inv5	MoM1	MoM2	MoM3	MoM4	MoM5
Size 1	−0.64 ***	0.16	0.46 ***	0.78 ***	1.38 ***	−0.05	0.48 ***	0.54 ***	0.67 ***	0.55 ***
	3.48	1.13	3.37	5.47	5.85	0.31	3.27	3.74	4.90	3.66
Size 2	−0.52 ***	0.13	0.44 ***	0.73 ***	1.09 ***	−0.03	0.35 ***	0.36 ***	0.52 ***	0.71 ***
	2.75	1.00	3.77	6.02	5.53	0.23	2.98	2.94	4.19	5.21
Size 3	−0.32 *	0.17	0.35 ***	0.60 ***	0.83 ***	−0.02	0.32 ***	0.46 ***	0.35 ***	0.53 ***
	1.79	1.46	3.42	5.53	4.41	0.19	3.28	4.70	3.36	4.68
Size 4	−0.27	0.21 **	0.35 ***	0.49 ***	0.75 ***	−0.05	0.26 ***	0.35 ***	0.45 ***	0.43 ***
	1.44	2.16	3.90	4.81	4.68	0.63	2.85	4.13	5.19	5.12
Size 5	−0.32 *	0.10	0.30 ***	0.37 ***	0.43 **	−0.23 *	0.18 **	0.22 **	0.18 ***	0.37 ***
	1.79	0.85	4.08	4.00	2.55	1.84	2.02	3.15	2.62	3.83

Table 9 ASIA-PACIFIC: Time-series regressions intercepts in percentage of the monthly excess returns of panels A, B, C, and D with the CAPM estimated with GMM$_d$: November 1990 to February 2021

Market model intercepts estimated with GMM$_d$ (in%)

	BM1	BM2	BM3	BM4	BM5	OP1	OP2	OP3	OP4	OP5
Size 1	−0.04	−0.11	0.18	0.48*	0.89***	0.59*	0.73***	0.79***	0.56**	0.01
	0.13	0.41	0.78	1.89	2.84	1.87	3.45	2.97	2.24	0.02
Size 2	−0.52***	−0.23	−0.23	0.09	0.28	0.02	0.34*	0.15	0.07	−0.50**
	2.77	1.20	1.41	0.52	1.17	0.09	1.84	0.93	0.29	2.20
Size 3	−0.35*	−0.08	0.13	0.15	0.20	0.02	0.48***	0.13	0.20	−0.38**
	1.81	0.52	0.78	0.97	1.05	0.13	2.96	0.90	1.14	2.06
Size 4	0.21	0.28*	0.12	0.40***	0.28*	0.12	0.32**	0.46***	0.34**	−0.04
	1.38	1.78	0.90	2.80	1.70	0.90	2.49	3.25	2.28	0.19
Size 5	0.13	0.28***	0.27***	0.23	0.30	0.46***	0.20*	0.23**	0.23**	0.00
	1.05	2.97	2.75	1.84	1.47	3.22	1.75	2.53	2.11	0.01

	Inv1	Inv2	Inv3	Inv4	Inv5	MoM1	MoM2	MoM3	MoM4	MoM5
Size 1	−0.32	0.32	0.75***	1.18***	1.11***	0.22	0.82***	0.68***	0.72***	0.67***
	1.14	1.41	3.47	4.84	3.68	0.67	3.03	2.96	2.77	3.05
Size 2	−1.15***	0.08	0.29*	0.54***	0.65**	−0.37	−0.03	0.23	0.27	0.25
	5.03	0.44	1.73	3.13	2.24	1.37	0.13	1.37	1.38	1.54
Size 3	−0.83***	0.05	0.25*	0.61***	0.46*	−0.42**	0.21	0.03	0.39***	0.32*
	4.08	0.31	1.72	4.10	1.82	2.28	1.24	0.23	2.74	1.88
Size 4	−0.37*	0.08	0.30**	0.47***	0.39	−0.19	0.30**	0.27	0.40***	0.47***
	1.86	0.51	2.43	3.19	1.62	1.28	2.06	1.44	3.27	3.77
Size 5	0.16	0.07	0.34***	0.37***	0.52**	−0.09	0.21	0.28***	0.40***	0.25*
	0.67	0.43	3.18	3.19	2.48	0.57	1.57	2.82	3.48	1.87

Table 10 JAPAN: Time-series regressions intercepts in percentage of the monthly excess returns of panels A, B, C, and D with the CAPM estimated with GMM$_d$: November 1990 to February 2021

Market model intercepts estimated with GMM$_d$ (in%)

	BM1	BM2	BM3	BM4	BM5	OP1	OP2	OP3	OP4	OP5
Size 1	0.31	0.43 **	0.48 ***	0.45 ***	0.56 ***	0.42 *	0.43 **	0.55 ***	0.45 **	0.53 **
	1.20	2.00	2.70	2.61	2.62	1.95	2.26	2.91	2.23	2.48
Size 2	0.25	0.06	0.21	0.36 **	0.27	0.27	0.25	0.29 *	0.34 *	0.15
	1.02	0.33	1.28	2.32	1.45	1.31	1.50	1.69	1.89	0.86
Size 3	0.01	0.07	0.16	0.19	0.33 *	0.21	0.23	0.19	0.15	0.16
	0.07	0.57	1.05	1.28	1.87	1.24	1.44	1.25	0.98	1.02
Size 4	-0.02	0.16	0.22 **	0.27 **	0.27	0.20	0.20	0.30 ***	0.11	0.19
	0.13	1.59	2.05	2.07	1.60	1.51	1.59	2.81	0.92	1.63
Size 5	0.13	0.22 ***	0.22 **	0.33 ***	0.47 ***	0.21	0.14	0.11	0.26 **	0.18
	0.92	2.60	2.34	2.86	2.67	1.63	1.37	1.26	2.58	1.40
	Inv1	Inv2	Inv3	Inv4	Inv5	MoM1	MoM2	MoM3	MoM4	MoM5
Size 1	0.47 *	0.57 ***	0.54 ***	0.62 ***	0.42 *	0.36 *	0.52 ***	0.47 **	0.46 **	0.72 ***
	1.83	2.74	2.81	3.05	1.68	1.68	2.74	2.42	2.37	3.26
Size 2	0.18	0.25	0.32 *	0.30 *	0.31	0.11	0.26	0.31 *	0.32 *	0.34 *
	0.75	1.39	1.71	1.68	1.61	0.58	1.60	1.75	1.85	1.77
Size 3	0.25	0.13	0.21	0.28 *	0.24	0.12	0.17	0.22	0.22	0.26
	1.17	0.79	1.36	1.89	1.26	0.69	1.09	1.59	1.57	1.54
Size 4	0.26	0.25 *	0.19	0.12	0.30 *	-0.01	0.18	0.32 ***	0.32 ***	0.17
	1.27	1.87	1.55	1.09	1.78	0.09	1.39	2.80	3.14	1.49
Size 5	0.19	0.07	0.03	0.26 ***	0.26	0.06	0.17	0.32 ***	0.22 **	0.27 ***
	0.89	0.57	0.38	2.70	1.36	0.42	1.55	3.62	2.30	2.63

$$\text{(CAPM)} \quad r_{i,t} - r_{f,t} = \begin{cases} \alpha_i + \beta_i^{OLS}(r_{M,t} - r_{f,t}) + \epsilon_{i,t} \\ \alpha_i + \beta_i^{GMM}(iv_{r_{M,t}-r_{f,t}}) + \epsilon_{i,t} \\ \alpha_i + \beta_i^{CGA}(r_{M,t} - r_{f,t}) + \epsilon_{i,t} \end{cases}$$

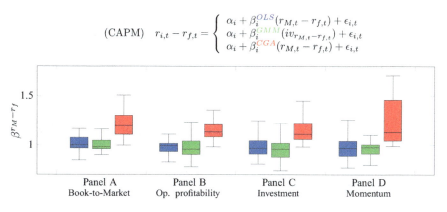

Fig. 1 WORLD: Tukey box plots of the $\beta^{r_M - r_f}$ for the CAPM model for each panel: November 1990 to February 2021. The figures below present, for the CAPM, the Tukey box plots of the $\beta^{r_M - r_f}$ for every single panel. Portfolios are sorted by firms' characteristics: Size-Book to market (Panel A); Size-Operating profitability (Panel B); Size-Investment (Panel C), and Size-Momentum (Panel D). Time-series regressions of monthly excess returns run from November 1990 to February 2021 using 1. ordinary-least-square method (blue box), 2. Hansen's generalized method of moments using instrumental variables based on higher moments (green box) and 3. A compact genetic algorithm (red box)

$$\text{(CAPM)} \quad r_{i,t} - r_{f,t} = \begin{cases} \alpha_i + \beta_i^{OLS}(r_{M,t} - r_{f,t}) + \epsilon_{i,t} \\ \alpha_i + \beta_i^{GMM}(iv_{r_{M,t}-r_{f,t}}) + \epsilon_{i,t} \\ \alpha_i + \beta_i^{CGA}(r_{M,t} - r_{f,t}) + \epsilon_{i,t} \end{cases}$$

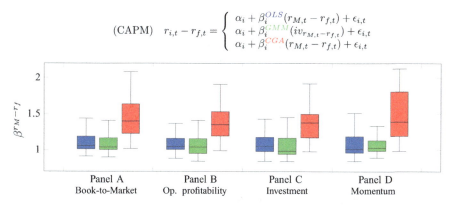

Fig. 2 NORTH AMERICA: Tukey box plots of the $\beta^{r_M - r_f}$ for the CAPM for each panel: November 1990 to February 2021. The figures below present, for the CAPM, the Tukey box plots of the $\beta^{r_M - r_f}$ for every single panel. Portfolios are sorted by firms' characteristics: Size-Book to market (Panel A); Size-Operating profitability (Panel B); Size-Investment (Panel C), and Size-Momentum (Panel D). Time-series regressions of monthly excess returns run from November 1990 to February 2021 using 1. ordinary-least-square method (blue box), 2. Hansen's generalized method of moments using instrumental variables based on higher moments (green box) and 3. A compact genetic algorithm (red box)

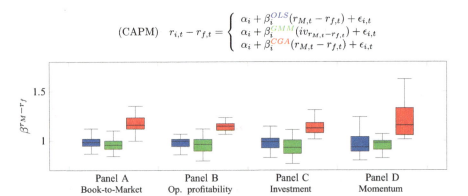

$$\text{(CAPM)} \quad r_{i,t} - r_{f,t} = \begin{cases} \alpha_i + \beta_i^{OLS}(r_{M,t} - r_{f,t}) + \epsilon_{i,t} \\ \alpha_i + \beta_i^{GMM}(iv_{r_{M,t}-r_{f,t}}) + \epsilon_{i,t} \\ \alpha_i + \beta_i^{CGA}(r_{M,t} - r_{f,t}) + \epsilon_{i,t} \end{cases}$$

Fig. 3 EUROPE: Tukey box plots of the $\beta^{r_M - r_f}$ for the CAPM model for each panel: November 1990 to February 2021. The figures below present, for the CAPM, the Tukey box plots of the $\beta^{r_M - r_f}$ for every single panel. Portfolios are sorted by firms' characteristics: Size-Book to market (Panel A); Size-Operating profitability (Panel B); Size-Investment (Panel C), and Size-Momentum (Panel D). Time-series regressions of monthly excess returns run from November 1990 to February 2021 using 1. ordinary-least-square method (blue box), 2. Hansen's generalized method of moments using instrumental variables based on higher moments (green box) and 3. A compact genetic algorithm (red box)

$$\text{(CAPM)} \quad r_{i,t} - r_{f,t} = \begin{cases} \alpha_i + \beta_i^{OLS}(r_{M,t} - r_{f,t}) + \epsilon_{i,t} \\ \alpha_i + \beta_i^{GMM}(iv_{r_{M,t}-r_{f,t}}) + \epsilon_{i,t} \\ \alpha_i + \beta_i^{CGA}(r_{M,t} - r_{f,t}) + \epsilon_{i,t} \end{cases}$$

Fig. 4 ASIA-PACIFIC: Tukey box plots of the $\beta^{r_M - r_f}$ for the CAPM model for each panel: November 1990 to February 2021. The figures below present, for the CAPM, the Tukey box plots of the $\beta^{r_M - r_f}$ for every single panel. Portfolios are sorted by firms' characteristics: Size-Book to market (Panel A); Size-Operating profitability (Panel B); Size-Investment (Panel C), and Size-Momentum (Panel D). Time-series regressions of monthly excess returns run from November 1990 to February 2021 using 1. ordinary-least-square method (blue box), 2. Hansen's generalized method of moments using instrumental variables based on higher moments (green box) and 3. A compact genetic algorithm (red box)

$$(\text{CAPM}) \quad r_{i,t} - r_{f,t} = \begin{cases} \alpha_i + \beta_i^{OLS}(r_{M,t} - r_{f,t}) + \epsilon_{i,t} \\ \alpha_i + \beta_i^{GMM}(iv_{r_{M,t}-r_{f,t}}) + \epsilon_{i,t} \\ \alpha_i + \beta_i^{CGA}(r_{M,t} - r_{f,t}) + \epsilon_{i,t} \end{cases}$$

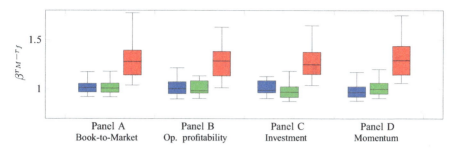

Fig. 5 JAPAN: Tukey box plots of the $\beta^{r_M - r_f}$ for the CAPM model for each panel: November 1990 to February 2021. The figures below present, for the CAPM, the Tukey box plots of the $\beta^{r_M - r_f}$ for every single panel. Portfolios are sorted by firms' characteristics: Size-Book to market (Panel A); Size-Operating profitability (Panel B); Size-Investment (Panel C), and Size-Momentum (Panel D). Time-series regressions of monthly excess returns run from November 1990 to February 2021 using 1. ordinary-least-square method (blue box), 2. Hansen's generalized method of moments using instrumental variables based on higher moments (green box) and 3. A compact genetic algorithm (red box)

5.3 Adjusted R^2

Figure 6 shows the adjusted R^2's for the CAPM. The blue line is for OLS results and the red one is for CGA. From left to right, we give the results for panels A, B, C, and D successively for World, North America, Europe, Asia-Pacific, and Japan (a total of 500 adjusted R^2).

First, we can observe that overall the dispersion of the adjusted R^2 is higher for OLS regressions. For example, in the case of World, the minimum (maximum) value of adjusted R^2 is about 66.2% (95%) with OLS versus 74.5% (87.2%) with the CGA estimations (à actualiser). For North America, the 100 different adjusted R^2 values range between 57% and 90.7% for the OLS estimations (à actualiser). The same range collapses to 75.7% and 87.9% with the CGA (à actualiser). Similar results for the adjusted R^2's are observed for other geographies, namely, Europe, Asia-Pacific, and Japan. For example, while the lowest adjusted R^2 of the CAPM regressions for European portfolios is 63.7%, this lower bound rises to 75% for the same geography when we implement the measurement error correction model. When we look at the results for the Asia-Pacific portfolios, the single factor adjusted R^2 exhibit also less variability with the CGA as the adjusted R^2 values range between 75.8 and 86.5% in contrast to the OLS R^2's between 57.1 and 91.5% (à actualiser).

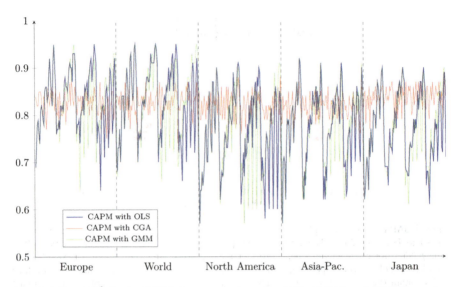

Fig. 6 Adjusted R^2 for the CAPM for every region using OLS, GMMd, and CGA: November 1990 to February 2021. The graph below presents, for the CAPM, the adjusted R^2 values (y-axis) obtained from CAPM regressions for all geographic regions and portfolios sorted by firm characteristics (x-axis) using 1. Ordinary-least-square method (blue curve), 2. Hansen's generalized method of moments using Instrumental variables based on higher moments (green curve) and 3. a compact genetic algorithm (red curve). Time-series regressions of portfolio excess returns on systematic risk factor run from November 1990 to February 2021

Second, for all regions, the average adjusted R^2 for all panels are systematically lower with CGA-based estimations compared to OLS. For example, in the case of World, we obtain a mean adjusted R^2 about 82.84% with CGA versus 83.28% with OLS. For Europe, the mean adjusted R^2 for all panels (100 portfolios) is 82.59% with CGA compared to 83.22% with OLS method.

To sum up, we can retain two main results for the adjusted R^2. Compared to the OLS method, the CGA method reduces the extreme values of the adjusted R^2 for the portfolios (higher values for the minimum and lower values for the maximum). Otherwise, as a consequence of this lower dispersion, the average value of the adjusted R^2 for all regressions is lower with CGA compared to OLS. We turn back to this discussion in the next section to add some other interesting remarks about the adjusted R^2.

5.4 GRS Test

For clarity and shortness, we summarize the results of GRS tests in Table 11 and Fig. 7. We plot the GRS test statistics in blue for OLS results and those derived by the CGA estimations in red. We run the test for each panel of portfolio and for

Table 11 Gibbons, Ross, and Shanken statistics per panel and per region: November 1990 to February 2021

		Book-to-Market		Op. Profitability		Investment		Momentum	
		OLS	CGA	OLS	CGA	OLS	CGA	OLS	CGA
World	CAPM	17.99	3.39	19.31	5.23	20.34	4.70	11.42	8.10
		Book-to-Market		Op. Profitability		Investment		Momentum	
		OLS	CGA	OLS	CGA	OLS	CGA	OLS	CGA
North Am.	CAPM	13.43	3.66	12.55	3.41	12.30	4.17	7.21	5.60
		Book-to-Market		Op. Profitability		Investment		Momentum	
		OLS	CGA	OLS	CGA	OLS	CGA	OLS	CGA
Europe	CAPM	15.37	2.51	25.34	5.31	16.75	2.84	12.15	11.40
		Book-to-Market		Op. Profitability		Investment		Momentum	
		OLS	CGA	OLS	CGA	OLS	CGA	OLS	CGA
Asia-Pac.	CAPM	9.97	4.71	13.43	5.48	11.58	5.52	11.27	8.54
		Book-to-Market		Op. Profitability		Investment		Momentum	
		OLS	CGA	OLS	CGA	OLS	CGA	OLS	CGA
Japan	CAPM	7.35	1.74	12.21	1.96	5.86	1.32	3.16	1.93

each region. We thus obtain 20 (4 panels $\times$ 5 regions) GRS $\mathcal{F}$-statistic for each pair of "portfolio vs. geography." In short, lower GRS test statistics indicate jointly less significant intercepts and thus provide empirical support to the model under inspection. In Fig. 7, this is equivalent to a series on average narrower and closer to the center of the plot. In all cases, this is the case of the red series compared to the blue one. Numerical values of these statistics as shown in Table 11 also clearly show the overall difference between the results of the OLS and CGA estimations. Overall, for all regions and all panels, we obtain systematically lower GRS values for the CAPM with the CGA methodology.

Specifically, if we consider the CAPM as the true model of the risk-reward trade-off, the message carried out by Fig. 7 is inspiring: Regardless of the geography and/or the portfolio, the contour of the GRS statistics delimited by the CGA method considerably shrunks the one drawn by the OLS estimations ignoring the EIV in the market portfolio. The $\mathcal{F}$-statistics are much lower in all cases. This points out to a significant improvement in favor of the CAPM's fundamental prediction that the intercepts must be collectively equal to zero. For some cases like Japan, we even come up with such lower GRS statistics that we cannot reject the null that the intercepts are jointly zero, giving thus empirical support to CAPM. Estimations that overlook the EIV correction in the market risk premium, however, hardly explain the variability in portfolio returns.

$$(CAPM) \quad r_{i,t} - r_{f,t} = \begin{cases} \alpha_i + \beta_i^{OLS}(r_{M,t} - r_{f,t}) + \epsilon_{i,t} \\ \alpha_i + \beta_i^{GMM}(iv_{r_{M,t}-r_{f,t}}) + \epsilon_{i,t} \\ \alpha_i + \beta_i^{CGA}(r_{M,t} - r_{f,t}) + \epsilon_{i,t} \end{cases}$$

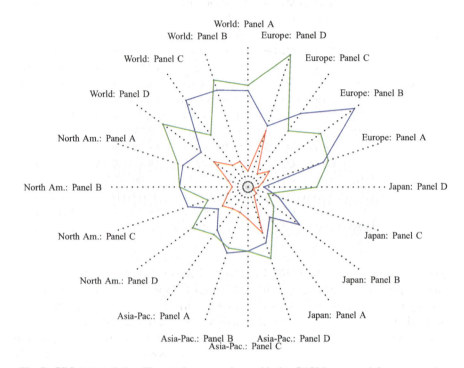

Fig. 7 GRS test statistics: Time-series regressions with the CAPM per panel for every region: November 1990 to February 2021. The figure shows the GRS test statistics were $GRS = \frac{T-N-K}{N} \times \left(1 + \widehat{\mu}_f^\top \widehat{\Omega}_f^{-1} \widehat{\mu}_f\right)^{-1} \times \left(\widehat{\alpha}^\top \widehat{\Sigma}_\epsilon^{-1} \widehat{\alpha}\right) \sim \mathcal{F}_{N,T-N-K}$ with T, the number of observations, N the number of dependent variables, K the number of risk factors, $\widehat{\alpha}$ the vector of Jensen's α, $\widehat{\mu}_f$, the mean vector of the explanatory variables, Σ_ϵ the covariance matrix of residuals, and Ω_f the covariance matrix of explanatory variables for the CAPM for all portfolios sorted by firms' characteristics: Size-Book to market (Panel A); Size-Operating profitability (Panel B); Size-Investment (Panel C), and Size-Momentum (Panel D). Time-series regressions of monthly excess returns run from November 1990 to February 2021 using 1. ordinary-least-square method (blue line), 2. Hansen's generalized method of moments using Instrumental Variables based on higher moments (green line) and 3. A compact genetic algorithm (red line) such as

5.5 Additional Results

After outlining the main outputs of our regressions in the previous subsections, we highlight here additional interesting results. We focus on three main observations. First, we compare the idiosyncratic volatility between OLS and CGA for the CAPM (Fig. 8). Overall, we can observe that the idiosyncratic volatility of the CGA method has lower disparity than that of OLS method for all regions (World,

$$r_{i,t} - r_{f,t} = \begin{cases} \alpha_i + \beta_i^{OLS}(r_{M,t} - r_{f,t}) + \epsilon_{i,t} \\ \alpha_i + \beta_i^{CGA}(r_{M,t} - r_{f,t}) + \epsilon_{i,t} \end{cases}$$

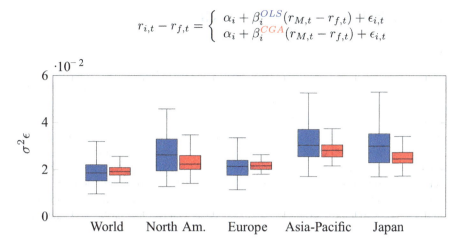

Fig. 8 Distribution of idiosyncratic volatilities (σ_ϵ^2) for each strategy for all regions based on OLS and CGA for the CAPM: November 1990 to February 2021: November 1990 to February 2021. The figure shows the distribution with box plots of the idiosyncratic volatilities of each strategy for the five regions (World, North America, Europe, Asia-Pacific, and Japan) estimated with 1. ordinary-least-square method (blue box), and 2. a compact genetic algorithm (red box)

North America, Europe, Asia-Pacific, and Japan). More specifically, we obtain a minimum idiosyncratic volatility of 0.96%, a maximum of 5.4%, and an average of 2.58% with OLS method versus a minimum of 1.41%, a maximum of 3.93%, and an average of 2.37% with CGA. In summary, the CGA method reduces the extreme values of the idiosyncratic volatility for the portfolios (higher values for the minimum and lower values for the maximum). Otherwise, as a consequence of this lower dispersion, the average value of the idiosyncratic volatility for all regressions is lower with CGA compared to OLS.

Second, we suggest here to see in depth the results for small portfolios. As mentioned above in the literature review, the size effect is much debated. However, we can state easily that many empirical studies pointed out to the difficulty of asset pricing models to explain returns of small firms. Primary results of our study give an interesting orientation for the future research about the size effect. If we consider all small portfolios of our sample, a total of 100 portfolios (5 portfolios of quintile 1 size for each panel and each region), our results show that the CAPM with the CGA method explains on average 82.38% of portfolios' returns (average adjusted R^2) compared to an average of only 69.49% with the OLS method. Moreover, the mean idiosyncratic volatility is about 2.47% with CGA versus 3.29% with OLS. Finally, the attenuation bias of the market beta β_M is reduced through CGA. On average, the market beta for small portfolios is about 0.99 with OLS regressions and becomes 1.44 with CGA.

6   Conclusion and Future Research

We propose a new methodology to mitigate the errors-in-variables (EIV) problem inherent in the estimation of asset pricing models. With the well-known Roll's critique in mind (Roll, 1977), we focus on the market portfolio, still at the center of almost all theoretical or empirical efforts deployed to understand the basic risk-reward relationship in finance. Given the definition of the market portfolio and in line with the existing literature, we presume that the true values of the returns on this hypothetical portfolio are at best observed with some measurement error and, consequently, the widespread least-squares regressions of the risk-return relationships ignoring this issue yield to biased and inconsistent parameters estimates. In the case of CAPM regressions, for example, such measurement errors generate systematically downward-biased coefficients on the market risk factor even in large samples.

We apply an estimation method based on a compact genetic algorithm devised by Satman and Diyarbakirlioglu (2015) to compare the results of time-series and cross-sectional regressions on the CAPM using portfolio returns data over the period 1990–2021. We consider five geographic regions and four different panels of portfolios sorted by size, book-to-market, operating profitability, and momentum. We verify that the CGA-based estimations reduce the impact of EIV in the market risk factor.

Based on fitted intercepts $\widehat{\alpha}$, market betas $\widehat{\beta}_M$, adjusted R^2, and the GRS statistics, we conclude that the CGA-based estimations outperform the traditional OLS. Collectively, we obtain on average higher adjusted R^2 values, and the GRS statistics are substantially lower when we use the CGA estimator. These results provide evidence that naive OLS estimations are unsatisfactory as a tool to run time-series regressions of stock returns in the case of measurement error in at least one of the explanatory variables. We also note that neglecting the measurement error in the market portfolio generates significant attenuation bias in the coefficient estimates as the market risk factor loadings can be underestimated by as much as 25% with CAPM regressions. Finally, the CGA estimators outperform the GMM with IV estimators for all regions and all portfolios.

We can outline at least three main contributions from our study. First, on the empirical side, we can assert that OLS time-series regressions are unsatisfactory regardless of the specification due to presence of measurement errors not only in the market portfolio M but potentially in other variables. Second, if we consider the CAPM as the *true* model that describes expected returns, OLS regressions exhibit major pitfalls due to attenuation bias in market risk loading. It is essential to take into account the EIV and implement an alternative estimation method to overcome this econometric problem in time-series regressions. OLS regressions that ignore the EIV in market risk premium underestimate substantially the market risk, whereas with the CGA we correct this bias. Third, the improvements of regressions output of the CAPM (attenuation bias of market beta β_M, adjusted R^2, idiosyncratic volatility) with the CGA method compared to the OLS method in the case of small firms give promising explanation for the size effect for future research.

Our findings have several theoretical, empirical, and managerial implications. First, on the theoretical side, we revive the critique of Roll (1977) and restart the debate again about the *true* market portfolio. Second, for empirical studies, we show that it is more than necessary to question the OLS method and the GMM with IV in time-series regressions. Third, our findings lead to many managerial implications related to portfolio management (performance measurement, stock picking, etc.), asset pricing (stock valuation, risk-return trade-off, etc.), and corporate financial and investing decisions (cost of capital, valuation, funding).

Appendix: Pseudo-Code of the Algorithm

This appendix provides a plain language description of the EIV-CGA approach developed by Satman and Diyarbakirlioglu (2015). All functions and methods necessary to implement the approach are available with the R package `eive` (see Satman and Diyarbakirlioglu (2018)).

We conceive the process in two subsequent parts and a penalty function, which establishes the convergence criterion. The first part sets the initial parameter values and generates the search space within which the CGA will search the solution.

```
1   # PART I ─────────────────────────────────────────
2   # initializing
3   set n:= Number of observations
4   set d:= Number of dummies
5   set popSize := Population size
6   # setting up the search space for CGA
7   # {1 * d} probability vector for {n * 1} chromosomes
8   chromosomeSize := n x d
9   set P := [0.5, ..., 0.5]
10  # initialize the probability vector with P[i] = 0.5
11  P[i] := generatePopulation(chromosomeSize)
```

Next, we start the iterations until the "best" offspring is obtained among all possible combinations we can extract from the search space. This goes through random sampling of two parent vectors with elements coming from the current state of $P[i]$. Then, we attach the parents, e.g., the samples, a cost function such that the winner to survive the next generation is the one who has the lowest penalty. Next, we update the $P[i]$ using a simple rule in a loop over the entire search space. The algorithm converges when all elements of $P[i]$ are either equal to 0 or 1.

```
1   # PART II ─────────────────────────────────────────
2   # sample two binary random vectors using P[i] as
3       parent1 := sample(P)
4       parent2 := sample(P)
5   # evaluate parent1 and parent2
6       costParent1 := costFunction(parent1)
7       costParent2 := costFunction(parent2)
8   # winner with lowest cost function survives as
```

```
9        winner := selectBest()
10       loser  := selectWorst()
11  # updating P[i]
12  For i in 1:chromosomeSize{
13       if (winner[i] != loser[i]{
14           if (winner[i] == 1){
15               P[i] := P[i] + (1 / popSize)
16           }
17           Else{
18               P[i] := P[i] - (1 / popSize)
19           }
20       }
21   }
22  }
23  # iterate until each P[i] = 0 or 1
```

The cost function returns the sum of squared residuals from the regression given in Eq. 9 between two candidate solutions sampled from the search space and declares the "winner" as the one for which this score is lowest. The end result yields the series X^{CGA} that we consider as a *filtered* version of original observations.

```
1   # Defining the cost function ─────────────────────────────
2   costFunction := function(chromosome){
3       # observed X's = true X's + measurement error
4       # generate {n * d} matrix of dummies using P[i]
5       candidateDummies[] := extractVariables(chromosome)
6       # fit the auxiliary regression:
7       # X = phi[0] + phi[1] * D[1] + ... + phi[d] * D[d]
8       auxiliaryRegression := regress(X on candidateDummies)
9       # extract fitted series X^{CGA}:
10      X^{CGA} := predictedValues(auxiliaryRegression)
11      # fitting the main regression
12      # Y = alpha + beta * X^{CGA} + gamma * otherX + error
13      mainRegression := regress(Y on X^{CGA}, otherX)
14      # objective: minimize the sum of squared residuals
15      min{resid := sumOfSquaredResiduals(mainRegression)}
16      # return sum of squared residuals
17      return(resid)
18  }
```

References

Amihud, Y. (2002). Illiquidity and stock returns: Cross-section and time series effects. *Journal of Financial Markets, 5*(1), 31–56.

Andersson, J., & Møen, J. (2016). A simple improvement of the IV-estimator for the classical errors-in-variables problem. *Oxford Bulletin of Economics & Statistics, 78*(1), 113–125.

Ashenfelter, O., & Krueger, A. (1994). Estimates of the economic return to schooling from a new sample of twins. *American Economic Review, 84*(5), 1157–1173.

Baluja, S., & Caruana, R. (1995). *Removing the genetics from the standard genetic algorithm.* Pittsburgh, PA: Carnegie Mellon University.

Banz, R. W. (1981). The relationship between return and market value of common stocks. *Journal of Financial Economics, 9*(1), 3–18.

Basu, S. (1977). Investment performance of common stocks in relation to their price-earnings ratios: A test of the efficient market hypothesis. *Journal of Finance, 32*(3), 663–682.

Black, F. (1972). Capital market equilibrium with restricted borrowing. *The Journal of Business, 45*(3), 444–455.

Breeden, D. T., Gibbons, M. R., & Litzenberger, R. H. (1989). Empirical tests of the consumption-oriented CAPM. *Journal of Finance, 44*(2), 231–262.

Buonaccorsi, J. P. (2010). *Measurement error: Models, methods, and applications*. Boca Raton, FL: Chapman & Hall.

Carhart, M. M. (1997). On persistence in mutual fund performance. *Journal of Finance, 52*(1), 57–82.

Carmichael, B., & Coën, A. (2008). Asset pricing models with errors-in-variables. *Journal of Empirical Finance, 15*(4), 778–788.

Carroll, R. J., Ruppert, D., Stefanski, L. A., & Crainiceanu, C. M. (2006). *Measurement error in nonlinear models: A modern perspective*. Boca Raton, FL: Chapman & Hall.

Chan, L. K. C., Hamao, Y., & Lakonishok, J. (1991). Fundamentals and stock returns in Japan. *Journal of Finance, 46*(5), 1739–1764.

Cheng, C.-L., & Van Ness, J. W. (1999). *Statistical regression with measurement error*. London: Wiley.

Cochrane, J. H. (2005). *Asset pricing*. Princeton University Press.

Cochrane, J. H. (2011). Presidential address: Discount rates. *Journal of Finance, 66*(4), 1047–1108.

Coen, A., Hübner, G., & Desfleurs, A. (2010). Hedge fund return specification with errors-in-variables. *Journal of Derivatives and Hedge Funds, 16*(1), 22–52.

Coën, A., & Racicot, F. E. (2007). Capital asset pricing models revisited: Evidence from errors in variables. *Economics Letters, 95*(3), 443–450.

Cragg, J. G. (1994). Making good inferences from bad data. *Canadian Journal of Economics, 27*(4), 776–800.

Cragg, J. G. (1997). Using higher moments to estimate the simple errors-in-variables model. *RAND Journal of Economics, 28*, 71–91.

Dagenais, M. G., & Dagenais, D. L. (1997). Higher moment estimators for linear regression models with errors in the variables. *Journal of Econometrics, 76*(1), 193–221.

De Bondt, W. F. M., & Thaler, R. (1985). Does the stock market overreact? *Journal of Finance, 40*(3), 793–805.

Dimson, E., & Marsh, P. (Winter 1999). Murphy's Law and market anomalies. *Journal of Portfolio Management, 25*(2), 53–69.

Durbin, J. (1954). Errors in variables. *Revue de l'institut International de Statistique, 22*(1/3), 23–32.

Fama, E. F., & French, K. R. (1992). The cross-section of expected stock returns. *Journal of Finance, 47*(2), 427–465.

Fama, E. F., & French, K. R. (1993). Common risk factors in the returns on stocks and bonds. *Journal of Financial Economics, 33*(1), 3–56.

Fama, E. F., & French, K. R. (1995). Size and book-to-market factors in earnings and returns. *Journal of Finance, 50*(1), 131–155.

Fama, E. F., & French, K. R. (1997). Industry costs of equity. *Journal of Financial Economics, 43*(2), 153–193.

Fama, E. F., & French, K. R. (2012). Size, value, and momentum in international stock returns. *Journal of Financial Economics, 105*(3), 457–472.

Fama, E. F., & French, K. R. (2015). A five-factor asset pricing model. *Journal of Financial Economics, 116*(1), 1–22.

Fama, E. F., & French, K. R. (2016). Dissecting anomalies with a five-factor model. *The Review of Financial Studies, 29*(1), 69–103.

Fama, E. F., & French, K. R. (2018a). Choosing factors. *Journal of Financial Economics, 128*(2), 234–252.

Fama, E. F., & French, K. R. (2018b). Long-horizon returns. *The Review of Asset Pricing Studies, 8*(2), 232–252.

Fama, E. F., & French, K. R. (2018c). Volatility lessons. *Financial Analysts Journal, 74*(3), 42–53.

Fama, E. F., & French, K. R. (2020). Comparing cross-section and time-series factor models. *The Review of Financial Studies, 33*(5), 1891–1926.

Fama, E. F., & MacBeth, J. D. (1973). Risk, return, and equilibrium: Empirical tests. *Journal of Political Economy, 81*(3), 607–636.

Ferson, W. (2019). *Empirical asset pricing: Models and methods.* Cambridge, MA: MIT Press.

Fuller, W. A. (1987). *Measurement error models.* New York, NY: John Wiley & Sons, Inc.

Gibbons, M. R., Ross, S. A., & Shanken, J. (1989). A test of the efficiency of a given portfolio. *Econometrica, 57*(5), 1121–1152.

Goldberg, D. E. (1989). *Genetic algorithms in search, optimization and machine learning.* Boston, MA, USA: Addison-Wesley Longman Publishing Co., Inc.

Greene, W. H. (2018). *Econometric analysis.* Essex: Pearson.

Hansen, L. (1982). Large sample properties of generalized method of moments estimators. *Econometrica, 50*(4), 1029–1054.

Harik, G. R., Lobo, F. G., & Goldberg, D. E. (1999). The compact genetic algorithm. *IEEE Transactions on Evolutionary Computation, 3*(4), 287–297.

Harik, G. R., Lobo, F. G., & Sastry, K. (2006). Linkage learning via probabilistic modeling in the extended compact genetic algorithm (ECGA). In M. Pelikan, K. Sastry, & E. CantúPaz (Eds.), *Scalable optimization via probabilistic modeling* (pp. 39–61). Berlin, Heidelberg: Springer.

Harvey, C., Liu, Y., & Zhu, H. (2016). ... and the cross-section of expected returns. *Review of Financial Studies, 29*(1), 5–68.

Hausman, J. A. (2001). Mismeasured variables in econometric analysis: Problems from the right and problems from the left. *Journal of Economic Perspectives, 15*(4), 57–67.

Hausman, J. A., & Watson, M. W. (1985). Errors in variables and seasonal adjustment procedures. *Journal of the Americal Statistical Association, 80*(391), 531–540.

Holland, J. H. (1973). Genetic algorithms and the optimal allocation of trials. *SIAM Journal on Computing, 2*(2), 88–105.

Holland, J. H. (1975). *Adaptation in natural and artificial systems: An introductory analysis with applications to biology, control and artificial intelligence.* University of Michigan Press.

Holland, J. H. (1987). Genetic algorithms and classifier systems: Foundations and future directions. In *International Conference on Genetic Algorithms* (pp. 82–89). Cambridge, Massachusetts, USA.

Hou, K., Xue, C., & Zhang, L. (2015). Digesting anomalies: An investment approach. *The Review of Financial Studies, 28*(3), 650–705.

Huang, C.-f., & Litzenberger, R. H. (1988). *Foundations for financial economics.* North-Holland.

Iwata, S. (1992). Instrumental variables estimation in errors-in-variables models when instruments are correlated with errors. *Journal of Econometrics, 53*(1), 297–322.

Jensen, M. C. (1968). The performance of mutual funds in the period 1945–1964. *Journal of Finance, 23*(2), 389–416.

Leamer, E. (1987). Errors in variables in linear systems. *Econometrica, 55*(4), 893–909.

Lintner, J. (1965). The valuation of risk assets and the selection of risky investments in stock portfolios and capital budgets. *The Review of Economics and Statistics, 47*(1), 13–37.

Markowitz, H. (1952). Portfolio selection. *Journal of Finance, 7*(1), 77–91.

Mossin, J. (1966). Equilibrium in a capital asset market. *Econometrica, 34*(4), 768–783.

Novy-Marx, R. (2013). The other side of value: The gross profitability premium. *Journal of Financial Economics, 108*(1), 1–28.

Olea, J. L. M., & Pflueger, C. (2013). A robust test for weak instruments. *Journal of Business and Economic Statistics, 31*(3), 358–369.

Pal, M. (1980). Consistent moment estimators of regression coefficients in the presence of errors in variables. *Journal of Econometrics, 14*(3), 349–364.

Pástor, L., & Stambaugh, R. F. (2003). Liquidity risk and expected stock returns. *Journal of Political Economy, 111*(3), 642–685.

Racicot, F.-E. (2015a). Engineering robust instruments for GMM estimation of panel data regression models with errors in variables: a note. *Applied Economics, 47*(10), 981–989.

Racicot, F.-E. (2015b). Errors in economic and financial variables. *La Revue des Sciences de Gestion, 3–4*(267–268), 79–103.

Racicot, F.-É., Rentz, W. F., & Kahl, A. L. (2017). Rolling regression analysis of the Pástor-Stambaugh model: Evidence from robust instrumental variables. *International Advances in Economic Research, 23*(1), 75–90.

Racicot, F.-E., Rentz, W. F., Kahl, A., & Mesly, O. (2019). Examining the dynamics of illiquidity risks within the phases of the business cycle. *Borsa Istanbul Review, 19*(2), 117–131.

Racicot, F.-É., Rentz, W. F., & Théoret, R. (2018). Testing the new Fama and French factors with illiquidity: A panel data investigation. *Finance, 39*(3), 45–102.

Racicot, F.-E., & Theoret, R. (2015). The Pastor-Stambaugh empirical model revisited: evidence from robust instruments. *Journal of Asset Management, 16*(5), 329–341.

Racicot, F.-E., & Theoret, R. (2016). Testing Fama-French's new five-factor asset pricing model: Evidence from robust instruments. *Applied Economics Letters, 23*(6), 444–448.

Reinganum, M. R. (1981). Misspecification of capital asset pricing: Empirical anomalies based on earnings' yields and market values. *Journal of Financial Economics, 9*(1), 19–46.

Roll, R. (1977). A critique of the asset pricing theory's tests Part I: On past and potential testability of the theory. *Journal of Financial Economics, 4*(2), 129–176.

Rosenberg, B., Reid, K., & Lanstein, R. (1985). Persuasive evidence of market inefficiency. *Journal of Portfolio Management, 11*(3), 9–16.

Satman, M. H., & Diyarbakirlioglu, E. (2015). Reducing errors-in-variables bias in linear regression using compact genetic algorithms. *Journal of Statistical Computation and Simulation, 85*(16), 3216–3235.

Satman, M. H., & Diyarbakirlioglu, E. (2018). eive: An Algorithm for Reducing Errors-in-variables Bias in Linear Regression. R package version 2.3.

Shanken, J. (1992). On the estimation of beta-pricing models. *Review of Financial Studies, 5*(1), 1–33.

Sharpe, W. F. (1964). Capital asset prices: A theory of market equilibrium under conditions of risk. *Journal of Finance, 19*(3), 425–442.

Stock, J. H., Wright, J. H., & Yogo, M. (2002). A survey of weak instruments and weak identification in generalized method of moments. *Journal of Business and Economic Statistics, 20*(4), 518–529.

Tobin, J. (1958). Liquidity preference as behavior towards risk. *The Review of Economic Studies, 25*(2), 65–86.

Wooldridge, J. M. (2015). *Introductory econometrics: A modern approach.* Cengage Learning.